Children of Color

Psychological Interventions with Culturally Diverse Youth

Jewelle Taylor Gibbs

Larke Nahme Huang

and Associates

Forewords by

Congressman George Miller

Stanley Sue, Ph.D.

Jossey-Bass Publishers • San Francisco

Substantial discounts on bulk quantities of Jossey-Bass books are available to corporations, professional associations, and other organizations. For details and discount information, contact the special sales department at Jossey-Bass Inc., Publishers (415) 433–1740; Fax (800) 605–2665.

For sales outside the United States, please contact your local Simon & Schuster International Office.

 Manufactured in the United States of America on Lyons Falls Turin Book. This paper is acid-free and 100 percent totally chlorine-free.

Library of Congress Cataloging-in-Publication Data

Gibbs, Jewelle Taylor.
    Children of color : psychological interventions with culturally
diverse youth / Jewelle Taylor Gibbs, Larke Nahme Huang. — Updated
ed.
        p.   cm. — (The Jossey-Bass psychology series)
    Includes index.
    ISBN 0–7879–0871–1 (pbk. : alk. paper)
    1. Children of minorities—Mental health—United States.
I. Huang, Larke.   II. Title.   III. Series.
RJ507.M54G53   1997
618.92'89'008900973—DC21

97–17209
CIP

UPDATED EDITION
PB Printing   10 9 8 7 6 5 4 3 2 1

Contents

Foreword

Over the last several decades, we in the United States have witnessed dramatic changes that have profoundly affected our young people and their families demographically, economically, socially, and psychologically and that pose enormous challenges to which the nation must respond.

Perhaps nowhere are these changes more evident and compelling than in the rapidly increasing cultural and demographic diversity of our citizenry. Minority group members—blacks, Hispanics, American Indians, and Asians—constitute 14 percent of all adults in the country and 20 percent of children under seventeen. By the year 2000, it is projected that one-third of all school-age children will fall into this category.

This changing demographic tapestry in the United States promises not only the richness that diversity brings but also many difficult challenges in extending the American dream to all of our citizens. Historically, people of color have found themselves at the bottom of the economic and social order. They are disproportionately represented among the poor, the unemployed, the homeless, the sick, the inadequately educated, and those who are ill-prepared for full participation in American life. For children of color, the toll has been even greater. Infant mortality in the black community is double that in the white community, and the gap is widening. Half of all black children and one-third of all Hispanic children live in poverty. School dropout rates for minority youth remain at alarming levels, with rates reaching more than 60 percent in some urban areas.

Concomitant economic changes and increasing isolation of communities of color compound the challenges. The number of blue-collar manufacturing jobs—which allowed past generations of minorities and immigrants to climb into the economic mainstream—

is declining. The opportunities now available to minority adults increasingly are in low-paying service-sector jobs that provide far fewer opportunities for upward mobility.

In addition, we have seen an upswing in race-related violence and other racially motivated incidents in diverse communities around the country. Apart from their tragic personal significance, incidents of racial antipathy give us important lessons about larger economic and demographic trends in our society and about the environments in which our children are growing up.

Children of color face daily challenges to their success and self-esteem. In investigations by the U.S. Select Committee on Children, Youth, and Families, we have documented the disparate treatment of minority and white children with mental health problems. The understanding and treatment of children's mental health is still in its infancy in America. Nearly ten million children suffer from mental health problems that need attention. Yet an estimated 70 to 80 percent of these children get inappropriate mental health services or no services at all. For children of color, the problems are even more severe. Due to a mental health system that is poorly funded and all too frequently insensitive to race and ethnic origin, these children are often misdiagnosed and mistreated, if they are treated at all.

The importance of addressing these issues cannot be overstated: they must be at the core of America's agenda. This book provides an important contribution to defining and making more visible these concerns, which have remained under wraps for far too long. Children are our future, and we must give them the opportunity to do a good job of it. They and the nation deserve no less.

February 1989
(for first edition)

CONGRESSMAN GEORGE MILLER
Chairman, Select Committee
on Children, Youth, and Families
U.S. House of Representatives

Foreword

Hodgkinson (1983) has indicated that in the next few years the motive for working with and knowing about people of color will be not political liberalism or obligation but enlightened self-interest. It is obvious that the interest of everyone is served by the ability to work with diverse ethnic populations. The population of American society is increasingly diverse, and if we are to achieve economic, social, educational, and democratic ideals, we must develop multicultural knowledge and skills. In the mental health field, the need for enlightenment is particularly acute. Many minority individuals experience stress, which contributes to adjustment problems and psychopathology, but we lack adequate institutional resources and mental health services to address their problems. There are many economic, sociocultural, and political reasons why these problems continue to exist. For mental health professionals, one major barrier to attending to these problems has been inadequate knowledge and training.

Many of us who have studied the effect of ethnicity on mental health are frequently asked such questions as: What are the cultural values of particular ethnic groups? How do cultural conflicts affect mental health? What assessment instruments are valid to use with these groups? Must psychotherapeutic techniques be modified to be effective with minority clients? What is meant by the term *culturally sensitive therapist?* Do minority group members demonstrate a great deal of heterogeneity? What kinds of psychotherapeutic and societal interventions are required to address the mental health needs of ethnic minorities? In view of the growing diversity of U.S. society, how can we plan for the future?

In this book, Jewelle Taylor Gibbs, Larke Nahme Huang, and their colleagues address some of these questions with respect to children of color and their families. The work is a significant contribution for several reasons. First, because little has been written about children of color, researchers, practitioners, and decision makers often must operate without much knowledge of the issues involved. This book provides an up-to-date analysis of the state of knowledge about developmental/ecological and intervention issues. Second, the book is strongly oriented toward both scholars and practitioners. Researchers should find many of the ideas amenable to further study; practitioners will gain a better understanding of how to assess and treat minority children. While no simple answers are given, the cultural, sociopolitical, and clinical contexts presented by the various contributors should enable practitioners to work better with members of diverse cultural groups. Third, unlike many books of readings that lack integration and coherence, this book consists of chapters in which a standard format is used to discuss issues, and the authors illustrate their ideas with case studies. Particularly interesting are the analyses of specific cases by the different contributors. These analyses provide a most enlightening lesson in how cases can be meaningfully approached by experts who have broad knowledge of cultural diversities and the issues of psychological assessment and intervention. No longer do we have to restrict our discussions about working with culturally diverse clients to abstract admonitions. We now have an adequate knowledge base and the expertise to begin to respond truly to the needs of ethnic minority groups.

February 1989 (for first edition)

STANLEY SUE, PH.D.
Professor of Psychology
University of California, Los Angeles

Reference

Hodgkinson, H. L. "Guess Who's Coming to College?" *Academe*, 1983, *69*, 13–20.

Preface

Children and adolescents of color constitute the most rapidly growing segment of the youth population in the United States, yet relatively little literature is available to enlighten clinicians, educators, health professionals, and social workers about the problems and needs of these young people. When we wrote the first edition of this book in 1989, we recognized the need for a comprehensive text on the psychological assessment and treatment of ethnic minority children and adolescents, a group that generally had been neglected in the proliferation of textbooks on minority mental health in the 1980s. In general, these books focused on the mental health problems of minority adults and the implications of ethnicity for family therapy, yet all of the major ethnic minority groups are characterized by disproportionately youthful populations as compared to the dominant white majority. Our experiences as teachers, supervisors, and consultants further emphasized the need for a book that would encompass theoretical, empirical, and clinical perspectives on the assessment and treatment of these youth of color.

The response of mental health professionals, educators, and students to our book was so positive that our publisher encouraged us to revise and update it for this new paperback edition. To date there are still only a few books that address the unique problems and special needs of ethnic minority children and adolescents with psychological and behavioral problems. Although in recent years there has been an increase in the knowledge base about ethnic minority populations, this knowledge has only recently been effectively translated into a few comprehensive handbooks for use in clinical intervention and in the training of mental health and human service professionals. Because the population of nonwhite and Hispanic-speaking youth in the United States is rapidly increasing and expected to reach 36 percent of all youth by the year

2000, the need for educational and clinical resources relevant to this group is clearly evident (U.S. Bureau of the Census, 1996). In fact, ethnic minority youth now constitute 35 percent of the U.S. public school population and more than 50 percent of the student population in many large urban school districts, with concomitant increases in academic and behavioral challenges, which teachers and counselors often are unprepared to handle effectively. The objective of this book, therefore, is to meet the needs of these educators and of professionals in the mental health and human service professions, such as psychiatry, psychology, social work, psychiatric nursing, and counseling.

The book is designed to fulfill several goals and to be useful in a wide variety of clinical, professional, and educational settings. First, its primary purpose is to present a well-balanced discussion of the issues involved in the clinical assessment and treatment of children and adolescents from six major ethnic groups and two emerging special population groups. A broad range of interventions is covered by the various contributors, from psychodynamic to social cognitive to systems-oriented approaches, with an ecological perspective providing a common thread across groups and serving to integrate the conventional with the more culturally based methods of intervention.

Second, a comparative, cross-cultural approach to the book provides an overarching framework around which each chapter is organized, enabling the reader to compare selected topics (such as socialization practices, identity formation, coping strategies, assessment issues, and treatment approaches) across ethnic groups.

Third, the book also reflects a major commitment to an ecological perspective that recognizes the significant impact of social and environmental factors such as poverty, discrimination, immigration, and family structure on the adaptation and coping patterns of children and adolescents of color. We strongly believe that some knowledge of a group's history in the United States, of their traditional value system and family organization, and of their current demographic realities is essential for accurate clinical assessment and effective intervention with youth from diverse ethnic backgrounds. Thus, relevant background information is briefly summarized for each group in order to provide a sociocultural context that justifies the recommendations for differential strategies of assessment and treatment.

The most difficult aspect of planning the scope of this book was the initial decision concerning which groups to include and which groups to exclude. Our decision was to focus on children and adolescents from six of the largest ethnic minority groups in the United States—African Americans, Chinese Americans, Japanese Americans, American Indians, Mexican Americans, and Puerto Rican Americans—as well as from two emerging groups—Southeast Asian refugee youth, and biracial youth. The six ethnic groups were selected for several reasons: first, they have historically been the largest minority groups with the longest period of residence in this country; second, more literature and a greater range of reliable sources were available for writing about these groups; and third, these particular groups represent a range of demographic, linguistic, and acculturation differences. For example, in terms of population trends, Chinese Americans are a rapidly increasing group, while Japanese Americans are stabilizing and perhaps even declining due to high rates of out-of-group marriage. The route of entry to the United States of the groups chosen varies, from American Indians, who were indigenous, to African Americans, who were imported as slaves, to Japanese and Chinese Americans, who were imported as laborers, to the most recent Southeast Asians, who were initially admitted as political refugees. Along with these differences in migration history, there is a continuum of acculturation among these groups that is reflected in linguistic and cultural patterns ranging from the bilingualism of many second-generation Spanish-speaking Americans to the rapid assimilation of many third-generation Japanese Americans. It is also important to underscore the wide diversity *within* each ethnic group. The attitudes, behaviors, and values of members of each group are strongly influenced by their degree of acculturation, their socioeconomic status, and their ties with ethnic institutions and communities. For example, there may be greater differences between the first and third generations of Japanese Americans than between middle-class Japanese Americans and middle-class white Americans. Thus, although our contributors have attempted to describe the traditional history, culture, and mental health attitudes and beliefs of these ethnic groups, we recognize that all of these groups are in the process of continual change and adaptation to the dominant society and that the generalizations made in these chapters are not equally applicable to all the members of a specific ethnic group.

As noted earlier, there are also two chapters that address the unique problems of two emerging groups in the youth population: refugee youth from Southeast Asia, and biracial adolescents. Although there is very little in the clinical literature about these two groups, they are a rapidly growing segment of the youth population in this country, and we believe they pose particular dilemmas to mental health practitioners who may be unfamiliar with their cultural and social experiences. The two chapters offer an initial attempt to consolidate the ethnographic, developmental, clinical, and empirical literature that provides useful information for clinicians who work with these youth.

Although we are aware that there are many other minority groups that have recently grown in size and made significant contributions to U.S. society—such as Koreans, Filipinos, Cubans, Central Americans, Asian Indians, and Caribbean blacks, among others—we have not been able to include all of these groups due both to limitations of space and to inadequate databases concerned with the mental health issues of children in these groups. However, throughout this book there are sections on assessment and treatment that will have some relevance for these groups, as well as many references that are directly applicable to them.

In planning the topics to be included, we preferred to present in-depth discussion about selected treatment modalities rather than to produce a survey text with a superficial coverage of all modalities of treatment for minority children and adolescents. Because most of these youth are seen in outpatient clinics and practice settings, the authors focus on appropriate individual and family treatment modalities. Few of the authors address the issues of residential treatment or hospitalization, because these are specialized settings that frequently involve medication and more restrictive forms of intervention. Finally, psychological testing is not covered in this book because the issues of testing minority youth have been effectively addressed in many other textbooks.

The twelve chapters of this book are organized to reflect natural groupings within the broad category of ethnic minority populations, as well as historical differences in their relationship to the dominant culture. The first chapter, by Jewelle Taylor Gibbs and Larke Nahme Huang, provides an introduction to the book and an overview of the issues. In this chapter the coauthors describe the purpose and goals of the book, its conceptual framework, and its integrative cross-cultural perspective. Examples from each of the topical chapters are included to illustrate specific points and to highlight particular themes.

Nine topical chapters follow, each focusing on a particular minority group or special population. The authors of each chapter are psychologists who have personal and professional knowledge as well as extensive clinical experience with the ethnic groups they describe. The content of these chapters adheres to a similar format: they each include demographic data, epidemiological data regarding the incidence of psychological and behavioral disorders (where available), historical information about entry into and migration to the United States, discussion of significant issues of family structure and functioning and of sociocultural issues in assessment (attitudes, values, and beliefs about mental health and illness; symptom patterns; help-seeking; and utilization patterns), and implications for effective intervention strategies and treatment techniques. Brief case vignettes are presented in each chapter to illustrate the appropriate role of sociocultural factors in the assessment of symptomatology, defensive strategies, and coping behaviors in emotionally troubled minority children and adolescents, and for the purpose of developing specific treatment techniques and/or alternative intervention strategies.

In Chapter Two, Larke Nahme Huang and Yu-Wen Ying describe the mental health issues of Chinese American children and adolescents and provide a unique model of "active exchange" in intervention with these youth and their families. Donna K. Nagata focuses in Chapter Three on the implications of bicultural identity for Japanese American children, who are particularly vulnerable to parental and societal pressures to fulfill the expectations of the "model minority" stereotype as they cope with the dual pressures of adolescent developmental tasks and acculturation. In Chapter Four, Teresa D. LaFromboise and Kathryn Graff Low propose a combination of indigenous and Western therapeutic methods for treating the psychological and behavioral problems of American Indian youth, whose problems often result from the poverty, social isolation, and cultural discontinuities of reservation or urban life.

In Chapter Five, LaRue Allen and Shayda Majidi-Ahi emphasize the resiliency and adaptability of African American children, whose psychosocial development is frequently influenced by poverty, racial discrimination, and single-parent families. Jewelle Taylor Gibbs builds on this theme in Chapter Six as she describes the psychosocial problems of African American adolescents, whose behavioral disorders often mask underlying psychological problems that are exacerbated by their disadvantaged socioeconomic status. Together these two chapters provide a comprehensive portrait of the challenges facing African American youth, the largest group of minority youth in American society.

In Chapter Seven, Oscar Ramirez points out the dual impact of biculturalism and bilingualism on the psychosocial development of Mexican American children, who often find themselves in conflict between the traditional Latino values of their parents and the values of contemporary Anglo American society. Jaime E. Inclán and D. Gloria Herron echo many of these themes in Chapter Eight as they characterize the mental health issues of Puerto Rican American youth. In both of these chapters, the authors emphasize the importance of involving the family in any treatment program for a Hispanic child or adolescent.

Larke Nahme Huang presents in Chapter Nine an overview of the adjustment issues facing Southeast Asian refugee and immigrant children, who have experienced multiple separations and losses, forced relocation, and pressures for rapid acculturation to an unfamiliar society. In Chapter Ten, Jewelle Taylor Gibbs examines the implications of biracial heritage for the psychosocial adjustment of adolescents, whose identity development may be exacerbated by conflicts about their dual racial heritage.

Huang and Gibbs illustrate in Chapter Eleven the diverse ways in which the contributing authors view a standardized case of a child or adolescent, depending on the child's and the author's respective sociocultural contexts. The objective of this chapter is to highlight how clinicians' cultural sensitivity can influence their conceptualization of a case, their diagnostic assessment, and their treatment recommendations, particularly when they are taking into account the sociocultural background of the child or adolescent client. In Chapter Twelve, Huang and Gibbs integrate the common themes developed in the topical chapters, highlighting the similarities and differences in mental health issues among the various groups of children and adolescents of color. In addition, they propose an ecological model of clinical inquiry and assessment appropriate for children and adolescents, who share characteristics that set them apart from the dominant majority. Finally, they present a set of recommendations for further research on the mental health of youth of color, for greater expansion and improvement in the training of mental health professionals to treat these clients, and for significant restructuring of the mental health delivery system to meet the needs of the growing minority population.

In summary, we feel that this book is an important contribution to the field for three reasons: first, it will fill a significant gap in the clinical literature on the treatment of children and adolescents of color, because so few books are currently available; second, it will be a valuable tool for use in the training of all mental health and human service professionals, many of whom are required to gain knowledge of ethnic minority groups for their licensing examinations in psychiatry, psychology, social work, and family and marriage counseling; and third, it will be extremely useful for mental health and human service professionals in all public and private agencies, which according to current demographic trends and projections will serve an increasingly higher proportion of minority youth and their families well into the twenty-first century.

We should add one caveat for our readers: our goal is not to create "experts" or "specialists" in the field of minority mental health but to provide an introduction to and a way of conceptualizing the mental health problems of ethnic minority youth. We hope that this book will not only expand the knowledge base of clinicians who work with these youth but will also increase their sensitivity to the similarities and differences among and between groups in our society. Toward that end, we especially appreciate the efforts of our contributors to respond promptly and enthusiastically to our request to update their chapters with current demographic and epidemiological information for this revised edition.

Children of color constitute one of the fastest-growing segments of the population, yet social scientists have paid little attention to their development, educators have demonstrated little understanding of their special needs, and mental health professionals have expressed little awareness of their special problems. It is our hope that this revised paperback edition will not only increase the accessibility of this important information but will also further contribute to increasing the understanding of the needs of these youth, improving the assessment of their mental health, and developing more effective methods of intervention and treatment for their behavioral and psychological disorders.

August 1997   JEWELLE TAYLOR GIBBS
                                                     Berkeley, California

                                                     LARKE NAHME HUANG
                                                     Washington, D.C.

Reference

U.S. Bureau of the Census. *Statistical Abstract of the United States: 1996.* (116th ed.) Washington, D.C.: U.S. Department of Commerce, 1996.

Acknowledgments

Children of Color truly represents a collaborative undertaking, not only of the contributing authors but also of many others who made direct and indirect contributions to the project. First, we would like to thank the contributing authors, whose enthusiasm and cooperation sustained us through the challenges inherent in such a project. We would also like to express our appreciation for the encouragement and support of the late Dean Harry Specht and of other colleagues in the School of Social Welfare, University of California, Berkeley.

We are grateful for the advice and counsel of the late Sheldon J. Korchin and of other colleagues in the Psychology Clinic, University of California, Berkeley. A special thanks to Forrest B. Tyler of the University of Maryland, whose knowledge and ideas instilled precious life values and the wisdom of diversity.

We owe thanks to several research assistants who assisted with the research on our chapters in this book, including Helen Ahn, Kathryn Chun, Holly Danforth, Alice Hines, Karen Huang, Mary Leong Lam, Huong Mai Le, Lawrence Liese, Joseph Merighi, Martha Sue Skinner, and Alberta Wu. We also want to acknowledge the helpful comments and insights offered by graduate students in our courses on minority mental health, and participants in our workshops from 1981 through 1997. We further express our thanks to James Steele, Norma Harrison, and all of the office staff who were so cooperative in facilitating our work in countless ways. To Gracia Alkema, our editor at Jossey-Bass, we express our deep appreciation for her belief in this project, her consistent support and patience, and her prompt and insightful feedback. We also owe a debt of gratitude to Alan Rinzler, editor for this revised edition, who proposed the paperback version and shepherded us through the project with enthusiasm and good humor.

Our special thanks to Sharon Ikami, who typed several versions of this manuscript with professionalism, patience, and graciousness.

We wish also to acknowledge the indirect contributions of the professors who taught us and the clinicians who supervised us during our graduate and postgraduate training in clinical and community psychology at the University of California, Berkeley (J.T.G.), Yale University (L.N.H.), Mt. Zion Hospital in San Francisco (J.T.G.), Stanford University (J.T.G.), George Washington University Medical Center (J.T.G.), and Langley Porter Psychiatric Institute, University of California Medical Center, San Francisco (L.N.H.).

We are grateful to our families and friends for their unwavering support and sustenance throughout the two years of our intense involvement in this project: Leonard and Dorothy Nahme, Andrew and Diana Huang, Donna and Charles Salcetti, Scott Ren Nahme, Earnestine Singletary, Phyllis Elperin Clark, and all of the Taylor clan and the Gibbs extended family in the San Francisco Bay Area. To our respective spouses, James and Kirk, and to our children, Geoffrey, Lowell, Christina, and Kevin, we owe a special debt of gratitude for their patience and forbearance.

Finally, this volume is the culmination of a joint effort between two friends and colleagues from different ethnicities and backgrounds. We have learned much from and about each other, and in the spirit of diversity, our own lives have been enriched and the bonds of friendship and knowledge strengthened through this relationship.

J.T.G.

L.N.H.

Children of Color

To my beloved parents
Margaret Taylor Hancock
and the late Reverend Julian Augustus Taylor
whose high expectations
inspired two generations of black youth to achieve
—J.T.G.

To my family
Christina Lee Huang and Kevin Nahme Huang
for timely inspiration and constant distraction
and E. Kirk Huang
for loving companionship and rejuvenating enthusiasm
—L.N.H.

Chapter One

A Conceptual Framework for the Psychological Assessment and Treatment of Minority Youth

Jewelle Taylor Gibbs
Larke Nahme Huang

The field of minority mental health has grown rapidly since it was fostered by the community mental health movement in the late 1960s. Although the movement has spawned dozens of books on a range of minority mental health issues, nearly all of these books have focused on the problems of minority adults and families (see, for example, Atkinson, Morten, and Sue, 1989; Jones and Korchin, 1982; McGoldrick, Pearce, and Giordano, 1996; Paniagua, 1994; Pedersen, Draguns, Lonner, and Trimble, 1989; Sue and Sue, 1990). In spite of their growing numbers in the population, minority children and youth have generally been ignored and neglected in the mental health literature.

Between 1960 and 1995, the proportion of nonwhites in the U.S. population increased dramatically. Demographers have predicted that nonwhite and Hispanic-speaking youth under age eighteen will constitute 36 percent of the nation's youth population in the year 2000 and 48 percent by 2020 (U.S. Bureau of the Census, 1996). These population changes and projected trends are largely the result of four factors: (1) increased immigration from Latin America, Asia, Africa, and the Caribbean; (2) higher birthrates among these immigrant groups and resident minority groups; (3) increased longevity of the minority population; and (4) lower birthrates of the resident white population.

These population trends have created a "demographic imperative" for the social institutions that serve youth to modify their traditional programs and services in order to serve these minority youth more effectively (Ozawa, 1986). The impact of this changing population has already been felt by schools, social services, health and mental health agencies, juvenile probation services, and all other family- and youth-oriented programs. For example, in 1995 nonwhite and Hispanic youth constituted 35 percent of the nation's public school population, more than 40 percent of the students in states such as California, Florida, New York, and Texas, and well over half of the students in many large urban school districts throughout the country ("Quality Counts," 1997). As this minority youth population has continued to grow, however, it has become increasingly clear that most of the human service and mental health professionals who serve them do not have adequate information, applicable training, or appropriate resources to address the problems and needs of these young people. This problem is particularly acute in urban areas, where high rates of poverty among these minority groups contribute to social isolation and social disorganization, further magnifying ethnic and cultural differences (Edelman, 1987; Wilson, 1987).

In 1978, the President's Commission on Mental Health noted that low-income minority children and adolescents were particularly at risk for psychological disorders and behavioral problems because of their low socioeconomic status, their often stressful environments, and their lack of access to mental health services. Two decades later, this situation has not measurably improved and children of color are still triply disadvantaged by their ethnicity, their poverty, and their social isolation (Children's Defense Fund, 1996; Rodgers, 1986; Schorr, 1986).

The purpose of this book is to provide a balanced and comprehensive overview of psychological intervention with minority children and adolescents experiencing psychological and behavioral problems. Toward this objective, the book will (1) provide basic demographic and sociocultural information about these minority youth, (2) present data on the incidence of behavioral and

psychological disorders in these groups, and (3) propose an ecological and culturally sensitive framework for the psychosocial assessment and treatment of these youth. The book is intended not
to present a comprehensive survey of all possible treatment modalities for children and adolescents but rather to concentrate on in-
depth coverage of clients seen in outpatient clinical settings, where
the great majority of these young people are treated. Thus the contributors do not devote much attention to such topics as psychological testing, residential treatment, or hospitalization.

The book will focus on school-age children and youth from ages
five through twenty-one in four major ethnic minority groups in the
United States: Asians, African Americans, Hispanics, and American
Indians. In recognition of the diversity within the Asian and Hispanic populations, chapters are devoted to two of the largest ethnic groups within each of these categories: Chinese American and
Japanese American youth represent Asians, and Mexican American and Puerto Rican youth represent Hispanics. In addition, there
are chapters on the unique experiences and problems of youth in
two emerging special population groups: refugee children from
Southeast Asia and biracial/bicultural children and adolescents.
Although the literature on these latter groups is sparse, they constitute a rapidly growing segment of society and pose particular
challenges to mental health professionals who may be unfamiliar
with the cultural and social experiences of these groups.

The choice of these particular groups was not random or
capricious but based on several important considerations. First,
the six groups chosen are among the largest minority groups with
a long period of residence in the United States. Second, there is
a significant database on these groups that includes ethnographic,
demographic, empirical, and clinical studies. Third, the groups
chosen represent a continuum of acculturation, from the most assimilated (Japanese Americans) to the least assimilated (Southeast Asian refugees), with a wide spectrum between these extremes
that reflects different patterns of migration, different degrees of
bilingualism, and different levels of adaptation to mainstream customs, values, and behaviors. Additionally, these groups represent contrasting demographic trends, from the Chinese Americans and Hispanic Americans, who are rapidly increasing in the
population, to the Japanese Americans and African Americans,

who are stabilizing or declining in numbers or in their relative proportion in the population.

While we are aware that there are many other minority groups that have recently grown in size and made significant contributions to society—such as Asian Indians, Koreans, Filipinos, Cubans, Central Americans, Caribbean blacks, and Pacific Islanders, among others—we have not been able to include all of these groups due to both limitations of space and inadequate databases concerning children's mental health issues among these groups. However, throughout this book there are sections on assessment and treatment that will have some relevance for these groups, as well as many references that are directly applicable to them. Our decision was to select a few representative groups to discuss in depth rather than a larger number of groups to discuss in more general terms.

It is important to point out the diversity that exists within each of these groups in terms of migration history, socioeconomic status, level of acculturation, lifestyle, values, and behaviors. Although we acknowledge this diversity, we also emphasize the shared history, cultural traditions, and social experiences of the members of these groups relative to the dominant society. In some cases, there may be greater differences between Hispanic and non-Hispanic blacks, for example, or between American Indians from different tribal backgrounds, than between some members of these groups and white Americans. It is not our intention to create or reinforce stereotypes or myths about any of these groups; rather, we intend to present the available information that will inform mental health clinicians about some of the central characteristics of the cultural heritage of these groups in order to enable them to deliver more effective and culturally sensitive services to these youth and their families.

Our Conceptual Framework

This book is organized around three primary conceptual perspectives: a developmental perspective, an ecological perspective, and a cross-cultural or minority mental health perspective. These perspectives are described briefly, followed by a discussion of their relevance to the assessment and treatment of minority children and adolescents.

Developmental Perspective

The developmental perspective provides a framework for examining the influence of race and ethnicity on the psychosocial tasks of growing up in American society. While maturational processes are undeniably universal and occur with only minor variations across racial and cultural groups, many social science researchers have shown that these processes are subject to wide ethnic variations in their behavioral manifestations, their symbolic meanings, and their societal responses (Phinney and Rotheram, 1987).

Erikson (1959) proposes that there are five psychosocial stages from birth to late adolescence, each one posing a specific developmental challenge for the growing child to master. The outcomes of each stage are determined by an interaction of the individual's personality attributes, his or her relationships with significant others, and the opportunities available in the environment. The psychosocial crises to be resolved in these five stages depend on a favorable interaction of these three variables, which would result in a sense of trust rather than mistrust in the infant, autonomy rather than shame and doubt in the toddler, initiative rather than guilt in the preschool child, industry rather than inferiority in the latency-age child, and identity consolidation rather than identity diffusion in the adolescent. In discussing these psychosocial crises, Erikson points out that children from minority and low-income backgrounds may experience more difficulties in achieving these positive outcomes because of prejudice, discrimination, or barriers to full opportunity for personal growth.

It is important to note two major contributions of Erikson's theory to the study of minority children and youth, as well as to recognize certain limitations in the theory. First, this framework enables mental health clinicians to evaluate a child's level of psychosocial development at various ages in terms of certain salient characteristics, such as dependency, competence, interpersonal skills, and sense of personal identity. Second, this framework is useful for assessing a child's relationships with significant others (such as parents, teachers, and peers) and adjustment to the environment (home, school, and community).

Although Erikson's stage-related theory of psychosocial development is quite relevant for children reared in nuclear families in highly industrialized societies, his conceptual scheme may be less applicable to children reared in extended families in nonindustrial societies where the emphasis might be placed on different psychosocial outcomes. Awareness of this potential bias is an important caveat in assessing specific characteristics in children of recent immigrants, those reared on reservations, and those reared in other culturally homogeneous environments.

A second major limitation of Erikson's theory is its assumption that the self-concept and the self-esteem of minority children are significantly affected by the stigma of membership in a devalued ethnic group. This assumption is contradicted by the work of Mead (1934), who proposes that the child develops a self-concept and self-esteem from the reflected appraisals of family, close relatives, and friends and not from the broader society, which only later affects the adolescent, when he or she leaves the relative social insulation of the family and ethnic community. Recent surveys of the literature on the self-esteem of minority children and adolescents support the view that their level of self-esteem is as high as or higher than that of their white peers (Powell, 1985; Rosenberg and Simmons, 1971; Taylor, 1976). Cross (1991) further describes the complexity and diversity of black identity and the various factors that contribute to self-esteem for African Americans. In spite of these limitations, Erikson's conceptual scheme provides the clinician with a framework for viewing important areas of psychosocial growth and development. By complementing this scheme with the ecological and cross-cultural perspectives, the clinician will obtain a more comprehensive and differentiated view of minority youth.

Ecological Perspective

The ecological perspective as proposed by Bronfenbrenner (1979) is useful in viewing the growing child or adolescent as an active agent in a series of interlocking systems, ranging from the microsystems of the family and the school to the macrosystem of governmental social and economic policies. Each of these systems poses risks and opportunities for the child or adolescent interacting with the environment at successive developmental stages. The ecological perspective is especially relevant in analyzing the impacts of poverty, discrimination, immigration, and social isolation on the psychosocial development and adjustment of minority children and youth.

Extensive research on poor families has shown that poverty has negative impacts on nearly all aspects of their children's lives, including nutrition, health care, housing, education, and recreation (American Public Welfare Association, 1986; Rodgers, 1986; Schorr, 1986). When children are both poor and members of ethnic minority groups, the negative and long-term impact of poverty increases significantly (Wilson and Aponte, 1985; Committee for Economic Development, 1987; Edelman, 1987). Recent immigration status and language problems are increased sources of stress for children of immigrants and refugees, who must cope not only with adjustment to a strange new culture but also with the loss of their native land and indigenous culture (Sluzki, 1979; Gong-Guy, Craveks, and Patterson, 1991; Padilla, 1995; Lefley, 1989).

Historical forces, economic factors, and political realities shape the macrosystem of minority youth. First, for example, Asian and Hispanic immigrants are often compared to European immigrants of the late nineteenth and early twentieth centuries, yet these contemporary nonwhite immigrants and their children encounter a very different set of attitudes and experiences among the dominant society than did the earlier waves of white immigrants. Second, structural changes in the economy and technological changes in the workforce have resulted in high rates of unemployment among minority adults, many of whom do not have the education or skills to compete in a highly industrialized urban economy (Wilson and Aponte, 1985). Third, since the demise of the War on Poverty, political attitudes have become more conservative and there has been a backlash against affirmative action programs in employment and higher education. All of these trends have had a heavy impact on low-income minority families, resulting in increased levels of stress, which in turn have diminished their ability to provide a stable and nurturant environment for their children (Edelman, 1987). In spite of these ecological stressors, these families have demonstrated remarkable resiliency, creativity, and competence in meeting the tasks of socializing their children in an often hostile and alien environment.

The ecological perspective is also useful in the assessment of the child's psychosocial functioning in the family, the school, the peer group, and the community (Gustavsson and Balgopal, 1990; Spencer and Dornbusch, 1990). The impact of these systems on minority youth cannot be overestimated because they provide the environmental context in which socialization occurs. As Larke Nahme Huang points out in her chapter on Southeast Asian refugee children, in families with a recent history of immigration, children and adolescents are often in conflict with two competing sets of values and norms, and this conflict requires them to develop one set of behaviors for the family setting and another set of behaviors for school and community settings. When these behaviors are diametrically opposed, it inevitably leads to emotional stress and may be expressed in somatic symptoms, behavior disorders, school adjustment problems, delinquency, depression, or suicidal behavior.

Cross-Cultural Perspective

The cross-cultural perspective, developed by anthropologists to establish a comparative framework for the analysis of all human societies, assumes that all behavior has meaning and serves an adaptive function, and that behavior is governed by a set of rules and norms that promote stability and harmony within a society. Dysfunctional or deviant behavior, as defined by the group, disrupts group functioning and must be regulated by some type of institutionalized control mechanisms, such as shamans, spiritualists, faith healers, and mental health practitioners (Gaw, 1993; Price-Williams, 1975).

This cross-cultural perspective has been employed by many minority mental health researchers to provide a comparative context for viewing psychological phenomena among diverse ethnic groups in the United States (Atkinson, Morten, and Sue, 1989; Comas-Diaz and Griffith, 1988; Pedersen, Draguns, Lonner, and Trimble, 1989). While these efforts are still in their infancy, research on mental health in a variety of ethnic groups has encompassed a wide range of topics, including attitudes toward mental health and mental illness; belief systems about the causes of mental illness and dysfunctional behavior; differential symptomatology, defensive patterns, and coping strategies; help-seeking behaviors; utilization of services; and responsiveness to treatment.

Ethnicity and Mental Health

Research on minority mental health has documented the numerous ways in which ethnicity influences the psychological well-being of minority adults and families, but little attention has been paid to its influence on the developing child and adolescent (Powell, Yamamoto, Romero, and Morales, 1983; Phinney and Rotheram, 1987; Spencer and Dornbusch, 1990). Obviously its influence is mediated to children through their parents and other significant adults in their immediate social environment.

First, ethnicity shapes the child's belief systems about what constitutes mental health and mental illness, in terms of both general criteria and specific behavioral traits. Second, ethnicity influences the child's manifestation of symptoms, defensive styles, and patterns of coping with anxiety, depression, fear, guilt, and anger. Some ethnic groups reinforce "acting in" neurotic symptoms, others reward "acting out" characterological symptoms, and still others reward somatic symptoms; thus children learn patterns of illness and dysfunctional behavior that are culturally reinforced and tolerated. Third, ethnicity largely determines the help-seeking patterns that parents use to seek relief for children or adolescents with dysfunctional behaviors or symptoms. The person consulted for help may range from a priest or minister to a spiritualist or native healer to an herbalist or acupuncturist to a tribal council or family elder. Fourth, ethnicity is a major factor in shaping the way the child or adolescent utilizes and responds to treatment. The level of initial trust and openness, the attitude toward self-disclosure, the willingness to discuss certain topics, the motivation to participate in insight-oriented treatment—all of these aspects of the treatment relationship are filtered through the screen of ethnicity.

Sue and Sue (1977) have identified three variables that are important to assess in minority clients: culture-bound variables, language-bound variables, and class-bound variables. These variables are particularly relevant to children and adolescents, whose daily lives are circumscribed by their family and community experiences. In order to conduct an adequate assessment of a young client, the clinician should have some knowledge of the cultural background, attitudes, norms, and childrearing practices of the family; some familiarity with the language, the immigration history, the belief systems, and the level of acculturation of the family; and an understanding of the impact of socioeconomic status on the family's lifestyle, community experiences, opportunities, and aspirations.

Ethnicity, Social Class, and Adaptation

Ethnicity is a term that has been defined in various ways by various authors, but it will be used here to mean "those who share a unique social and cultural heritage, that is passed on from generation to generation" (Mindel and Habenstein, 1981, p. 5). Green (1982) further points out that "members of an ethnic group believe themselves to be distinctive from others in some significant way" (p. 9). Race and ethnicity are not identical, but they frequently overlap, as with Chinese Americans or African Americans. Hispanics, conversely, are defined by their common cultural heritage (Mexican or Latin American) and their language (Spanish), but they can be white, black, Indian, or a mixture of all three.

Membership in an ethnic group provides an individual with a cultural identity and a set of prescribed values, norms, and social behaviors. Ethnic identity provides a significant framework through which the growing child views himself or herself, the world, and future opportunities. It also provides meaning to the child's subjective experiences, structure to interpersonal relationships, and form to behaviors and activities. For example, ethnicity may be a factor in determining the kind of family in which a child grows up, the language that he or she speaks first, the kind of neighborhood he or she lives in, the church he or she attends (if any), the kind of school he or she attends, and the role models that are available.

Ethnic identity, when combined with membership in a minority race, creates a dual challenge to the child or adolescent. In a country where the dominant majority is Caucasian, there are many "white" ethnic groups, such as the Jews, the Poles, the Irish, and the Italians (Mindel and Habenstein, 1981). Members of these groups can practice their cultural customs in their homes and religious institutions, but they can also blend into the mainstream social institutions, such as schools, businesses and professional organizations, and government. Ethnic minority groups, however, are visibly identified by their racial or linguistic differences. Minority groups have been defined as "those groups that have unequal access to power, that are considered in some way unworthy of sharing power equally, and that are stigmatized in terms of assumed inferior traits or characteristics" (Mindel and Habenstein, 1981, p. 8). Ethnic minority status has traditionally been associated with a restricted range of options in education, employment, and lifestyle, as well as with reduced opportunities for mobility and success in the wider society (Farley and Allen, 1989; Omi and Winant, 1986). Thus a child growing up in a minority family may be exposed to different family dynamics, different school experiences, and different community responses than a child from a white family.

Social class is another dimension that describes and defines the child's world by ascribing a specific position and value to his or her family's socioeconomic status (SES). The family's SES will largely determine the child's social environment, lifestyle, level of education, and occupational aspirations. For an adolescent, social class will also influence the choice of friends, activities, and social roles. Thus membership in a social class provides a set of parameters within which the growing child and adolescent will experience a restricted range of opportunities, choices, and challenges in particular social contexts.

In American society there is an important interrelationship among ethnicity, race, and social class, with high status associated with membership in white, Anglo-Saxon, middle-class families and low status associated with membership in nonwhite, ethnic minority, lower-class families (Hacker, 1992; Omi and Winant, 1986). It follows that children and adolescents in many Asian, black, Hispanic, and American Indian families are triply stigmatized in American society because they differ from the norm in three major respects: they are nonwhite by race (except for white Hispanics), non–Anglo-Saxon by ethnicity, and predominantly non-middle-class by socioeconomic status.

An Interactive Model

It is obvious that ethnicity, race, and social class overlap considerably and may be conceived parsimoniously as three interacting dimensions of the child's life experience. We propose that ethnicity is the overarching dimension that provides the child with a framework for perceiving and responding to the world; that it shapes the child's personal and social identity; that it establishes values, norms, and expectations for appropriate behaviors; and that it defines parameters for choices and opportunities for the child's social, educational, and occupational experiences. Ethnicity is a major influence on the child's socialization in the family; it provides the structures through which developmental tasks are mediated. Moreover, ethnicity has a significant impact on the way the child is perceived and treated in the school, by peers, and in the broader community.

It is also important to point out that parents from different ethnic groups may use different criteria to measure independence, competence, and interpersonal skills, or they may differentially value these behaviors as either relevant or irrelevant to the child's successful adaptation to the social environment. Thus childrearing practices reflect broad diversity in the strategies and techniques employed to socialize children according to the belief system, values, and norms of their ethnic group. DeAnda (1984) describes the process of bicultural socialization through which minority parents teach their children how to function in two distinct sociocultural environments. She posits six factors that influence the outcome of this process of dual socialization: (1) the degree of overlap or commonality between the two cultures with regard to norms, values, perceptions, and beliefs; (2) the availability of cultural translators, mediators, and models; (3) the amount and type of corrective feedback provided by each culture regarding a person's behaviors in the specific culture; (4) the congruence of conceptual and problem-solving styles of the minority individual with those of the mainstream culture; (5) the individual's degree of bilingualism; and (6) the degree of similarity in physical appearance to the mainstream culture. DeAnda's model of bicultural socialization is an example of the incorporation of the developmental, ecological, and cross-cultural frameworks in conceptualizing the socialization of ethnic minority children.

Implications for Assessment

An understanding of the three overlapping perspectives—the developmental, the ecological, and the cross-cultural—offers a comprehensive framework for the clinician to assess the five major domains of the functioning of the individual child or adolescent: (1) level of psychosocial adjustment, (2) relationships with family, (3) school adjustment and achievement, (4) relationships with peers, and (5) adaptation to the community (Kestenbaum and Williams, 1987; Oldham, Looney, and Blotcky, 1980).

Assessment of Individual Psychosocial Adjustment

There are a number of areas in which variations in these domains have significant implications for differences in the child's psychosocial adjustment and, by extension, implications for psychological evaluation. These areas are (1) physical appearance, affect, self-concept and self-esteem; (2) interpersonal competence; (3) attitudes toward autonomy; (4) attitudes toward achievement; (5) management of aggression and impulse control; and (6) coping and defense mechanisms.

Physical appearance. In evaluating the physical appearance of the minority child or adolescent, the clinician must bear in mind that low-income minority children often suffer from malnutrition, which causes stunted growth, low hemoglobin levels, and skin and hair problems (Homel and Burns, 1989; Kovar, 1982; Egbuono and Starfield, 1982; U.S. Department of Health and Human Services, 1991). Diet can also affect their levels of energy, sleep, and elimination, so a complete physical examination may be indicated to rule out physiological causes of emotional and behavioral problems. In addition, variations from the preferred Anglo norms in height, weight, or physique can be a source of stress for minority adolescents.

Affect. The affective expression in children is influenced by cultural norms, so some children appear to be more animated while others are more reserved. Culturally appropriate norms of expressing affect should not be confused with lack of affect or depressed affect (Canino and Spurlock, 1994). Similarly, direct eye contact between children and adults is discouraged in some ethnic groups, yet this should not be interpreted by the clinician as a sign of disrespect or evasiveness.

Self-concept and self-esteem. Groups vary in the value they attach to particular characteristics and abilities, which become the sources of self-concept and self-esteem for the child and adolescent (Parham and Helms, 1985; Phinney and Rotheram, 1987). It is important for the clinician to know the differential value placed on specific attributes within each ethnic group in order to evaluate the minority youth's criteria for self-evaluation.

Interpersonal competence. Ethnic groups also vary in the values they attach to certain kinds of interpersonal skills (Phinney and Rotheram, 1987). Behaviors that are highly valued and reinforced in one group may be considered inappropriate in other groups. Clinicians should be familiar with the norms of interpersonal competence in each group in order to determine whether or not a child or adolescent is behaving in ways that are socially appropriate to his or her sociocultural milieu.

Attitudes toward autonomy. Parents in different ethnic groups place differential emphasis on early training for independence and later encouragement of adolescent autonomy (Phinney and Rotheram, 1987). The clinician must have sufficient knowledge of the value the ethnic group places on independence training at each level of development in order to determine whether a family has respected or violated its own cultural norms in regard to the development of autonomy, whether the family's norms are in serious conflict with the norms of the child's school and/or community environment, and whether the degree of dependence or autonomy is adaptive in terms of the youth's overall life situation.

Attitudes toward achievement. Cultural attitudes toward educational achievement vary widely among ethnic groups as a function of historical traditions, philosophical systems, opportunity structures, and school-related experiences (Gilmore, 1985; Fordham and Ogbu, 1986). Those groups that have been cut off from their original cultures through slavery and forced relocation have been divorced from a meaningful connection with their previous cultural achievements. Subjected to continuing barriers to social mobility, parents in these groups frequently subscribe to the value of education but find it difficult to demonstrate to their children the connection between education and occupational success. Often the achievement motive will be communicated to these youth in other ways, and their aspirations will be shaped accordingly.

In evaluating achievement, attitudes, and behaviors in minority youth, the clinician should not only examine traditional channels of educational achievement but should also include other areas such as sports, music, social relationships, and so on. When minority youth are referred for treatment because of academic or behavioral problems in the classroom, their failure often reflects low teacher expectations, chaotic school environments, inflexible or inappropriate curricula, or inappropriate placement (Reed, 1988). The clinician should assess achievement motives, interests, aptitudes, and abilities and try to determine the most effective way to facilitate a match between the client's motives and abilities on the one hand, and the available role models and opportunities on the other.

Management of aggression and impulse control. There is great ethnic variation in the socialization practices used by families to teach children how to channel their aggression and sexual impulses (Phinney and Rotheram, 1987). While some minority parents typically induce shame in order to teach children appropriate ways to manage their impulses, other parents prefer to induce guilt in order to achieve the same goals. Still other parents are more likely to use harsher methods of discipline to create external sanctions for inappropriate expressions of aggression and sexuality. These different approaches have implications for the development of internal controls, the ability to delay gratification, and the choice of subliminatory channels in these youth.

Coping and defense mechanisms. Parents from different ethnic groups employ culturally prescribed strategies to teach children how to cope with anxiety (Canino and Spurlock, 1994). The two basic strategies are (1) to reinforce externalizing (acting-out) behaviors, or (2) to reinforce internalizing (acting-in) behaviors. The clinician should be familiar with the cultural preference for handling anxiety, the defense mechanisms that are reinforced, and the adaptive strategies that are employed to handle stress.

An important caveat cannot be stated too frequently throughout this book: the clinician should always use the knowledge about a child's ethnic background as a *general* guide to psychosocial assessment, but the clinician should always be mindful of the individual child's unique characteristics, situation, symptoms, defenses, and coping strategies.

Assessment of Family Relationships

Roles and functions of children in families vary according to the type of family structure, size, traditions, communication patterns, and expectations, all of which are influenced by the ethnicity and social class of the family (Mindel and Habenstein, 1981; Mc-Goldrick, Pearce, and Giordano, 1996). Sex and birth order of the child frequently determine the imposition of a set of norms and expectations that prescribe appropriate behaviors and attitudes for that child. Physical characteristics (such as skin color), physical or mental disability, and certain personality traits may be irrelevant to the child's status in some families but highly salient in others. Socialization practices during the preschool years result in a broad spectrum of parent-child and sibling relationships in minority families (Phinney and Rotheram, 1987).

Family relationships in some ethnic groups tend to be defined in terms of age and sex-role hierarchies, with a strong emphasis on filial obedience to parental authority, respect for elders, acceptance of male authority, loyalty to the extended family, and strong conformity to community norms and expectations. Other ethnic groups are characterized by greater egalitarianism in age and sex roles, greater emphasis on shared household responsibilities, individual decision making, flexibility in marital roles, and moderate conformity to community norms and expectations.

In some ethnic families, children assume household chores and child care at earlier ages than is the norm among Anglo families. These roles should not be confused with the premature "parentified" role that is often assumed by the first generation immigrant child, who may serve as an interpreter and mediator between parents and the dominant society. Parentified children are also found in single-parent families, where they may provide emotional support and companionship as well as household help to an overly stressed parent. The clinician should be able to make a distinction between children who are fulfilling supportive roles in accordance with their age and abilities and those who are acting inappropriately as substitute parents.

If family communication patterns are hierarchical and children are not encouraged to express their opinions or to engage in free-flowing conversations, they may have trouble adapting to the teacher's expectations of verbal participation in the classroom. Traditional communication patterns in some ethnic families, for example, are not wholly compatible with the demands of the American educational system, which rewards assertive behavior, verbal fluency, and competitiveness in students (Committee for Economic Development, 1987).

The ways in which parents use their authority and enforce discipline are reflected in the ways children respond to authority and rule setting, which varies considerably among different ethnic groups. The child who does not fit the ideal cultural familial norm may be scapegoated and identified as "the problem child" or "the difficult child" and may be perceived as the rule breaker and the norm violator.

School Adjustment and Achievement

As the second major institution of socialization for latency-age children and adolescents in American society, school is an important arena for the evaluation of a child's adjustment. There are four broad areas in which the child's school adjustment should be measured: psychological adjustment to the school setting, behavioral adjustment in the school setting, academic achievement, and relationships with peers.

Psychological adjustment. Minority children, particularly those from low-income families, often experience difficulties making the transition from the home to the school environment. A number of factors may account for this difficult transition, including parental lack of education, negative parental attitudes or experiences with the school system, lack of familiarity with the norms and expectations of the classroom, language problems, and social class differences (Dokecki and others, 1975). The lack of fit between the child's background or home culture and the school environment has been associated with poor school performance (Comer, 1984; National Coalition of Advocates for Students, 1988) and a limited, sometimes disruptive parent-school relationship (Huang and Gibbs, 1992). Furthermore, for the latency-age child, this lack of congruence may be reflected in separation anxiety, school phobia, somatic symptoms, sleeping and eating problems, enuresis, and depression.

In adolescents, school phobia or truancy may actually represent fear of a violent or chaotic school environment or fear of social rejection due to some cultural, racial, or economic difference from the majority of the student body. For many minority adolescents, the transition from elementary school to the middle school or junior high school is often stressful because they leave a neighborhood school where they form a majority of the students to go to a larger school where they may become a numerical minority—a process that is repeated in the transition from junior high to high school. The stress of being a minority adolescent in a dissonant social context has been discussed by Rosenberg (1979), who points out the potential negative effects of this situation on the self-concept and self-esteem of these teenagers. Such a transition also typically requires the adolescent to become accustomed to a new set of criteria for evaluating academic competence, social skills, and extracurricular abilities. These new standards of evaluation can create considerable anxiety and depression for minority students who previously excelled in their neighborhood schools but must adjust to new criteria that generally place them at an initial disadvantage. School psychologists and social workers who evaluate students for placement in special classes need to take these various factors into account in order to avoid the misidentification of minority students, who are overrepresented in classes for students with emotional problems and learning disabilities (Reed, 1988; Mercer, 1975).

Behavioral adjustment. Minority children and adolescents are also overrepresented in special education classes for children with behavior problems (Jones, 1988; Mercer, 1975; Reed, 1988; Rivers and others, 1975). While some children are socialized to internalize their anxiety through symptoms of depression, withdrawal, somatization, and phobic behaviors, other children are reinforced for externalizing their anxiety through fighting, acting out, and delinquent behaviors. The incidence of school violence, delinquency, substance abuse, and gang activity is much higher in inner-city schools than in middle-class urban and suburban schools (Dryfoos, 1990; Fitzpatrick and Boldizar, 1993; Schubiner, Scott, and Tzelepis, 1993). More inner-city students display disruptive behaviors in the school setting, there are more disciplinary problems for teachers, and there are fewer mental health professionals to handle the referrals. When these students are referred for problem behaviors, the clinician should conduct a careful assessment of their home situation (some homes do not have adequate sleeping or study facilities), their nutrition (some students are hyperactive or lethargic due to poor diets), their family situation (some students are victims of child abuse, family violence, or absent parents), and their health status (some students have undetected vision, hearing, and other physical problems) (Kovar, 1982; Children's Defense

Fund, 1987; Powell, Yamamoto, Romero, and Morales, 1983). A careful evaluation of these students will reveal that behavior problems are usually symptomatic of more serious underlying psychological and physical problems, which are often chronic and have been neglected because of poverty, lack of access to health care, and in some cases, parental unawareness and neglect.

Academic achievement. In the area of academic achievement, low-income minority children and adolescents have generally not performed as well as their middle-class counterparts on standardized achievement tests, in Carnegie units earned toward high school graduation, or in grade-point averages (Children's Defense Fund, 1987; Quality Education for Minorities Project, 1990; Reed, 1988). As a result, these minority students have had particular difficulties in achieving parity with the non-Hispanic white students in the public school system. (This book does not tackle the controversy over the use of intelligence tests with minority students because other researchers have discussed the problems of norms and the inappropriate use of these tests with children from culturally different backgrounds. See Jones, 1988; Mercer, 1975; Samuda, 1975; and Snowden and Todman, 1982.) Because of these test results, many minority students are mislabeled as educationally handicapped, placed in remedial classrooms, and channeled into educational programs that are neither challenging nor useful. This mislabeling and misplacement probably contributes to feelings of alienation among many minority students, who have higher dropout rates and higher rates of expulsion and suspension than white students (Children's Defense Fund, 1987; Reed, 1988).

When clinicians assess the academic performance of minority youth, they should pay careful attention to the verbal skills of these children (they may have much greater fluency in their native language), to their attitudes toward school (they may feel stigmatized by placement in a special education class), to their motivation for learning (they may see no relationship between school and the "real world"), to their study habits (they may not have a safe and quiet place to study at home or a schedule for studying), and to their level of family support (their parents may not be able or willing to assist and reinforce their efforts to succeed academically) (Irvine and Irvine, 1995; Jones, 1988). Because poor academic achievement is more often a consequence of cultural, social, and environmental factors than the result of lack of ability, a sensitive clinician can identify those factors that impede the performance of minority students and develop an intervention plan to improve their academic skills.

Peer relationships in the school setting. The child's relationship with peers in the school setting should be evaluated, because it is easier to obtain independent ratings of peer interactions in the school than in the community setting (Thompson, 1990; Way, 1996). The clinician should assess the child's ability to form friendships, to display empathy, to engage in cooperative and competitive activities in the classroom and in extracurricular activities, to manage aggressive and sexual impulses, and to engage in socially appropriate same-sex and opposite-sex activities.

As minority children move into adolescence and enter schools with more heterogeneous student bodies, they are more likely to become aware of their particular ethnic or minority status and its associated degree of desirability. Biracial and bicultural adolescents in particular may have trouble joining a peer group because they do not fit into the rigid ethnic categories that define peer group membership in adolescence (Gibbs and Moskowitz-Sweet, 1991; Root, 1992). At this stage, it is also important to assess the formal and informal labels and identity of the peer group to which the adolescent belongs, because these labels supply valuable clues to the teen's self-perception and preferred activities. The minority teenager's choice of extracurricular activities and level of involvement are also important clues to his or her self-confidence, sense of competence, and degree of comfort in relating to peers.

Peer relationships in the community. In addition to the child's peer relations in the school setting, relationships with peers in the neighborhood and community should also be evaluated. Minority children and adolescents often have two sets of peer relationships: one in the school setting, and another in the community setting (Boykin and Ellison, 1995; Spencer and Dornbusch, 1990). Members of the latter group are more likely to be from the child's own ethnic group in their immediate neighborhood, from their church, or from their community activities (such as Black History Week, Chinese New Year, Cinco de Mayo Festival, and so on). Thus the usual question about having a best friend should include reference to both school and neighborhood to determine the primary locus of the child's peer affiliations. Minority children who are social isolates at a predominantly white school may be sociometric stars in their segregated neighborhood. Moreover, adolescents are more mobile and can select their friends from a wider geographical area, so inquiries should be made about the scope of their social networks. When teens are referred for problem behaviors, substance abuse, and delinquency, the clinician should determine whether these behaviors represent individual maladaptation or conformity to the peer-group culture that exists in many inner-city ghettos and barrios. The choice of intervention for a teenager who is a socialized delinquent will be very different than for one who is an antisocial delinquent (Gibbs, 1982; Gold and Petronio, 1980; Thompson, 1990). Assessment of peer relationships should focus on the social skills of the adolescent as defined by the ethnic group, that is, according to the criteria used to measure social competence, group acceptance, and group leadership (Boykin and Ellison, 1995; Phinney and Rotheram, 1987).

Heterosexual relationships in adolescents are an important area in the assessment of peer relationships. The clinician should inquire about dating practices, sexual preference, involvement in sexual activity, attitudes toward contraception, knowledge about sexually transmitted diseases, and attitudes toward intraracial versus interracial dating, particularly for biracial and bicultural youth.

Adaptation to the Community

The latency-age child's experiences in the community usually revolve around church activities, youth groups, and language schools. Involvement in these activities should be assessed to obtain a complete picture of the child's areas of interest, mobility in the community, sense of security about nonfamily activities, behavioral adjustment, and quality of relationships with adult authority figures. Minority children are sometimes "token" members of community groups, including children's drama, dance, and music groups, which can be prestigeful for their parents but stressful for them. Minority children are also sometimes scapegoated by other children who subtly reward them for assuming the role of the group's clown, rebel, or victim. Alternately, a meaningful community activity can provide the minority child with a sense of competence and with special skills that may not be available within the school or home situation. It is important for the clinician to determine the role and function of the child in community activities that can either enhance development or siphon off energy that could be used more productively in the regular school setting.

The adolescent's role in the community expands from the role of the child to include the possibility of work, organized sports and cultural activities, and volunteer activities (Feldman and Elliott, 1990). If a teenager has a part-time or full-time job, it may be essential to assess job performance, interaction with employers and coworkers, and management of money. Minority adolescents often have trouble finding jobs, and this has an impact on their sense of self-worth and on their ability to develop good work habits (Sum, Harrington, and Goedicke, 1987; Larson, 1988). If the adolescent is involved in a major activity such as an athletic team, a drama group, a rock band, or volunteer work, the clinician should assess the impact of this activity on the adolescent's self-concept, sense of competence, and educational and occupational aspirations. The clinician should also determine whether this involvement has created any family conflicts, affected academic performance, or contributed to any dysfunctional behavior, such as delinquency or drug abuse.

Implications for Treatment

The distinction between assessment and treatment is often artificial, because many clinicians believe that treatment begins with the first contact with the client. For the sake of this discussion, the assessment process is separated from treatment on the assumption that some children and adolescents will not be referred for psychological treatment per se but instead may be offered alternatives such as medication or environmental modification of a family, school, or peer system.

Because a number of studies have shown that minority clients have higher dropout rates than whites in the initial stages of treatment, clinicians should be particularly alert to the issues of involving minority children and youth in the treatment process after an initial diagnostic assessment and treatment recommendation has been completed (Sue, 1977). Clinicians who adopt the multidimensional conceptual framework outlined earlier in this chapter will be more effective in selecting and implementing appropriate interventions for minority youth with psychological and behavioral problems. We propose that if these youth are referred for psychological treatment, there are certain issues that must be addressed irrespective of the therapeutic theoretical framework or the treatment modality (such as individual, group, or family treatment). These issues, though common to all therapeutic encounters, take on special significance in the treatment of children of color and will be discussed in depth in the following chapters. A brief summary here will highlight the issues that are salient to the culturally sensitive treatment of these youth.

Entry to Treatment

The initial task of the clinician is to relieve the child's anxiety and fears about treatment, particularly those of minority youth, who are less likely than white youth to have had experience with and knowledge about therapy. They may also have entered treatment with negative attitudes about the helping professions, based on their families' previous experiences with the health and social welfare bureaucracy. Moreover, they may be concerned about being stigmatized by their families, teachers, and peers as "crazy," because formal mental health treatment is still a source of shame and embarrassment for many minority families (Canino and Spurlock, 1994; Ho, 1992; Paniagua, 1994).

Clinicians have found several strategies to be effective in their initial contacts with these clients. First, some minority youth respond favorably to an informal, friendly style in which the clinician chats with them to put them at ease. Called "personalismo" by the Hispanics and "interpersonal competence" by others, this approach defuses anxiety and establishes initial rapport with the client (Munoz, 1982; Gibbs, 1985). Other youth, however, may prefer a more formal style of authority. Second, the ethnic group's traditional sex and age roles and relationships should be respected if a child is initially interviewed with the family; this is a signal to the family that the clinician understands and respects their cultural norms, even if the family does not actually conform to those norms. Third, clinicians should offer a brief explanation of therapy, its similarity to familiar roles of healers in the client's culture (such as curandero or medicine man), and the expectation that it will bring some symptomatic relief to the client (Acosta, Yamamoto, and Evans, 1982; Frank and others, 1978).

Establishing a Relationship

Having overcome the initial barriers to treatment, the clinician faces the next challenge of establishing a therapeutic alliance with the minority youth. Major issues in the development of this relationship are establishing trust, facilitating open communication, and negotiating boundaries (Canino and Spurlock, 1994; Vargas and Koss-Chioino, 1992). Trust is a central issue in the treatment of minority clients, who have often been misperceived, mislabeled, and mistreated by other helping professionals. A certain degree of "cultural paranoia" is frequently expressed by these clients, who initially behave with suspicion and skepticism in clinical encounters (Gibbs, 1985; Ridley, 1984). Clinicians should consciously communicate warmth to and acceptance of these clients, who may be expecting a distancing and superior attitude.

To facilitate open communication of information and feelings, the clinician should be willing to share some limited personal information. Minority clients will vary in their degree of self-disclosure, but generally they are not as comfortable as Anglo clients in discussing their feelings and the intimate details of their lives. By respecting the client's pace of discussing culturally sensitive topics, the clinician will gradually build rapport and increase the client's level of self-disclosure over the course of treatment.

As the treatment relationship develops, it will be important for the clinician to negotiate boundaries within which the treatment will occur. These boundaries are an extension of the treatment contract, but they focus more specifically on the client's expectations of the therapist. Since many of these clients are unfamiliar with the therapeutic process as well as the relationship, it is important for clinicians to emphasize confidentiality, to define the relationship in business rather than social terms, and to structure sessions with flexible but clear guidelines. Negotiating boundaries in the treatment of minority youth and their families is a process of mutual accommodation between the clinical concerns of the therapist and the cultural norms of the clients.

Summary

This chapter has presented an overview of the issues in the assessment and treatment of minority children and adolescents from four major ethnic groups and two emerging population groups. Throughout this book the mental health issues of these young people will be viewed from three primary conceptual perspectives: developmental, ecological, and cross-cultural. Each contributor employs these perspectives with varying levels of emphasis, but all of them are committed to a person-in-environment approach to these issues. This multidimensional conceptual framework allows each author to analyze the interaction of sociocultural factors, developmental factors, and environmental forces.

Children of color are described as a population at risk for behavioral and psychological problems because of their minority status, their often low socioeconomic status, and their limited access to health and mental health services. Yet in spite of their greater vulnerability to problematic outcomes, the majority adapt successfully to their environments and grow up to function effectively as adults. Obviously many of these children enjoy protective factors that provide effective buffers against the stresses of poverty, prejudice, and social isolation. These protective factors may include extended families, supportive kin and social networks, strong religious beliefs, and traditional sources of help or healing, such as religious leaders, curanderos, medicine men, and herbalists.

The remainder of this book is organized to reflect the experiences of minority groups that have followed different historical pathways in American society. Nine topical chapters follow this one, each focusing on a particular minority group or special population. The authors of each chapter are psychologists who have personal and professional knowledge as well as extensive clinical experience with the ethnic groups they describe. The content of each of these chapters adheres to a similar format, providing demographic data, epidemiological data regarding incidence of psychological and behavioral disorders (where available), historical information about entry and migration to the United States, discussion of significant issues of family structure and functioning, and sociocultural issues in assessment (attitudes, values, and beliefs about mental health and illness; symptom patterns; help-seeking; and utilization patterns); and discussion of implications for effective intervention strategies and treatment techniques. Each author presents brief case vignettes that illustrate the appropriate role of sociocultural factors in the assessment of symptomatology, defensive strategies, and coping behaviors in emotionally troubled minority children and adolescents, for the purpose of developing specific treatment techniques and/or alternative intervention strategies.

The first two of these chapters describe, respectively, Chinese American youth and Japanese American youth, groups categorized by Mindel and Habenstein (1981) as "early-arriving ethnic minorities" because they first emigrated to the United States before 1900. The next four chapters describe, respectively, American Indians, African American children, African American adolescents, and Mexican Americans, all of whom are categorized by Mindel and Habenstein as "historically subjugated but volatile ethnic minorities" because of their history of slavery, forced relocation, or exploited labor. The next chapter is on Puerto Rican youth, whom these authors categorize as a "recent and continuing ethnic minority." The final two topical chapters are on, respectively, Southeast Asian refugee youth and biracial adolescents, whom we have categorized as "emerging special populations."

The next chapter deviates from the format of the others and represents a unique attempt to provide a cross-cultural comparison of clinical material in which the only variables that change are the ethnicity of the client and of the clinician. The objective of this chapter is to highlight how clinicians' cultural sensitivity can influence their conceptualization of a case, their diagnostic assessment, and their treatment recommendations, particularly when they take into account the sociocultural background of the child or adolescent client.

In the concluding chapter, the similarities and differences among the minority groups are discussed in terms of their implications for a culturally sensitive, culturally competent approach to assessment and treatment of minority youth in general. Three other important issues are also discussed: the need for further research on minority mental health issues, the need for expanded and improved training programs for mental health professionals, and the need for major changes in the mental health service delivery system to meet the needs of this growing segment of the population.

At this point we do not have sufficient, valid, and reliable data about some ethnic groups to constitute the final word on their mental health status problems or needs. Yet, as the minority populations continue to increase, we strongly feel that we cannot wait to address their mental health needs until more years of research provide this information. We believe that this book represents an initial step in providing mental health practitioners and educators with a framework for understanding the impact of ethnicity and socioeconomic status on the psychosocial development and adaptation of minority youth. Although we hope that by reading this book clinicians will gain a better understanding of these youth and their families, we must caution that the book alone will not make them experts in minority mental health. Ideally, this book will help clinicians to become more knowledgeable about the particular ethnic groups discussed and more sensitive to the similarities and differences that exist among and between all human groups.

The number of children of color in the United States is rapidly increasing, yet they remain literally and figuratively misunderstood, mislabeled, and mistreated. This book is a modest effort to increase the understanding of their needs, to improve the assessment of their problems, and to develop more effective methods of intervention and treatment for their behavioral and psychological disorders.

References

Acosta, F. X., Yamamoto, J., and Evans, L. A. *Effective Psychotherapy for Low-Income and Minority Patients.* New York: Plenum, 1982.

American Public Welfare Association. *One Child in Four.* New York: American Public Welfare Association, 1986.

Atkinson, D., Morten, G., and Sue, D. W. *Counseling American Minorities: A Cross-Cultural Perspective.* Dubuque, Iowa: W. C. Brown, 1989.

Boykin, A. W., and Ellison, C. M. "The Multiple Ecologies of Black Youth Socialization: An Afrographic Analysis." In R. L. Taylor (ed.), *African-American Youth: Their Social and Economic Status in the United States.* New York: Praeger, 1995.

Bronfenbrenner, U. *The Ecology of Human Development: Experiments by Nature and Design.* Cambridge, Mass.: Harvard University Press, 1979.

Canino, I. A., and Spurlock, J. *Culturally Diverse Children and Adolescents: Assessment, Diagnosis and Treatment.* New York: Guilford Press, 1994.

Children's Defense Fund. *A Children's Defense Budget.* Washington, D.C.: Children's Defense Fund, 1987.

Children's Defense Fund. *A Children's Defense Budget.* Washington, D.C.: Children's Defense Fund, 1996.

Comas-Diaz, L., and Griffith, E. E. (eds.). *Clinical Guidelines in Cross-Cultural Mental Health.* New York: Wiley, 1988.

Comer, J. "Home-School Relationships and How They Affect the Academic Success of Children." *Education and Urban Society,* 1984, *16*(3), 323–337.

Committee for Economic Development. *Children in Need: Investment Strategies for the Educationally Disadvantaged.* New York: Committee for Economic Development, 1987.

Cross, W. E. *Shades of Black: Diversity in African-American Identity.* Philadelphia: Temple University Press, 1991.

DeAnda, D. "Bicultural Socialization: Factors Affecting the Minority Experience." *Social Work,* 1984, *29,* 101–107.

Dokecki, P. R., and others. "Low Income and Minority Groups." In N. Hobbs (ed.), *Issues in the Classification of Children: A Sourcebook on Categories, Labels, and Their Consequences.* Vol. 1. San Francisco: Jossey-Bass, 1975.

Dryfoos, J. *Adolescents at Risk: Prevalence and Prevention.* New York: Oxford University Press, 1990.

Edelman, M. W. *Families in Peril: An Agenda for Social Change.* Cambridge, Mass.: Harvard University Press, 1987.

Egbuono, L., and Starfield, G. "Child Health and Social Status." *Pediatrics,* 1982, *69,* 550–556.

Erikson, E. H. "Identity and the Life Cycle." *Psychological Issues,* 1959, *1*(entire issue 1).

Farley, R., and Allen, W. R. *The Color Line and the Quality of Life in America.* New York: Oxford University Press, 1989.

Feldman, S., and Elliott, G. (eds.). *At the Threshold: The Developing Adolescent.* Cambridge, Mass.: Harvard University Press, 1990.

Fitzpatrick, K. M., and Boldizar, J. P. "The Prevalence and Consequences of Exposure to Violence Among African-American Youth." *Journal of the American Academy of Child and Adolescent Psychiatry,* 1993, *32,* 424–430.

Fordham, S., and Ogbu, J. "Black Students' School Success: Coping with the Burden of 'Acting White.'" *Urban Review,* 1986, *18,* 176–206.

Frank, J. D., and others. *Effective Ingredients of Successful Psychotherapy.* New York: Brunner/Mazel, 1978.

Gaw, A. C. *Culture, Ethnicity, and Mental Illness.* Washington, D.C.: American Psychiatric Press, 1993.

Gibbs, J. T. "Personality Patterns of Delinquent Females: Ethnic and Sociocultural Variations." *Journal of Clinical Psychology,* 1982, *38,* 198–206.

Gibbs, J. T. "Treatment Relationships with Black Clients: Interpersonal Versus Instrumental Strategies." In C. Germain (ed.), *Advances in Clinical Social Work Practice.* Silver Spring, Md.: National Association of Social Workers, 1985.

Gibbs, J. T., and Moskowitz-Sweet, G. "Clinical and Cultural Issues in the Treatment of Biracial and Bicultural Adolescents." *Families in Society,* 1991, *72*(10), 579–592.

Gilmore, P. "'Gimme Room': School Resistance, Attitude, and Access to Literacy." *Journal of Education,* 1985, *167,* 111–128.

Gold, M., and Petronio, J. "Delinquent Behavior in Adolescence." In J. Adelson (ed.), *Handbook of Adolescent Psychology.* New York: Wiley, 1980.

Gong-Guy, E., Craveks, R., and Patterson, T. "Clinical Issues in Mental Health Service Delivery to Refugees." *American Psychologist,* 1991, *46*(6), 642–648.

Green, J. W. *Cultural Awareness in the Human Services.* Englewood Cliffs, N.J.: Prentice Hall, 1982.

Gustavsson, N. S., and Balgopal, P. R. "Violence and Minority Youth: An Ecological Perspective." In A. R. Stiffman and L. E. Davis (eds.), *Ethnic Issues in Adolescent Mental Health.* Thousand Oaks, Calif.: Sage, 1990.

Hacker, A. *Two Nations: Black and White, Separate, Hostile, Unequal.* New York: Scribner, 1992.

Ho, M. K. *Minority Children and Adolescents in Therapy.* Thousand Oaks, Calif.: Sage, 1992.

Homel, R., and Burns, A. "Environmental Quality and Well-Being of Children." *Social Indicators Research,* 1989, *21,* 133–158.

Huang, L. N., and Gibbs, J. T. "Partners or Adversaries: Home-School Collaboration Across Culture, Race, and Ethnicity." In S. Christenson and J. Conoley (eds.), *Home-School Collaboration: Enhancing Children's Academic and Social Competence.* Silver Spring, Md.: National Association of School Psychologists, 1992.

Irvine, J. J., and Irvine, R. W. "Black Youth in School: Individual Achievement and Institutional/Cultural Perspectives." In R. L. Taylor (ed.), *African-American Youth: Their Social and Economic Status in the United States.* New York: Praeger, 1995.

Jones, E. E., and Korchin, S. J. (eds.). *Minority Mental Health.* New York: Praeger, 1982.

Jones, R. L. (ed.). *Psychoeducational Assessment of Minority Group Children: A Casebook.* Berkeley, Calif.: Cobb & Henry, 1988.

Kestenbaum, C., and Williams, D. (eds.). *Clinical Assessments of Children and Adolescents.* New York: New York University Press, 1987.

Kovar, M. G. "Health Status of U.S. Children and Use of Medical Care." *Public Health Reports,* 1982, *97,* 3–15.

Larson, T. E. "Employment and Unemployment of Young Black Men." In J. T. Gibbs (ed.), *Young, Black, and Male in America: An Endangered Species.* Westport, Conn.: Auburn House, 1988.

Lefley, H. P. "Counseling Refugees: The North American Experience." In P. B. Pedersen, J. G. Draguns, W. J. Lonner, and J. E. Trimble (eds.), *Counseling Across Cultures.* (3rd ed.) Honolulu: University of Hawaii Press, 1989.

McGoldrick, M., Pearce, J. K., and Giordano, J. (eds.). *Ethnicity and Family Therapy.* (2nd ed.) New York: Guilford Press, 1996.

Mead, G. H. *Mind, Self, and Society.* Chicago: University of Chicago Press, 1934.

Mercer, J. R. "Psychological Assessment and the Rights of Children." In N. Hobbs (ed.), *Issues in the Classification of Children: A Sourcebook on Categories, Labels, and Their Consequences.* Vol. 1. San Francisco: Jossey-Bass, 1975.

Mindel, C. H., and Habenstein, R. W. (eds.). *Ethnic Families in America: Patterns and Variations.* (2nd ed.) New York: Elsevier, 1981.

Munoz, R. F. "The Spanish-Speaking Consumer and the Community Mental Health Center." In E. E. Jones and S. J. Korchin (eds.), *Minority Mental Health.* New York: Praeger, 1982.

National Coalition of Advocates for Students. *New Voices: Immigrant Students in the U.S. Public Schools.* Boston: National Coalition of Advocates for Students, 1988.

Oldham, D. G., Looney, J. G., and Blotcky, M. "Clinical Assessment of Symptoms in Adolescents." *American Journal of Orthopsychiatry,* 1980, *50,* 697–703.

Omi, M., and Winant, H. *Racial Formation in the United States: From the 1960s to the 1980s.* New York: Routledge, 1986.

Ozawa, M. "Nonwhites and the Demographic Imperative in Social Welfare Spending." *Social Work,* 1986, *31,* 440–446.

Padilla, A. M. (ed.). *Hispanic Psychology: Critical Issues in Theory and Research.* Thousand Oaks, Calif.: Sage, 1995.

Paniagua, F. A. *Assessing and Treating Culturally Diverse Clients.* Thousand Oaks, Calif.: Sage, 1994.

Parham, T., and Helms, J. "Attitudes of Racial Identity and Self-Esteem of Black Students: An Exploratory Investigation." *Journal of College Student Personnel,* 1985, *26,* 143–147.

Pedersen, P. B., Draguns, J. G., Lonner, W. J., and Trimble, J. E. (eds.). *Counseling Across Cultures.* (3rd ed.) Honolulu, Hawaii: University of Hawaii Press, 1989.

Phinney, J. S., and Rotheram, M. J. *Children's Ethnic Socialization: Pluralism and Development.* Thousand Oaks, Calif.: Sage, 1987.

Powell, G. J. "Self-Concepts Among Afro-American Students in Racially Isolated Minority Schools: Some Regional Differences." *Journal of the American Academy of Child Psychiatry*, 1985, *24*, 142–149.

Powell, G. J., Yamamoto, J., Romero, A., and Morales, A. (eds.). *The Psychosocial Development of Minority Group Children*. New York: Brunner/Mazel, 1983.

President's Commission on Mental Health. *Mental Health in America: 1978*. Vol. 1. Washington, D.C.: U.S. Government Printing Office, 1978.

Price-Williams, D. R. *Explorations in Cross-Cultural Psychology*. Novato, Calif.: Chandler and Sharp, 1975.

"Quality Counts: A Report Card on the Condition of Public Education in the Fifty States." *Education Week*, 1997, *16*, 61.

Quality Education for Minorities Project. *Education That Works: An Action Plan for the Education of Minorities*. Cambridge: Massachusetts Institute of Technology, 1990.

Reed, R. "Education and Achievement of Young Black Males." In J. T. Gibbs (ed.), *Young, Black, and Male in America: An Endangered Species*. Westport, Conn.: Auburn House, 1988.

Ridley, C. R. "Clinical Treatment of the Nondisclosing Black Client: A Therapeutic Paradox." *American Psychologist*, 1984, *39*, 1234–1244.

Rivers, L. W., and others. "Mosaic of Labels for Black Children." In N. Hobbs (ed.), *Issues in the Classification of Children: A Sourcebook on Categories, Labels, and Their Consequences*. Vol. 2. San Francisco: Jossey-Bass, 1975.

Rodgers, H. R. *Poor Women, Poor Families*. Armonk, N.Y.: Sharpe, 1986.

Root, M. P. (ed.). *Racially Mixed People in America*. Thousand Oaks, Calif.: Sage, 1992.

Rosenberg, M. *Conceiving the Self*. New York: Basic Books, 1979.

Rosenberg, M., and Simmons, R. *Black and White Self-Esteem: The Urban School Child*. Rose Monograph Series. Washington, D.C.: American Sociological Association, 1971.

Samuda, R. *Psychological Testing of American Minorities: Issues and Consequences*. New York: Dodd, Mead, 1975.

Schorr, A. *Common Decency: Domestic Policies After Reagan*. New Haven, Conn.: Yale University Press, 1986.

Schubiner, H., Scott, R., and Tzelepis, A. "Exposure to Violence Among Inner-City Youth." *Journal of Adolescent Health*, 1993, *14*, 214–219.

Sluzki, C. "Migration and Family Conflict." *Family Process*, 1979, *18*(4), 379–390.

Snowden, L., and Todman, P. A. "The Psychological Assessment of Blacks: New and Needed Developments." In E. E. Jones and S. J. Korchin (eds.), *Minority Mental Health*. New York: Praeger, 1982.

Spencer, M. B., and Dornbusch, S. "American Minority Adolescents." In S. Feldman and G. Elliott (eds.), *At the Threshold: The Developing Adolescent.* Cambridge, Mass.: Harvard University Press, 1990.

Sue, D., and Sue, E. "Barriers to Effective Cross-Cultural Counseling." *Journal of Counseling Psychology,* 1977, *24,* 420–429.

Sue, D. W., and Sue, D. *Counseling the Culturally Different.* (2nd ed.) New York: John Wiley, 1990.

Sue, S. "Community Mental Health Services to Minority Groups: Some Optimism, Some Pessimism." *American Psychologist,* 1977, *32,* 616–624.

Sum, A., Harrington, P. E., and Goedicke, W. "One-Fifth of the Nation's Teenagers: Employment Problems of Poor Youth in America, 1981–1985." *Youth and Society,* 1987, *18,* 195–237.

Taylor, R. L. "Psychosocial Development Among Black Children and Youth: A Reexamination." *American Journal of Orthopsychiatry,* 1976, *46,* 4–19.

Thompson, C. L. "In Pursuit of Affirmation: The Antisocial Inner-City Adolescent." In A. R. Stiffman and L. E. Davis (eds.), *Ethnic Issues in Adolescent Mental Health.* Thousand Oaks, Calif.: Sage, 1990.

U.S. Bureau of the Census. *Statistical Abstract of the United States, 1996.* (116th ed.) Washington, D.C.: U.S. Department of Commerce, 1996.

U.S. Department of Health and Human Services. *Health Status of Minorities and Low-Income Groups.* (3rd ed.) Washington, D.C.: U.S. Government Printing Office, 1991.

Vargas, L. A., and Koss-Chioino, J. D. (eds.). *Working with Culture: Psychotherapeutic Interventions with Ethnic Minority Children and Adolescents.* San Francisco: Jossey-Bass, 1992.

Way, N. "Between Experiences of Betrayal and Desire: Close Friendships Among Urban Adolescents." In B. J. Leadbetter and N. Way (eds.), *Urban Girls: Resisting Stereotypes, Creating Identities.* New York: New York University Press, 1996.

Wilson, W. J. *The Truly Disadvantaged.* Chicago: University of Chicago Press, 1987.

Wilson, W. J., and Aponte, R. "Urban Poverty." *Annual Review of Sociology,* 1985, *11,* 231–258.

Chapter Two

Chinese American Children and Adolescents

Larke Nahme Huang
Yu-Wen Ying

A chapter on psychological problems in the Chinese American population may seem surprising to some because Asian Americans in general seldom use mental health services and because most professionals in the field have had minimal if any contact with Chinese American clients. Add to this the popular media stereotype of Asians as the "model minority" and one is justified in asking, Do such problems actually exist in this community? The answer, of course, is yes; but unfortunately utilization rates and media stereotypes obscure the reality. The Special Populations Task Force of the President's Commission on Mental Health (1978) concluded that ethnic minorities are underserved or inappropriately served by existing mental health services and that utilization rates are not reliable indicators of need in minority communities. Ethnic minority clients often find mental health services strange, intimidating, stigmatizing, and not particularly helpful. Chinese Americans have tended to use mental health services only as a last resort, when family and community resources have been exhausted.

In addition, cultural definitions of mental health problems vary considerably within the Chinese community and most dramatically between Asian and Western cultures. These conceptualizations often direct the person's search for resolution, so if the disorder is thought to result from weak will or organic factors, a teacher, elder, or physician may be sought rather than a psychiatrist, psychologist, or mental health worker. These unconventional help-seeking patterns further obfuscate the true incidence of psychological disorder in this population.

Finally, the model-minority stereotype oversimplifies the issues for Chinese Americans and obscures important realities in the community. Without a doubt, some Chinese Americans have "made it" socially and economically. However, many have not. Although Chinese Americans have among the highest median family incomes of many ethnic minorities, they are also underemployed and receiving lower salaries than other people doing comparable work. In the 1970s, the poverty rate for Chinese Americans in New York City was 15 percent—4 points higher than the national rate (Chen, 1981). Chinese American youth, in particular, suffer under this stereotype as it obscures the heterogeneity among this population and places undue stress and expectations on them.

The objective of this chapter is to familiarize the reader with the Chinese American population in the United States, to highlight the mental health issues for children and adolescents in that population, and to recommend appropriate intervention strategies. This is a task easier said than done, because Chinese Americans are an extremely heterogeneous group—socially, politically, and culturally. Although it is impossible to provide a picture of the typical Chinese American, it is reasonable to try to present a framework for examining the Chinese experience in the United States. One such framework that allows for multiple levels of analysis is an ecological systems approach (Bronfenbrenner, 1979), which enables the examination of the interaction between individual and environment. So, for example, to understand the experience of Chinese American youth in this country, it is necessary not only to understand the childrearing strategies of Chinese and Chinese American parents, but also to comprehend the impact of restrictive immigration laws in the 1900s; of miscegenation and exclusion laws, which were only repealed in the 1960s; and of racism and discrimination. These larger societal issues have an impact on Chinese American families, on their composition, on their descendants, and on the community as a whole. It is similarly important to grasp the influence of Confucian traditions, which are passed from one generation to the next and, although they are becoming increasingly diluted and Westernized, still impose an Eastern philosophy of order on Chinese American families. Although these events and traditions will have varying effects depending on the degree of the family's acculturation, they represent levels of analysis critical to an understanding of Chinese American youth and their manifestation of psychological problems.

To begin to understand these youth, it is first necessary to obtain an overview of the Chinese in the United States, of the critical events in their history and patterns of migration, and of the traditions carried from China that have influenced family formation in this country.

The Chinese in America

According to the 1990 census, there are 1,645,472 Chinese residing in the United States, of whom the majority are foreign-born (U.S. Bureau of the Census, 1990). This is a population still in the process of acculturating and establishing a Chinese American culture, for whom the migration process is still a fresh experience and integration of the old with the new is still ongoing. The rate of immigration has significantly increased since the elimination of quotas on immigrants from Asia in 1965, and it is expected to continue to rise into the next century.

Geographically, the majority of the Chinese American population is found along the West and East Coasts, primarily in and around major metropolitan centers. More than half (53 percent) live in the western states, including California (33 percent) and Hawaii (3 percent) (Lee, 1996). Since the 1980 census, the Chinese American population has become geographically dispersed throughout the rest of the United States, with the significant concentrations found in the northeastern states and New York State, followed by lower concentrations in the South and in the north central states.

The median age of Chinese Americans is 29.6 years. Youth make up 30 percent of the population, with a fairly even distribution across the ages (U.S. Bureau of the Census, 1983a).

Education is highly valued within this culture. This is demonstrated in the high percentage of school enrollees at all ages. Of persons 25 years and older, 71.3 percent are high school graduates and the median number of school years completed is 13.4. Seventy-five

percent of males over 25 and 67.4 percent of females have completed high school (U.S. Bureau of the Census, 1983b). Yet, in
contrast to these statistics, 11 percent of Chinese Americans are illiterate, a percentage seven times that of whites and three times
that of blacks (Chen, 1981).

Socioeconomically, Chinese Americans span a wide range, with
some families living at or below the poverty level and others among
the most wealthy of the general population. Median household income in 1980 was $19,561. Of 250,585 households, 31,022 (12 per-
cent) exist on an annual income of less than $5,000; at the other
extreme, almost 20,000 households make more than $50,000 (U.S.
Bureau of the Census, 1983b). In 1990, the Chinese had the highest number of persons (13.3 percent) living below the poverty level
of all Asian groups in the United States except for Southeast Asian
refugees (Asian American Health Forum, 1990).

History and Patterns of Migration

The history of Chinese migration to the United States is sporadic
and uneven. Small numbers of Chinese first arrived in this country
in 1820. The catalyst for increased migration was the discovery of
gold in California in the 1840s, in conjunction with increasingly
harsh living conditions in China due to oppressive, feudalistic control by the Manchu dynasty, repeated floods and famine, and ongoing civil wars. These immigrants and those who followed came with
the intent of making a fortune in America, the "Gold Mountain,"
and then returning to China (Sung, 1967). Most of these immigrants
were from areas around Hong Kong, Macao, and Guangdong (Can-
ton) province and were Cantonese-speaking males.

These earliest immigrants were received with little animosity
and much indifference. However, as the United States entered its
own economic downturn in the late 1870s, and as the numbers of
Chinese immigrants increased into the thousands, anti-Chinese
sentiment grew. It culminated in the Chinese Exclusion Act of
1882, which was the first legislation to ban a particular race from
entering the United States. In 1924 the Oriental Exclusion Act
banned all Oriental immigration from Asia. From 1890 to 1945,
more Chinese left than entered the United States. Those who remained lived under the oppression of the exclusion laws, suffering

innumerable humiliations, racial violence, loss of property and livelihood, and sometimes loss of life. In spite of the hostile environs, many Chinese elected to stay in the United States, but to do so they needed to change their status from laborers (who were targets of deportation) to merchants or businessmen. Chinatowns became the basis for this economic conversion, drawing on traditional structures such as clans and family associations to organize an urban economic community built on the service industries, such as restaurants, small shops, domestic work, and laundries (Chen, 1981; Lyman, 1976).

The next wave of immigrants reflected the changing social structure in China. When imperial China fell in 1911, a new middle class of businessmen and entrepreneurs emerged. The families of this class, as well as affluent landowners, began to send their children overseas to obtain an American or European education or to establish an overseas branch of the family business. These new immigrants came from a wealthier social class, usually spoke a different dialect than the earlier Chinese, often originated from such cosmopolitan cities as Shanghai, were better educated, and did not settle in Chinatowns. They had little in common with the earlier settlers, so the two groups initially had minimal interaction. However, like the earlier immigrants, many of these immigrants were sojourners who intended to return to China and, with their modern education, secure prestigious positions in their province. With the Communist takeover of China in 1949, these immigrants were stranded overseas and became unintended permanent residents of the United States.

In 1965, in the midst of the civil rights movement, the Immigration and Nationality Acts Amendments ended legislated discrimination and resulted in yet another wave of immigrants. Some of these post-1965 immigrants were unskilled laborers, but many were from middle-class or affluent families, and they spoke Mandarin rather than the Cantonese dialects, were sometimes fluent in English, and possessed higher-level skills and education. They usually came by way of Hong Kong or Taiwan and attempted to establish themselves in businesses, industry, and professions for which they had been trained (Chen, 1981). Although many of these immigrants eventually became successful, they often suffered a period of underemployment or downward mobility because their training or degrees were initially less valued than and noncompetitive with comparable degrees in the United States.

Culture and Family Traditions

Although Chinese American families show much diversity and variation, the following discussion conveys some of the historical and cultural antecedents for Chinese American family structure. The nature and structure of the Chinese family derived from Confucian philosophy, which fostered a sense of order by prescribing the roles to be assumed in Chinese society. Guidelines for specific family relationships, patterns of communication, and negotiations with the outside world were clearly delineated, with the goal of harmonious existence (Lin, 1938).

Family Roles

Confucian ethics placed a strong emphasis on roles within the family and on the proper behavior associated with each role. The obligations, responsibilities, and privileges of each role were delineated according to a vertical, hierarchal role structure, with the father as the undisputed head. His authority was unchallenged, and he was the recipient of total respect and loyalty from all family members. In return, he assumed maximum responsibility for the family's social status and economic well-being. The mother was responsible for the emotional nurturance and well-being of the family, her primary role being to serve the father and raise the children. She was accorded respect from her children, although her role was less removed and distant than the father's. She would often intercede with the father on behalf of the children. Mothers were generally discouraged from taking on work roles outside the family (Shon and Ja, 1982).

Gender and birth position were also associated with certain duties and privileges. Sons were more highly valued than daughters; family lineage was passed through the male, while females were absorbed into the families of their husbands. The first-born son, the most valued child, received preferential treatment as well as more familial responsibilities. The prescriptive roles for daughters were less rewarding; females often did not come into positions of authority or respect until they assumed the role of mother-in-law.

These family roles were predominant in imperial, feudal China. Of course, as China has modernized, these roles have altered radically. Similarly, in acculturated Chinese families in the United States, only derivatives of these rigidly defined roles remain. For example, females are not entirely relegated to subservient roles. Fathers are often the figurative heads of families, especially when dealing with the public, while the mother may in fact be the driving force in the family and the decision maker behind the scenes. First sons continue to be highly valued, but the discrepancies between the sexes in duties and privileges, though still there, are not so glaring.

The extended family rather than the nuclear family was the primary family unit in China. The process of migration disrupted these relationships, but many Chinese in America have attempted to reconstruct this kinship network. For some, the extended family is clearly identified as an important source of social and sometimes financial support. However, for some highly Westernized families, the extended family may also be experienced as a burden and as a restriction on one's autonomy.

Patterns of Communication

Congruent with a rigid system of role relationships, rules of communication were governed by the attributes of the parties involved. Within families, usually gender and age governed the degree of open expression allowed, the initiator of conversation, the structure of the language used, and the topics to be addressed. Communication was often indirect, and outright confrontation was eschewed. Even today, expression of emotion is generally frowned upon, and suppression of undesirable thoughts or emotions is highly valued. These rules for communication contrast markedly with American values of expression and the tendency to speak one's mind or "let it all hang out" (Shon and Ja, 1982).

Obligation, Shame, and "Face"

In contrast to the Western concept of contractual obligation and reciprocity, unspoken and obligatory reciprocity in interaction is of paramount importance in Chinese culture and continues to be evident among Chinese in America. Obligations are determined by one's role (for example, the obligation of the child to the parent, or filial piety) or incurred through acts of kindness or helpfulness. Behavior is often dictated by a sense of obligation or by a desire to avoid being in a position of obligation.

Shame and "loss of face" are similarly guiding principles of behavior and powerful motivating forces for conforming to societal or familial expectations (Shon and Ja, 1982). Even truthfulness and honesty in the abstract are secondary to "saving face" for oneself and others. Bringing shame on one's family is avoided at all costs. Ability to place the group's or family's wishes above one's individual desires is held as a virtue. Given that interdependence is the foundation of Chinese culture, everything an individual does is viewed as a reflection on the family as a whole.

Mental Health Issues for Chinese American Children and Adolescents

The literature on psychological and behavioral disorders in Chinese American children and adolescents is quite limited, as Asian Americans in general have not been the focus of systematic inquiry concerning mental health issues. Several studies of Chinese American adults examine psychiatric hospitalization rates, patterns of service utilization, and comparison of inpatients and outpatients (Berk and Hirata, 1973; Brown, Stein, Huang, and Harris, 1973; Sue and McKinney, 1975); however, none of these studies looks at the youth population. Even the Special Populations Task Force of the President's Commission on Mental Health, which submitted an extensive report on the mental health of Asian/Pacific Americans in 1978, neglected to examine the mental health needs of Chinese American youth.

Only recently have studies begun to examine the mental health needs of Asian American children and adolescents. In a longitudinal study of mental health service utilization rates for ethnic minority youth in California between the years 1983 and 1988, Bui and Takeuchi (1992) concluded that Asian American adolescents were underrepresented in mental health facilities, and of those seen, most were referred by the school system. In contrast to African American and Hispanic adolescents, who were more frequently diagnosed with conduct disorder, Asian American adolescents were given nonpsychiatric diagnoses, such as organic brain syndrome, drug problems, or cognitive impairments, or a deferred diagnosis.

The County of Los Angeles Department of Mental Health (1985, 1986) reports serving a total of 652 Chinese American clients, 97 of whom were children under age eighteen, during the 1984–85 fiscal year. In the following fiscal year, the number rose to 873, and of these, 115 were under eighteen. Diagnostically, these clients ranged from adjustment disorder to psychotic disorders. Unfortunately, the specific diagnostic breakdown for these Chinese American children is not available.

Data from various urban community mental health service agencies and programs provide a better diagnostic picture. At Asian Community Mental Health Services in Oakland, California, sixteen Chinese American children and adolescents were seen during the 1987–88 fiscal year (D. Li-Repac, personal communication, Aug. 8, 1988). Of these, six were under age thirteen and ten were between thirteen and seventeen; six were female and ten were male. Diagnostically, three suffered from disorders that usually are first evident in infancy, childhood, or adolescence; two suffered from schizophrenic disorder, one from a psychotic disorder not elsewhere classified, three from affective disorder, and seven from adjustment disorder.

At San Francisco's Galileo High School Adolescent Program, fifty adolescents (twenty-nine males and twenty-one females, aged fourteen to twenty) were seen during the 1987–88 school year (L. Lee, personal communication, July 28, 1988). Fifteen of these young people received a diagnosis of adjustment disorder with depressed mood; twelve were diagnosed as having adjustment disorder with mixed emotional features; and seven were diagnosed with adjustment disorder with mixed disturbance of emotions and conduct. The remaining sixteen met criteria for a variety of other disorders, ranging from anxiety disorder to schizophrenic disorders. The major precipitating factors appeared to be immigration adjustment and change of school.

At the Asian Bicultural Clinic of Gouverneur Hospital in New York City, fourteen adolescents (aged twelve to nineteen) were seen for suicidal gestures or attempts from 1985 to 1988 (Ma, Cohen, and Yeung, 1988). Six were male, eight were female; six were U.S.–born and eight were foreign-born (mostly from Hong Kong). Their diagnoses ranged from affective disorder (seven clients), schizoaffective disorder (two), schizophrenic disorder (one), and atypical psychosis (one) to adjustment disorder (two) and life circumstance problem (one). Eight of the adolescents made one suicidal gesture or attempt during this period, and the other six made two or three. The precipitating events were family conflicts (four), problem relationships with the opposite sex (three), school adjustment (three), psychotic delusion (three), and conflict with peers (three).

In a study of a nonclinical population, Lorenzo (1995) found that 99 Asian American ninth grade students exhibited less delinquent behavior and performed better academically than 404 ninth grade white adolescents. However, the Asian American students were significantly more isolated, more depressed and anxious, and less involved in after-school activities than their white classmates. Furthermore, they tended to internalize social problems, were less likely to seek help, and had fewer role models and less social support.

These data provide a rough picture of the range of psychological difficulties experienced by Chinese American children and adolescents. However, the relatively small number of Chinese American youth in these programs likely reflects underutilization of the services and thus gives only an incomplete picture. Our limited information on the psychological problems of Chinese American youth makes it necessary to extrapolate from other areas of the literature that may bear on the experiences of these children and their mental health. Three such areas are studies of migration and relocation of youth, self-concept studies, and empirical personality studies.

Touliatos and Lindholm (1980) compared the incidence of psychological disturbance in American-born Caucasian children and children of foreign-born parents. Among the sample of ninety-seven children of foreign-born parents, forty-two were of Chinese, Japanese, or Southeast Asian descent. Some of these children were American-born, some were foreign-born. The types of disorders examined were conduct problems, personality problems, inadequacy/immaturity problems, socialized delinquency, and psychotic symptomatology. In all five areas, the children of foreign-born parents showed less psychopathology than the native-born Caucasian children. Further analysis revealed that children of Chinese, Japanese, or Southeast Asian descent exhibited significantly fewer conduct and inadequacy/immaturity problems than native-born Caucasian children.

The results of this study are consistent with Aronowitz's (1984) review, which concluded that immigrant children do not necessarily show a higher incidence of disorder than their native peers. None of the studies that Aronowitz reviewed focused specifically on Chinese children; however, his conclusions about immigrant children in general may be pertinent. Acknowledging that the incidence of disorder is not greater for immigrant children, he nevertheless documented that when disorders do occur, there is a certain predictability. These children tend to present with anxiety, depression, and conduct disorders rather than with acute psychiatric symptoms. An extensive survey of West Indian children in London revealed that conduct disorders among the immigrant children were manifest almost entirely at school and not at home (Rutter and others, 1974). The authors suggested that this may be due to possible learning difficulties, racial discrimination, and high pupil turnover in the predominantly immigrant schools.

The developmental literature indicates that relocations may be stressful for children (Garmezy and Rutter, 1983). The subjective experience and manner of coping are, of course, related to the developmental stage of the child. For the latency-age child or adolescent, relocations or migrations are experienced directly and may represent a significant loss and at least temporary instability and uncertainty. Anxiety and depression may initially outweigh the excitement associated with the move. For the infant and toddler, the relocation is more often experienced through the parents. As long as the parents remain constant figures in the child's life, the impact of a move may be less dramatic. However, the anxiety experienced by the parents may be inadvertently transmitted to the young child. Rutter (1983) indicates that children may be affected by their parents' attitudes and psychological states as well as by any actual event. Thus a relocation, though indirectly experienced, may still have a dramatic impact on the very young child.

Children and adolescents may assume rather passive roles in the early stages of migration and then become quite active and mobilized in the later stages. They generally have little say in the decision-making process and the actual arrangements for migrating; however, once in the new country, they tend to acculturate more rapidly and then assume a more active role in the family. These children become "parentified," assuming roles that previously had been those of their parents. Because of their rapid ease with the new language, they become the negotiators of the outside world for their parents. They do the shopping, they pay the bills, they answer the telephone; they are their parents' interpreters. For some children, this new role may be novel and exciting. However, when prolonged, it can become burdensome and tedious and a threat to the traditional configuration of roles within the family.

Ou and McAdoo (1980) examined the self-concept, ethnic preference, and cognitive development of American-born latency-age children of Chinese immigrant parents. The children in this study generally had high self-concept, low anxiety, and high cognitive functioning. A child's mental health was related to the parents' attitude toward their heritage. For the older (fifth and sixth grade) boys, the more Chinese was spoken between parents and children, the higher was the boys' anxiety. Additionally, the more positive parents' attitudes were toward Chinese culture, the lower was the older boys' self-concept. The researchers concluded that speaking English in the home lowered the boys' anxiety because it lessened the bicultural and bilingual pressure on the child. These findings may reflect the uncertainty and difficulty that latency-age bicultural children experience in establishing a sound self-concept. Even though their parents demonstrate a strong attachment to the Chinese culture, the older boys in this sample may be more acculturated to mainstream American society, resulting in some confusion over self-concept.

In a similar vein, Hisama (1980) speculates about the relation between immigrant acculturation patterns and psychological disorders manifested by children. In traditional Asian families, children may be expected to give unquestioning obedience to their parents and to strive at any cost for the academic excellence expected of them. Their parents remain unacculturated, creating a substantial gap between the home and school environments. Hisama indicates that the children of these families tend to internalize their distress, thus manifesting more anxiety reactions, psychosomatic disorders, and school phobia. In contrast, marginal families are characterized by uncertainty in identification with the new and old cultures. Unquestioning obedience to parents is not present in these families. Role relationships within the family have become confused and disorganized. The children may tend to externalize their anxiety and manifest behavioral disorders.

For adolescent immigrants, problems seem to center on self-concept, identity conflicts, and generational conflicts with parents. Although these are typical issues that confront adolescents, migration seems to exacerbate these normal developmental conflicts (Aronowitz, 1984). Studies of minority immigrants reveal self-depreciation and low self-worth among these adolescents (Nann, 1982; Osborne, 1971), many of whom feel driven to make the difficult choice between the values and identities of their old and new cultures. These conflicts and role stresses may result in deviant behavior and, occasionally, serious psychopathology (Naditch and Morrissey, 1976).

First-born males in Chinese American families are under extreme pressure and may be especially vulnerable to psychological disorders (Hisama, 1980). This point is reiterated by Lee (1982), who states that the positions of oldest son and youngest daughter are associated with the highest rates of psychopathology in Chinese American culture. Oldest sons are expected to provide emotional support to the mother, to assume responsibility for the educational and character development of younger siblings, and to bring honor and financial support to the family. The youngest daughter may resent being left with responsibility for the parents as her older siblings leave home, as well as the unequal treatment she receives in comparison with her brothers. As the youngest, she may also be the most acculturated and the most vulnerable to cultural conflicts and disagreements with her parents.

Empirical personality studies of Chinese American college students found them to be more inhibited, conventional, and socially withdrawn than their white American counterparts (Sue and Kirk, 1973). A study using the Minnesota Multiphasic Personality Inventory revealed that Chinese American college students in Los Angeles have problems with dependency, inferiority feelings, ruminations, somatic complaints, and limited social skills (Sue and Sue, 1974). Sue and Frank (1973) report that Chinese American college students suffer from more stress than nonminority American students and tend to feel more isolated, lonely, rejected, and anxious. The results of these studies must be interpreted with caution because the norms for the assessment instruments used were established with white middle-class populations.

In the past, cultural restraints against aggression contributed to a relatively low rate of juvenile delinquency among Chinese Americans. In recent years, however, this rate has been rising, with a particularly marked increase in aggressive offenses such as assault and robbery (Abbott and Abbott, 1973; Sue, Sue, and Sue, 1983). In San Francisco, where approximately 12 percent of the population is Chinese American, 5 percent of the eight thousand juvenile offenders each year are identified as Chinese American (Millard, 1987). As Chinese American youth become more acculturated, parental authority begins to erode and constraints against aggression become less effective. Parents are often distracted from family issues as they try to make a living in the new country; frequently both parents work, a change from the previous role structure, so there is less direct supervision in the home. For adolescents living in Chinatown, which has all the characteristics of an urban ghetto, the unemployment rate among youth is high and the impoverished conditions and poor housing are glaring. The arrival of immigrant youth who speak little or no English and possess no job skills compounds the existing problems.

The phenomenon of gangs among Chinese American youth, which often receives sensational coverage by the news media, is becoming increasingly alarming to the Chinese community. The process of gang formation in the Chinese community is not unlike that in other communities; however, the gangs' involvement in criminal activities, including assault and extortion within the community, intermittently brings them into the public limelight (Fong, 1968). The antecedents for this behavior are similar to the socioenvironmental conditions associated with delinquency, in conjunction with poor self-image resulting from language problems, poor academic performance in school, self-depreciation internalized from the outside dominant community, and provincial rivalries stemming from place of birth.

This discussion has focused primarily on immigrant and first-generation youth. Later generations of Chinese American youth will be more acculturated; however, they may retain some ethnic traditions and differences in cultural values. Their manifestations of disorder and their attitudes regarding mental health may be more similar to those of mainstream American youth than to those of their predecessors, but ethnic identity issues are frequently involved. Identity conflicts may be the primary presenting problem, or they may be interwoven with other psychological disorders.

Sociocultural Issues in Assessment

Clinicians working with children and adolescents are generally in agreement that working with the family system and the school system facilitates effective psychological treatment (Pothier, 1976; Reisman, 1973). The following ecological approach to assessment focuses on the individual person system and the family system, and briefly on the school and societal systems. For each of these interacting subsystems, relevant sociocultural factors are presented, as they are key to an accurate interpretation of the data.

The Individual Person System

The categories of data for assessment of Chinese American youth may be similar to those used with white American youth, with the addition of two dimensions: level of acculturation and immigration history. However, the actual data may have very different meanings when examined in a sociocultural context.

Level of acculturation. Level of acculturation is an extremely significant factor because it will affect the interpretation of data obtained throughout the assessment. A recent immigrant child may be very unfamiliar with American customs and values and may possess a distinctly Chinese worldview. Chinese values, traditions, and behavior may be the standards for this child. For a child who is third-generation and very Westernized, however, ethnic differences may be minimal. English may be spoken in the home, and values may be very Americanized. Excessive attention to cultural explanations will be inappropriate in this situation. Somewhere in the middle range is the bicultural child who incorporates both Chinese and American values and behaviors. For some children, biculturalism engenders stress and even psychopathology when the values come into conflict. Other children, however, negotiate competently between the two cultures, mastering both and skillfully employing situation-appropriate behaviors.

Immigration history. The child's age at the time of immigration and resettlement may influence the degree of acculturation and socialization to American society. Younger children usually adjust more rapidly than older children, who may experience more difficulty in acquiring the new language. Country of origin, socioeconomic status in that country, process of actual migration, and persons accompanying the child may also influence the ease of the transition and the adjustment of the child. While many children migrate with intact families, many others are sponsored by relatives in the United States and are joined later by their parents. Some children migrate with older siblings and are separated from parents for a long period. Readjustment to nuclear family life or to parents who are recent immigrants and unacculturated may be the source of much disharmony in the newly reunited family. Although this factor may not seem to be as critical for American-born Chinese children, it is important to understand the immigration history of their parents or grandparents. Many Chinese parents immigrate to America for the futures of their children. This becomes a powerful dynamic in the family, and the burdens and responsibilities placed on the children to justify the parents' sacrifices play an important role in these children's development.

Physical appearance. For children, any deviation from the norm may garner undesired attention. Conformity in appearance and behavior is highly valued. For the Chinese American child, who differs in physical appearance and, depending on degree of acculturation, may also differ in dress, behavior, and mannerisms, this may be a point of conflict or sensitivity. In addition, the generally smaller physique of Chinese American children makes them vulnerable to the "heightism" so prevalent in American society (Okie, 1988).

Speech and language. The importance of language as an issue will vary depending on degree of acculturation. It is important to assess the degree of fluency in English and Chinese, especially if this may be affecting competence in schoolwork. Language may not be as critical an issue for the American-born as for the foreign-born child, although assessing its role in family dynamics would be important. The combination of monolingual parents with bilingual children may upset the traditional role configurations within the family. Additionally, a child's rejection of the culture of origin is often manifested as refusal to speak the native language, much to the chagrin and displeasure of the parents or grandparents.

Affect. What is often considered excessively restrained or non-expressive affect in Chinese Americans may in fact be culturally appropriate. Overt expression of feelings is encouraged in Western culture but not in Chinese culture. On the contrary, suppression of emotion, particularly in public situations, is highly valued. Expression of affect, especially negative affect, is thought to reflect poor upbringing. Again, this is related to degree of acculturation. The highly expressive Chinese American child may be behaving culturally appropriately if from a very Americanized family or highly adapted to Western manners.

Interpersonal relations. The quality of relatedness to other children and adults must be examined for appropriate dependence, affection, closeness, and separation. In contrast to the rugged individualism espoused by American society, interdependence, and often prolonged dependence, is highly encouraged within the Chinese family. Acknowledgment of roles and associated proper behavior contribute to a sense of formality, especially when adults are involved. For example, Chinese children are expected to address all adults by a formal title, such as Uncle, Aunt, Mr., or Mrs., not by first names.

Attitude toward self. This category includes one's feelings about oneself, stability of self-identification, self-esteem, and sense of competence. Studies of minority children conducted before the civil rights movement in the 1960s often found negative self-images (Brody, 1968; Clark and Clark, 1947). More recent studies have generated mixed results. Many Chinese American children have experienced some sort of ethnicity-related insult, either internal or external, to their sense of self. This may range from simple yet painful teasing at school to recurrent ethnic-derogatory comments by other significant persons that become internalized by the child, to total denial of one's ethnicity.

Anxiety and patterns of defense. The degree of anxiety, the way it is manifested, and under what conditions are important to assess. With children in general, and Chinese American children in particular, the earliest manifestations are often somatic concerns and complaints, sleep and appetite disturbances, and disruptions in school performance. Given the importance placed on academic excellence in the Chinese culture, this last manifestation is a frequent presenting problem.

Issues of sexuality. For adolescents, it is important to assess how sexuality is manifested and its role in family dynamics. Sexuality remains a taboo subject in many Chinese American families. A therapist must treat this topic with much discretion and develop a strong alliance with the family before broaching issues of sexuality.

The Family System

In working with Chinese American children or adolescents, it is important to involve the family in the treatment program because family is the critical unit of social organization in the Chinese culture.

Acculturation. In addition to the typical generation gap within families, Chinese American families may experience "acculturation gaps." Individual members may adapt to a new environment at quite different rates. In recent immigrant families and even in some second-generation families, parents are much more reluctant to accept the values and behaviors of the American culture than their children, who readily become Americanized in dress and behavior and, subsequently, in values. These different rates of acculturation are often the source of family disharmony.

Stage in migration history. Sluzki (1979) identifies five discrete stages in the migration process, each of which is associated with different types of family conflict and coping patterns. The first two stages are *preparation* and the actual *act of migration.* The third stage, a period of *overcompensation,* is characterized by a heightened level of activity focused on survival and the satisfaction of primary needs. The fourth stage is a stormy, crisis-ridden period of *decompensation.* The family is confronted with the task of reshaping its new reality and maximizing its compatibility with the new environment. Family members may also begin to step back and take a more realistic view of their situation. Disappointment may be acknowledged, and realization of the losses associated with leaving their homeland may penetrate the defense system that initially spawned the period of overcompensation. The final stage involves a *clash between generations,* which is often both intercultural as well as intergenerational.

Offspring raised in the United States often clash dramatically with their parents in terms of values, norms, and behaviors. It is in these latter two stages that families are most prone to have contact with mental health services.

Attitudes about mental health. When explaining mental disorders, the Chinese rarely draw on psychological causes. Explanations usually involve social, moral, or organic factors (Ishisaka and Takagi, 1982; Tseng and McDermott, 1981). In social explanations, the individual is seen as the victim of some unfortunate and uncontrollable circumstance. Fate may be implicated in this event rather than individual factors. In moral explanations, mental disorder is considered a punishment for a violation of values. For example, a violation of filial piety or bringing shame to the family may trigger mental disorder. Guilt arises from transgression of interpersonal obligations deriving from cultural traditions. Occasionally, the misconduct of one's ancestors may lead to misfortune in later generations. This is exemplified in the popular belief that "one wrong marriage leads to three generations of disorder." Finally, organic and genetic explanations are probably the most common. Physical disease or an imbalance of yin and yang, the two basic life forces, is seen as the source of mental disorder. Somatic explanations are consistent with the Eastern concept of unity of mind and body, which links physical and emotional functioning.

Pattern of help-seeking. Consistent with the foregoing explanations for mental disorder, Chinese Americans rarely approach formal psychological helpers except as a last resort. Intrafamilial help from family elders or extended family members is often considered more appropriate because of fears of what might happen to the disordered individual if the problems are revealed to outside authorities, and also because of the powerful sense of family shame and obligation.

Family communication. As discussed earlier, what may appear to be formal and somewhat stilted communication may in fact be culturally determined. Patterns of communication are often indirect, not free-flowing, and roles are not egalitarian. A reluctance to disclose family problems may be not resistance but, rather, culturally appropriate propriety and an attempt to save face.

Socioeconomic status. Chinese Americans span the entire socioeconomic range, and multiple wage earners are often found within a household. This category of data may be important in assessing the resources available to a family, and it may also shed light on the role arrangements within the family as these arrangements relate to occupational status. Particularly for recent immigrant families, traditional wage-earner relationships may be disrupted, generating disharmony within the family.

Support system. It is also critical to assess the degree to which a family is isolated or integrated within its community. If the family is most comfortable with traditional Chinese culture, does it interact with other families with similar values, or is it isolated among primarily non-Asian families? Or if it is highly assimilated, does it maintain any ties with the Chinese American community and culture? The support network in which a family is embedded may affect identity development and conflict for its children and adolescents.

The School System

In working with children, it is useful to obtain information about their school experience and performance. For the ethnic minority child, certain variables are especially important.

Racial/ethnic composition. Is the child or adolescent the only Chinese American student in the class? Is he or she American-born or foreign-born? Is this of significance to the child? For some children, it is isolating and intimidating. For others who are more acculturated, it is of no consequence. However, the way the child experiences peer relationships and internalizes the views of peers is important to assess, because it may strongly influence the child's attitudes toward himself or herself.

Attitudes of the teacher. The stereotype of the Chinese American student as bright, conscientious, and quiet is pervasive. Although stereotypes may contain seeds of reality, they are nevertheless harmful and limiting to individual growth. Unfortunately, many teachers may have expectations of Chinese students based on these stereotypes. Because of the recent influx of immigrants, many Chinese students are entering school with limited English skills. Teachers in port-of-entry areas are becoming frustrated and annoyed with the difficulties in and lack of support services for dealing with these students. Some teachers are tired of teaching "foreigners." Other teachers minimize cultural differences and expect these students to mirror white majority students. They would like assertive, active participants in class, but they do not realize that this expectation may contrast with the child's home environment, where quiet, obedient behavior is expected. The Chinese American student in this situation must negotiate between the conflicting expectations of the two settings.

Societal Issues

The attitude of American society toward its minority populations fluctuates in relation to a number of factors, politics and economics being primary ones. The growth of civil rights, the development of affirmative action policies, the encouragement of minority businesses, and the endowment of scholarships for minority students may be the priority of one administration, only to be rapidly discarded by the succeeding one. In the mid-1980s, Asian groups were the targets of considerable anti-Asian sentiment. At the college level, Asian American students faced a backlash in response to their increasingly successful penetration of exclusive colleges and universities. This resulted in unofficial yet discriminatory quotas on admissions (Nakao, 1987) as well as negative attitudes and anti-Asian bias among non-Asian students and college personnel. Other sources of hostility included the growth and proliferation of Asian American small businesses, mounting trade deficits with Japan and Taiwan, numerous stories heralding Asian American superachievers in education, and increasing visibility of Asian Americans moving into previously all-white or all-black communities (Fong, 1987). This resentment resulted in a resurgence of violence toward Asian Americans.

Chinese American children and adolescents, though not always immediate victims of this violence, were often unknowing and unintended victims. This hostility penetrated systems in which these children were direct or indirect participants—schools, families, peer groups, parents' places of employment, neighborhood playgrounds, and communities. Even though there may be no obvious link between such a societal attitude and a youngster's psychological disorder, it is important to examine the larger societal issues that may form the backdrop for a child experiencing difficulties.

Intervention and Treatment

In the psychological treatment of Chinese Americans, it is necessary but not sufficient to understand sociocultural factors. The therapist must go beyond cultural awareness to an understanding of how these factors translate into concrete therapeutic behaviors. The following discussion uses clinical cases to illustrate pertinent issues in two phases of the therapeutic process: entering treatment and establishing the working alliance.

Entering Treatment

For many Chinese Americans, contacting mental health services represents a last-ditch effort to resolve a problem. Usually other sources of help have been exhausted, as the following case example illustrates.

Rose was an eighteen-year-old adolescent who had immigrated from China with her parents as a young child. She was brought to an inpatient mental health crisis unit by her mother and seventeen-year-old brother, with the assistance of a mental health outreach worker. At intake she was hostile and belligerent and needed to be restrained. She was disheveled and unkempt, was disoriented, and had delusions of meeting Chairman Mao in Chinatown. She was angry at her parents for "incarcerating" her, and she claimed that she had important appointments to keep.

Rose's mother spoke only Toishanese, so a history was obtained using the brother as translator. The mother noted a gradual deterioration in Rose's behavior following completion of high school about one and a half years earlier. At that time she had become sullen and withdrawn, had lost all her friendships, and had experienced difficulty maintaining a job in the family's small restaurant. She had begun using makeup in a garish fashion, staying out late at night, and verbally abusing her mother. The precipitating incident for admission to the crisis unit was increasingly bizarre behavior in the home followed by a physical assault on her mother.

During the first six months of Rose's deterioration, the mother had sought help from an acupuncturist, relatives, the family doctor, and a minister. When nothing seemed to relieve the problem, the family, very ashamed and desperate, began to lock Rose in her room. It was during this eight-month period that she would escape at night and wander the streets. Her brother would find her, usually quite delusional, and bring her home. Rose's mother was tearful as she provided this history; the brother seemed nonexpressive but tense. After completion of the intake procedure and medical exam, it was discovered that Rose was six to seven months pregnant. The mother and brother said they were totally unaware of this.

This case vividly illustrates the difficulty with which some Chinese Americans approach formal mental health services. Rather than seek help from unfamiliar sources, this family had lived with their daughter's deteriorating condition for over a year with limited resources and no formal assistance. It was not until she became unmanageable that they sought help. By that time, the daughter had become so psychotic that inpatient treatment was required. The family's reluctance to seek help reflected their feelings of shame and embarrassment, their lack of familiarity with mental health services, and their defensive pattern of denial, which they also mobilized in regard to Rose's sexuality and pregnancy. For the therapist or mental health worker, it is critical to understand the significance of the family's decision to come to the crisis unit—the profound sense of failure, the loss of face, and the exposure of inner family problems that may provoke feelings of guilt and uneasiness. Conversely, the family may also be yearning for relief and a close supportive relationship. Appreciating this ambivalence may be crucial to the therapeutic relationship.

This case also highlights the role of interpreter. Although family members may often be used, for expedience, there is always a potential conflict of interest. It is therapeutically more advantageous to have an interpreter experienced in psychological issues, because of the difficulty of translating English expressions or emotional terms into Chinese. It is important to use the same person as interpreter each time, if possible, and to reassure the client of confidentiality. In addition, it is often useful to schedule pretherapy sessions with the interpreter in order to establish a relationship, discuss the translation format, and allow the interpreter to raise questions (Lee, 1982).

Another issue in the entering phase of treatment is the therapist's credibility in the eyes of the Chinese American client. In the mental health literature on people of color, there has been much discussion about the therapist/client match: Should Asian clients see Asian therapists, should blacks see blacks, and so forth? Sue and Zane (1987) have provided a useful reformulation of this issue based on ascribed credibility (the position or role that the therapist is assigned by the client on the basis of sex, age, and expertise) and achieved credibility (the therapist's skills in culturally appropriate interventions and general therapeutic abilities). Traditionally, in Asian cultures women have been subordinate to men and youth have been subordinate to elders; hence a young female would have a low ascribed status in contrast to an elderly male. In the entering phase of treatment, the young, female therapist must rapidly demonstrate effective therapeutic skills in order to improve the level of achieved credibility and maintain the client in therapy.

> Mrs. Wong, an immigrant from Hong Kong, traveled one hour to the university mental health clinic for evaluation and treatment of her child, who was manifesting behavior problems. In opposition to a referral from the school, she bypassed the biculturally staffed neighborhood psychiatric clinic. When she was assigned to a Chinese American therapist at the university clinic, she was very disappointed, refused to see the therapist, and indicated that she wanted to see one of the "real" doctors, like Dr. Smith.

> Mrs. Chu brought her six-year-old son to the university mental health clinic at the urging of her family doctor, who speculated that the child was developmentally delayed. She was very relieved to be assigned a Chinese American therapist. She immediately and tearfully described her son's problems as well as her own personal and family difficulties in adjusting to life in the United States.

In these two cases, the therapist's ascribed status had different implications. For Mrs. Wong, expertise was associated with being white, as is the case in Hong Kong, a British colony, where one may be socialized to believe this and where, in fact, British people are in power. If the therapist's ascribed status as a Chinese American interferes with Mrs. Wong's attempts to engage in therapy, this should be acknowledged, and perhaps another therapist should be assigned to the case. An underlying issue is whether to deal with Mrs. Wong's internalized feelings of self-devaluation and ethnic inferiority or to respond to her overt wishes. In this initial stage, the subjective experience of the client is crucial, and if one is to engage the family in treatment, responding to her expressed wishes will be necessary. An additional issue in this case may be Mrs. Wong's concerns about confidentiality, reflected in her traveling beyond her familiar community to one where no one would recognize her.

In contrast, Mrs. Chu valued the opportunity to meet with a Chinese American therapist. This facilitated her rapid self-disclosure and immediate engagement in therapy. For her, the therapist's ethnicity was associated with a high level of ascribed credibility.

Establishing the Working Alliance

A major problem in the treatment of Chinese Americans is their tendency to drop out after the initial sessions. They often do not see the efficacy of talking, nor do they experience any sense of personal relief or connection with the helping services. For these reasons, the working alliance needs to be reconceptualized as an *active exchange,* in which the client immediately feels there is reciprocal giving and receiving and that he or she is gaining something definite by participating in the interaction. For example, extensive evaluations or lengthy history-taking sessions may often result in parents' removing a child from treatment because they feel they have gained nothing in exchange for their time and information. Some of the components in this active exchange include, on the client's part, being willing to come to therapy, disclosing information and feelings, listening to the therapist, and providing some form of payment for services. The therapist's part in this exchange includes willingness to share information about his or credentials and personal qualifications, providing education about the therapeutic process and the mental health system, giving reassurance, empathizing with the client's pain and frustrations, accepting the client's formulations of the problem, and acknowledging appropriate social and cultural etiquette. This reciprocity, or *mutual exchange,* enables the client to feel an immediate and direct benefit from the treatment. The following case illustrates this reciprocity.

Wei Lee, a nineteen-year-old male, was referred to the therapist by an inpatient mental health crisis unit for follow-up treatment on an inpatient basis. Wei's diagnosis was paranoid schizophrenia. Many of his delusions were race related; his feelings of persecution were based on being Chinese American and being rejected by his surrounding community. After one session with Wei, and with Wei's consent, the therapist invited his parents to meet with her. Mr. and Mrs. Lee, immigrants from China, had resided in the United States for more than twenty years, and both worked as civil servants for the city government. They were a rather traditional couple, Mr. Lee being the clear, dominant authority and Mrs. Lee being silent, in the background, and considerably more emotional. Wei was their fourth child and had been born in the United States.

Although Mr. and Mrs. Lee recognized the bizarre behavior of their son, they expressed anger and frustration toward the mental health system. They said that very little information had been shared with them, that there was no discussion of his diagnosis or treatment plan, and that after he was discharged Wei had returned home, again became withdrawn, and stopped his medications. They reported that this was Wei's second hospitalization in two years and the pattern was exactly the same. Their questions remained unasked and unanswered, and Wei had refused to continue treatment.

The therapist discussed the diagnosis and range of possible implications, answered questions about the hospitalization and the mental health system, discussed insurance and disability payments, and employed the parents as collaborators in the treatment plan. She acknowledged the boundaries and limits of confidentiality in the individual therapy with Wei, but she also invited any calls or questions from the parents. She listened and empathized with their frustrations with their son and the mental health system, and she acknowledged Mrs. Lee's concerns about possible relations between events during her pregnancy and Wei's disorder. The meeting went beyond the designated fifty minutes.

The therapy with Wei continued for three and a half years with the support of his parents. The payment of a reduced fee was shared by Wei and his parents. Wei learned to identify environmental and personal factors that triggered his delusions and developed methods to cope with them. He began to be able to distinguish reality-based racism from his own projections. No further meetings were held with his parents, although they initiated telephone contact with the therapist about once a month. Wei made considerable gains, lived independently, worked as a grocery clerk, and visited his family regularly.

In working with children and their families, it is important to establish a working relationship with the parents, because they can make or break the therapy. In this case, the therapist exchanged information, education, and supportive empathy for parental support of the treatment. She acknowledged Mrs. Lee's emotion-filled hypotheses about her son's illness while presenting other possible theories and hypotheses, based on her own expertise, for Mrs. Lee to consider. She clarified the treatment process in a clear, non-patronizing manner and engaged the parents as partners in the treatment. The parents felt comfortable in calling whenever they had questions or concerns, but they did not pry into the specifics of Wei's therapy sessions, thus accepting the therapist's limits. In contrast to previous therapists, who had attempted to disengage Wei from his family with the implication that they were not therapeutically good for him, this therapist tried to specify behaviors that would help or hinder Wei's progress. In conjunction with Wei and his parents, she reached the conclusion that an independent residence with regular visits home for meals would be in Wei's best interest and would satisfy the cultural value of family interdependence.

In the active exchange with Wei, the therapist provided the following: support, empathy, and constancy; acknowledgment of his delusions and methods for gaining control over them; acceptance of his belief that racism was partly responsible for his condition; and an examination of his relevant settings—work, residence, and family—and factors in each that triggered his decompensation. Together they outlined methods for coping with these factors. For Wei's part of the exchange, he disclosed conflicts, difficult emotions, and his previously private and protective delusions, and he complied with the overall treatment plan. The alliance with Wei and his parents was grounded in a mutual exchange and a sense of reciprocity. Each participant dispelled any feeling of obligation by giving and providing in the relationship.

The appropriate pacing of self-disclosure and the management of communication are a delicate process with Chinese American clients. Personal disclosure of problems is antithetical to the cultural value of preserving "face" and keeping one's troubles within the family. In group or family therapy, often used with adolescents, this is particularly problematic, because the Chinese American adolescent, perhaps already feeling guilty for needing special treatment, is asked to reveal problems to a group of strangers, in direct contrast to family norms. Thus the adolescent may feel doubly conflicted. Disclosure of family problems may also have different implications for various family members, as seen in the next case.

> Mrs. Chow requested therapy for her family because of her fourteen-year-old son's outbursts in the home, his poor school grades, and her concerns that he would become a "delinquent." Their first session was with a Chinese American female therapist. Mrs. Chow and her son did most of the talking. She focused on her son's unmanageable behavior, speaking angrily toward him, and then began blaming the father for his inability to control his son. The son, experiencing severe identity conflicts, also seemed angry and accused his father of being too "Chinesey." His father remained quiet, contributing little to the interaction. However, the family failed to return for subsequent sessions, never directly canceling the session with the therapist but leaving messages with excuses in response to the therapist's inquiries.

In this case, the therapist lost control of the session, and the rapidity of disclosure had resulted in a loss of face for the father. The public humiliation by his son and his wife made it too difficult for him to return or to allow his family to return. The therapist failed to manage communication with respect to the cultural hierarchy and did not intercede quickly enough to stem the verbal abuse from son to father. The father, receiving nothing positive in this exchange, refused to participate. Additionally, the therapist's low ascribed credibility as a young female further impeded the development of a therapeutic relationship.

In the cases presented so far, the concept of active exchange to establish a working alliance has focused primarily on the parents. This concept is also pertinent to the therapeutic relationship with the child or adolescent. In this situation, the active exchange may involve using tangible, specific techniques such as role-playing, global assessment scaling, or play therapy.

> Michael, a seventeen-year-old Chinese American high school senior born in the United States, was referred to an outpatient adolescent crisis unit by his school counselor for depression and suicidal ideation. Michael was failing in several subjects, was repeatedly absent or late for school, and was sleeping much of the time.

Michael's parents (his mother had immigrated from Taiwan more than twenty years earlier, his father was American-born) were both successful professionals. They said, "There's nothing wrong with us or with Michael's younger brother and sister, so what's wrong with Michael?" The parents expected their children to be doctors and were frustrated and angered by Michael's academic failure. Michael was the first-born son and received the most pressure from the parents.

The therapist arranged a family meeting and then met several times with the parents, met regularly with Michael in individual sessions, and had regular phone contact with his school counselor. In the session with the parents, the active exchange involved the following: In response to their indirect queries, the therapist shared her academic and professional qualifications, knowing that education and advanced degrees were particularly meaningful to this couple and would raise her ascribed credibility. She underscored the importance of diminishing pressure on Michael and gently introduced more realistic expectations for their son (who was not interested in becoming a doctor and lacked the requisite academic record), guiding them toward recognition of Michael's other areas of strength. The parents reciprocated by supporting Michael's therapy and attempting to adjust their expectations for Michael. Empathically, the therapist guided them through the process of grieving as they relinquished their unrealistic aspirations for Michael.

The individual work with Michael involved psychodynamic therapy supplemented with behavioral techniques. It was important that an active exchange with Michael produce meaningful gains early in the relationship. The therapist validated Michael's interests and empathized with the pressure he endured from his parents. Michael became most animated and excited when talking about enrolling in a course to become a volunteer firefighter, but he would occasionally become unrealistic and impassively state his goal of becoming a neurosurgeon (his parents' wishes). He ventilated his own frustrations and his envy of his younger brother, who was enrolled in an academically exclusive high school. Michael's dreams and fantasies revealed a very active fantasy life, internalized feelings of failure, and much aggression. The therapist noticed much disorganization in his task orientation and problem-solving style. To deal with his disorganization, the therapist used the Global Attainment Scaling (GAS) to accomplish different objectives. This was done with school attendance, focusing on getting to school on time more frequently, which was necessary in order to graduate. This technique was also used in relation to study habits. Michael was a socially awkward, highly introverted adolescent. Role-playing was used to prepare him for upcoming social situations. In general, the therapy focused on discrete behavioral goals (important indicators of progress for both Michael and his parents) as well as on in-depth work on emotional areas.

The active exchange was a critical process in this therapy. Both Michael and his parents needed to experience benefits from therapy as soon as possible. Early on, Michael experienced relief from anxiety, understanding from an adult, validation for his interests, and some success using the GAS. As Michael's attendance improved and the number of hours spent sleeping diminished, his parents noted these changes and continued support of his therapy. Michael's case also illustrates the destructiveness of the media stereotype of the Asian American "whiz kids" (Brand, 1987). Parents accept this stereotype and place unrealistic and injurious academic pressure on their children. For Michael, this was an added stress, compounding already serious emotional problems.

For many Chinese American children, play therapy may be a useful vehicle for dealing with the problem of self-disclosure and saving face, as the following case illustrates.

Billy was a nine-year-old fourth grader, referred for disruptive behavior in school, marked deterioration in academic performance, and difficult behavior at home. He had been born in the United States of parents who had immigrated from China as adolescents. Billy was the shortest boy in his class.

Billy repeatedly brought homework into the playroom. He ignored the toys, concentrated on doing his homework, and engaged in minimal communication with the therapist. He would occasionally ask the therapist to correct his homework. The therapist began to use the homework as a vehicle for communication. Eventually, Billy admitted that he was coming here as punishment and that he thought the therapist was a teacher or some kind of tutor. After the therapist's role was clarified, Billy began to move toward the toys. Over several sessions, he played with army men who were all repeatedly killed by a single "hero." Probing revealed this hero to be "a big white guy and new in town," while the other men were all different colors and not as smart. Symbolically, the play revealed Billy's poor self-esteem and conflicts around being a new Chinese American boy in a predominantly non-Asian suburban school. Further play revealed anger toward his parents for removing him from his old neighborhood and friends, most of whom were also Chinese American.

Because Billy could not talk directly about these issues or express anger toward his parents to a stranger, play served as a face-saving modality. Unlike verbal disclosure, symbolic play does not provoke guilt or shame for revealing family difficulties or secrets to an outsider. Some children initially have difficulty using the play materials. Most commonly, Chinese American children view the therapist as a teacher, and bringing in homework is sometimes even encouraged by parents, who may not be familiar with the therapeutic process. A decline in academic performance is often a first indicator of problems and, for some Chinese parents who stress academic excellence, a most important symptom to alleviate. When using play therapy, it is important to educate parents about its efficacy, as they may often view it as frivolous and not educational or healing.

Billy's case also illustrates that cultural identity conflicts may be the core problem or entangled with the main presenting problem. His feelings of not fitting in and of feeling inferior and different generated much anger and hostility, which in turn interfered with his schoolwork and his relations with his parents.

Summary and Conclusions

Chinese Americans are a very diverse population within the United States. They come from different provinces of China and countries in Asia, they speak different dialects, their descendants are quite variable in their degree of acculturation to American society, and their manifestations and conceptualizations of psychological disorders are numerous. Among Chinese American youth, psychological problems span the entire range from severe psychotic illness to quasi-normative adolescent identity conflicts. What is striking, however, is the degree to which ethnic and racial issues are interwoven with the presenting disorder. The psychotic delusions often involve themes of racial persecution; the adolescent identity conflicts involve such questions as Am I Chinese or American? Where do I fit? Where do I belong? Consequently, in treating these youth it is important to understand the dynamic blending of generic and culture-specific features.

An ecological perspective is conducive to a fuller understanding of the disorders of these youngsters. The individual psychodynamics are intertwined with the primary cultural and social unit, the family; in turn, the family continually negotiates with outside institutions, whether they are schools, offices, neighborhoods, or family associations. As the case studies illustrate, some families experience frustrating and bewildering contact with mental health agencies. Therapists in these situations need to be guides for the youngster and family, not only collecting data for an assessment but simultaneously unraveling the intersystem conflicts that contribute to the presenting psychological problems.

This chapter has offered a framework for intervention with Chinese American families, children, and adolescents. Although awareness of the culture is important for good intervention, it is not enough. A dynamic understanding of sociocultural factors in assessment, a knowledge of techniques for establishing therapist credibility, and a working alliance based on a reciprocal active exchange are essential for effective treatment.

References

Abbott, K., and Abbott, E. "Juvenile Delinquency in San Francisco's Chinese-American Community: 1961–1966." In S. Sue and N. Wagner (eds.), *Asian-Americans: Psychological Perspectives*. Palo Alto, Calif.: Science and Behavior Books, 1973.

Aronowitz, M. "The Social and Emotional Adjustment of Immigrant Children: A Review of the Literature." *International Migration Review,* 1984, *18*(2), 237–257.

Asian American Health Forum. *Asian and Pacific Islander American Population Statistics* (Monograph Series 1). San Francisco: Asian American Health Forum, 1990.

Berk, B., and Hirata, L. "Mental Illness Among the Chinese: Myth or Reality?" *Journal of Social Issues,* 1973, *29*(2), 149–166.

Brand, D. "The New Whiz Kids." *Time,* Aug. 31, 1987, pp. 42–51.

Brody, E. (ed.). *Minority Group Adolescents in the United States.* Baltimore: Williams & Wilkins, 1968.

Bronfenbrenner, U. *The Ecology of Human Development: Experiments by Nature and Design.* Cambridge, Mass.: Harvard University Press, 1979.

Brown, T., Stein, K., Huang, K., and Harris, D. "Mental Illness and the Role of Mental Health Facilities in Chinatown." In S. Sue and N. Wagner (eds.), *Asian-Americans: Psychological Perspectives.* Palo Alto, Calif.: Science and Behavior Books, 1973.

Bui, T. K., and Takeuchi, D. "Ethnic Minority Adolescents and the Use of Community Mental Health Care Services." *American Journal of Community Psychology,* 1992, *20*(4), 403–417.

Chen, J. *The Chinese of America: From the Beginnings to the Present.* New York: HarperCollins, 1981.

Clark, K., and Clark, M. "Racial Identification and Preference in Negro Children." In T. Newcomb and E. Hartley (eds.), *Readings in Social Psychology.* Austin, Tex.: Holt, Rinehart and Winston, 1947.

County of Los Angeles Department of Mental Health. *Client and Service Summary Statistics for the Period July 1, 1984 to June 30, 1985.* Los Angeles: County of Los Angeles Department of Mental Health, 1985.

County of Los Angeles Department of Mental Health. *Client and Service Summary Statistics for the Period July 1, 1985 to June 30, 1986.* Los Angeles: County of Los Angeles Department of Mental Health, 1986.

Fong, S. "Identity Conflicts of Chinese Adolescents in San Francisco." In E. Brody (ed.), *Minority Group Adolescents in the United States.* Baltimore: Williams & Wilkins, 1968.

Fong, T. "Asian Small Business Growth Becomes Lightning Rod for Anti-Asian Sentiment." *East/West News,* July 9, 1987, p. 1.

Garmezy, N., and Rutter, M. (eds.). *Stress, Coping and Development in Children.* New York: McGraw-Hill, 1983.

Hisama, T. "Minority Group Children and Behavior Disorders: The Case of Asian-American Children." *Behavior Disorders,* 1980, *5*(3), 186–196.

Ishisaka, H., and Takagi, C. "Social Work with Asian- and Pacific-Americans." In J. Green (ed.), *Cultural Awareness in the Human Services.* Englewood Cliffs, N.J.: Prentice Hall, 1982.

Lee, E. "A Social Systems Approach to Assessment and Treatment for Chinese-American Families." In M. McGoldrick, J. K. Pearce, and J. Giordano (eds.), *Ethnicity and Family Therapy.* New York: Guilford Press, 1982.

Lee, E. "Chinese Families." In M. McGoldrick, J. K. Pearce, and J. Giordano (eds.), *Ethnicity and Family Therapy.* (2nd ed.) New York: Guilford Press, 1996.

Lin, Y. *The Wisdom of Confucius.* New York: Random House, 1938.

Lorenzo, M. K. "Emotional and Behavioral Problems of Asian American Adolescents: A Comparative Study." *Child and Adolescent Social Work Journal,* 1995, *12*(3), 197–212.

Lyman, S. "Conflict and the Web of Group Affiliation in San Francisco's Chinatown, 1850–1910." In N. Hundley (ed.), *The Asian American: The Historical Experience*. Santa Barbara, Calif.: Clio Press, 1976.

Ma, S. P., Cohen, N. L., and Yeung, W. "Assessing Suicide Risk Among Chinese-American Adolescents." Paper presented at annual meeting of the American Orthopsychiatric Association, San Francisco, Mar. 1988.

Millard, M. "Problem of Asian Juvenile Offenders Brings Outcry for Better System in S.F." *East/West News*, July 30, 1987, pp. 1, 8–9.

Naditch, M., and Morrissey, R. "Role Stress, Personality, and Psychopathology in a Group of Immigrant Adolescents." *Journal of Abnormal Psychology*, 1976, *85*(1), 113–116.

Nakao, A. "Thorny Debate over U.C.: Too Many Brainy Asians?" *San Francisco Examiner*, May 3, 1987, pp. A1, A12–13.

Nann, B. "Settlement Programs for Immigrant Women and Families." In R. Nann (ed.), *Uprooting and Surviving*. Dordrecht, Holland: Reidel, 1982.

Okie, S. "Children Reach for New Heights in Study of Growth Hormones." *The Washington Post*, Oct. 31, 1988, pp. A1, A4.

Osborne, W. "Adjustment Differences of Selected Foreign-Born Pupils." *California Journal of Educational Research*, 1971, *22*, 131–139.

Ou, Y. S., and McAdoo, H. "Ethnic Identity and Self-Esteem in Chinese Children." Unpublished report submitted to National Institute of Mental Health Center for Minority Group Mental Health Programs. Columbia, Md.: Columbia Research Systems, 1980.

Pothier, P. *Mental Health Counseling with Children*. New York: Little, Brown, 1976.

Reisman, J. *Principles of Psychotherapy with Children*. New York: Wiley, 1973.

Rutter, M. "Stress, Coping and Development: Some Issues and Some Questions." In N. Garmezy and M. Rutter (eds.), *Stress, Coping and Development in Children*. New York: McGraw-Hill, 1983.

Rutter, M., and others. "Children of West Indian Immigrants. Part 1: Rates of Behavioral Deviance and of Psychiatric Disorder." *Journal of Child Psychology and Psychiatry*, 1974, *15*, 241–262.

Shon, S., and Ja, D. "Asian Families." In M. McGoldrick, J. K. Pearce, and J. Giordano (eds.), *Ethnicity and Family Therapy*. New York: Guilford Press, 1982.

Sluzki, C. "Migration and Family Conflict." *Family Process*, 1979, *18*(4), 379–390.

Special Populations Task Force, President's Commission on Mental Health. *Report on the Mental Health of Asian/Pacific Americans Submitted to the President's Commission on Mental Health*. Washington, D.C.: U.S. Government Printing Office, 1978.

Sue, D., Sue, D. W., and Sue, D. M. "Psychological Development of Chinese-American Children." In G. J. Powell, J. Yamamoto, A. Romero, and A. Morales (eds.), *The Psychosocial Development of Minority Group Children.* New York: Brunner/Mazel, 1983.

Sue, D. W., and Frank, A. C. "A Topological Approach to the Psychological Study of Chinese- and Japanese-American College Males." *Journal of Social Issues,* 1973, *29*(2), 129–148.

Sue, D. W., and Kirk, B. "Differential Characteristics of Japanese-American and Chinese-American College Students." *Journal of Counseling Psychology,* 1973, *20,* 142–148.

Sue, S., and McKinney, H. "Asian-Americans in the Community Health Care System." *American Journal of Orthopsychiatry,* 1975, *45*(1), 111–118.

Sue, S., and Sue, D. W. "MMPI Comparisons Between Asian-American and Non-Asian Students Utilizing a Student Health Psychiatric Clinic." *Journal of Counseling Psychology,* 1974, *21*(5), 423–427.

Sue, S., and Zane, N. "The Role of Culture and Cultural Techniques in Psychotherapy: A Critique and Reformulation." *American Psychologist,* 1987, *42*(1), 37–45.

Sung, B. *Mountain of Gold.* Old Tappan, N.J.: Macmillan, 1967.

Touliatos, J., and Lindholm, B. "Behavior Disturbance of Children of Native-Born and Immigrant Parents." *Journal of Community Psychology,* 1980, *8*(1), 28–33.

Tseng, W. S., and McDermott, J. *Culture, Mind and Therapy.* New York: Brunner/Mazel, 1981.

U.S. Bureau of the Census. *1980 Census of Population: General Population Characteristics, United States Summary.* Washington, D.C.: U.S. Government Printing Office, 1983a.

U.S. Bureau of the Census. *1980 Census of Population: General Social and Economic Characteristics, United States Summary.* Washington, D.C.: U.S. Government Printing Office, 1983b.

U.S. Bureau of the Census. *Statistical Abstract of the United States, 1990.* (110th ed.) Washington, D.C.: U.S. Department of Commerce, 1990.

Chapter Three

The Assessment and Treatment of Japanese American Children and Adolescents

Donna K. Nagata

Japanese American adults are typically perceived as being successful, well acculturated, and mentally healthy, and their children are often seen as being obedient and educationally successful. However, mental health professionals have become increasingly aware that such perceptions are incomplete and inaccurate (Sue, Sue, Sue, and Takeuchi, 1995), and that there has been a failure to recognize the impact of cultural and sociohistorical factors on the mental health of Japanese American parents and their children. This chapter reviews literature on the assessment and treatment of Japanese American children and adolescents and their families. Because little information is available on this topic, it is hoped that this chapter will provide an initial framework for understanding the complex issues presented by this population.

For the purposes of this chapter, the term *Japanese American* refers to an individual who was born in the United States or who immigrated to this country near the beginning of the twentieth century. It does not include recent immigrants from Japan. The Japanese use specific terms to identify the various generations of Japanese Americans. The *Issei* were the first generation to come to the United States, and the *Nisei*, second-generation Japanese Americans, were born here. The offspring of the Nisei constitute the third genera-tion and are called *Sansei,* and the fourth and fifth generations are referred to respectively as *Yonsei* and *Gosei.* Because anti-Asian im-migration laws have regulated the numbers of Japanese immigrants to the United States, there is an unusual degree of distinction be-tween these generational categories. Most Issei immigrated between 1900 and 1924, and their American-born children, the Nisei, were generally born between 1910 and 1945 (Kitano, 1969b). In ad-dition, there are some Japanese Americans who were born in Amer-ican and therefore technically are Nisei but who also spent many of their early years in Japan. The term *Kibei* has been used to refer to these individuals. It is primarily the children and grandchildren of the Nisei or Kibei generations who constitute the current Japanese American youth population.

Demographic Data

In 1990 there were 866,160 Americans of Japanese ancestry in the United States, including 585,474 native-born and 280,686 foreign-born (U.S. Bureau of the Census, 1993a, Table 1). The geographic distribution of Japanese Americans includes a strong concentration in the West (75.9 percent) relative to the Northeast (8.8 percent), the Midwest (7.3 percent), or the South (7.9 percent) (U.S. Bureau of the Census, 1993b, Table 135). Geographic location is an im-portant variable to consider when reviewing the research literature. Although the two largest concentrations of Japanese Americans are in California (320,730) and Hawaii (252,291), a distinction must be made between these groups. Japanese Americans in Hawaii live in an environment with many Asian Americans, and mainland Japan-ese Americans live in a Caucasian-majority environment. In addi-tion, the government-enforced incarceration of Japanese Americans during World War II affected nearly all those on the mainland, in contrast to much smaller numbers in Hawaii. The impact of these varied environments can be seen in the finding that Hawaiian Japanese Americans tend to preserve their Japanese culture to a greater degree than their mainland peers (Johnson, 1977; Kitano, 1969b). There are also important distinctions between different mainland cities with Japanese American populations. Gehrie (1976) points out that there are differences between Japanese Americans who grew up in Los Angeles, where there is an identifiable, concentrated Japanese American population, and in Chicago, where Japanese Americans are more widely dispersed. Sansei interviewed by Gehrie in Chicago, for example, perceived California Sansei as less individualistic and more sheltered within the Japanese American community.

Educationally, Japanese Americans are above the national average. Nearly all graduate from high school. In 1990, the U.S. Census showed that more than 90 percent of native-born Japanese Americans aged fifteen to nineteen were enrolled in school (U.S. Bureau of the Census, 1993a, Table 3). More than 96 percent of all Japanese American males aged twenty-five to thirty-four were high school graduates, and more than 50 percent had a bachelor's degree or higher. Similarly, among Japanese American females aged twenty-five to thirty-four, 97 percent were high school graduates or higher, and more than 46 percent had a bachelor's degree or higher (U.S. Bureau of the Census, 1993b, Table 106). In addition, the majority of Japanese American children under eighteen (86 percent overall, and 84 percent of native-born) were living at home with two parents (U.S. Bureau of the Census, 1993a, Table 2). With a median family income in 1990 of more than $50,000 ($51,550, for Japanese American families overall, and $52,728 for natives), Japanese Americans have one of the lowest poverty rates (3.4 percent overall, and 2 percent for natives) in the country (U.S. Bureau of the Census, 1993a, Table 5). This "successful" economic picture of Japanese Americans must be viewed with caution, however. A separate 1980 report published by the U.S. Commission on Civil Rights points out that Japanese Americans (and other Asian Americans) are actually underemployed (U.S. Commission on Civil Rights, 1980). The report cites a study conducted by Cabezas (1979) that found that college-educated Japanese American males in four major mainland cities (Chicago, Los Angeles, New York, and San Francisco) made several thousand dollars less than their majority non-Asian peers in 1970.

Although Japanese Americans were the largest Asian American group at the time of the 1970 census, they are currently the third largest. (As of 1990, the largest group is Chinese Americans, followed by Filipino Americans.) Hence, Japanese Americans are becoming an increasingly smaller portion of the Asian American group. Whereas in 1980 they constituted nearly 21 percent of all Asian Americans, the percentage dropped to 12 percent in 1990 and a further decrease is expected by 2000 (Gardner, Robey, and Smith, 1985).

The census data reflect two important issues for Japanese American families. First, they illustrate how it is possible for stereotypes of Japanese American educational and economic success to be perpetuated. These stereotypes are then used by some to support the view that Japanese Americans are problem free and have assimilated well into American mainstream society. Information in this chapter challenges this viewpoint. Second, the data also reflect a cultural group whose proportion of representation in society is decreasing. This can have important implications for Japanese Americans' sense of community, identity, and role in the majority society. The current outmarriage rate is estimated to be greater than 60 percent (Kitano, Yeung, Chai, and Hatanaka, 1984). Many Japanese Americans worry that the Japanese American culture and values will disappear altogether in the near future. In the meantime, the diminishing numbers of Japanese Americans also reduces the degree to which they can maintain the political power necessary to advocate for their community's needs.

Utilization of Mental Health Facilities

To understand the mental health needs of Japanese American youth, it is useful to evaluate the degree to which this population is using services. Unfortunately, a review of the literature on the incidence and prevalence of psychological and behavioral disorders in children revealed no comprehensive data on Japanese American children and adolescents. This absence of information is not surprising given that there is very little information on the mental health of Japanese Americans in general, regardless of age (Kitano, 1969a). The data that have been reported for Japanese Americans indicate that they rarely seek mental health services and are underrepresented in their utilization of such services (Kitano, 1969a; Sue and Morishima, 1982; Uomoto and Gorsuch, 1984). Kitano (1969a), for example, found that admission rates to California state mental hospitals were proportionately lower for Japanese Americans. Similarly, Sue and McKinney (1975) found that although

Japanese Americans made up 1.2 percent of the population in the Seattle area, they represented only .1 percent of the cases seen at community mental health centers there.

There are numerous problems with this "treated cases" method of estimating the mental health needs of any group (see Sue and Morishima, 1982). One major problem is the assumption that low utilization rates imply a low incidence of problems in the community. Research indicates, however, that it may be only the most distressed Japanese Americans who seek public services, and that the absence of Japanese Americans in the mental health statistics reflects their culturally based hesitancy to use services, not that they have "superior" mental health (Kitano, 1969a; Sue and Morishima, 1982; Sue and Sue, 1974).

Rather than reflecting an absence of mental health problems, low utilization rates seem to indicate that Japanese Americans are reluctant to use the types of services for which such statistics are maintained. An informal study by Kitano (1969a) notes that Japanese American mental health professionals themselves agree that Japanese Americans rarely use professional services for emotional problems. One possible reason is that they rely more on the extended family and informal structures for support (Kitano, 1969b). This would not be surprising, because the family unit is of central importance in Japanese American culture. Kim (1978) conducted a needs assessment of Japanese Americans in the Chicago area and found support for this hypothesis. She reports that the Japanese Americans in her study relied more heavily on private resources (for example, family, friends, and relatives) than on public resources (such as hospitals, doctors, and the police).

Attitudes toward the utilization of mental health services may differ across generations, however. A recent study suggests that the supportive function of the Japanese American family around psychological problems may be less apparent today. Uomoto and Gorsuch (1984) examined the attitudes of second- and third-generation (Nisei and Sansei) Japanese Americans toward mental health and non–mental health referrals. Participants from Seattle and Los Angeles were presented with three vignettes describing various disorders (paranoid schizophrenia, major depression, and agoraphobia) and a fourth vignette describing marital and family problems. They were then asked to write two things they would do in response to each vignette. In contrast to earlier literature, family and friends were not seen as the primary source of referral. Referral to a mental health facility for problems related to schizophrenia, depression, and agoraphobia was at least as frequent a response as referral to family and friends. Sansei were more likely than Nisei to refer the cases in the vignettes to a psychiatrist or psychologist. Hence, it is possible that the cultural variables mentioned previously may be less apparent in the mental health attitudes of today's Japanese Americans. All respondents in the study were less likely, however, to turn to mental health professionals for referral of marital and family problems. This is particularly important given that many child/adolescent problems are related to family issues.

The surrounding ethnic environment may also influence the likelihood that a Japanese American family will utilize services. Prizzia and Villanueva-King (1977) found that in Hawaii Japanese Americans reported less discomfort in seeking counseling at a community center than their Samoan, Filipino, Hawaiian, Chinese, and Caucasian American counterparts. Although this finding seems to contradict previously cited findings indicating that Japanese Americans would be reluctant to seek services, it may also be seen as evidence of the influence of ethnic environments. Japanese Americans, and Asian Americans in general, form a much larger proportion of the population in Hawaii. Therefore they may experience greater comfort in seeking services there, because the greater availability and visibility of Asian ethnic mental health workers makes the services seem less alien and intimidating.

Epidemiological Data

Data on the incidence of specific problems among Japanese American children and adolescents are scarce. However, statistics gathered by the Clinical Information Service of the Department of Mental Health in Los Angeles, an area with a high concentration of Japanese Americans, illustrate the range of cases that have been treated in that city (S. G. Lubeck, personal communication, May 7, 1987). A total of 879 Japanese American clients received public mental health services in Los Angeles County from 1985 to 1986. Of this total, 12.5 percent (N = 110) were twenty-one years of age or younger. These 110 people represented less than one-tenth of 1 percent of the county's Japanese American population. The majority of clients from the youth group were between ages thirteen and twenty-one. More specifically, the breakdown by age was as follows: five clients were five years old or younger, fourteen clients were six to twelve years of age, forty-five clients were thirteen to eighteen years old, and forty-six clients were nineteen to twenty-one years of age. The most frequent mode of service was outpatient care (ninety-four cases), followed by inpatient care (nine cases), day treatment (five cases), and case-management/continuing care services (two cases). Almost all clients aged twenty-one or younger who were seen for inpatient and day treatment services were eighteen to twenty-one years of age.

The Los Angeles County statistics also showed that Japanese American boys (62 percent of the total cases seen) were seen more frequently for outpatient care than girls. In addition, the most frequent primary diagnoses for Japanese American youth at the time of initiating outpatient services were adjustment disorders, conduct disorders, affective-related disorders, and schizophrenia-related disorders. Approximately twelve to fifteen outpatient clients aged twenty-one or younger fell within each of these categories.

Overall, the Los Angeles County statistics reflect a very low incidence rate for Japanese American children and adolescents. A low incidence of referred Japanese American child and adolescent cases is also reflected in data reported by Sata (1983). Sata notes that information available through the Seattle Public Schools for the 1974–75 school year reflected an "extremely low" number of Sansei children who were identified as having behavioral or special education problems. In addition, out of 1,458 Sansei students enrolled in the Seattle school district that year, only 2 were suspended.

It should be noted that private mental health service utilization is not represented in either the Los Angeles County or Seattle public school data. Hence, a true estimate of utilization would be higher than this. In addition, the low incidence rate does not mean that Japanese American children do not suffer from psychological difficulties. The low numbers of documented treatment cases may actually reflect a tendency by Japanese American parents to deny or minimize certain behavioral problems in their children. Sata (1983) points out, for example, that cases of hyperactivity in Japanese American children may be infrequently reported because their parents minimize the clinical significance of overactivity and inattention.

Very low rates of delinquency for Japanese American youth have also been reported (Kitano, 1967). The Los Angeles County probation figures for 1960 indicate that Japanese Americans had the lowest number of arrests of all comparison groups (white, black, Chinese, and Native American). Kitano noted that those Japanese American children who were delinquent were more likely to come from broken homes, to have low identification with their ethnic community, to be distant from their families, and to be essentially "marginal" socially. More recent investigations suggest that the low rates of the 1960s might have underestimated the arrests of Japanese American juveniles because of early intervention by Nisei parents to correct the problem. Since parental action can increase the likelihood that formal charges or further prosecution will be dropped, it seems likely that a higher proportion of Japanese American juveniles than reported were engaged in delinquent behavior but this was not reflected in formal arrest records (Sata, 1983). Data on the specific offenses committed by Japanese American juveniles were unavailable, although Morales, Ferguson, and Munford (1983) report that the most frequent offenses committed by Asian Americans in general were burglary, petty theft, auto theft/joyriding, and possession of marijuana.

Some information exists about alcohol and drug abuse. Japanese Americans have been observed to drink less alcohol than Caucasian Americans. However, increasing acculturation has resulted in an increase in alcohol consumption by Japanese American youth (Sue and Nakamura, 1984). Today's Sansei and Yonsei adolescents and young adults are more likely to drink than their parents or grandparents. Sue and Nakamura point out that a fourth-generation Japanese American adolescent has parents whose cultural attitudes about and behavior toward alcohol are much closer to those of the more permissive American society. Hence this adolescent may be more at risk for developing alcohol-related problems. Data from Nakagawa and Watanabe's (1973) survey of drug use by Japanese Americans in junior and senior high schools also support the hypothesis that current Japanese American youth may be more at risk for chemical abuse than previous generations. Of the Japanese

Americans polled, 29 percent reported having had some experience with drugs.

In contrast, Japanese American families remain underrepresented in statistics on child abuse. Dubanoski and Snyder (1980) report that although Japanese Americans accounted for approximately 27 percent of the population in Hawaii in 1976 and 1977, only 3.45 percent of abuse and 4.65 percent of neglect cases were attributed to them. Interestingly, neglect was more common than abuse. The authors suggest that this finding may reflect the Japanese American family's emphasis on shame and ostracism as forms of punishment rather than direct confrontations involving physical violence.

The lack of documented psychological or behavioral difficulties in Japanese American children and adolescents should not be seen as evidence of the absence of psychological problems. Sue and Morishima (1982) point out that psychological distress is not always presented in the form of pathology. It might also be reflected in a diminished degree of positive mental health or in a failure to live up to one's potential. There is evidence, for example, that Japanese American children aged nine to twelve have a less positive self-concept than their Caucasian American peers with respect to physical characteristics, and that this dissatisfaction may endure into young adulthood (Arkoff and Weaver, 1966). Sata (1983) suggests that early adolescence and the onset of dating may be particularly stressful times for Japanese American children. These are times when the realities of their ethnicity may create difficulties (for example, encountering parents of other racial groups who have negative attitudes toward the Japanese or Japanese Americans). The transition between high school and college may also be problematic. Emphasis from Nisei parents on doing well in school can create pressures on those Sansei who do attend college. Furthermore, because of the high numbers of Japanese Americans attending college, a stereotype exists that all Japanese Americans are high academic achievers. Sata points out that those youth who do not go on to college may be at particular risk for emotional problems. Not only do they fail to live up to the stereotype of Japanese American success, but they are also more likely to be exposed to discrimination in the nonprofessional labor market.

Cultural and Family Characteristics

The lack of information on the incidence of diagnoses for Japanese American children and adolescents is reflective of a larger phenomenon—the lack of data on Japanese American mental health in general. Kitano (1969a) notes that it is curious that so little scientific interest in Japanese Americans has been generated. He hypothesizes that perhaps this lack of interest can be attributed to the perception that Japanese Americans have been successful in adapting to life in the United States. Stereotypes of Japanese Americans as a "model minority" have caused many people to assume that Japanese Americans are no different from nonminority Caucasian Americans. Yet a brief glance at the history of Japanese in this country shows that this is far from true.

Historical Perspectives on the Family

Japanese Americans first immigrated to the United States after 1885, when Japan legalized emigration (Knoll, 1982). The major portion of Japanese immigration occurred between 1890 and 1924. This first generation of immigrants (the Issei) were young males who hoped to earn a fortune and return to Japan. Most did not return but settled instead in Hawaii and along the Pacific Coast, working as farm laborers. Issei men eventually requested wives from Japan and the arrival of these Issei women marked the beginnings of the Japanese American family. The number of Japanese in America grew; by 1920 there were approximately 111,000 people of Japanese ancestry. However, the Immigration Act of 1924 curtailed the relatively free immigration of all Asians, and fewer than 7,000 Japanese Americans came to the United States between 1925 and 1941 (Knoll, 1982). When World War II began in 1941, no Japanese were allowed into the country.

The children of the Issei were born in America, and most spent the larger part or all of their lives in this country. These second-generation Japanese Americans (the Nisei) were raised with a mixture of Japanese and American values. It was not unusual for a Nisei child to attend Japanese-language school immediately after American school, or to go from speaking English at school to speaking Japanese at home. Because Japanese Americans tended to stay within their own community, the Nisei associated primarily with other Japanese Americans and hence were exposed to the same pressures to conform that the Issei experienced. Marriages for both the Issei and Nisei generations were also primarily within-group because of antimiscegenation laws as well as ethnic preference. For example, a law preventing intermarriage with whites existed in California, where the majority of non-Hawaiian Japanese Americans were located, until 1948 (Tinker, 1982).

Laws preventing Japanese from marrying whites represent only a portion of the discriminatory legislation and racism experienced by Japanese Americans in this country. Numerous immigration quotas and restrictions were applied to them as well, and it was not until the McCarran-Walter Act of 1952 that the Issei were allowed to apply for citizenship. The most blatant act of discrimination toward Japanese Americans took place during World War II when all persons of Japanese ancestry were removed from their homes along the West Coast and placed in internment camps for periods of up to four years. Following the bombing of Pearl Harbor in 1941, more than 110,000 Japanese Americans were ordered by the United States government to live in army barracks located in desolate desert areas of the country (Kitano, 1969b). Two-thirds were U.S. citizens (primarily Nisei). They could take to the camps only what they could carry and were given little time in which to prepare for the move. Many had only twenty-four hours' notice that they were being uprooted. Japanese Americans remained in the camps for an average of two to three years. The impact of this internment, as is discussed later in this chapter, was great (Nagata, 1987, 1990, 1993).

The third generation of Japanese Americans, the Sansei, differ markedly from their grandparents and parents, particularly with respect to outmarriage. Kitano, Yeung, Chai, and Hatanaka (1984) report that in 1979 in Los Angeles, Japanese American rates of outmarriage were 60.6 percent; half of the marriages were to non-Asians. This high rate of outmarriage is important to note, because it means that the structure of the present-day Japanese American family is qualitatively different in many ways from that of earlier generations. Today's child or adolescent of Japanese American ancestry is as likely to come from a family where a second racial or cultural background is present as from a family where both parents are Japanese American.

Family Structure

Although Japanese American families have tended to remain intact, with low rates of separation and divorce, generational changes over time and outmarriage rates have certainly affected the nature of the family for this ethnic group. Even in families in which both parents are Japanese Americans it is impossible to predict the degree to which family structure and values brought to the United States by the Issei generation have been retained. Nonetheless, it is highly likely that the Japanese values of the Issei have, albeit perhaps indirectly, shaped important characteristics of the present-day Japanese American family. Therefore an overview of these values is useful.

The Issei were raised in Japan entirely with Japanese concepts of social and familial structure. Kitano and Kikumura (1976) summarize key aspects of Japanese social structure that have been identified by Nakane (1970), including the following: (1) an emphasis on *ie*, or the household unit, as the most important structure for early socialization and upbringing; (2) an emphasis on the group as opposed to the individual and on roles within the group structure; (3) the importance of loyalty; and (4) the importance of rank and status. In essence, the Japanese social structure for the Issei stressed high in-group unity, group consensus, and discouragement of individuality. Additional terms that are useful in understanding Japanese behavior include *on* and *giri*, which emphasize the importance of recognizing ascribed and contractual obligations, respectively, and *amae*, which is not directly translatable into English but very generally involves the concept of dependency and the need to be loved and cherished (Kitano, 1969b).

In comparing the structure of families in Japan and those in the United States, Yamamoto and Kubota (1983) describe the Japanese family as emphasizing the priority of the family group over the individual, vertical relationships, conformity to societal norms, and social control based on shame, guilt, and an appeal to duty and responsibility. In contrast, American families are seen as emphasizing individualism, equalitarian relationships, independent behavior in society, and social control based on love and punishment. Other characteristics of the Japanese American family that are seen as representative of Japanese values include a vertical structure with authority vested in the father and older males, a stress on duty and obligation over love, an emphasis on prolonged family dependence, encouragement of obedience and conformity in children, and an emphasis on indirect, nonconfrontational techniques of parenting that rely on nonverbal communication (Kitano and Kikumura, 1976). In addition, Kitano (1969b) notes the importance of the extended family as a source of social support.

Enryo, a Japanese concept that means to be reserved, not to express one's wishes or preferences, and to defer to those in authority (Yamamoto and Kubota, 1983), has also influenced the Japanese American family. This can be seen in such behaviors as a reluctance to praise achievements, a hesitancy to speak out, or a reluctance to ask questions. *Gaman,* another Japanese term, is used to describe the importance of repressing or internalizing rather than externalizing emotions. In the Japanese American family, gaman is often demonstrated by an emphasis on keeping emotions such as anger or hostility inside. This, in conjunction with the value of nonconfrontational and indirect communication, serves to minimize overt outbursts of aggression.

Although the indirect communication style can be a strength for the Japanese American family, it can be problematic around certain topics. Sexuality, according to Kitano (1969b), was rarely discussed between the Issei and Nisei generations; a language difference created an obvious communication barrier. However, data from Abramson and Imai-Marquez (1982) suggest that even members of the Sansei generation, who do not have a communication barrier with their children, may experience difficulty in discussing sexuality within the family. According to their study, although the level of sex-related guilt has been decreasing with each successive generation, Japanese Americans as a group still express significantly greater sex-related guilt than Caucasian Americans. The research did not explore the relationship between sex guilt and parental communication about sexual issues. However, it seems plausible that higher degrees of sex guilt would be associated with greater discomfort in discussing sexual matters.

Some characteristics of family role structure appear to be similar in Japanese and Japanese American families, and others have been adapted to the American lifestyle. For example, although the Issei father was structurally in the position of greatest authority, he was culturally disadvantaged in the United States and had to rely on his Nisei son or daughter to handle issues where communication outside the Japanese community was necessary (Kitano, 1969b). A number of researchers have pointed to the fact that each successive generation of Japanese Americans is more acculturated than the last, and today's Sansei are depicted as being much less influenced by Japanese values and more influenced by American values than their parents and grandparents (see, for example, Connor, 1974; Masuda, Matsumoto, and Meredith, 1970; Padilla, Wagatsuma, and Lindholm, 1985). At the same time, there is evidence that differences do remain between Japanese American and Caucasian American families. O'Reilly, Tokuno, and Ebata (1986) found that Hawaiian Japanese American parents differed from their Caucasian American peers in their rankings of valued competencies to be encouraged in children. Although the Caucasian American parents ranked the characteristic "self-directed" highest in importance, Japanese American parents rated "behaves well" as most important. In another study, Caudill and Frost (1972) note that although some behaviors of Sansei mothers from Hawaii resembled those of Caucasian American mothers more than those of mothers in Japan, the Sansei also retained characteristics of mothering that were more like the Japanese mothers (for example, spending greater amounts of time carrying, lulling, and playing with their babies). Finally, although the Sansei are generally portrayed as being highly acculturated, this may not necessarily be true. Gehrie (1976) suggests that the individualistic behaviors that some interpret as reflecting acculturation may actually be more reflective of the Sansei's mode of handling their anxiety about being different in a white-majority environment. Clearly, further research is necessary to explore the dynamics underlying observed behaviors of acculturation.

The Internment Experience

The preceding paragraphs highlight several important characteristics of the Japanese American family and the ways they have persisted. However, perhaps the most important historical event to influence Japanese American families and their retention of

Japanese characteristics was the internment during World War II. Hence this event warrants special attention.

Several researchers have discussed the psychological impact of the internment camps on the Japanese American family (for example, Morishima, 1973; Mass, 1986). These effects included severe economic loss, the psychological stress of being uprooted and incarcerated for a prolonged period, blatant questioning of national loyalty, the experience of victimization and fearfulness about the future, and a change in family structure due to barrackslike communal conditions and disruption of normal family roles. Mass (1986) has suggested that these stressful conditions led those who were interned to adopt defense mechanisms such as repression, denial, rationalization, and identification with the aggressor. Perhaps the most noticeable impact of the camps is how little the Issei and Nisei have discussed their experiences from the years in which they were interned. For more than forty years, open discussion of the internment was absent. Some writers have attributed this silence to the hypothesis that the internees were similar to victims of rape (Hansen and Mitson, 1974). Like rape victims, they had done nothing wrong, yet they experienced shame and guilt for what had happened to them.

The impact of the internment extends beyond those who were incarcerated. As literature on the children of survivors of the Holocaust demonstrates (for example, Danieli, 1982; Nadler, Kav-Venaki, and Gleitman, 1985), the children of those who underwent such severe and disruptive trauma are also likely to experience cross-generational psychological effects. One way in which the Sansei and Yonsei have been affected is through the childrearing practices of their parents. Morishima (1973) notes that many Nisei parents who were interned indicated that they made a concerted effort to raise their children to be as American as possible. Given this context, it is not surprising that very few Sansei speak or understand Japanese. Kitano and Kikumura (1976) also point out that as a result of the camp experience, Japanese Americans were especially concerned that their children not "rock the boat" or "stick out" in their communities. In essence, there was a strong desire for invisibility. Parental expectations of the younger generation have also been affected. Henkin (1985) suggests that the Nisei may have responded to racial discrimination in part through an emphasis on high achievement, which created stress for the Sansei.

Many Sansei may experience as shameful a level of accomplishment that others might see as a success. A Sansei student, for example, may be embarrassed by a less-than-perfect A- grade point average. At the same time, Henkin notes, the Sansei are caught in a double bind between being as American as possible (which includes becoming independent) and remaining Japanese by following their parents' expectations to maintain close family ties.

The author's research (Nagata, 1990, 1993) indicates that the internment has affected the Sansei even though most were born after the war. For example, survey data show that Sansei whose parents were interned were less confident in their rights in this country and had a greater preference for affiliating with other Japanese Americans than did Sansei whose parents were not interned. In addition, interview comments from research participants suggest that the lack of parental communication about the internment itself had an impact. For some offspring, the silence created a sense of emotional distance; for others, it created frustration. Although Sansei wanted to learn more about this part of their parents' lives, they were reluctant to ask, partly out of respect for their parents' privacy and partly out of fear of uncovering negative emotions or information within their family. Despite a lack of communication about the camps, the internment continues to be an important issue for many Sansei. One interviewee, for example, felt that his mother's camp experience had influenced his upbringing. He stated: "I'm sure it affected how she dealt with that part of her life. . . . It shaped her temperament and instilled in her that her children need to succeed in life." This pressure, he noted, resulted in high expectations for success, expectations that both he and his sister found difficult to bear. Eventually, both sought therapy to help them deal with their difficulties.

The full extent to which the internment has affected the children in today's Japanese American families remains to be seen. What is apparent is that the internment has had an important impact on these families in multiple ways.

Sociocultural Issues in Assessment

As we have seen, Japanese Americans and their families are not likely to utilize public mental health facilities. Clinicians must therefore recognize that once a Japanese American child and family do seek services, their needs may be especially great, because they have already overcome important barriers to obtaining treatment. Assessment of Japanese American clients should reflect the importance of three basic areas of information: (1) client attitudes toward psychological problems and services, (2) therapist sensitivity to cultural issues in case conceptualization, and (3) the appropriateness of various assessment techniques.

Client Attitudes

The first area of information is the attitudes that a Japanese American client may have about psychological problems and seeking services. Kitano (1970) notes that the Issei brought with them from Japan a view of mental illness as something that is inherited and "taints" the bloodline. For this reason, a great deal of shame, or *haji*, may be associated with mental disturbances. This suggests the importance of assessing any concerns that a Japanese American family or client might have about confidentiality and seeking services. These concerns may not be expressed directly or verbally, however, and the therapist may wish to reduce a family's feeling of shame by actively recognizing the personal nature of the information being shared and reassuring them that this information will be held in confidence. It may be helpful to ask family members directly about their conceptualization of emotional problems and how they view the current presenting complaint.

Kitano (1970) also notes that Japanese Americans tend to view mental illness as inappropriate behavior or malingering. Recognizing this, a clinician should explore the degree to which parents feel a child's behavior problems are willful or manipulative. This would be particularly critical in cases that involve family therapy or collateral work with parents.

Japanese American clients may differ from non-Asian clients not only in their attitudes toward emotional difficulties but also in the very manner in which their complaints are presented. Sue and Sue (1974) note that Japanese American college students tended to report more somatic complaints than their Caucasian American counterparts. Similarly, Kitano (1982) describes a study by Okano (1977) in which Japanese Americans from Los Angeles reported that they did not experience frequent emotional or psychological problems. The majority of respondents saw themselves as mentally healthy. They did acknowledge, however, that their major personal problems were related to their physical health. Japanese Americans, then, may be more likely to express emotional difficulties through somatization, so a thorough assessment of both psychological and physical factors is especially important when working with these clients.

Therapist Sensitivity in Case Conceptualization

The issues just presented point to the importance of assessing the attitudes held by Japanese American children and families who seek services. However, therapists must also assess their own biases and attitudes toward Japanese Americans. Clinicians must be careful not to misinterpret culturally influenced responses to the treatment setting or interview as evidence of simple defense mechanisms. Reservations about being seen at a clinic, for example, should not be interpreted merely as signs of resistance. Rather, a culturally sensitive therapist would view this as a reasonable response from a member of a cultural group that perceives any psychological problem negatively and that, because of past discrimination by the majority environment, is concerned about being perceived as different.

Gray and Cosgrove (1985) indicate that an ethnocentric clinician might also negatively misconstrue characteristics of a Japanese American family that are in actuality nonpathological. Avoiding open praise or expecting that children should spend much of their free time studying might be viewed as emotionally harmful or punitive by a naive evaluator. In fact, such behaviors can be culturally congruent and valued.

In working with adolescents, therapists must also be aware that their own stereotypes of Japanese Americans may influence their case conceptualization. Assessment of academic strengths and weaknesses and how these fit into decisions about goals for the future can play an important role in many adolescent cases. Many people believe that all Asian Americans are good in math and poor in verbal subjects. Sue and Frank (1973), however, found that Japanese American male college students did not differ from Caucasian American subjects in their mathematical ability and did not differ from other students in the physical or social sciences in their choice of occupations. Sata (1983) also has reported that Sansei are increasingly majoring in diverse disciplines. Consequently, a Japanese American adolescent who is failing math should not be seen as suffering from any greater academic failure than a non-Asian peer. Nor should a failing grade in a social science be dismissed as less important because of assumptions that this is an area in which such a student might be expected to have difficulties.

Therapists must maintain sensitivity to Japanese American culture when gathering information at the individual, family, and community levels. The following outline provides specific questions a therapist might explore at each of these levels, although it should be recognized that the answers to questions presented at any one level may draw on information across several levels.

Individual Assessment Issues

Issues to be explored at the individual level include the following:

- *To what degree is ethnicity an issue for this child or adolescent?* Issues of ethnicity will be different for a newly acculturated Japanese American child, for example, than for a fourth-generation Japanese American.
- *How does the child feel about his or her physical attractiveness and aptitude?* Because Japanese Americans may be smaller in stature than their Caucasian American counterparts, they may feel that they cannot do well in certain sports (such as basketball). They may also feel self-conscious or unsatisfied with their racial characteristics because they do not fit the Caucasian American standards for attractiveness. Some Japanese American adolescent girls, for example, use cellophane tape to create Western-looking double eyelids. If a client does this, it can be useful to explore their sense of personal attractiveness and ethnicity.
- *How does the child or adolescent respond to persons with authority?* Because Japanese American culture stresses obedience to authority, the client may defer to teachers and parents as well as to the therapist. A child who has been referred for poor school performance may "suffer" from a lack of communication rather than from actual cognitive limitations. The child may be unclear about classwork instructions but feel it is rude to ask the teacher for clarification or assistance. At the other extreme, a therapist might encounter a Japanese American adolescent who rebels against all authority fig-

ures. In this case, the adolescent may be striking out against the pressure within the family to obey authority.

- *If the client is an adolescent, how does he or she feel about issues related to dating and sexuality?* The onset of dating and the development of self-consciousness about appearance can raise a young person's awareness of being of a racial minority to new levels of intensity (Sata, 1983). At the same time, rebelling against parental authority and exhibiting nonconformist behavior to establish a unique identity can put the Japanese American adolescent into conflict with cultural values that emphasize conformity and deference to parents. Issues around sexuality are likely to intensify, and as has been noted, it may be difficult for the Japanese American family to respond to the adolescent's sexual issues.

Family Assessment Issues

Additional areas for exploration occur at the family level. For example:

- *How much contact is there with the extended family?* If there is close and constant contact with the extended family, the therapist should explore further the nature of this contact. Do the client's parents view the contact as a joy, a burden, or a mixture of both? If a grandparent lives in the home, is that person the parent of the mother or the father? When significant extended family members are part of the household, it may be valuable to include them in the assessment and treatment process. Lack of contact with an extended family should also be explored. A child's family may, for example, experience isolation because they lack access to the extended family. Or they may have deliberately curtailed visits with the extended family because of familial conflicts.

- *How much emphasis do the parents place on their child's achievement?* If great emphasis is placed on achievement, the child may feel pressured to do well and may experience a disproportionate sense of failure if goals are not attained. Parental pressure to achieve might also create conflict within the family itself. For example, the child may want to participate in after-school sports, but the parents may see this as a frivolous use of time.

- *What is the generational status for each parent and the child?* If the parents are Nisei or older Sansei (for example, born during World War II), it would be important to know whether or not they were interned and, if so, at what age and for how long. A clinician should not expect the parents to discuss their internment at length because this is a topic that is difficult for many former internees. However, most who were in camps will give brief factual information about their experiences. Further, the parents may themselves be of different generations and may differ in their philosophies of parenting and in their styles of interaction with their child.

• *How has the family responded to changes in the generational family life cycle?* If, for example, the parents are Sansei, in what ways are their family roles and attitudes about interracial dating similar to or different from those of their Nisei parents?

Community Assessment Issues

The community surrounding each Japanese American family should also be evaluated. For example, what is the ethnic/cultural composition of the child's current and past neighborhood and school? A Japanese American child who lives in a community with a sizeable number of Japanese Americans will have a different sense of cultural identity than a child who lives in an all-white community. A child in a community where the majority of its members are non-Asian minorities will have yet another sense of cultural identity; for example, there are Japanese Americans who grew up in the predominantly black community of Crenshaw, Los Angeles, and adopted both the dialect and mannerisms of African Americans. If the community includes other Asian Americans who are not Japanese, the therapist must recognize that this may not necessarily be a positive factor. There have historically been many tensions between Japan and China and Korea, and a similarity of racial characteristics with other Asian Americans does not ensure smooth intergroup interactions. A Japanese American boy who wants to date a Chinese American girl may encounter prejudice and rejection from her parents just as he might from the parents of a Caucasian American girl.

Selection of Assessment Techniques

Clinicians should also recognize that commonly used assessment techniques may have limited utility with Japanese American children and adolescents. Asian Americans frequently expect mental health professionals to be directive and action oriented (Leong,

1986). This fits well with cultural expectations that emphasize deference to authority. As a result, ambiguous projective tests such as the Rorschach may be less useful than more structured behavioral assessments. Kim (1985) suggests that because many Japanese American parents are strongly committed to helping their children whenever possible, explicit enlistment of their help in early assessment techniques is useful. Behavioral questions present a structured way for parents to participate in their child's treatment.

Standardized objective tests may also have limited utility. Little research evaluates the degree to which particular objective measures are valid for Japanese Americans. The problem here is not one of language (as it is, for example, with Spanish-speaking children or recent Asian immigrants). The Sansei and Yonsei are native English speakers, but they have been raised with different sociocultural values than the majority Caucasian Americans who form the normative groups for most objective tests. A study by Saeki, Clark, and Azen (1985) illustrates the utility of examining the performance of Japanese American children. These researchers compared the responses for Japanese, Japanese American, and Caucasian American children on a developmental test for sensory integration. They found that the Japanese American children did better on the test than the Caucasian American children, but not as well as the Japan-born children of equivalent age. The researchers suggest that because norms for this measure are based only on Caucasian American children, the test may actually be underselective of Japanese and Japanese American children with sensory integration difficulties.

Whenever possible, clinicians should also obtain cross-situational assessments of behavior for their Japanese American clients (Sue and Morishima, 1982). In a study by Ayabe (1971), Japanese American and Caucasian American college students did not differ in vocal strength (used here as an indicator of deference) when in the company of another student. In the presence of a professor, however, the Japanese American students spoke with less vocal strength than their Caucasian American peers. Perceived deference in one setting may be absent in other situations. Younger Sansei and Yonsei might show assertive behaviors outside the home but deferent behaviors with parents. An adolescent who is outspoken or defiant at school may not behave similarly at home.

Finally, therapists should be aware of the way a Japanese American client responds to their evaluation results. Given that the Japanese American culture encourages deference to authority, a family may passively accept test results without asking for clarification. Diamond and Bond (1974) explored the possibility that Japanese American college students in Hawaii might be more likely to accept personality test interpretations than their Caucasian American peers. Their results do not support this hypothesis. However, the limited scope of their study prohibits any generalization of the results to other Japanese American clients, suggesting that therapists should make every effort to elicit questions or concerns from Japanese American children and families when presenting evaluation results.

Intervention and Treatment

Although little has been written on methods of intervention and treatment with Japanese American youth, there is a growing literature on clinical work with Asian Americans as a larger group (Leong, 1986; Uba, 1994) and with Japanese Americans more specifically (Fujii, Fukushima, and Yamamoto, 1993; Marsella, 1993). In part this literature has been triggered by data indicating underutilization of mental health services by Asian Americans and by additional data presented by Sue (1977) that reveal that significantly more Asian Americans (more than 50 percent) than Caucasian Americans (about 30 percent) drop out of treatment after one session. These facts highlight the need for culturally sensitive treatments and interventions for Asian American youth. In the following sections, specific therapeutic issues in working with Japanese American children and adolescents are discussed in relation to (1) initiation of treatment, (2) therapist style, (3) culture specifics in treatment, and (4) advantages and disadvantages of selected treatment methods.

Initiation of Treatment

Most initial sessions with a child or adolescent include a parent. In this sense, initial contacts are often family sessions. Kim (1985) states that although most therapists realize the importance of maintaining flexibility in any initial family session, a flexible approach at this early stage of work is especially critical for Asian American families. Hsu and others (1985) found, for example, that profiles of healthy families differed between Japanese American and Caucasian American families in Hawaii. The Japanese American families were rated as less direct, less overtly affectionate, less revealing of private matters, and displaying greater incongruence between their stated and observed behaviors. Observers rated the Japanese American families to be less competent and less "healthy," even though the research was conducted on nonclinical families. A therapist might similarly see "pathology" in a family when in fact what is really being observed is healthy culturally influenced family functioning.

Henkin (1985) points to another danger: a therapist may try to change Japanese American clients into mainstream ideals (either as individuals or as a family) that are antithetical to the client's cultural background. The following case presents a situation in which an evaluation of Japanese American cultural values would be useful before instituting a treatment strategy.

Ken, a sixteen-year-old Japanese American male, reported feeling depressed and fatigued. Upon further inquiry, Ken noted that his depression had increased at the same time that recent conflicts with his parents had arisen. Ken's parents, both Nisei who had been interned as adolescents, owned and operated a family grocery store that had been in the family for two generations. They hoped that Ken, the oldest son, would take over the store after they retired. Conflicts between Ken and his parents centered on his resistance to working in the store after school and on Saturdays. Ken's parents expected him to contribute his part to the family business, but Ken resented having to spend his free time working for his parents. He pointed out that none of his Caucasian American friends had such restrictions on their schedule. In fact, Ken stated, several of his peers made fun of the fact that he was "still tied to his parents' apron strings."

Ken noted that his mother and father just "didn't understand" him. Rather than listen to him, they admonished his verbal outbursts of anger by telling him it was disrespectful to challenge their authority. Ken grew increasingly frustrated with his situation and began experiencing depressive feelings and fatigue as he internalized his frustration more and more, withdrawing from his parents, and eventually his peers as well.

In this case, the therapist might be tempted to view Ken's rebellion as an example of his growing independence from the family and focus treatment goals on facilitating Ken's separation from the family. Aoki (cited in Henkin, 1985), however, notes that whereas the Western goal of family therapy is to resolve family issues by encouraging family members to individuate and develop their independence, this goal may be inappropriate for Japanese American families. Because Japanese American families place a high value on cohesiveness and interdependence, it might not be appropriate to assume that Ken's separation from the family is desirable.

Much more is at stake in this case than whether or not Ken is to work at his parents' store. For example, the store represents a link with past family generations as well as with traditional Japanese ethics regarding work, responsibility, and obligation to the family. As a result, Ken is under considerable pressure to help his parents. This pressure may be compounded by the fact that Ken's parents were interned during the war. First, because they were about the same age as Ken when they were imprisoned behind barbed wire, they may view his need for free time as extravagant. In comparison with their experience as adolescents, Ken already has a great deal of freedom. Second, the internment experience may have caused Ken's parents to be extrasensitive to issues of financial stability and maintaining the family business. After seeing their own parents struggle with the losses of the internment, they may be especially intent on making plans for Ken to participate in the store.

Encouraging Ken to separate from his family could also be detrimental in other ways. Although some therapists might see his verbal outbursts as a healthy sign of self-assertion, Ken himself may have great ambivalence about losing control and challenging his parents. Clinicians need to be aware that adopting Westernized styles of expression may cause discomfort even for third- and fourth-generation Japanese Americans. The fact that Ken's Caucasian American peers compare his family's standards of interaction to those of their own families and mock the cultural pressures he experiences complicates the situation. Ken is caught between saving face with his peers and saving face with his family. Hence, assessment would need to take into account the ramifications of self-assertion and independence in relation to both Ken's specific cultural-familial background and his interactions with the larger majority culture.

Because Japanese Americans tend to defer to authority figures and view their emotional problems as physically based, they are likely to approach the therapist in a manner somewhat like a patient seeking concrete medical advice from a physician (Tsui and Schultz, 1985). Given such expectations, in initial sessions the therapist should attempt to establish a clear-cut structure for counseling and explain the therapy process itself (Henkin, 1985; Kim, 1985; Root, 1985). Without concrete explanations of what is to be expected, Asian American clients are less likely to return for services (Root, 1985). Hsu (1983) states that therapists should also avoid extensive diagnostic evaluations with Asian American clients and work towards tangible, problem-focused goals as soon as possible. Patience may be required of the therapist during these early sessions (Henkin, 1985). Japanese Americans may view self-disclosure as self-centered, losing control, and/or losing face in the presence of the therapist or other family members. Therapists, then, must recognize the need for early structure and goal setting as well as the need to avoid hasty diagnoses based on incomplete data. In dealing with these realities, a therapist might early on set immediate primary goals (some of which might incorporate enlisting the family's help in providing more information in certain areas) but allow for the formation of secondary goals as additional information emerges from the family work.

Related to assumptions that the therapist is an expert are expectations regarding age and sex. Respect for age is evident in Japanese American culture. The following case example illustrates how younger therapists may be received with less confidence than older therapists.

While an intern, the author was treating a Sansei adolescent who was extremely depressed and anxious. After several meetings the client's mother appeared in the waiting room after a session. The client introduced the therapist, at which point the mother's face dropped in disappointment. Her remark was simply, "Oh, so young!"

The young, female therapist clearly did not meet the hopes and expectations of this concerned mother, despite the mother's stated preference for a Japanese American therapist. I responded by acknowledging the mother's concerns, then briefly described my professional background and training. Once the mother heard I was a "doctor," she visibly relaxed. Describing one's credentials may seem egotistical. However, this case example demonstrates that it can serve a beneficial purpose in working with a Japanese American client.

Therapist Style

The way therapists present themselves can clearly influence the client's degree of comfort in sharing information. Most experts agree that an active rather than a passive therapist style works best with most Asian American clients (Yamamoto and Acosta, 1982). Henkin (1985), however, suggests that therapists should be aware that such Western behaviors as intense eye contact, physical gestures, and direct questions may be seen as intrusive by Japanese American clients. At the same time, an overly aloof therapeutic style may be construed as a sign of lack of interest, as the following vignette illustrates.

> A sixteen-year-old Japanese American adolescent girl was suicidal following the breakup of a relationship. The therapist adopted an analytically oriented, nondirective approach to the case and met with the family and the girl to discuss the current family structure. Unfortunately, the family did not feel they had established a trusting relationship with the therapist, nor did the therapist make an attempt to direct the interactions during the sessions. The net result was that the daughter felt awkward and embarrassed for having her family subjected to her therapy (which seemed a waste of time) and the family felt ineffectual in aiding their daughter. The therapist did not investigate the impact of the family session and the client terminated treatment.

This termination might have been avoided if the therapist had adopted a more active role with the client and her family, explaining the goals of the family session and eliciting any concerns from the parents and their daughter. This would have provided a structure for the therapy and would have encouraged interaction between the clients and the therapist.

Suggestions have been made concerning the style of therapy that is most effective for Japanese American clients. Atkinson, Maruyama, and Matsui (1978) found that college-aged Japanese American students rated high a counselor who used a logical, rational, and structured approach rather than an affective, reflective, ambiguous one. Henkin (1985) suggests that the therapist take on a nonthreatening yet defined role with Japanese American clients that allows them to ask questions. Japanese American clients may be hesitant to ask questions, however, because the cultural dynamic of *enryo* may cause them to feel they should not assert their own viewpoint and challenge the therapist's authority. One solution is to enlist the client's questions as a specific task. Doing so enables clients to assist in the therapy by allowing them to ask questions in a culturally consonant way (that is, in a role of responding to an authority's request and also in a role of helping to alleviate the problem). This approach might be especially desirable in family therapy, because the enlistment of the Japanese American family as a mobilizing force to augment individual work can be extremely useful.

The preceding suggestions concerning therapeutic style could be incorporated by any therapist who desires to work effectively with Japanese Americans. Questions have been raised, however, about the degree to which Japanese American children and adolescents and their families can be treated effectively by non-Japanese American therapists. Research supporting the importance in the therapeutic process of therapist-client match for Japanese Americans is as yet unclear. Atkinson, Maruyama, and Matsui (1978) report mixed results on this topic. One sample of Japanese American subjects in their study felt that racial similarity was highly significant in determining the credibility of a therapist, but a second sample did not indicate this preference. It is clearly desirable to have more trained Japanese American therapists who could be available to Japanese American clients. However, given the decline in the Japanese American population, it is also important to train non-Japanese American therapists to be aware of the clinical issues raised here.

Culture Specifics in Treatment

Broader cultural issues, in addition to those related to therapeutic style, can affect a therapist's treatment interventions with Japanese

Americans. A lack of culturally sensitive services has been seen as contributing to the high therapy dropout rate of Asian Americans. Unfortunately, the provision of culturally sensitive services is extremely complex. Clinicians working with a Japanese American child and family have a difficult task. On the one hand, they must be cognizant of Japanese American cultural differences, some of which are rooted in more general Asian American heritage and tradition. On the other hand, they must also be aware that current Japanese American parents and children are likely to be highly acculturated and American in many of their attitudes, values, and behaviors. Blind application of clinical style based only on a knowledge of Asian American families would be offensive to a fourth-generation Yonsei. At the same time, complete ignorance of the ways in which such a client may differ from Caucasian Americans may also jeopardize the effectiveness of an intervention. Recognizing this, the following discussion serves more as a menu of issues that clinicians might consider in their work than as an exhaustive list of how-to's to be followed dogmatically. Family therapy is used as a primary focus because family work is often indicated in both child and adolescent interventions.

First, treatment strategies must take into account two very important variables: (1) the structure of the Japanese American family, and (2) the degree to which the family has become acculturated. Lack of appreciation for the family structure may impede therapy. Kim (1985) and Hsu (1983) note that it is safest to respect the family's vertical hierarchy (for example, addressing the father as the authority), at least initially, thus allowing the parent to save face until groundwork is laid to address the family in other ways. However, the issue of generational status must also be considered before implementing such a suggestion. If, for example, the parents are Sansei in their thirties with an egalitarian relationship, they may not adhere to the vertical hierarchy that was once present in most Japanese American families. In this case, attempts to address a vertical hierarchy within the family could be offensive.

The clinician must also be alert to differences in acculturation that may exist among family members. Literature suggests that today's Japanese American adolescent may in many ways differ little from his or her Caucasian American peers. McDermott and others (1984) found that Japanese American and Caucasian American adolescents in Hawaii did not differ in their family values. Interestingly, however, their parents differed significantly on several dimensions. Japanese American parents strongly emphasized the need for important family decisions to include family discussion as a group, and they took a more cognitive attitude toward interactions. Caucasian American parents emphasized the importance of individual decisions and open expressions of affect in interactions. These findings indicate that the clinician must be aware of the conflicts a Japanese American adolescent might face with parents concerning family values and styles of interaction. A case described by Sue and Morishima (1982, p. 141) illustrates how such issues might present themselves in therapy:

> A Japanese American adolescent was brought in by his parents because he was constantly using drugs, had been arrested several times for shoplifting, and was associating with "the wrong crowd." He complained that his parents were too "Japanesey" and did not understand him.

In this situation, the adolescent is clearly pointing to a barrier that exists between his parents and himself, a barrier that consists of both generational and value differences. Realistically, his parents may not be able to understand his world. At the same time, however, the adolescent is expressing another difficulty. The fact that his parents are "too Japanesey" suggests that they may also be a source of embarrassment for him. Most adolescents are concerned about fitting in with their peers. Having parents who do not fit the majority stereotype of parents can cause added tensions in the family. The "Japaneseness" of this client's parents may also have caused discomfort by serving as a constant reminder of his cultural heritage in a social world where he is trying to be like everyone else.

Another situation described by Sue and Morishima (1982, p. 142) illustrates similar issues.

> An eighteen-year-old Japanese American student was upset over her family's reaction to her Caucasian American boyfriend. Her parents refused to meet him and on several occasions threatened to disown her. The reactions from her brothers was more extreme. They threatened to beat up that "white bastard." Furthermore, the parents were disturbed by her low grades. Although she had done well in high school, her grades in college were now below average.

The student in this case is hurt by the animosity displayed by both her parents and her brothers. In the case of the parents, generational issues may be contributing to their rejection of the boyfriend. First, it is quite likely that they experienced strong social sanctions against dating whites when they were growing up and were legally prevented from outmarrying. Second, if her parents were interned, they were imprisoned and dominated by Caucasian Americans during the war. Placed in this context, their threats of disownment become clearer. The student's brothers may be expressing a somewhat different reaction to the Caucasian boyfriend. As Sansei who grew up in the 1960s and 1970s, when ethnic pride and solidarity were highly valued, the brothers may see dating a Caucasian American as evidence of selling out one's own ethnic group. Hence, even within a generational cohort, there may be value differences.

In both of the cases just discussed, the differences between the parents' and the adolescent's cultural values and experiences are apparent. What is not described in these cases but may also be a contributing factor is the degree to which the adolescents' retention of Japanese American values can exacerbate the dilemma. For both adolescents, family upbringing that discourages open confrontation with (or even doubt of) a parent's opinion or behavior can make it especially difficult to express disagreement or disappointment openly.

Advantages and Disadvantages of Selected Treatment Methods

Research suggests that not all treatment methods will be equally effective with Japanese American children and adolescents. Kim (1985) believes that the strategic/behavioral framework may be most useful for therapy with Asian American families, because this approach focuses on active problem solving and structure. It is important to note, however, that such approaches also require the therapist to have a clear idea of the structure of the Japanese American family before intervening in that structure.

Miyoshi (1980) found a unique application of family therapy based on Boszormenyi-Nagy and Spark's (1973) theory of multi-generational dynamics. Miyoshi adopted this framework because she was interested in using family sessions as a way to encourage discourse between Nisei parents and their children. More specifically, sessions focused on discussing the internment experience. It was hoped that a discussion of this difficult topic would uncover the intergenerational burdens shared by both the Nisei and Sansei. Miyoshi conducted ten family therapy sessions with each of three Japanese American families and seven sessions with a fourth Japanese American family. Although she did not publish empirical outcome data from her work, her writing did document the rich information that emerged from the family sessions. Clinicians who work with Japanese American families in which the impact of the internment appears especially central would benefit from reviewing Miyoshi's intervention technique.

Behavioral problems are likely to be presenting issues for younger Japanese American children who appear for services. As previously noted, there are several advantages to using behavioral, directed therapies when working with Japanese American families. The following case exemplifies some of these advantages.

Mr. and Mrs. Y., both Sansei-generation Japanese Americans, contacted the clinic with concerns about their son Eric. Eric, six years old and the younger of two sons, was reported to be "unmanageable" at home. Both parents had postponed calling the clinic several times and admitted that they were somewhat embarrassed for "using up" the clinician's time with a problem they should have been able to correct themselves. Mrs. Y. was in particular distress over Eric's behavior and tearfully reported that she could not cope much longer with his tantrums and uncooperativeness. She carried the majority of child-care responsibilities in addition to working part-time. Mr. Y. indicated that although he supported his wife's desire to work, he had been raised to see child care as a woman's role and felt ill-equipped to help Mrs. Y. with Eric's tantrums. An intake interview with Eric revealed him to be a bright, outgoing child. Although he was cooperative with the clinician, he became increasingly disruptive and whiny when his parents entered the room.

Further assessment revealed that the Y.'s lived within fifteen minutes of Mrs. Y.'s parents. Visits between the two families were frequent. Mrs. Y. had asked her own mother for advice about Eric's behavior but found her unsupportive. In fact, Mrs. Y. noted that her mother blamed her for Eric's problems, suggesting that he would not be so difficult if his mother stayed at home full-time with the children. Mrs. Y.'s mother felt that family should always come first. Because Mrs. Y. worked, she was seen by her mother as compromising the family.

Mrs. Y.'s mother had also discouraged the Y.'s from contacting the clinic and was worried that friends might find out that Eric was having problems. This, said Mrs. Y.'s mother, would reflect on the entire family. Consequently, by the time the Y.'s did show up for therapy, Mrs. Y. was anxious not only about whether or not she could get help with Eric but also about risking the family's reputation by seeking treatment.

A behavioral approach to treating Eric's tantrums was implemented. After a thorough behavioral assessment, the Y.'s were instructed in the use of rein-forcements and contingencies to reduce the frequency of Eric's problem behaviors. Charts were used to monitor progress as the treatment progressed.

Like other forms of treatment, behavioral therapy must be sensitive to the fact that many Japanese Americans are wary of seeking mental health services. The Y.'s, for example, have already expressed shame about seeking help. To enlist family confidence and alleviate feelings of shame, a clinician might label the Y.'s help-seeking as positive evidence of their parenting ability and concern for Eric's well-being rather than as a sign of weakness.

A behavioral treatment is particularly useful in this case for several reasons. First, by asking Mr. and Mrs. Y. to identify the antecedents and consequences of Eric's behaviors and to give detailed descriptions of his tantrums, the clinician provided a clear structure within the interview itself. The clarity of these questions helped to ease the Y.'s discomfort and alleviated their sense of hopelessness about the problem. The clinician provided hope by assuming the role of an "expert" who could provide straightforward guidance on ways to handle Eric. At the same time, because the clinician's questions were ones that Mr. and Mrs. Y. could answer, they enabled the Y.'s to recognize that they knew more about Eric's problem than they had realized.

The behavioral approach also provided Mr. Y. with a way to become involved in the treatment without challenging his culturally influenced conceptions of sex roles. The clinician stressed that Mr. Y.'s observations and participation were critical in implementing a consistent behavioral program, but she did not suggest that he directly take on more child-care responsibilities or that he should question the origins of his attitudes toward child care. In fact, Mr. Y. looked forward to actively participating in the treatment and saw his involvement as an important way to help his wife and strengthen his family.

Mrs. Y. faced an especially difficult situation. As a Sansei, many of her behaviors and attitudes were the same as her Caucasian American peers. Like many women today, she found work outside the home important and gratifying. Her Nisei mother, however, constantly compared her to a more traditional Japanese standard of motherhood. Mrs. Y. felt close to her mother and did value the importance of family a great deal. This was evidenced, in part, by her decision to live near her parents. However, she also enjoyed working and felt guilty when her mother accused her of abandoning the children. A behavioral approach to Eric's behavior could not alleviate the friction between Mrs. Y. and her mother. However, it did provide Mrs. Y. with tools to feel more confident in handling her mother's criticisms and doubts. A nondirective or intrapsychic treatment might have seemed nonproductive to Mrs. Y.'s mother, but a behavioral treatment allowed Mrs. Y. to point to concrete interventions she was implementing to help her son, as well as to charts documenting Eric's progress.

Additional cultural variables may play a role in the application of behavioral techniques with a Japanese American family. Behavioral modification treatment emphasizes the importance of observable and measurable behaviors. Much of the communication in a Japanese American family, however, may be nonverbal and not obvious to a Western therapist. Therefore, therapists using behavioral assessments and interventions may need to look for behaviors that are absent as well as for those that are apparent in order to develop useful interventions. For example, they should be aware that Japanese Americans tend not to give overt praise or verbal feedback to their children. This may reflect a general hesitancy to provide verbal feedback. When comparing Japanese American and Caucasian American Hawaiian students engaged in a discussion task, Ogawa and Welden (1972) found that the Japanese American students engaged in significantly less verbal feedback than their Caucasian peers. Hence, simply instructing the Y.'s to verbally reinforce Eric's appropriate behaviors ignores the cultural conflict inherent in such a request. As an alternative, a clinician might explore with the family other, perhaps nonverbal ways in which approval may be communicated.

Individual play therapy for Japanese American children has not been explored in the literature, and it is difficult to know what its potential effectiveness might be. Nonetheless, the following case description shows that play therapy can be an important form of treatment for Japanese American children.

> Lisa, a seven-year-old fourth-generation Japanese American girl, was referred to the clinic by her school after becoming increasingly withdrawn and tearful. Lisa's teacher reported that she would not participate in class, did not play with other children in the classroom or at recess, and frequently asked to go home during the middle of the day. Her parents noted that Lisa frequently wanted to stay home to avoid school. They were worried by the fact that she had become increasingly withdrawn from them at home as well.

> When Lisa was invited into the play therapy room, she appeared nervous and withdrawn. Although she did not speak to the therapist, she immediately went to a shelf lined with dolls, selected one with dark hair and one with blond hair, and staged a fierce battle between the two. The blond doll eventually knocked the dark-haired doll to the ground and exclaimed, "I win!" Additional dark-haired dolls then tried to "save" the defeated dark-haired doll but were unable to lift her from the floor.

> Defeat of dark-haired dolls by blond-haired dolls became a recurrent theme in Lisa's play. At times the battles were fought between light-colored animals and dark-colored animals. Whatever the characters, the light-colored character emerged the victor, and the efforts of other dark-colored characters to rescue the defeated would fail.

> As therapy continued, Lisa eventually revealed that children at school made fun of her "tiny eyes" and black hair and did not pick her for their sports teams. Lisa's play in sessions indicated that she wished she were not Japanese, and that she felt anger toward her parents and blamed them for her difference. In her eyes, if her parents were not Japanese she would not be experiencing the ostracism she now faced. Because her parents were Japanese like herself, she did not feel they could rescue her from the "blond attackers."

In Lisa's case, play therapy proved to be an important vehicle for expressing a number of painful thoughts and feelings about ethnicity and peer relations that would be unlikely to emerge in family therapy or a behavioral treatment. In the safe context of play and fantasy she could express her identity conflicts without directly challenging her parents or peers.

Although play therapy worked well for Lisa, other young Japanese American children may find the play situation somewhat confusing. If their families have encouraged them to respect and obey authority figures, they will want to comply with the therapist's requests. At the same time, if their families have also emphasized the importance of doing homework during free time and frowned upon excessive play as a frivolous activity, the therapist's invitation to play may be difficult to accept. (For these reasons, other projective techniques that are similar to schoolwork, such as telling and writing stories or drawing pictures, may be useful.) Similarly, it is important to explain clearly to the child's parents the function and goals of play therapy. Given that Japanese American parents will likely be seeking concrete signs of progress in their child, they may see play therapy as fruitless and indulgent. Once again, however, the degree to which these hypotheses hold true will depend greatly on the particular Japanese American family being seen and on their life experiences. For a Sansei couple who know about the principles underlying play therapy and who are highly acculturated, these issues may be less relevant.

Role-playing can also present difficulties for the Japanese American child, because it requires a client to step out of a structured, prescribed role and assume one that is ambiguous. Once again, the child may feel conflict between (1) pleasing an authority figure by complying with the therapist's request, and (2) experiencing the request as culturally inappropriate or aberrant. This conflict can have countertherapeutic effects. Sue (1981) presents a case illustration in which role-playing in the form of the Gestalt "empty chair" technique was used with an Asian American client and had an unintended negative consequence.

> A student was in conflict with his parents about his career choice but could not openly express his conflict with them. After the therapist used the empty chair technique to encourage him to express his anger towards his parents, the student became less actively involved in the therapy.

Several factors that are common in Japanese American culture could have contributed to the "failure" of this technique. The role-play required the client to assert himself and his anger. However, he had been brought up to respect his parents and elders, not to talk back or confront them, and to keep negative emotions within. Simply to encourage behaving assertively is to ignore the network of associations a Japanese American adolescent might have around the meaning of assertive behavior.

Group therapy might provide a less individually focused, less intensive form of intervention with adolescents and might also serve to reduce shame about receiving services. However, Schlesinger (1981) has suggested that the implications of being a member of a therapy group may be greater for a Japanese American client than for a Caucasian American client. Because group membership is taken very seriously in Japanese culture and cooperation within the group is strongly encouraged, a Japanese American client might be reluctant to become involved in the group process.

Finally, artwork may provide a useful form of intervention, given that the Japanese American child may have been raised in an environment where nonverbal communication is as important as verbal communication. If the child's work can be shared with the parents, this may also provide a way for the parents to gain an understanding of their child's issues without entering into a more confrontational verbal exchange. As a cautionary note, before incorporating artwork into the therapy, therapists should be aware of any preconceptions they may have of Asian Americans as artistic, quiet, and inarticulate. Certainly not all Japanese Americans would fit this stereotype.

Summary and Conclusions

Assessment and treatment of Japanese American children and adolescents and their families present the clinician with challenging tasks. As this chapter has shown, Japanese Americans cannot be simplistically categorized into either Caucasian American or Japanese stereotypes. Variables such as generational status, composition of a child's ethnic community, level of acculturation, and the potential long-term impact of the internment on the family can influence the effectiveness of a therapist's efforts.

A major point in this chapter is that Japanese Americans, as well as other Asian Americans, underutilize mental health services. Many of the suggestions for therapeutic intervention may rarely be implemented, because data indicate that Japanese American children appear for treatment infrequently. It also is clear, however, that the underutilization of services does not diminish the need for culturally sensitive interventions. The question becomes, What type of intervention would be most useful? A "culturally sensitive" service is often defined as including the provision of (1) bilingual, bicultural, or culturally sensitive therapists; (2) parallel services in areas with large concentrations of ethnic communities; and (3) nonparallel services for ethnic minority clients (Sue and Zane, 1987). For Japanese Americans, however, these recommendations are less clear. Language is not a factor, because contemporary Japanese Americans are English-speaking; and their decreasing numbers, combined with the increasing geographic dispersal of Sansei and Yonsei, make the second and third suggestions difficult to implement.

Additionally, Uba (1982) notes that given the diversity of individuals within any Asian American population, one cannot assume that culturally relevant services are automatically applicable to the same degree for all clients. Educating non–Japanese American therapists about the culture of Japanese Americans is important but insufficient, and any suggestions for the assessment and treatment of Japanese Americans must clearly be balanced with an understanding that each client, whether child, adolescent, or adult, brings to the therapeutic relationship a unique personal history of acculturation.

Interventions designed to enhance well-being need to be developed, in recognition that the effects of discrimination may have diminished the positive mental health of Japanese Americans (Sue and Morishima, 1982). Future research is needed to illuminate the stresses experienced by Japanese American children and their families. In particular, as health psychology has begun to explore the interplay among stress, physical health, and psychological well-being, efforts should be made to explore the somatic complaints presented by Japanese Americans. Research and interventions sensitive to the increasing numbers of Japanese American children and adolescents from mixed marriages are another important area for future emphasis. Moritsugu, Foerster, and Morishima (1978) found that the Eurasians interviewed in their study (ages seventeen to twenty-one) reported experiences of alienation because of their mixed ancestry, despite providing positive self-descriptions. Research is needed on the complex issues facing these children and on the ways in which these issues might be integrated into assessment and intervention.

Finally, attention should be paid to the international and political environment in which Japanese American children and adolescents find themselves. As tensions between the United States and Japan are strained due to economic conditions, Japanese American children and their families may experience increased racism and discrimination. Prejudice against other Asian groups within the United States can also affect Japanese American families because many people fail to distinguish among the various Asian American ethnic groups. A *Wall Street Journal* report, for example, reported a 62 percent increase in anti-Asian incidents between 1984 and 1985 (Wong, 1986). Awareness of the larger sociopolitical climate surrounding Japanese Americans, and Asian Americans in general, will clearly be important for mental health professionals who work with this population.

References

Abramson, P. R., and Imai-Marquez, J. "The Japanese-American: A Cross-Cultural, Cross-Sectional Study of Sex Guilt." *Journal of Research in Personality*, 1982, *16*, 227–237.

Arkoff, A., and Weaver, H. "Body Image and Body Dissatisfaction in Japanese Americans." *Journal of Social Psychology*, 1966, *68*, 323–330.

Atkinson, D. R., Maruyama, M., and Matsui, S. "Effects of Counselor Race and Counseling Approach on Asian Americans' Perceptions of Counselor Credibility and Utility." *Journal of Counseling Psychology*, 1978, *25*, 76–83.

Ayabe, H. I. "Deference and Ethnic Differences in Voice Levels." *Journal of Social Psychology*, 1971, *85*, 181–185.

Boszormenyi-Nagy, I., and Spark, G. M. *Invisible Loyalties: Reciprocity in Intergenerational Family Therapy*. New York: HarperCollins, 1973.

Cabezas, A. Y. "Disadvantaged Employment Status of Asian and Pacific Americans." In U.S. Commission on Civil Rights, *Civil Rights Issues of Asian and Pacific Americans: Myths and Realities.* Washington, D.C.: U.S. Commission on Civil Rights, 1979.

Caudill, W., and Frost, L. "A Comparison of Maternal Care and Infant Behavior in Japanese-American, American and Japanese Families." In U. Bronfenbrenner (ed.), *Influences on Development.* Orlando, Fla.: Dryden Press, 1972.

Connor, J. W. "Acculturation and Family Continuities in Three Generations of Japanese-Americans." *Journal of Marriage and the Family,* 1974, *36,* 159–165.

Danieli, Y. "Families of Survivors of the Nazi Holocaust: Some Short- and Long-Term Effects." In C. D. Spielberger, I. G. Saragon, and N. A. Milgram (eds.), *Stress and Anxiety.* Vol. 8. Bristol, Pa.: Hemisphere, 1982.

Diamond, M. J., and Bond, M. H. "The Acceptance of 'Barnum' Personality Interpretations by Japanese, Japanese-American, and Caucasian American College Students." *Journal of Cross-Cultural Psychology,* 1974, *5,* 228–235.

Dubanoski, R. A., and Snyder, K. "Patterns of Child Abuse and Neglect in Japanese- and Samoan-Americans." *Child Abuse and Neglect,* 1980, *4,* 217–225.

Fujii, J. S., Fukushima, S. N., and Yamamoto, J. "Psychiatric Care of Japanese Americans." In A. C. Gaw (ed.), *Culture, Ethnicity, and Mental Illness.* Washington, D.C.: American Psychiatric Association Press, 1993.

Gardner, R., Robey, B., and Smith, P. "Asian Americans: Growth, Change, and Diversity." *Population Bulletin.* Washington, D.C.: Population Reference Bureau, 1985.

Gehrie, M. J. "Childhood and Community: On the Experience of Young Japanese-Americans in Chicago." *Ethos,* 1976, *4,* 353–383.

Gray, E., and Cosgrove, J. "Ethnocentric Perception of Childrearing Practices in Protective Services." *Child Abuse and Neglect,* 1985, *9,* 389–396.

Hansen, A. A., and Mitson, B. E. *Voices Long Silent: An Oral Inquiry into the Japanese American Evacuation.* Fullerton: California State University Oral History Program, 1974.

Henkin, W. A. "Toward Counseling the Japanese in America: A Cross-Cultural Primer." *Journal of Counseling and Development,* 1985, *63,* 500–503.

Hsu, J. "Asian Family Interaction Patterns and Their Therapeutic Implications." *International Journal of Family Psychiatry,* 1983, *4,* 307–320.

Hsu, J., and others. "Family Interaction Patterns Among Japanese-American and Caucasian Families in Hawaii." *American Journal of Psychiatry,* 1985, *142,* 577–581.

Johnson, C. L. "Interdependence, Reciprocity, and Indebtedness: An Analysis of Japanese American Kinship Relations." *Journal of Marriage and the Family,* 1977, *39,* 351–363.

Kim, B.L.C. *The Asian Americans: Changing Patterns, Changing Needs.* Montclair, N.J.: Association of Korean Christian Scholars in North America, 1978.

Kim, S. C. "Family Therapy for Asian Americans: A Strategic-Structural Framework." *Psychotherapy,* 1985, *22,* 342–348.

Kitano, H.H.L. "Japanese-American Crime and Delinquency." *Journal of Psychology,* 1967, *66,* 253–263.

Kitano, H.H.L. "Japanese-American Mental Illness." In S. C. Plog and R. B. Edgerton (eds.), *Changing Perspectives in Mental Illness.* Austin, Tex.: Holt, Rinehart, and Winston, 1969a.

Kitano, H.H.L. *Japanese Americans: The Evolution of a Subculture.* Englewood Cliffs, N.J.: Prentice Hall, 1969b.

Kitano, H.H.L. "Mental Illness in Four Cultures." *Journal of Social Psychology,* 1970, *80,* 121–134.

Kitano, H.H.L. "Mental Health in the Japanese American Community." In E. E. Jones and S. J. Korchin (eds.), *Minority Mental Health.* New York: Praeger, 1982.

Kitano, H.H.L., and Kikumura, A. "The Japanese American Family." In C. H. Mindel and R. W. Habenstein (eds.), *Ethnic Families in America.* New York: Elsevier, 1976.

Kitano, H.H.L., Yeung, W. T., Chai, L., and Hatanaka, H. "Asian-American Interracial Marriage." *Journal of Marriage and the Family,* 1984, *2,* 179–190.

Knoll, T. *Becoming Americans: Asian Sojourners, Immigrants, and Refugees in the Western United States.* Portland, Oreg.: Coast to Coast Books, 1982.

Leong, F.T.L. "Counseling and Psychotherapy with Asian Americans: A Review of the Literature." *Journal of Counseling Psychology,* 1986, *33,* 196–206.

Marsella, A. J. "Counseling with Japanese Americans: Cross-Cultural Considerations." *American Journal of Orthopsychiatry,* 1993, *63,* 200–208.

Mass, A. I. "Psychological Effects of the Camps on Japanese Americans." In R. Daniels, S. C. Taylor, and H.H.L. Kitano (eds.), *From Relocation to Redress.* Salt Lake City: University of Utah Press, 1986.

Masuda, M., Matsumoto, G. M., and Meredith, G. M. "Ethnic Identity in Three Generations of Japanese Americans." *Journal of Social Psychology,* 1970, *81,* 199–207.

McDermott, J. F., and others. "Cultural Variations in Family Attitudes and Their Implications for Therapy." In S. Chess and A. Thomas (eds.), *Annual Progress in Child Psychiatry and Child Development.* New York: Brunner/Mazel, 1984.

Miyoshi, N. "Identity Crisis of the Sansei and the American Concentration Camp." *Pacific Citizen,* 1980, *91,* 41–55.

Morales, A., Ferguson, Y., and Munford, P. R. "The Juvenile Justice System and Minorities." In G. J. Powell, J. Yamamoto, A. Romero, and A. Morales (eds.), *The Psychosocial Development of Minority Group Children.* New York: Brunner/Mazel, 1983.

Morishima, J. K. "The Evacuation: Impact on the Family." In S. Sue and N. N. Wagner (eds.), *Asian Americans: Psychological Perspectives.* Palo Alto, Calif.: Science and Behavior Books, 1973.

Moritsugu, J., Foerster, L., and Morishima, J. K. "Eurasians: A Pilot Study." Paper presented at the Western Psychological Association Convention, San Francisco, 1978.

Nadler, A., Kav-Venaki, S., and Gleitman, B. "Transgenerational Effects of the Holocaust: Externalization of Aggression in Second Generation of Holocaust Survivors." *Journal of Consulting and Clinical Psychology,* 1985, *53,* 365–369.

Nagata, D. K. "Long-Term Effects of the Japanese Internment Camps: Impact on the Children of the Internees." Paper presented at the Second National Convention of the Asian American Psychological Association, New York, Aug. 1987.

Nagata, D. K. "The Japanese American Internment: Exploring the Transgenerational Consequences of Traumatic Stress." *Journal of Traumatic Stress,* 1990, *3,* 47–69.

Nagata, D. K. *Legacy of Injustice: Exploring the Cross-Generational Impact of the Japanese American Internment.* New York: Plenum, 1993.

Nakagawa, B., and Watanabe, R. *A Study of the Use of Drugs Among the Asian American Youth of Seattle.* Seattle: Demonstration Project of Asian Americans, 1973.

Nakane, C. *Japanese Society.* Berkeley: University of California Press, 1970.

Ogawa, D. M., and Welden, T. A. "Cross-Cultural Analysis of Feedback Behavior Within Japanese American and Caucasian American Small Groups." *Journal of Communication,* 1972, *22,* 189–195.

Okano, Y. *Japanese Americans and Mental Health.* Los Angeles: Coalition for Mental Health, 1977.

O'Reilly, J. P., Tokuno, K. A., and Ebata, A. T. "Cultural Differences Between Americans of Japanese and European Ancestry in Parental Valuing and Social Competence." *Journal of Comparative Family Studies,* 1986, *17,* 87–97.

Padilla, A. M., Wagatsuma, Y., and Lindholm, K. J. "Acculturation and Personality as Predictors of Stress in Japanese and Japanese Americans." *Journal of Social Psychology,* 1985, *125,* 295–305.

Prizzia, R., and Villanueva-King, O. *Central Oahu Community Mental Health Needs Assessment Survey. Part III: A Survey of the General Population.*

Honolulu: Management Planning and Administration Consultants, 1977.

Root, M. P. "Guidelines for Facilitating Therapy with Asian American Clients." *Psychotherapy,* 1985, *22,* 349–356.

Saeki, K., Clark, F. A., and Azen, S. P. "Performance of Japanese and Japanese American Children on the Motor Accuracy-Revised and Design Copying Tests of the Southern California Sensory Integration Tests." *American Journal of Occupational Therapy,* 1985, *39,* 103–109.

Sata, L. S. "Mental Health Issues of Japanese-American Children." In G. J. Powell, J. Yamamoto, A. Romero, and A. Morales (eds.), *The Psychosocial Development of Minority Group Children.* New York: Brunner/Mazel, 1983.

Schlesinger, R. "Cross-Cultural Psychiatry: The Applicability of Western Anglo Psychiatry to Asian Americans of Chinese and Japanese Ethnicity." *Journal of Psychosocial Nursing and Mental Health Services,* 1981, *19,* 26–30.

Sue, D. W. *Counseling the Culturally Different: Theory and Practice.* New York: Wiley, 1981.

Sue, D. W., and Frank, A. C. "A Typological Approach to the Psychological Study of Chinese- and Japanese-American College Males." *Journal of Social Issues,* 1973, *29*(2), 129–148.

Sue, S. "Community Mental Health Services to Minority Groups: Some Optimism, Some Pessimism." *American Psychologist,* 1977, *32,* 616–624.

Sue, S., and McKinney, H. "Asian-Americans in the Community Health Care System." *American Journal of Orthopsychiatry,* 1975, *45*(1), 111–118.

Sue, S., and Morishima, J. K. *The Mental Health of Asian Americans: Contemporary Issues in Identifying and Treating Mental Problems.* San Francisco: Jossey-Bass, 1982.

Sue, S., and Nakamura, C. Y. "An Integrative Model of Physiological and Social/Psychological Factors in Alcohol Consumption Among Chinese and Japanese Americans." *Journal of Drug Issues,* 1984, *14,* 349–364.

Sue, S., and Sue, D. W. "MMPI Comparisons Between Asian-American and Non-Asian Students Utilizing a Student Health Psychiatric Clinic." *Journal of Counseling Psychology,* 1974, *21*(5), 423–427.

Sue, S., Sue, D. W., Sue, L., and Takeuchi, D. "Psychopathology Among Asian Americans: A Model Minority?" *Cultural Diversity and Mental Health,* 1995, *1,* 39–51.

Sue, S., and Zane, N. "The Role of Culture and Cultural Techniques in Psychotherapy: A Critique and Reformulation." *American Psychologist,* 1987, *42*(1), 37–45.

Tinker, J. N. "Intermarriage and Assimilation in a Plural Society: Japanese-Americans in the United States." *Marriage and Family Review,* 1982, *5,* 61–74.

Tsui, P., and Schultz, G. L. "Failure of Rapport: Why Psychotherapeutic Engagement Fails in the Treatment of Asian Clients." *American Journal of Orthopsychiatry,* 1985, *55,* 561–569.

Uba, L. "Meeting the Mental Health Needs of Asian-Americans: Mainstream or Segregated Services." *Professional Psychology,* 1982, *13,* 215–221.

Uba, L. *Asian Americans: Personality Patterns, Identity, and Mental Health.* New York: Guilford Press, 1994.

U.S. Bureau of the Census. *1990 Census of the Population: Asian and Pacific Islanders.* Washington, D.C.: U.S. Bureau of the Census, 1993a.

U.S. Bureau of the Census. *1990 Census of the Population: Social and Economic Characteristics—United States.* Washington, D.C.: U.S. Bureau of the Census, 1993b.

U.S. Commission on Civil Rights. *Success of Asian Americans: Fact or Fiction?* Clearinghouse Publication no. 64. Washington, D.C.: U.S. Government Printing Office, 1980.

Uomoto, J. M., and Gorsuch, R. L. "Japanese American Response to Psychological Disorder: Referral Patterns, Attitudes, and Subjective Norms." *American Journal of Community Psychology,* 1984, *12,* 537–550.

Wong, J. "Asia Bashing: Bias Against Orientals Increases with Rivalry of Nations' Economies." *Wall Street Journal,* Nov. 28, 1986, pp. 1, 12.

Yamamoto, J., and Acosta, F. X. "Treatment of Asian Americans and Hispanic Americans: Similarities and Differences." *Journal of the American Academy of Psychoanalysis,* 1982, *10,* 585–607.

Yamamoto, J., and Kubota, M. "The Japanese-American Family." In G. J. Powell, J. Yamamoto, A. Romero, and A. Morales (eds.), *The Psychosocial Development of Minority Group Children.* New York: Brunner/Mazel, 1983.

Chapter Four

American Indian Children and Adolescents

Teresa D. LaFromboise
Kathryn Graff Low

For centuries, American Indians have been uprooted, relocated, educated, and socialized in attempts to integrate them into the dominant culture and extinguish their tribal identity and traditions. Many demographic trends, such as the increasing urbanization of American Indian families, tend to interfere with cultural practices and facilitate assimilation. The survival of American Indian tribal cultures and identity despite relocation, poverty, and disease attests to the strength and flexibility of the first Americans.

Over the last two decades, mental health services delivered to American Indians have expanded and contracted in terms of both general availability and range of care. These fluctuations have resulted from shifts in federal funding priorities and apart from careful consideration of questions concerning the essential components of psychological treatment. Often, immediate need outstrips existing knowledge and resources for gathering epidemiological data, identifying salient help-seeking pathways, detecting assessment bias, or designing and evaluating appropriate interventions. It is time to assess the strengths of American Indians, their beliefs about mental health, and the existing knowledge about American Indian youth. Toward this end, this chapter selectively reviews the literature pertinent to the assessment and treatment of American Indian children and adolescents. A series of clinical and research issues are posed as points of departure for further inquiry, the answers to which we believe will form the basis for competence in the delivery of psychological services to American Indian youth.

Demographic Data

The designator "American Indian" refers to all North American native peoples, including Indians, Alaska Natives, Aleuts, Eskimos, and Metis or mixed bloods. For brevity, the terms American Indian, Indian, and Native American are used interchangeably throughout this chapter to denote these varied peoples from diverse tribes. Bureaucratic ambiguity complicates the eligibility criteria for individuals of American Indian descent. Federal and state-managed treatment programs generally require one-quarter genealogically derived Indian blood for eligibility, rather than accepting tribally defined memberships or community consensus. However, private agencies and Indian community programs generally respect the right of tribes to define membership.

The American Indian population, once estimated at 10 million, has been reduced through what some have called cultural genocide to 1.9 million (U.S. Bureau of the Census, 1996). This population is double the population determined by the 1970 census and is currently characterized as mobile, urban, and young. About 564,000 Indian people are under the age of 15 (U.S. Bureau of the Census, 1996). The median ages are 27.3 years for American Indians and 23.1 years for Alaska Natives, both significantly lower than the national average of 34.3 years (U.S. Bureau of the Census, 1996). Each of the 556 federally recognized tribal entities (226 in Alaska and 330 in the lower forty-eight states) maintains unique customs, traditions, social organizations, and ecological relationships. There are two hundred distinct tribal languages still spoken today (Leap, 1981).

Rural poverty and federal reductions in tribal budgets have forced Indians into cities for employment, scattering families across the country and increasing the prevalence of intertribal and interethnic marriages (Sandefur and McKinnell, 1986; Snipp, 1996). In 1990, 22 percent of American Indians lived on reservations, 10 percent lived in tribal jurisdiction statistical areas (the historically Indian areas of Oklahoma), 2 percent lived in Alaska Native villages, 3 percent lived on tribal designated statistical areas, and 63 percent lived elsewhere in the United States (Snipp, 1996).

Frequent relocation, substandard living conditions, and chronic unemployment in both urban and reservation areas have taken their toll on Indian people. Malnutrition, an alcoholism mortality rate 6.3 times higher than that of other races, a rate of cirrhosis of the liver 3.5 times higher, a homicide rate 1.5 times higher, and a suicide rate 1.4 times higher, in addition to environmental contamination, continue to have significant impacts on Indian life expectancy and prevalence of illness. The Indian mortality rate is about 2.6 times higher than that of other races for motor vehicle accidents (May, 1996). The Indian infant mortality rate in the postnatal period (one month to one year) is 29 percent higher than that of the white population. Indian life expectancy is 71.5 years, 6 percent less than that of the white population (Snipp, 1996). There is some glimmer of hope that health care progress has been made. Government reports established that the infant mortality rate and the infectious disease death rate for American Indians have declined in recent years (May, 1996).

American Indians report a median family income of $21,619, compared to $24,698 for black families and $40,884 for white families (U.S. Bureau of the Census, 1996). From 1979 to 1989, Native American women had a 9 percent loss in the income ratio compared to white women. For Native American men who had not completed high school, average real income fell 22 percent, and for those who had completed high school, real income fell 12 percent. Twenty-seven percent of American Indian families live in poverty, compared to 9.1 percent of whites (Gregory, Abello, and Johnson, 1996). On reservations, average income varies from tribe to tribe. Notable are the absence of a large middle class and the substantially lower incomes on reservations. In 1989, according to a report from twenty-three reservations, 51 percent of families lived below the poverty threshold. The unemployment rate for American Indians in general is 14.4 percent, while the unemployment rate on the reservations is 45.6 percent, compared to the total U.S. rate of 6.3 percent (Trosper, 1996).

In light of this pervasive hardship, it is not surprising that Indians attain fewer years of formal education than members of other minority groups. For some, scholastic functioning is severely impaired, and lags in academic performance of one to two years in elementary school and two to four years in secondary school are not uncommon (Demmert and Bell, 1991). About 40 percent of American Indians have less than a high school education, 35 percent have completed high school, and 20.9 percent have some college education (Cunningham, 1996). Academic performance is also hampered by neurosensory disorders and developmental disabilities, and by other physically handicapping conditions (otitis media, or middle ear disease, for example, a condition that is estimated to occur in more than half of Indian children).

According to the National Center for Educational Statistics (1988), the average dropout rate of American Indian students is 35.5 percent. Dropout rates in urban high schools are particularly high, sometimes reaching 51 percent. American Indians have the highest rate of dropout among ethnic groups, and the lowest rate of return.

The dearth of college-educated American Indians (7.7 percent according to Snipp, 1989) has a substantial impact on this population. At the graduate level, the underrepresentation of American Indians is even more dramatic. For example, of 42,000 doctoral degrees awarded in 1993 nationwide, only 106 were to American Indians, and only 22 of those degrees were in psychology (U.S. Department of Education, 1995). Without psychologists, social workers, psychiatrists, and researchers who are sensitive to the complexity of American Indian cultural values, tribal customs, family ecology, and communication styles, collaboration and service delivery with American Indians will continue to be ineffective. Thus the low college enrollment of American Indians and the low priority placed on mental health professions by tribes perpetuates the underdevelopment of the current mental health service delivery system.

Epidemiological Studies

Much of the literature on American Indian and Alaska Native mental health emphasizes the cultural factors that influence treatment: beliefs about the causes of psychological disturbance and expectations about help-seeking and help-giving. Unfortunately, the empirical study of treatment decisions about goals of therapy and methods of intervention has not kept pace with the recognition of their clinical importance. Many epidemiological studies, particularly those concerning American Indian children, have methodological difficulties because of the use of culturally biased instruments. Community tolerance makes deviance difficult to decipher, and psychological disturbance is often camouflaged by alcoholism (Green, Sack, and Pambrun, 1981). In addition, conducting research with isolated Indian communities is difficult logistically and politically (LaFromboise and Plake, 1983).

For these reasons, only three community-wide psychiatric epidemiological studies have been conducted among American Indians and Alaska Natives. Each of these studies reports alarmingly high rates of psychological dysfunction and major mental disorder according to diagnostic criteria refined on the general population (Roy, Chaudhuri, and Irvine, 1970). Shore, Kinzie, Hampson, and Pattison (1973) report that 57 percent of their sample were definitely disturbed and another 15 percent were probably disturbed. Sampath (1974) found that 37 percent of Eskimo adults met *DSM-III* criteria for psychological disorders.

Little research has focused systematically on the psychological development of Indian children and adolescents, but some studies have estimated the prevalence of psychological disorders among them. Green, Sack, and Pambrun (1981) noted problems of abuse, neglect, foster care, school delinquency, and suicide. Boyce and Boyce (1983) found that for both male and female Indian youth there is a trend toward higher numbers of clinic visits among those whose families were poorly matched with the surrounding community with respect to cultural identity. The U.S. Congress Office of Technology Assessment (1990) reports that Native Americans have more serious mental problems than all other races in the U.S. population with respect to developmental disabilities, depression, suicide, anxiety, alcohol and substance abuse, self-esteem and alienation, running away, and school dropout. Blum and others (1992) found that 6 percent of a sample of Native American youth showed signs of severe emotional distress. Although juvenile psychopathology is on the rise, there is only one service provider available for every twenty thousand Indian youths. More than one-fifth of the population in Indian health service areas are children and adolescents. None of the twenty-one inpatient psychiatric beds for Indians are set aside for adolescent patients (U.S. Congress, Office of Technology Assessment, 1990).

Child abuse and neglect appear to be increasing among Indians (Hart, Echohawk, Harjo, and Humetewa, 1995; Lujan, DeBruyn, May, and Bird, 1989). In a study by Blum and others (1992), 18 percent of a sample of Indian youth had experienced some sort of abuse. Most of the children who experience neglect are also the ones who experience abuse and who have families with alcoholism and other major problems (Lujan, DeBruyn, May, and Bird, 1989).

As they enter school, American Indian youth often feel stranded between two cultures. Many of them speak an entirely different first language, practice an entirely different religion, and hold different cultural values from the dominant culture, yet they are expected to perform successfully according to conventional Anglo educational criteria. They encounter their parents' often hopeless attitudes resulting from overwhelming impoverishment and discrimination. They are also increasingly reminded of economic, experiential, and social discrepancies that exist between the Indian and Anglo cultures.

A fundamental problem for Indian youth continues to be the high incidence of alcohol and drug abuse. Alcohol abuse alone has critical consequences for young children in the form of fetal alcohol syndrome, which can lead to mental and/or psychosocial retardation (Boyce and others, 1986; May, 1982). Indian youths come into contact with both legal and illegal drugs at an early age. According to Bachman and others (1991), Native Americans continue to sustain the highest rates of alcohol and drug abuse. Substance abuse is a widely modeled means of coping with depression, anxiety, hostility, feelings of powerlessness, and stress reactions among Indians (Bobo, 1985; Oetting, Beauvais, Edwards, and Velarde, 1983). For adolescents, this coping mechanism exacerbates rather than solves the problems that contribute to educational underachievement, teen pregnancy, self-destructive behavior patterns, and high delinquency and arrest rates.

The growing literature on Indian youth suicide and accidental death attests to their special place among mental health concerns. Blum and others (1992) found that youth who were at high risk for suicide had problems with drug abuse, had or caused a pregnancy, believed that family is not caring, and had relatives or friends who had committed suicide. A study on suicide risk factors among Indian adolescents at a boarding school reported that

23 percent of high school students had attempted suicide (Manson, Beals, Dick, and Duclos, 1989). Indian youth experience traumatic loss of family and friends at a rate much higher than the general population because of accidental and premature death (Blum and others, 1992) and long separations from family for medical treatment or educational and employment opportunities (Long, 1983). Those who come from tribes classified as traditional (maintaining the old ways) are less likely to commit suicide than youth from transitional (neither highly traditional nor modern) or acculturated tribes (May, 1987).

American Indian Families: Strengths and Stresses

Complex and richly diverse, American Indian family life is difficult to describe because the roles of specific family members and the structure of extended families vary across tribes and among families within tribes. Nonetheless, obvious contrasts emerge when American Indian families are compared with Anglo families.

Traditionally, Indian people live in relational networks that serve to support and nurture strong bonds of mutual assistance and affection. Many tribes still engage in a traditional system of collective interdependence, with family members responsible not only to one another but also to the clan and tribe to which they belong. The Lakota Sioux use the term *tiospaye* to describe a traditional community way of life facilitated by well-functioning extended families, in which an individual's well-being remains the responsibility of the extended family (Red Horse, Lewis, Felt, and Decker, 1978). When problems arise among Indian youth, they become problems of the community as well. The family, kin, and friends join together to observe the youth's behavior, draw him or her out of isolation, and integrate that person back into the activities of the group.

Relationships between family members and the community can be quite complex. The amount of social and governing control exhibited by women or men depends on the tribe. In the traditional matriarchal Navajo family, for example, an older woman might reside with her husband, her unmarried children, her married daughter, and the daughter's husband and children (Ryan, 1980).

Generally, in patriarchal tribes a major role of the male as head of the family is to make important decisions. Women in these tribes influence family functioning as the core of the family, maintaining primary responsibility for the welfare of the children. Uncles and aunts are important teachers: they share wisdom, impart values, often serve as role models, and reinforce tribal traditions. Grandmothers and aunts often supply child care. In some tribes, child care is shared by the men. Mescalero Apache men, for example, take responsibility for children when not working away from the family (Ryan, 1980). Grandparents and other elders are particularly important in that they are the safekeepers of tribal stories and songs and often spend time with children sharing their oral tradition.

Traditionally speaking, tribal spirituality is the same as tribal life; the two are not deliberately separated (Hungry Wolf and Hungry Wolf, 1987). Early introduction of children to the spiritual life of the tribe fosters a loving respect for nature as well as independence and self-discipline.

Indian childrearing practices are largely shaped by Indian worldviews, which regard children as beloved gifts (Hill Witt, 1979). Time spent caring for, admiring, and playing with Indian children is cherished (Morey and Gilliam, 1974). Early childhood is often marked by a variety of celebrations that honor an infant's developmental milestones, such as the first smile, first laugh, first steps, or first attempts at using language. Although American Indian families celebrate these developments, they feel little pressure over the timing of such events. Their beliefs involve acceptance of a child's own readiness, and restraint from pressuring a child to perform (Everett, Proctor, and Cartmell, 1983; Dell, 1980). Historically, children were seldom physically punished in Indian households. After misbehaving, a child might quickly experience disapproving words, "tsk-tsk" sounds from the adults, or being ignored.

Communication patterns in Indian families differ from tribe to tribe. In general, these patterns might be characterized as hierarchal and diffuse. For example, information about a youth's misbehavior might be passed from the mother to her parents and sisters or from the mother or father to an aunt or uncle who has been designated as responsible for guiding the youth's character development. Restitution for the wrongdoing on the part of the youth may involve an apology to each of the family members who worry about the youth or are embarrassed by the youth's misbehavior. This indirect line of communication serves to protect the bonds between parents and youth and reinforces extended family involvement in maintaining standards of behavior. Similarly, when a youth is worthy of praise for a significant accomplishment, one of the family members might share this information with others in the community through a person known as the camp crier. One role of the camp crier is to convey good news about members of the community while maintaining each family's humility.

Because autonomy is highly valued among American Indians, children are expected to make their own decisions and operate semi-independently at an early age. In this childrearing style, family members allow children choices and the freedom to experience the natural consequences of those choices. The impact of a child's behavior on others is also emphasized. This seemingly diffuse approach to childrearing has often been labeled as permissive or negligent by social service providers because it appears to them that Indian parents exercise minimal observable control over their children (Gray and Cosgrove, 1985).

An adequate historical coverage of the voluntary migration patterns of American Indian families, their forced dispossession of traditional homelands, and governmental sponsorship of relocation efforts to urbanize and acculturate Indians is beyond the scope of this chapter. Excellent treatment of this subject is contained in Fixico (1986), Jacobs (1985), Kerri (1976), and Sandefur (1986).

In recent years, increased movement to urban areas has complicated Indian extended family functioning. Many Indians who have relocated to cities from reservations and other traditional Indian areas have felt isolated from their families and other Indian social support networks. To combat this sense of alienation, Indian people in urban environments often seek support from other Indians, neighbors, and nonfamily members, and over time reconstitute their extended family network. Unfortunately, some contemporary Indian families are less able to establish social support networks and, without the benefit of extended family life, may experience greater stress in daily living than their more traditional relatives. Boyce and Boyce (1983) argue that cultural "fit" between the family and the surrounding community may be a more critical determinant of health and illness than isolated measures of individuals' levels of acculturation.

Indian youth from extended family networks in either reservations or urban areas face special problems. Family responsibilities and expectations become problematic at times for all youth. Because tribal spirituality remains paramount among Indian people, families encourage and expect their children and adolescents to participate in various ceremonies. Unfortunately, their participation in these ceremonies sometimes violates the attendance policies of Anglo-operated schools and work sites. Students living away from home in boarding schools or universities often want to return home from great distances in order to participate in important family activities and ceremonies. Negative consequences often ensue for young people who opt to attend tribal ceremonies during school or work hours.

The high premium placed on individual achievement and success in academic institutions often causes conflict for Indian students and their families. For instance, Indian university students receiving scholarships may feel they should share their financial awards with family members even though financial aid packages are designed to fund subsistence support for students. Furthermore, American Indian students quickly discover that the academic success for which they receive praise on campus may yield further estrangement from their own people. Sometimes the community will actively discourage ambitions that involve leaving the reservation or the family (Lefley, 1975). Failing to meet community expectations can create dissent and generate guilt over social responsibility and noncompliance.

Sociocultural Issues in Assessment

The psychological assessment of American Indian children and adolescents presents a perplexing array of considerations. This section highlights some assessment issues that must be considered in working with Indian youth: the testing situation, the use of standardized assessment instruments, and diagnostic procedures for the three psychological interventions presented in the intervention and treatment section that follows this section.

In the testing situation, a person seeking information in intake interviews and standardized assessment situations must consider the testing environment; the biases, questioning style, and physical features of the test administrator; the biases inherent in the diagnostic instrument; and sociocultural factors that may affect the youth's perceptions of the assessment event and his or her consequent performance.

It is crucial that interpretations of assessment results take into account environmental factors that may facilitate or hinder the youth's response tendencies. These include the social organization that the test administrator represents, the physical features and location of the classroom or testing room, and the presence or absence of contextually relevant materials (for example, pictorial stimuli of children with pale faces). The clinician must also be aware of his or her personal biases in noting, scoring, and interpreting responses to test items.

Hynd and Garcia (1979) summarize behaviors of American Indian children during diagnostic interviews that may negatively affect assessment outcome: nonassertive, nonspontaneous, and soft-spoken verbal interaction; limited eye contact; discomfort and decreased performance on timed tasks; reluctance to offer self-disclosures; and selective performance of only those skills that contribute to the betterment of the group. In addition, because many tribal cultures emphasize perfection, American Indian children may be apprehensive about creating a block design or enacting some other task without long periods of observation or previously established competence in performing the task.

Use of standardized tests with minority children is, of course, controversial. Most assessment instruments have built-in biases; in fact, some researchers argue that there is no such thing as a culturally unbiased instrument. Tests are designed and validated according to middle-class values and lifestyles, and thus discriminate against other socioeconomic and nondominant cultural groups (Hynd and Garcia, 1979). Primarily, the biases involve the assumptions that children are fluent in English and that they have had a high degree of exposure to Anglo culture.

Test instructions assume a minimum vocabulary. They often use temporal concepts and terms that may be alien to Indian worldviews. In addition, many tribal languages are vastly different from English in vocabulary and structure. Even when there is semantic equivalence, "language evokes a specific culture frame, with selective demand characteristics for the assessment of one's own behavior or the protection of personality variables" (Lefley, 1975, p. 36).

Special considerations apply as well at the stage of making a psychological diagnosis. In his review of methodological limitations of Indian children's mental health assessment, Beiser (1981) recommends a multiaxial model for conducting evaluations that takes into account not only mental status and academic potential but additional information about the youth's strengths, about the age-appropriateness of the youth's behavior, about the youth's social environment, and about the youth's culture.

For example, a service provider considering social cognitive interventions might first conduct a functional analysis of the cognitive, behavioral, and social elements of disturbance associated with the target problem so as not to overlook essential cultural information. Consideration is given to both external (social and environmental) and internal (cognitive and emotional) antecedents and consequences (Bandura, 1986). Particular attention is paid to the youth's personal and cultural schemata, or beliefs about self and relationships with others, that may contribute to the onset and maintenance of the problem behavior. This analysis relies on the ability of the service provider to establish trust and credibility early in treatment. Another professional or an extended family member may be able to assist in interpreting cultural cognitions and designing culturally appropriate reinforcement regimens.

A service provider considering family systems therapies would search for information about how the presenting problem affects the identified client and other extended family members as individuals and as a social unit. Information about how families might be mobilized to support the client in dealing with problems can be gathered during network analysis (Attneave, 1969; Red Horse, 1982). Network analysis includes an assessment of the cultural fit between the family and the surrounding community regardless of the family's absolute degree of acculturation.

A service provider considering Indian traditional methods can be aided by recent advances in research on indigenous concepts of mental well-being, and by the development of measurement scales specific to American Indian cultures. Mohatt and Blue (1982) used these methods to develop a scale to rate *tiospaye,* or degree of traditionality, among members of the Lakota Sioux.

Manson, Shore, and Bloom (1985) have pioneered the use of culturally adjusted psychiatric diagnostic measures among diverse American Indian groups and, in the process, have delineated patterns of depressive symptoms and clinical presentation among the Hopi. Preliminary analysis of pretest data from a national study of Indian freshmen's adjustment to academic life, conducted by the Center for American Indian and Alaska Native Mental Health Research (J. Jordan, personal communication, Sept. 17, 1987), has uncovered tribally distinct factor structures on the Center for Epidemiologic Studies Depression Scale (Radloff, 1977), a commonly used self-report scale to measure depression. These recent advances in assessment provide useful alternatives to conventional diagnostic procedures and allow the clinician to make data-based decisions in the selection of traditional treatment.

Intervention and Treatment

American Indian youth may consider mental illness a justifiable outcome of human weakness or of a tendency to avoid the discipline necessary to maintain traditional cultural values. Indian people value social responsibility, honesty, independence, reciprocity, kindness, and self-control over the cultivation of social skills (Plas and Bellet, 1983; Trimble, 1989). Several qualities important to Anglo culture, such as individualism and competitiveness, may be actively discouraged by tribes. The Coyote stories, for example, carried from one generation to the next, warn of the danger associated with excessively individualistic and manipulative behavior.

Tribal diversity makes it difficult to generalize about therapeutic issues. It is clear that Indian youth may have different values and priorities than other youth. Does it follow that American Indian youth considering counseling or being referred for treatment have different needs and expectations than clients from the dominant culture? Recent research lends empirical support to the importance of considering culture in the application of counseling interventions as well in the use of assessment procedures with school-age Indian youth.

A study of perceived problems and sources of help among American Indian high school students by Dauphinais, LaFromboise, and Rowe (1980) found that, compared with Anglo youth,

Indian youth preferred to talk with friends and parents when they had problems rather than with school counselors or other support personnel. Their problems included concerns about the future, depression, apathy, decisions that needed to be made, ways of maintaining good grades, class scheduling problems, and whether to stay in school. Indian youth generally sought formal help only when they had been referred to psychological services by school officials or tribal judges.

Studies of Indian students' assessments of positive counselor attributes have rendered conflicting findings on the importance attached to counselor race. Three studies found a strong preference for an Indian person (Dauphinais, Dauphinais, and Rowe, 1981; Haviland, Horswill, O'Connell, and Dynneson, 1983; Littrell and Littrell, 1982); yet other investigations (LaFromboise and Dixon, 1981; LaFromboise, Dauphinais, and Rowe, 1980) did not confirm these results. These conflicting findings may be attributed to methodological differences among the studies. Preferences for same-sex counselors among Indian high school students have been supported (Haviland, Horswill, O'Connell, and Dynneson, 1983; Littrell and Littrell, 1982).

Trustworthiness is obviously important in every counseling relationship, regardless of the client's race or cultural background. This counselor attribute was shown to be even more crucial for Indian clients, who have learned from their past that authorities purporting to give help may have ulterior motives.

In general, Indian youth are looking for someone who understands the practical aspects of their culture and can give them sound advice about their lives, not someone who reflects and restates their feelings for the purpose of analysis (Dauphinais, Dauphinais, and Rowe, 1981). In fact, a study by LaFromboise, Davis, and Rowe (1985) indicates that in many cases conventional psychological training is not necessary to enable one to be a good counselor with Indian adolescents.

Compared with the research on preferred attributes of helpers, little empirical evidence exists on the comparative efficacy of psychological interventions with American Indian youth. The three therapeutic approaches discussed shortly—social cognitive interventions, systems therapy, traditional Indian interventions—are by no means the only interventions available to service providers working with American Indians. Although there are major differences among these psychological treatment approaches, they have one important commonality: they incorporate the Indian youth's environment or social context into treatment and therefore better accommodate Indian cultural practices (Attneave, 1982).

Social Cognitive Interventions

Social cognitive interventions have been considered less culturally biased than other theoretical approaches because they recognize the impact of culture on personal and environmental variables and allow each culture to define its own appropriate behaviors or targets for intervention (LaFromboise and Rowe, 1983). This is particularly important in light of tribal differences. Because social cognitive interventions include the examination of belief systems associated with target behaviors, they have heuristic appeal for accommodating cultural values and expectations (LaFromboise and BigFoot, 1988). A counselor working with an American Indian population is well advised to research the specific cultural practices and traditions of the tribes represented in his or her clientele. Generalizing about Indian cultural practices or making assumptions about tribe-specific conventions such as family structure may be insulting to an Indian client and damaging to the therapeutic process (Attneave, 1982).

External stimuli and reinforcers in an American Indian social environment may differ dramatically from stimuli and reinforcement in the dominant culture. Consequently, a therapist working with American Indian clients must be sensitive to the important philosophical differences between traditional cultures and the dominant culture. Dell (1980) describes an intervention for families and children based on Hopi worldviews that illustrates the importance of understanding Indian culture before designing an intervention or attempting to analyze stimuli and reinforcers.

Essentially, the Hopi feel that repetitive "bad" behaviors have a cumulative effect and that accrual of these behaviors leads to eventual change. A Hopi parent might therefore welcome the repetition of negative behavior as a sign of imminent change. A therapist unaware of Hopi philosophy might point out that the parents appear to be reinforcing poor behavior with their continual optimism and refusal to intervene. An intervention designed to eliminate these reinforcing behaviors would strike at the underpinnings of Hopi philosophy. Tailoring an intervention to the particular tribe while reinforcing the importance of Hopi optimism regarding outcome reduces the client's justified concern that psychological interventions might dilute culture-specific behaviors and norms, and it allows the therapist to enlist tribal belief and tradition as resources.

In addition to individual therapy, social cognitive group interventions have been used successfully in the areas of parenting (BigFoot, 1987), assertiveness and other professional skills (LaFromboise, 1988; LaFromboise and Rowe, 1983), and substance abuse (Schinke and others, 1985). Group skills training may be particularly effective because it reduces the emphasis on individual disclosure, which is difficult for some Indians, and introduces collective responsibility. Because a collective approach is characteristic of some Indian tribes and families, a group format may draw on an already familiar and powerful cultural ethic.

In contrast to the disease model of psychopathology, the theory behind cognitive therapies holds that most psychological problems are learned within the social milieu and maintained through cognitive reinforcement (Meichenbaum, 1977). When analyzing "faulty" or irrational cognitions, a therapist working with American Indian clients must be highly sensitive to the fact that self-deprecating beliefs may reflect an internalization of the dominant culture's attitude toward ethnic minorities. Likewise, beliefs that are irrational by the standards of the dominant culture may be perfectly reasonable in light of American Indian history. Faith in a medicine man, tribal prophecies, or tribal traditions may seem irrational in the dominant culture but may have substantial healing power in therapy with Indians. An American Indian youth who has broken a cultural taboo may experience anxiety that a therapist in the dominant culture would label "catastrophic." Yet given the power of some Indian beliefs, the youth's fear of retribution or spiritual consequences may be well founded. A therapist must assess the rationality of beliefs within the context of the culture. Once a therapist has identified dysfunctional thoughts within the cultural context, treatment focuses on the current determinants of behavior (as distinct from past or unconscious factors) and involves the analysis of components of the behavior or beliefs and the modification of these components in accordance with specific subgoals.

It is important that the therapist balance the need for successfully establishing trust with the need for effecting change. Some Indian clients may expect immediate results and will be frustrated by a slow rate of change. In addition, they may be quite reticent, expecting the therapist to supply the therapeutic answers. Asking Indian clients to keep behavior logs or to solicit help from the extended family may actively engage them in therapy earlier and allow some immediate insight or feedback on the nature of the problem.

The following case illustrates the use of a social cognitive intervention.

> Mark, a sixteen-year-old Indian male of average intelligence, has been "acting out" for more than a year. Often truant, Mark has fallen behind in his academic work. He uses drugs and alcohol, has had several violent encounters with fellow students, and has been in minor trouble with local authorities. Mark has lived with his maternal aunt and uncle on the reservation for the last ten years. His mother is a chronic alcoholic and Mark rarely sees her. The identity of Mark's father is unknown. Recently, Mark's uncle lost his job and began to disappear for days on end. Mark has been referred by a school counselor, who has become increasingly concerned about his apparent depression.

Clearly, an initial goal in therapy with Mark would be to establish the therapist's credibility and trustworthiness. A variety of techniques are available, but strategies for engaging Mark in therapy may depend on tribal and family tradition. Conferences with the family and enlistment of the support of extended family members are crucial. In particular, relatives may help ensure that Mark attends therapy sessions. In addition, tribal elders or other adults with whom Mark interacts might be consulted. The power of the extended family or tribe should not be underestimated.

Early in therapy, American Indian clients may feel more comfortable if the therapist practices some self-disclosure and indicates a desire for reciprocity (LaFromboise, 1985). Mark should not be pushed to make disclosures or assume a familiarity that he does not feel. Considerable time could be spent developing a definition of the problem from Mark's personal and cultural point of view. Asking Mark to help define the problem and provide input for establishing treatment goals may increase comfort and trust during the early stages of therapy.

The therapeutic problem, when defined through cognitive and behavioral assessment techniques, would involve exploring Mark's thoughts about himself and the cues and reinforcements for his negative behavior. His substance abuse may be a way of coping with peer and family pressure, or it may be the only way he has learned to make himself "feel good." In addition, Mark may be struggling with identity issues involving both his paternity and his need to function adequately in Anglo and Indian cultures. His inability to function in either environment may be painful enough to prompt his angry behavior.

The counselor's goal in therapy would be to influence Mark to change his irrational thoughts, internal dialogue, and negative self-assessments by means of self-monitoring, discrimination training, behavior change, and social validation. Typical intervention strategies might include identifying the origin of his negative beliefs about himself (particularly if they are internalized from the dominant culture); exploring the effects of negative stereotypes about Indian drinking patterns; recording his irrational thoughts to help him discover self-statements that contradict these negative cognitions; verbal persuasion; modeling positive thoughts and appropriate drinking behavior from tribal leaders; and specific techniques such as problem solving and increasing pleasant activities.

Because school is a problematic environment, a specific sub-goal of therapy might involve rehearsal of school situations, starting with those in which Mark is quite comfortable (for example, talking with a friend), in order to develop his coping skills. With rehearsal of ever more stressful scenarios, Mark's confidence will increase, ultimately improving his performance. Through consultation with Mark's teachers, methods of classroom participation might be modified to include cooperative learning activities that structure small-group activities and presentations rather than individual presentations to the entire class (Cohen, 1983).

In general, cognitive behavior therapy should not replace traditional Indian behaviors or therapeutic processes but should expand the adolescent's repertoire of coping options. For Mark, participation in social gatherings such as basketball tournaments, rodeos, powwows, feasts, and giveaways would be an important first step in helping him reaffirm his Indian identity. Gradually, we would hope to see an increase in Mark's self-esteem, the confirmation of personal identity and the emergence of a stronger Indian identity, improved academic performance, and comfortable and effective interactions in diverse and multicultural contexts.

Systems Therapy

Therapies based on systems theory effectively integrate the ongoing strengths inherent in Indian extended family networking. Systems theory includes a variety of specific therapeutic interventions, including transactional analysis, family therapy, and group therapy. These interventions share the assumption that the individual and the environment have continuous reciprocal interactions, that a client is one portion of a dynamic and interrelated whole. Systems theory argues that the most helpful therapeutic interventions are those that enhance an individual's interaction with others or with the environment and therefore ensure lasting change outside the context of the therapeutic relationship (Ivey, Ivey, and Simek-Downing, 1987). This approach takes advantage of the potentially supportive extended family in American Indian life while seeing that family members become aware of their own maladaptive patterns that may contribute to an individual's dysfunction.

The extended family, rather than conventional service delivery agencies, has remained the forum for problem solving and support in Indian communities, and most traditional interventions involve the extended family to ensure success. A therapist who persists in focusing primarily on an Indian youth's relationships within the nuclear family may be missing important contributions from more distant family members.

Shangreaux, Pleskac, and Freeman (1987) have developed an excellent systems intervention program for Indian families. Aspects of systems interventions that are particularly important for Indian families are summarized in the following paragraphs.

Defining the family may be a difficult task for some Indian families, and the therapist must make sure that salient family members are included in the client's therapy. Asking Indian youth to draw a genogram, draw a portrait of the family, or tell a story about their family may elicit important information about family function. Generally, family members who have a reasonable amount of contact with the youth (for example, living in the same household) should be included in systems analysis. Engaging the family in therapy may be difficult and may require the support of the tribe or Indian community, persistent requests by the therapist or referring agency, or frequent visits to the home to establish trust and rapport before beginning treatment.

Shangreaux, Pleskac, and Freeman (1987) suggest specific techniques for engaging a family in therapy. These include exercising patience, using self-disclosure to establish trust, allowing time for relationship building using humor and small talk, and establishing credibility through genuine concern and caring. Active listening techniques that focus on the client and family, work with the extended family, and asking community members to lend support by accompanying the family on initial visits are also recommended.

Once key family members are attending therapy, they should be asked to define the family and its structure, addressing such issues as hierarchy, triangulation, and alliances. The therapist must keep in mind that extended family interchanges and interdependence are encouraged in many Indian families, in contrast to the independence valued by Anglo families. The therapist who labels Indian families "enmeshed" often mistakes interdependence for inadequate boundaries. Further, therapists should be sensitive to problems in defining family and alliances. In particular, intergenerational conflicts around traditional practices, inappropriate family expectations (for example, that students should miss school to attend tribal events), and dependence issues may be problematic. Shangreaux, Pleskac, and Freeman (1987) suggest family sculpting as a useful tool for clarifying and demonstrating a variety of possible relationships in Indian families. Drawing, storytelling, or using family models may elicit information about structure and alliances without being threatening.

Family roles, often crucial in systems therapy, may be quite different in Indian families. The role of aunts and uncles in the guidance of Indian youth has already been noted. The youth may feel as if he or she has several "parents" in the form of grandparents, aunts, uncles, and cousins, and he or she may use all of these as role models. The systems therapist working with an Indian family must explore the degree to which the family utilizes extended family roles, and the nature of these roles.

Family values may also reflect the values of American Indian culture. Reverence for elders, emphasis on interdependence and community, and the ethic of sharing are all values typical of traditional Indian culture. The therapist who insists on promoting Anglo values in therapy is likely to meet substantial resistance and may not be acting in the best interest of the client. Instead, an intervention that focuses on increasing the cooperation, connectedness, and patience of the child may be a more culturally consonant approach.

Techniques that may be particularly effective with American Indian families in early sessions include employing ecomaps and genograms, assessing level of acculturation, having various family members monitor family function, and asking the family to share a story that represents the family history (Shangreaux, Pleskac, and Freeman, 1987).

In the case of Mark, a therapist conducting a systems intervention might want to assemble Mark's extended family in hopes of defining and solving his specific problems and eliciting the cooperation and support of family members. In addition, the therapist might explore ways in which the family contributes to or reinforces Mark's current maladaptive behavior. Particularly helpful may be the Indian belief that the behavior of any single family member reflects on the entire family or clan and is therefore the concern and responsibility of all family members. In addition, other significant community members may be helpful resources for Mark, assisting in monitoring, supporting, and rewarding positive behavior.

Group therapy involving a peer group or, in Mark's case, a group of alcohol abusers might also be effective (Kahn, Lewis, and Galvez, 1974). Social skills training interventions for alcohol abuse have been relatively successful with American Indian youth because such interventions deemphasize the individual and instead focus on the harm that substance abuse has brought to Indian people (Bobo, 1985).

Traditional Indian Interventions

Several traditional interventions may be used effectively in the treatment of Indian youth, particularly those who have been raised in more traditional Indian ways. Any of these could be incorporated into Mark's treatment. A counselor's decision to collaborate with a traditional healer usually begins with an assessment of the client's desire for ceremonial healing. These ceremonies are conducted either before or in conjunction with therapy.

Sweat lodge ceremonies are frequently conducted among American Indian groups for purification and prevention purposes. Participation in the sweat lodge consists of preparatory fasting, prayer, and offerings throughout serial purification sessions referred to as "rounds." The ceremony lasts several hours while participants make offerings for health and balance in life (Manson, Walker, and Kivlahan, 1987).

Manson, Walker, and Kivlahan suggest two other American Indian treatment strategies based on traditional healing practices: the "four circles" and the "talking circle." The four-circles intervention involves the symbolic organization of the important relationships in one's life. The centermost of four concentric circles represents the Creator, the second circle symbolizes the relationship with a partner or spouse, the third represents the extended or immediate family, and the fourth signifies tribal members. Four circles is a symbolic search for balance in relationships and is a useful tool for clarifying and assigning priorities to allegiances and social responsibility.

The talking-circle intervention resembles conventional group therapy. The participants form a circle and remain in the circle until the ceremony is complete. Sweet grass is burned to produce purifying smoke and provide direction for the group conversation. The leader begins by sharing feelings or thoughts about the group. Each participant is free to speak and no one is allowed to interrupt. Often a sacred object is circulated, and the ceremony ends with a joining of hands in prayer.

These traditional practices might be particularly effective in a case like Mark's, in which an adolescent is struggling to assert his tribal identity and feelings of self-worth. A traditional intervention like the talking circle would reaffirm Mark's Indian identity and acceptance by the group. It could also offer him the opportunity to share his frustrations and concerns with supportive community members. In turn, older participants in the talking circle could model behaviors or make suggestions that might help Mark cope with diverse cultural demands and enhance his self-esteem. Finally, the fact that a number of community members would engage in this level of support could enhance his estimate of self-worth. A combination of traditional healing and contemporary psychotherapy can solidify social support, facilitate communication with and cooperation from the community, and offer opportunity for purification.

All of the techniques described here can be adapted in a multimodal intervention and used effectively with American Indian youth. The case of Carol illustrates this blended approach.

> A group of adolescents, mostly males, had gathered in a remote area of the reservation for a drinking party. After the late-night affair, Carol, a thirteen-year-old member of the group, was raped by a distant cousin. She reported the incident to her parents. They felt, however, that she had "brought the problem on herself" and refused to take any action. Carol was referred to therapy by school authorities because of noticeable weight loss and symptoms of depression.

An approach that combines a variety of intervention techniques might help Carol. Therapy could explore her negative thoughts, particularly those relating to having been "violated" and to feeling dirty. The tribe's attitude toward early sexual activity and possible strong taboos against incest and forced copulation might be revealed as the cause of Carol's depression. The therapist might also incorporate behavioral techniques to relieve depression and improve Carol's eating habits. Such techniques might include increasing Carol's physical activity, monitoring her diet, and constructing a system of rewards for weight gain and positive interaction with others.

Meanwhile, traditional interventions such as a sweat lodge ceremony or a talking-circle ceremony might be particularly effective in Carol's case. The sweat lodge ritual could help relieve Carol's feelings of "dirtiness" or guilt through purification. The talking-circle ceremony could provide the opportunity for Carol to obtain support and reinforcement and give her a safe forum in which to express anger and pain. Systems therapy could focus on family interaction and provide an understanding of the parents' reaction to Carol's rape.

Defining the family is an important task. Carol's mother and father may not have been her primary caretakers. Other adults may have been equally supportive or influential in Carol's life. For what-

ever reason, Carol's family may be resistant to traditional interventions or to conventional therapeutic techniques. Nonetheless,
assembling even part of the family is beneficial. Parent/child interaction, family roles, the impact of the rape, and individual family members' attitudes should all be explored.

Summary and Conclusions

Although advances have been made toward understanding and
addressing the problems facing Indian youth today, extensive work
still needs to be done to offset the impact of pervasive poverty, underachievement, and poorly coordinated educational and social
services.

Despite past governmental policies of relocation, Indian cultural beliefs and practices prevail. American Indians not only assert that children are their most vital natural resource, they daily
acknowledge the importance of children through childrearing
practices. Indians realize that the pressures for acculturation will
not soon diminish and that they must continue to work diligently
for personal strength through traditionality. Even though Indians
are moving to urban areas in increasing numbers, they maintain
clan and extended family structures through frequent home visits
and reconstitution of networks with other Indians. Unfortunately,
this family structure and method of functioning can be misunderstood by professional helpers who fail to see the value of extensive
support systems in protecting against stress.

Some progress has been made in the refinement of psychological interventions for American Indians. The cultural adaptation of
psychological interventions must be accompanied by empirical validation of modified treatment procedures. Further progress toward
identifying effective areas of influence with Indian youth depends
on definitions of psychological dysfunction that take into account
local beliefs about mental health and mental illness.

Several directions for future epidemiological research have already been set forth (Manson, 1982; Manson and Trimble, 1982).
Research considerations of particular relevance to American Indian
youth include the need to better understand critical antecedents of
academic apathy, the need to distinguish among stages of intercultural and intracultural Indian identity development, the need to

determine tribe-specific traditional beliefs associated with self-esteem enhancement as well as self-destruction, and the need to delineate more tribe-specific behavioral manifestations of depression, anxiety, and anger.

It is time to reverse the emphasis on pathology in research and treatment with American Indians. Social cognitive interventions, systems approaches, and American Indian traditional healing methods are recommended because of their ability to focus on Indian cultural attributes and strengths. We propose that Indian traditional beliefs and healing practices be incorporated into conventional treatment designs whenever they are desired by the client and deemed appropriate by the community. Social cognitive interventions in particular lend themselves to application in educational settings with American Indian youth.

Research has shown that clinical treatment need not involve professionally trained caregivers to be effective with Indian youth (LaFromboise, Davis, and Rowe, 1985). In fact, it has been suggested that the natural skills of Indian helpers may be obviated by conventional clinical training experiences that impart Rogerian interviewing skills (Dauphinais, Dauphinais, and Rowe, 1981). Ways of legitimizing the work of Indian community advisers and strategies for incorporating their helping style into individual and family therapy should be explored. Increased collaboration between service providers and traditional healers is both exciting and challenging. American Indians should be encouraged to help fill the desperate need for community leaders in the mental health arena.

Mental health professionals can help Indian youth acquire the life skills and perspectives necessary for optimal development. For professionals to be successful at this, the Indian community must become the locus of intervention, and the relationships among Indian youth, their families, their schools, their communities, and the larger society must be clearly defined.

References

Attneave, C. L. "Therapy in Tribal Settings and Urban Network Intervention." *Family Process,* 1969, *8,* 192–210.

Attneave, C. L. "American Indians and Alaska Native Families: Emigrants in Their Own Homeland." In M. McGoldrick, J. K. Pearce, and J. Giordano (eds.), *Ethnicity and Family Therapy.* New York: Guilford Press, 1982.

Bachman, J. G., and others. "Racial/Ethnic Differences in Smoking, Drinking, and Illicit Drug Use Among American High School Seniors, 1976–1989." *American Journal of Public Health*, 1991, *81*, 372–377.

Bandura, A. *Social Foundations of Thought and Action: A Social Cognitive Theory*. Englewood Cliffs, N.J.: Prentice Hall, 1986.

Beiser, M. "Mental Health of American Indian and Alaska Native Children: Some Epidemiological Perspectives." *White Cloud Journal*, 1981, *2*, 37–47.

Berlin, I. N. "Anglo Adoptions of Native Americans: Repercussions in Adolescence." *Journal of the American Academy of Child and Adolescent Psychiatry*, 1978, *17*, 387–388.

Berlin, I. N. "Prevention of Emotional Problems Among Native American Children: Overview of Developmental Issues." *Journal of Preventive Psychiatry*, 1982, *1*, 319–330.

BigFoot, D. "Parent Training for American Indian Families." Unpublished doctoral prospectus, University of Oklahoma, Norman, 1987.

Blum, R., and others (1992). "American Indian–Alaska Native Youth Health." *Journal of the American Medical Association*, 1992, *267*, 1637–1644.

Bobo, J. K. "Preventing Drug Abuse Among American Indian Adolescents." In L. D. Gilchrist and S. P. Schinke (eds.), *Preventing Social and Health Problems Through Life Skills Training*. Seattle: School of Social Work, University of Washington, 1985.

Boyce, W. T., and Boyce, J. C. "Acculturation and Changes in Health Among Navajo School Students." *Social Sciences and Medicine*, 1983, *17*, 219–226.

Boyce, W. T., and others. "Social and Cultural Factors in Pregnancy Complications Among Navajo Women." *American Journal of Epidemiology*, 1986, *124*, 242–253.

Cohen, E. G. "Talking and Working Together: Status, Interaction and Learning." In P. Peterson, L. C. Wilkinson, and M. Hallinon (eds.), *The Social Context of Instruction: Group Organization and Group Processes*. Orlando, Fla.: Academic Press, 1983.

Cunningham, P. J. "Health Care Utilization, Expenditures, and Insurance Coverage for American Indians and Alaska Natives Eligible for the Indian Health Service." In G. D. Sandefur, R. R. Rindfuss, and B. Cohen (eds.), *Changing Numbers, Changing Needs: American Indian Demography and Public Health*. Washington, D.C.: National Academy Press, 1996.

Dauphinais, P., Dauphinais, L., and Rowe, W. "Effects of Race and Communication Style on Indian Perceptions of Counselor Effectiveness." *Counselor Education and Supervision*, 1981, *21*, 72–80.

Dauphinais, P., LaFromboise, T. D., and Rowe, W. "Perceived Problems and Sources of Help for American Indian Students." *Counselor Education and Supervision,* 1980, *20,* 37–44.

Dell, P. F. "The Hopi Family Therapist and the Aristotelian Parents. " *Journal of Marital and Family Therapy,* 1980, *6,* 123–130.

Demmert, W. G., and Bell, T. H. *Indian Nations at Risk: An Educational Strategy for Action.* Washington, D.C.: U.S. Department of Education, 1991.

Everett, F., Proctor, N., and Cartmell, B. "Providing Psychological Services to American Indian Children and Families." *Professional Psychology: Research and Practice,* 1983, *14,* 588–603.

Fixico, D. *Termination and Relocations: Federal Indian Policy, 1945–1960.* Albuquerque: University of New Mexico Press, 1986.

Gray, E., and Cosgrove, J. "Ethnocentric Perception of Childrearing Practices in Protective Services." *Child Abuse and Neglect,* 1985, *9,* 389–396.

Green, B. E., Sack, W. H., and Pambrun, A. "A Review of Child Psychiatric Epidemiology with Special Reference to American Indian and Alaska Native Children." *White Cloud Journal,* 1981, *2,* 22–36.

Gregory, R. G., Abello, A. C., and Johnson, J. "The Individual Economic Well-Being of Native American Men and Women During the 1980s: A Decade of Moving Backwards." In G. D. Sandefur, R. R. Rindfuss, and B. Cohen (eds.), *Changing Numbers, Changing Needs: American Indian Demography and Public Health.* Washington, D.C.: National Academy Press, 1996.

Hart, B., Echohawk, L., Harjo, R., and Humetewa, D. J. "Sorting Out Jurisdictional Issues of Indian Child Sexual Abuse Prosecution." Paper presented at Protecting Our Children, the thirteenth annual meeting of the National American Indian Conference on Child Abuse and Neglect, Minneapolis, Minn., Apr. 1995.

Haviland, M. G., Horswill, R. K., O'Connell, J. J., and Dynneson, V. V. "Native American College Students' Preference for Counselor Race and Sex and the Likelihood of Their Use of a Counseling Center." *Journal of Counseling Psychology,* 1983, *30,* 267–270.

Hill Witt, S. "Pressure Points in Growing Up Indian." Paper presented at eighty-seventh annual meeting of the American Psychological Association, New York City, Aug. 1979.

Hungry Wolf, A., and Hungry Wolf, B. *Children of the Sun.* New York: Morrow, 1987.

Hynd, G. W., and Garcia, W. I. "Intellectual Assessment of the Native American Student." *School Psychology Digest,* 1979, *8,* 446–454.

Ivey, A. E., Ivey, M. B., and Simek-Downing, L. *Counseling and Psychotherapy: Integrating Skills, Theory and Practice.* (2nd ed.) Englewood Cliffs, N.J.: Prentice Hall, 1987.

Jacobs, W. R. *Dispossessing the American Indian.* (2nd ed.) Norman: University of Oklahoma Press, 1985.

Kahn, M. W., Lewis, J., and Galvez, E. "An Evaluation Study of Group Therapy Procedure with Reservation Adolescent Indians." *Psychotherapy: Theory, Research and Practice,* 1974, *11,* 239–242.

Kerri, J. N. "Push and Pull Factor: Reason for Migration as a Factor in American-Indian Urban Adjustment." *Human Organization,* 1976, *35,* 215–220.

LaFromboise, T. D. "Effects of Race and Communication Style on American Indian Perceptions of Counselor Impact." Invited symposium presented at meeting of the American Educational Research Association, Chicago, Apr. 1985.

LaFromboise, T. D. *Circles of Women: Professionalization Training for American Indian Women.* Newton, Mass.: Women's Educational Equity Act, 1988.

LaFromboise, T. D., and BigFoot, D. "Cultural and Cognitive Considerations in the Prevention of American Indian Adolescent Suicide." *Journal of Adolescence,* 1988, *11,* 139–153.

LaFromboise, T. D., Dauphinais, P., and Rowe, W. "Indian Students' Perceptions of Positive Helper Attributes." *Journal of American Indian Education,* 1980, *19,* 11–16.

LaFromboise, T. D., Davis, B., and Rowe, W. "Verbal Response Patterns of Effective American Indian Helpers." Paper presented at annual meeting of the American Psychological Association, Los Angeles, Aug. 1985.

LaFromboise, T. D., and Dixon, D. "American Indian Perceptions of Trustworthiness in a Counseling Interview." *Journal of Counseling Psychology,* 1981, *28,* 135–139.

LaFromboise, T. D., and Plake, B. "Toward Meeting the Educational Research Needs of American Indians." *Harvard Educational Review,* 1983, *53,* 45–51.

LaFromboise, T. D., and Rowe, W. "Skills Training for Bicultural Competence: Rationale and Application." *Journal of Counseling Psychology,* 1983, *30,* 589–595.

Leap, W. L. "American Indian Language Maintenance." *Annual Review of Anthropology,* 1981, *10,* 271–280.

Lefley, H. P. "Differential Self-Concept in American Indian Children as a Function of Language and Examiner." *Journal of Personality and Social Psychology,* 1975, *31,* 36–41.

Littrell, J. M., and Littrell, M. A. "American Indian and Caucasian Students' Preferences for Counselors: Effects of Counselor Dress and Sex." *Journal of Counseling Psychology,* 1982, *29,* 48–57.

Long, K. "The Experience of Repeated and Traumatic Loss Among Crow Indian Children: Response Patterns and Intervention Strategies." *American Journal of Orthopsychiatry,* 1983, *52,* 116–126.

Lujan, C., DeBruyn, L. M., May, P. A., and Bird, M. E. "Profile of Abused and Neglected American Indian Children in the Southwest." *Child Abuse and Neglect,* 1989, *13,* 449–461.

Manson, S. M. (ed.). *New Directions in Prevention Among American Indian and Alaska Native Communities.* Portland: Oregon Health Sciences University, 1982.

Manson, S. M., Beals, J., Dick, R., and Duclos, C. "Risk Factors for Suicide Among Indian Adolescents at a Boarding School." *Public Health Reports,* 1989, *104*(6), 607–614.

Manson, S. M., Shore, J. H., and Bloom, J. D. "The Depressive Experience in American Indian Communities: A Challenge for Psychiatric Theory and Diagnosis." In A. Kleinman and B. Good (eds.), *Culture and Depression.* Berkeley: University of California Press, 1985.

Manson, S. M., and Trimble, J. E. "American Indian and Alaska Native Communities: Past Efforts, Future Inquiries." In L. R. Snowden (ed.), *Reaching the Underserved: Mental Health Needs of Neglected Populations.* Thousand Oaks, Calif.: Sage, 1982.

Manson, S. M., Walker, R. D., and Kivlahan, D. R. "Psychiatric Assessment and Treatment of American Indians and Alaska Natives." *Hospital and Community Psychiatry,* 1987, *38,* 165–173.

May, P. "Substance Abuse and American Indians: Prevalence and Susceptibility." *International Journal of the Addictions,* 1982, *17,* 1185–1209.

May, P. A. "Suicide and Self-Destruction Among American Indian Youths." *American Indian and Alaska Native Mental Health Research,* 1987, *1,* 52–69.

May, P. A. "The Health Status of Indian Children: Problems and Prevention in Early Life." In S. M. Manson and N. G. Dinges (eds.), *Behavioral Health Issues Among American Indian and Alaska Natives: Explorations on the Frontiers of the Biobehavioral Sciences.* Vol. 1: *American Indian and Alaska Native Mental Health Research.* Denver, Colo.: National Center, 1996.

Meichenbaum, D. H. (ed.). *Cognitive Behavior Modification: An Integrative Approach.* New York: Plenum, 1977.

Mohatt, G., and Blue, A. W. "Primary Prevention as It Relates to Traditionality and Empirical Measures of Social Deviance." In S. M. Manson (ed.), *New Directions in Prevention Among American Indian and Alaska Native Communities.* Portland: Oregon Health Sciences University, 1982.

Morey, S. M., and Gilliam, O. J. (eds.). *Respect for Life: The Traditional Upbringing of American Indian Children.* New York: Myrin Institute, 1974.

National Center for Education Statistics. *Dropout Rates in the United States.* Washington, D.C.: Department of Education, Office of Educational Research and Improvement, 1988.

Oetting, E. R., Beauvais, F., Edwards, B. W., and Velarde, L. *Drug Use Among Native American Youth: Summary of Findings (1975–81).* Fort Collins, Colo.: Western Behavioral Studies, 1983.

Plas, J. M., and Bellet, W. "Assessment of the Value-Attitude Orientations of American Indian Children." *Journal of School Psychology,* 1983, *21,* 57–64.

Radloff, L. S. "The CES-D Scale: A Self-Report Depression Scale for Research in the General Population." *Applied Psychology Measurement,* 1977, *1,* 385–401.

Red Horse, J. "American Indian Community Mental Health: A Primary Prevention Strategy." In S. M. Manson (ed.), *New Directions in Prevention Among American Indian and Alaska Native Communities.* Portland: Oregon Health Sciences University, 1982.

Red Horse, J., Lewis, R. G., Felt, M., and Decker, J. "Family Behavior of Urban American Indians." *Social Casework,* 1978, *59,* 67–72.

Roy, C., Chaudhuri, A., and Irvine, O. "The Prevalence of Mental Disorders Among Saskatchewan Indians." *Journal of Cross Cultural Psychology,* 1970, *1,* 383–392.

Ryan, R. A. "Strengths of the American Indian Family: State of the Art." In F. Hoffman (ed.), *The American Indian Family: Strengths and Stresses.* Isleta, N.Mex.: American Indian Social Research and Development Associates, 1980.

Sampath, H. M. "Prevalence of Psychiatric Disorders in a Southern Baffin Island Eskimo Settlement." *Canadian Psychiatric Association Journal,* 1974, *19,* 363–367.

Sandefur, G. D. "American Migration and Economic Opportunities." *International Migration Review,* 1986, *20,* 55–68.

Sandefur, G. D., and McKinnell, T. "American Indian Intermarriage." *Social Science Research,* 1986, *15,* 347–371.

Schinke, S. P., and others. "Preventing Substance Abuse with American Indian Youth." *Social Casework,* 1985, *66,* 213–217.

Shangreaux, V., Pleskac, D., and Freeman, W. *Strengthening Native American Families: A Family Systems Model Curriculum.* Lincoln, Nebr.: Lincoln Indian Center, 1987.

Shore, J. H., Kinzie, J. D., Hampson, D., and Pattison, E. M. "Psychiatric Epidemiology of an Indian Village." *Psychiatry,* 1973, *36,* 70–81.

Snipp, C. M. *American Indians: The First of This Land.* New York: Russell Sage Foundation, 1989.

Snipp, C. M. "The Size and Distribution of the American Indian Population: Fertility, Mortality, Residence, and Migration." In G. D. Sandefur, R. R. Rindfuss, and B. Cohen (eds.), *Changing Numbers, Changing*

Needs: American Indian Demography and Public Health. Washington, D.C.: National Academy Press, 1996.

Trimble, J. E. "Value Differentials and Their Importance in Counseling American Indians." In P. B. Pedersen, J. G. Draguns, W. J. Lonner, and J. E. Trimble (eds.), *Counseling Across Cultures.* Honolulu: University Press of Hawaii, 1989.

Trosper, R. L. "American Indian Poverty on Reservations, 1969–1989." In G. D. Sandefur, R. R. Rindfuss, and B. Cohen (eds.), *Changing Numbers, Changing Needs: American Indian Demography and Public Health.* Washington, D.C.: National Academy Press, 1996.

U.S. Bureau of the Census. *Statistical Abstract of the United States, 1996.* (116th ed.) Washington, D.C.: U. S. Department of Commerce, 1996.

U.S. Congress, Office of Technology Assessment. *Indian Adolescent Mental Health* (No. ANF 2689). Washington, D.C.: U.S. Government Printing Office, 1990.

U.S. Department of Education. *Minorities in Higher Education.* Washington, D.C.: National Center for Educational Statistics, 1995.

Chapter Five

African American Children

LaRue Allen
Shayda Majidi-Ahi

This chapter focuses on issues in the definition, assessment, treatment, and prevention of psychological problems in African American children, members of the country's second-largest racial group. The age range under consideration, five to twelve, has been called middle childhood, elementary school age, and latency age. These children and their families are descended largely from slaves who were brought to the United States from the sub-Saharan, middle West African coast, where relationships—political and economic as well as social—were based on patterns of kinship. In these societies, defining individuals by their ecological context (Comer, 1985)— for example, by their tribal affiliation, family membership, or geographical region—was preferred to using criteria based on individual characteristics. In this chapter, we have thus adopted the position that the functioning of black children is best understood when viewed as the product of an interaction between children and their various ecological niches, such as school, home, or church (Bronfenbrenner, 1979; Rickel and Allen, 1987).

Theoretical Orientation

This chapter reflects the belief, expressed also by Comer (1985) in his introduction to a special issue of the *Journal of the American Academy of Child Psychiatry* on black children and child psychiatry, that the one-to-one clinical, or medical, model does not encourage the examination of strengths but instead emphasizes the cataloguing of deficits. Given that most black children and their families adjust well despite poverty and racial discrimination (Hill, 1972), examination of the pathways to adaptive behavior may be even more informative than the study of the determinants of maladaptive behavior. Accordingly, we have adopted a social-ecological approach in discussing African American children, and we assume that promoting competence is no less important than treating maladjustment.

The social-ecological approach can be briefly described as an effort to understand the impact on development of person/environment interaction (Lewin, 1951). Bronfenbrenner (1979) offers a comprehensive ecological framework for understanding the developing child in context, incorporating four concentric systems that encompass the youth. *Microsystems* are those systems that have direct contact with and immediate daily effects on the child (for example, family, peers, school, and neighborhood). *Mesosystems* involve the relationships between and among the microsystems (for example, the interaction between family and school and the impact of that interaction on the child). *Exosystems* are settings that do not have immediate contact with the child but in which decisions are made that directly influence the child or the child's microsystems (for example, mental health agencies, school boards, and parents' employers). Finally, the *macrosystem* represents the values and mores of the institutions of society. Pervasive macrosystem values such as discrimination against blacks have both direct and indirect effects on the child. Such values can influence decisions made at all other levels of the ecological environment. For example, at the exosystem level, schools in black neighborhoods may not get a fair share of the school budget resources; at the mesosystem level, black parents and white teachers may fail to collaborate to remediate children's learning problems because of mutual mistrust stemming from years of exposure to racial stereotypes; and at the microsystem level, the black child who travels to a library in another part of the city may find that the extra resources available there are offered to him only grudgingly.

Demographic Data

In the United States, the black population is increasing in size relative to the white population. In 1995, the population of African Americans was 33,531,000 (12.7 percent of the total population)

(U.S. Bureau of the Census, 1996). Since 1990, the proportion of blacks has been in the 10 to 12.7 percent range. By the year 2000, their proportion in the population is expected to increase to 12.9 percent, or a total of more than 35 million.

Although African Americans are increasing in numbers, they continue to have a shorter life expectancy (69.6 years) than white Americans (76.4 years). This disparity continues despite techno-logical advances that have increased the life expectancy of whites to an all-time high. In 1995, the median age of the black popula-tion was 29.2 years, compared with 35.3 years for whites, a differ-ence largely attributable to differing life expectancies. Also in 1995, children aged 5 to 14 represented 18.7 percent of all blacks, while 14.2 percent of the white population were in that age group. It is projected that by the year 2000, 31.8 percent of blacks will be under 18 years old, compared with 24.6 percent of whites (U.S. Bureau of the Census, 1996).

From 1910, when 90 percent of all blacks lived on farms in the South, through 1970, blacks migrated from the South to the North and West. Between 1970 and 1990, the black population in the South declined from 60 to 52.8 percent of the total black popula-tion in the United States. African Americans form the highest pro-portion of the total population in the South (18.5 percent), the lowest in the West (5.4 percent), and intermediate proportions in the North Central (9.6) and Northeastern (11.0 percent) regions of the country (U.S. Bureau of the Census, 1996).

The black population is characterized by higher levels of poverty than among whites. In 1994, the median income for black families was $24,698, or 60 percent of white family income (U.S. Bureau of the Census, 1996). In high-income categories, blacks are underrepresented. Forty-three percent earn $25,000 or more, while more than 63 percent of white families do. At the lowest in-come levels, blacks are overrepresented, with 27.3 percent of fam-ilies living in poverty in 1994, compared with 9.1 percent of white families. Both race and poverty are risk factors for the development of psychological problems (Rickel and Allen, 1987). It is therefore important to note that in 1994, 43.3 percent of black children in the United States were poor, compared with 21.2 percent of chil-dren as a whole. Among blacks, 58.3 percent of children under eighteen lived in a female-headed household in 1995, compared with 21.3 percent of white children. And in 1994, 52.9 percent of children living at home in black female-headed households were poor (U.S. Bureau of the Census, 1996).

In 1995, levels of educational attainment were unequal for blacks and whites. Of blacks aged 25 and older, 26.2 percent had not attained a high school diploma, in contrast to 17 percent of whites aged 25 and older. At the college level, 13.2 percent of blacks had completed four years, while the comparable figure for whites was 24 percent (U.S. Bureau of the Census, 1996).

Epidemiological Data

Determining the scope of the problem—that is, the number of African American children who need, or who in the future are likely to need, assessment and/or intervention—is not a simple matter. Estimating the prevalence of psychological disorders among groups of children is an inexact science at best. Transient, developmentally appropriate changes in behavior may be difficult to distinguish from clinical disorders that should be treated. Compounding the problem is the fact that demographic variables such as race have rarely been evaluated in the few epidemiological studies done. Although the problem in classifying disorders has been acknowledged in the literature, to date there has been no scientifically sound resolution (Gould, Wunsch-Hitzig, and Dohrenwend, 1981).

Behavioral and Academic Problems

A significant percentage of referrals for school-aged black children are for academic and behavioral problems, particularly hyperactivity. In a survey of more than two hundred African American counselors and psychologists, poor academic achievement was the most frequently cited problem, followed closely by learning problems and excessive aggression (Gary, Beatty, and West, 1982).

Low levels of agreement among teachers, parents, and clinicians when rating the same child's behavior make diagnoses highly dependent on the source of data and the setting in which the data are collected. Parents and teachers appear to identify different children as maladjusted. Rutter, Tizard, and Whitmore (1970) found that reports of parents and teachers overlapped only 7 percent. The disparity between teacher and parent ratings of maladjustment correlates negatively with social class; agreement between ratings increases with higher social class (Glidewell and Swallow, 1968).

Even when the focus is on adaptive rather than maladaptive behavior, the rating disparity persists. For example, Wall and Paradise (1981) compared mother and teacher reports on two scales of the Adaptive Behavior Inventory for Children of the System of Multicultural and Pluralistic Assessment. Agreement on ratings of the behavior of African American boys and girls from lower-middle-income families averaged from 30 to 49 percent. Mothers consistently gave ratings that would indicate more competent functioning. Thus the children most at risk, such as those from lower socioeconomic groups, are most likely to have teachers who refer them for help with problem behavior that their parents do not identify. This potential for conflict rather than collaboration in the interaction of these two microsystems (the parent/teacher mesosystem) constitutes an additional risk factor for these black children.

Emotional Problems

Over the years, several panels of experts have assessed the prevalence of emotional problems in children (U.S. Congress, Office of Technology Assessment, 1986). The Joint Commission on Mental Health of Children (1968) adopted a broad definition of emotional disorder and estimated that 13.6 percent of children from birth to eighteen met its criteria. The Task Panel on Infants, Children, and Adolescents of the President's Commission on Mental Health (1978) estimated that 15 percent of children ages three to fifteen have mental problems that impair their functioning.

More recent epidemiological studies in the United States (for example, Gould, Wunsch-Hitzig, and Dohrenwend, 1981; Links, 1983) have concluded that 7.5 million children—12 percent of the population under age eighteen—need mental health intervention. This estimate does not distinguish the proportions of severe and mild disturbance. Nor does this survey or the two national studies assess racial differences.

Because the social ecology of black children as a group includes risk factors such as poverty and racial oppression, it is reasonable to predict that African American children will be overrepresented among children with psychological problems (Comer, 1985; Rickel and Allen, 1987). In fact, a Manhattan study reported that proportionately twice as many black as white children showed "psychiatric impairment" (Langner, Gersten, and Eisenberg, 1974). In a review of thirty-five studies of the epidemiology of childhood psychopathology, Gould, Wunsch-Hitzig, and Dohrenwend (1981) found that studies in poor, black, urban communities reported the highest rates of disorder. Vincenzi's (1987) study of black urban sixth graders found that at least 36 percent of the children at one school were at least mildly depressed as evidenced by scores on the Child Depression Inventory. At a second school, with three times the number of recipients of Aid to Families with Dependent Children, the depression rate was double that in the first school.

What little data are available do not, however, uniformly endorse the idea that disorder rates among black children are higher than those among whites. In a Midwestern study of personality differences among 433 black and 897 white schoolchildren (Gillum, Gomez-Marin, and Prineas, 1984), black parents rated their sons' levels of aggression, somatization, and sleep disturbance higher than white parents, and black girls were rated higher on sleep disturbance than white girls. The Missouri Children's Picture Series, a personality inventory for children, showed black boys significantly higher than white boys on aggression and somatization, and significantly lower on masculinity and maturity. Differences between black and white girls, however, were not significant. In the same vein, Achenbach and Edelbrock (1981) found in their normative sample for the Child Behavior Checklist that of 199 items analyzed for demographic differences, only 5 showed significant race effects, and all of these effects were quite small.

Cultural and Familial Factors

In order to work effectively with African American children, clinicians must be sensitive to the ecological context in which their clients exist. There is no single entity called "the black family." Black families vary in their backgrounds, their economic and social standing, their values, and the degree to which they are acculturated to the norms and values of mainstream America. There are, however, commonalities derived from the macrosystem devaluation of black people.

The present status of African Americans has been shaped by a three-hundred-year history that began with slavery, was succeeded by racism and oppression, and continues to be a story of persistent social and economic discrimination. Despite these obstacles, blacks in America have shown what Billingsley (1968) calls "an amazing ability to survive in the face of impossible conditions." A theoretical orientation called the "cultural variant" approach, proposed by Billingsley and other researchers, acknowledges the differing histories and ecological contexts of black and white families. This approach does not automatically assume that when differences between white and black family norms and behavior are encountered, the black family patterns are indicative of pathology. This orientation contrasts with Moynihan's (1965) earlier "cultural deviant" perspective, which assumes that any differences between black and white families are attributable to the inferiority of blacks.

The differences in ecological relations between African American and mainstream groups generate implications for treatment as well as for prevention. Research on how black families cope has pointed to elaborate arrangements that allow kin and friends to share resources, housing, and household tasks. Stack (1974) suggests that economic factors reduce the chances that lower-class black people can establish nuclear families, making extended families a plausible alternative for achieving family stability. Hill (1972), writing of black family strengths that most researchers ignore, cites the flexibility of roles between males and females and the presence of the extended family network as important survival resources. A clinician who can acknowledge these microsystem differences will be better able to plan contextually sensitive interventions that capitalize on available resources.

McAdoo (1977) points to potential class differences in resources that further complicate the picture. For middle-class blacks, the costs of remaining involved in the kinship network may be too high. She describes a typical scenario in which older children in a family leave school and go to work so that the youngest child can get an education. The family pools its efforts so that at least one member can rise above the poverty level. The upwardly mobile child, often a female, is expected to help her family as she was helped. Consequently, her emotional, financial, and physical resources cannot be devoted solely to her career. Thus the beneficiary of the family sacrifice faces a dilemma: she can continue to participate in the resource exchange network, with its obligation to give as needed, or she can isolate herself from her family of origin and concentrate on her own nuclear family and her career. This may account for the "alienation and antagonism that exist between working-class and middle-class blacks" (McAdoo, 1977, p. 78).

Differences in childrearing practices between African American families and the dominant culture constitute, for the child, an additional microsystem factor that contributes to a different social reality for blacks. Early studies found significant differences between black and white practices, including more permissiveness in feeding and weaning, greater restrictiveness in toilet training, and greater reliance on physical punishment among blacks (Davis and Havighurst, 1946). To some extent, these differences reflected social-class differences rather than racial differences (Bronfenbrenner, 1965). Evidence of this can be seen in the convergence of black and white childrearing behaviors as the economic position of blacks has improved. The extent of this convergence seems, however, to have an upper limit well before the point at which blacks' and whites' behaviors would be identical. Black parents are more likely to socialize children without strict differences based on the sex of the child, to share child care and decision making about childrearing, and to consider a child's competence in interpersonal relationships more important than his or her competence in dealing with the physical environment (Lewis, 1975). Highly significant differences between the races on all dimensions of Moos's (1974) Family Environment Scale have been found in a large Midwestern sample (Gillum, Gomez-Marin, and Prineas, 1984). For both male and female children, black families showed less openly expressed conflict, more achievement orientation and moral-religious emphasis, and more organization and control than white families.

The impact of these differences on child behavior and personality development, as well as their implications for child clinicians, is not yet clear. Some implications can be drawn, however, from research on sex-role socialization and on the development of the self-concept. The first implication comes from the absence of strict sex-role distinctions when black parents socialize children. Girls are encouraged to be aggressive and assertive; boys are encouraged to express emotion and be nurturant (Lewis, 1975). A clinician unaware of these possibilities might draw erroneous conclusions about the sex-role-appropriateness of black clients' behavior.

The quality of the self-concept is another socialization outcome that has generated research interest. Before the late 1960s, social science disseminated the notion that black parents' childrearing practices led to negative self-concepts in their offspring. This belief changed as the prevailing theory on black families changed from "cultural deviant" to "cultural variant." That change, along with the increase in racial pride that began for blacks with political activities in the late 1960s, led to new research that challenged the notion of negative self-concept. The work of McCarthy and Yancy (1971), among others (such as Hines and Berg-Cross, 1981; Hraba and Grant, 1970; Powell and Fuller, 1972; Rosenberg and Simmons, 1971; Soares and Soares, 1969), has shown higher self-concepts in black than in white children. Powell's (1985) research with 4,088 black and white children in three northern and southern cities is a reminder of the importance of ecological context in determining individual differences. Powell found that black children in segregated southern schools scored higher than any other group and attributes this, in part, to the cohesiveness that can develop in homogeneous African American communities as a defense against a hostile outside world. Clearly, earlier assumptions that blacks must have low self-esteem because of the negative evaluative feedback they receive from all levels of their ecological system are not correct. If blacks' self-esteem is determined by factors different from those that support whites' self-esteem, then the meaning of self-esteem for blacks is quite likely different from that for whites (Gray-Little and Appelbaum, 1979). Further, relationships between esteem and factors such as depression, typically found in white samples, may or may not be valid among blacks. Only empirical data can resolve this issue.

A final socialization issue, which exemplifies all that is distinct about the black experience in America, is teaching children how to cope with racism. Pierce (1974), a black psychiatrist, describes blacks' everyday experiences as riddled with multiple encounters with racism, creating a stressful environment filled with subtle to blatant incidents. The need to combat racism leads African American parents to emphasize the development of achievement motivation, self-confidence, and high self-esteem in their children (Peters, 1981).

Sociocultural Issues in Assessment

The views of ethnic minorities on the definition, etiology, and appropriate treatment of mental illness differ from those of Western mental health professionals (Flaskerud, 1984). Members of six ethnic groups differed significantly from mental health professionals both in labeling behaviors as mental illness and in recommending types of behavior management. Minorities' views of maladaptive behavior, including spiritual, moral, somatic, psychological, and metaphysical components, were broader than those of mental health professionals. Suggestions for management of disordered behavior included social, spiritual, economic, vocational, recreational, personal, physical, and psychological assistance, while professionals relied on traditional psychotherapeutic and psychopharmacological approaches (Flaskerud, 1984). These findings give some clues to the differing value that African American clients may place on various microsystem relationships. The well-prepared service provider needs to be familiar with the resources that could be made available to the client and family—from traditional churches and social service groups to social clubs, aid societies, and athletic leagues (Spurlock, 1985)—and the degree to which those resources enhance the fit between black clients and mental health interventions (Sue, 1977).

Assessment of symptom patterns and problem behaviors in African American children is complicated by the much-documented fact that racial and class biases influence diagnostic judgments, as well as by the lack of a reliable classification system for describing disorders. Hollingshead and Redlich's (1958) seminal work on class structure and mental illness showed that psychological disorder was rarer among members of the most affluent class, and twice the expected rate for members of the lowest social class. Hollingshead and Redlich also found that class influenced the diagnoses given to patients, with more severe diagnoses being given to the lower classes.

Traditional individually focused therapies *can* under the right circumstances be as effective with African American children and their parents as with any other group (Spurlock, 1985). But most therapeutic interventions, should they be made available, are likely to be conducted by a white, middle-class therapist. The historical difficulties between races make it extremely difficult, if not impossible, for most black clients to trust a white, or even a black middle-class, therapist. Jones and Seagull (1977) found that black clients defended themselves either by using lack of verbal clarity, uttering largely meaningless phrases, or by telling the therapist what they believed he wanted to hear.

On the therapist's part, there may be a tendency either to deny that race is an issue in the interaction or to overcompensate by attributing all of the client's problems to cultural and racial conflict. The effective therapist must be able to sift through presented behavior while considering the many alternative explanations for it and generating causal hypotheses consistent with the client's presentation of self and the therapist's knowledge of the ecology of the client's life. Therapists need to know, for example, that lower-income black people do not nod or say "Uh-huh" to indicate that they have heard something being said to them. Without this knowledge, therapists may call a black child who sits silently while being given directions "sullen" or "uncommunicative" when according to the African American community the child is interacting normatively.

An area that has received much attention is the examination of the validity and reliability of standard psychological tests as diagnostic tools for African American children. A full discussion of the controversy surrounding this issue is well beyond the scope of this chapter, but it is important to sketch the main points here and to lay out some of the implications for interventions with black children. It is important also to try to distinguish ethnic group differences from differences due to social class. The often-reported fifteen-point difference in IQ in favor of whites over blacks is reduced to five points when social class becomes more similar for the two groups (Nichols and Anderson, 1973). This finding does not, however, vitiate the need to discover whether these tests are differentially valid across sociodemographic subgroups. Identical test scores may have vastly different meanings if the tests were not measuring the same abilities or characteristics across groups.

The major argument against the use of psychological tests, particularly intelligence tests, with African American children is that these tests tend to be standardized on white, middle-class children and are insensitive to cultural differences (Flaugher, 1978; Sattler, 1988). Another charge is that tests that measure performance against national norms are inappropriate for use with black children. The countercharge is that the use of pluralistic norms rather than a single set can lead to invidious comparisons between subgroups of children (Sattler, 1988).

In evaluating the validity of either position, one must consider the purpose for administering the test and the qualifications of the tester. Use of national norms can provide information about *relative* performance among children, but they cannot be said to be a source of information about the *absolute* abilities of any child. The examiner can also reduce the negative impact that the lack of test-taking skills may have on a child's performance through rehearsal, explanations of tasks, and careful attention to establishing rapport before testing begins. An examiner from a racial group different than the child's must be sensitive to the possibility that this difference makes the child wary and mistrustful of the situation, thus threatening the validity of test results. For many African American children, mistrust of the white population and white institutions is the acceptable normative behavior. Consequently, multiple reassurances of confidentiality from a white examiner may have little effect on the black child's feelings of suspicion and mistrust. Further, speaking about certain topics outside the home, such as "family business," is most certainly a violation of family rules.

Children from different ethnic and social-class groups are motivated by different sets of reinforcers. Zigler and his colleagues found that rapport with the examiner was strongly related to academic performance for black students but not for whites (Zigler and Butterfield, 1968; Zigler, Abelson, and Seitz, 1973). Given this finding, it is particularly important for the therapist to attend to the relationship with the child in order to generate valid and reliable data.

Another factor that may undermine a positive relationship is the therapist's own feelings about interacting with African American children. Smith (1981) describes a white counselor who states that he is tired of having to prove himself to every new black client. White therapists who consider themselves "liberal" are sometimes aghast that black clients do not trust them. One way to address these feelings of frustration is to meet regularly with colleagues to discuss ways to foster positive cross-racial interactions. Once it can be acknowledged that *no one* has a simple formula, it should be easier for all to admit their uncertainty and fear.

Intervention

In working with the behavioral and emotional problems of African American children, the mental health interventionist must be cognizant of individual as well as ecological approaches to prevention and treatment. Because behavior is embedded within multiple systems that affect it both directly and indirectly (Bronfenbrenner, 1979), and because transactions in a child's relationships are bidirectional and reciprocal (Bell and Harper, 1977), interventions should focus simultaneously on children's individual behavior and on dysfunctional microsystem or mesosystem relationships. In addition, cultural dimensions of the African American family will influence the individual's interpretation of and response to these interventions.

Given the bias in the mental health profession toward assigning black clients to behavioral rather than insight-oriented therapies, relatively small numbers of African American parents and their children are referred for individual treatment. When they are referred, blacks are more likely than whites to drop out of treatment. According to one report, 52.1 percent of blacks dropped out compared with 29.8 percent of whites (Sue, 1977). These statistics underscore the importance of adapting interventions to the culturally determined preferences and expectations of the client.

One issue over which black clients and their middle-class therapists often clash is the interpretation of time. Wilkinson and Spurlock (1986) found that clients at a mental health center were consistently fifteen to thirty minutes late, despite clinicians' efforts to interpret the "resistance" and get clients to change their behavior. The concept of time varies in meaning from one culture to another, so each client's lateness might be handled differently. One might confront the issue with the client and negotiate some boundaries around the behavior that are mutually agreeable. In addition, alternative explanations for the lateness must be considered. Some clients may desire shorter sessions and thus have no motivation to arrive on time. Others may want the whole session but experience persistent transportation problems. This behavior may have been shaped by cultural differences in attitudes toward time, as well as by years of experience being kept waiting indefinitely in a health clinic despite having had "an appointment" for a particular time. For clinicians who work with children, who are dependent on adults to get them to their sessions, it is especially important at least to confront the lateness issue. Even though the child may not be able to effect a change in her parents' behavior, the existence of the time boundary should be acknowledged. Among middle-class African American clients who have become more acculturated to mainstream American values, lateness is more likely to be a manifestation of resistance and should be confronted as such by the clinician.

A second area of conflict and misunderstanding derives from differences in communication style. African Americans often converse among themselves while engaging in another activity. It is understood within the group that one can participate in the conversation without needing to maintain constant eye contact. However, among clinicians avoidance of eye contact is an important criterion of relatedness. Consequently, clinicians who work with black children must consider other indexes of social relatedness before concluding that a black child has problems in social development because of "poor" eye contact.

In addition to not making eye contact, African Americans are less likely to reinforce one another verbally in conversation. This means that a therapist might find herself explaining the purpose of an interview and the procedures and objectives for the next few sessions without getting any sign that the client has received or understood the information. In this situation, it is important to be attuned to body language, a dimension of communication generally considered more developed among blacks than whites (Smith, 1981).

Premature termination, often due to miscommunication and misunderstanding, is such a pervasive problem in reaching African American and other minority clients that programs have been designed to orient these clients to the therapeutic process (Acosta, Evans, Yamamoto, and Wilcox, 1980). Acosta and associates developed a multifaceted orientation program to prepare clients for psychotherapy. Their slide/cassette program uses twenty-four actors to represent a cross-section of ethnic backgrounds, age, and gender. Pilot testing of the program showed that clients' knowledge of the therapy process increased after exposure to the orientation program. This and other orientation curricula should be tested with children and their families to determine the most effective means of helping clients and therapists to adapt to each other.

Clients often come to the mental health system because of a crisis:

> Mrs. J., a working mother, had exhausted herself and her resources trying to improve the behavior of her son Mike, age twelve. After Mike was suspended from school, Mrs. J., concerned that he would be unsupervised during the day and on the streets, requested help from the mental health clinic. A social worker from the clinic visited the home to meet with all family members and discuss the situation. The social worker enabled them to express their frustrations with Mike and with the whole state of affairs. Together, they worked out a plan to defuse the situation and to get family members linked to the resources they needed to resolve the crisis. For example, a community-based mediation and dispute resolution service was called on to assist the family in negotiating the child's return to the classroom.

Families who continue follow-up work at the community mental health center or who accept referrals to other sources of mental health assistance might be offered a range of individual therapies, group therapy, or family therapy. The range of individual therapies that might be offered includes psychodynamic, cognitive, and behavioral approaches.

Psychodynamic Therapy

An assumption of psychodynamic therapy is that a client's symptoms or behaviors are not his or her "real" problem. Rather, it is assumed that these behaviors are surface manifestations of underlying problems that are buried so deeply in the client's psyche that he or she is unaware of what the underlying issues are (Achenbach, 1982). The primary goal of therapy is to help the child to achieve insight—to uncover underlying conflicts and deal with them directly. In showing a child the relationship between present and past feelings, the therapist interprets the child's utterances and play. To do this with any child, the therapist must learn the child's language and communicate warmth and acceptance. In working with African

American children, understanding the child's communications may be complicated by class and racial differences between therapist and child that limit the therapist's familiarity with the child's social reality.

Despite early reports in the literature that poor and/or black children and their families are not capable of insight, clinicians have documented the successful use of insight therapies with black clients (for example, Meers, 1970).

> A six-year-old boy, Bobby, born of a black father and white mother, was referred for a psychiatric evaluation by the Department of Social Services for suspected sexual abuse. Bobby, his mother, his fifteen-year-old stepbrother, his four-year-old sister, and his maternal grandmother lived in a two-bedroom apartment in an urban housing project. The referral was initiated by the school when Bobby was observed to be engaging in continuous masturbation, to be easily startled while napping, and to be enuretic. It was also reported that the child used sexually graphic language.

> For a six-year-old who was not fully able to express himself and resolve issues verbally, play therapy and drawings as communication media were useful for expressing uncomfortable thoughts and feelings. After nine months of intensive play therapy, Bobby disclosed the nature of the sexual abuse through a drawing of himself in his bed with a huge, muscular man "peeing" on him. This huge man was not identified at the time. In play depicting family events, however, the child expressed a lot of anger and fear toward his stepbrother, who was eventually identified as the abuser.

> Through play therapy, the therapist was able to introduce alternative ways of being and acting in situations similar to those that Bobby experienced. This exploration was designed to allow a corrective experience to take place that would facilitate the psychodynamic resolution of his feelings of hopelessness and hatred toward himself for "causing" the abuse and toward his mother for not protecting him. A turning point occurred in the establishment of the therapeutic relationship when the therapist expressed interest in Bobby's rapping, allowing him to teach her rap music—a language that became an integral part of their interactions and their efforts to communicate.

In many ways such an approach is similar to what would be done with a child from any other racial group. The therapist in this case, however, had to continually question her understanding of Bobby's communications. Such questioning alone will increase the sensitive therapist's chances of detecting subtle differences in meaning.

Behavioral Approaches

Behavioral approaches assume that maladaptive behaviors are learned because they have been reinforced in the child's social environment; thus these approaches are more sensitive than psychodynamic therapy to ecological variables (Bandura, 1977). The first task for the behavior therapist is to determine how often the undesired behaviors occur and in what settings. Then an intervention plan is designed and implemented. In operant conditioning, the most commonly applied behavioral model, adaptive behaviors are explicitly rewarded, while maladaptive behaviors are explicitly not rewarded or are extinguished.

Eight-year-old Sandra became enuretic after her mother's boyfriend moved into their apartment, leading her to feel neglected by her mother. Sandra was observed by her teachers to be suddenly quite needy and dependent. This observation resulted in a referral for psychological services provided by a school consultation team that was associated with a local community mental health center.

The consultation team implemented a behavioral program to reduce the frequency of bedwetting. Sandra and her therapist developed a chart for recording the frequency of bedwetting on a weekly basis. Whenever the child was able to stay dry for two consecutive nights, she would get a star. On collecting four stars, she was rewarded with a special outing with her mother to the local children's museum or a nearby shopping mall. At the same time, whenever she wet her bed, she had to get up, change her sheets, and take a shower. This plan was carefully monitored by the mother, who communicated the information to the consultation team. By the end of the second month, this intervention had reduced the bedwetting to fewer than three incidents a month.

In behavioral interventions, the assistance of a parent is often required. When interacting with African American parents, therapists approach the work in a collaborative mode. Black families are more likely than white families to judge a person's competence by his or her warmth and interpersonal skill rather than simply on the basis of instrumental competence (Gibbs, 1985). The clinician must convey competence as a caring person before attempting to document competence as a behaviorist. By collaborating with the family, the clinician also increases the chance that the program is truly addressing the conditions the clinician wants to address.

Cognitive Therapy

Cognitive therapy, which is based on research findings that disturbed children have different thought processes than other children (Luria, 1961), has been used to help children with behavioral, emotional, social, and learning problems. For example, cognitively based social skills training has been used in the Detroit public schools to teach high-risk children how to interact in an assertive yet nonaggressive manner in their social environment. Each child received a program tailored to his behavior problem, with intervention focused on substituting acceptable behaviors for the maladaptive ones that had prompted referral (Rickel and Allen, 1987).

Cognitive interventions are also useful as an adjunct to or component of other types of interventions, as the following case illustrates.

A group of fifth grade girls, all black, were identified by their teacher as having severe behavior problems in class and exhibiting "gang behavior" in their bullying of other children in the class. In extensive individual interviews, the girls identified threats to their safety, and the threat of sexual abuse in particular, as common concerns. Activity-oriented group therapy was chosen as the intervention for these girls.

One phase of the group intervention involved a workshop geared toward education about sexual abuse, in which the therapists defined abuse and provided concrete cognitive information about dimensions of abuse. The group then role-played the situation of a young girl approached by a man who intended to abuse her. This was followed by a discussion of problem-solving strategies. This exercise helped the girls to adopt a cognitive problem-solving style for this situation and enabled them to participate actively in developing effective coping behaviors and role-playing various alternatives.

The objective of the social skills training workshop was to provide these girls with the cognitive skills necessary to problem solve in frightening situations such as threatened sexual abuse. The cognitive intervention focused on the development of assertiveness, supportive behaviors toward peers, and skills for communicating feelings and facts that may be difficult to talk about. The purpose was also to empower these girls with a sense of competence that would generalize from the role-play environment to the other settings in which they frequently found themselves.

In working with African American clients, therapists will frequently encounter cognitions that are disturbing to them—cognitions about sexual abuse and other signs of very stressful lives. Therapists must guard against overidentifying with clients, because this renders the therapists less capable of objectively helping clients to master difficult situations.

Microsystem Interventions

Because ecological relationships are so important in a child's life, therapy using the peer group or family group as the unit of intervention should be used more commonly. Group therapy is often recommended when children might benefit from exposure to peers. Each child can serve as a model for his or her peers and can also see those peers model behaviors that the child is trying to learn. What actually happens in group therapy depends on the developmental level of the group members. The youngest elementary school–aged children might be involved in an activity group, using crafts or group play as a vehicle for verbal exchange and for generating material that the group leader or group members might interpret or comment on (Schamess, 1976).

Danny, aged seven, was seen in twice-weekly activity group therapy aimed at helping him to develop impulse control. Danny actively avoided any direct attempts to discuss his behavior problem, actually averting his head or covering his ears on many occasions. He listened intently, however, when the therapist discussed behavior control with other children in the group. As long as the therapist did not attempt to make eye contact with Danny or to involve him in such discussions directly, he remained involved. He was especially interested in what the therapist had to say about needing to fight back when you get picked on in your neighborhood but needing to turn the other cheek on the school playground or else get into big trouble.

The group therapist needs to know what is usual when African American children interact with one another. For instance, trading insults about each other's families is a game commonly played in low-income neighborhoods. A novice to "playing the dozens" might fear that physical conflict is imminent and inappropriately intervene. Checking with group members about the meaning of words and actions will give a therapist more credibility with a group than trying to bluff one's way through.

Another microsystem intervention, family therapy, is particularly important to consider for black families, given the importance of the extended family in the African American community. For family therapists, problems lie not in the individual child client but rather in disturbed family relationships (French, 1977). A child's delinquency at school, for example, might be seen as a form of acting out to deflect parental attention from a troubled marriage, thus delaying a feared parental separation or divorce. Some family therapists consider the family system the locus of intervention; others consider family therapy a chance to augment individual work with an examination of family dynamics to determine how they affect the "target patient."

Clinicians who work with black families need to ask questions about people who may live with the child, such as a mother's boyfriend, or who live outside the home but are an integral part of the child's life, such as an aunt who regularly provides after-school care (Hines and Boyd-Franklin, 1982). The presence of such individuals might not be detected using the usual intake forms. To establish credibility with the family, the family therapist needs to be flexible enough to abandon the therapist's usual job description and explore the impact of the family's environment on its functioning. Clinicians must be ready to address problems posed by systems external to the family (social, political, economic, religious, physical, and other) while also helping the family to improve its interactions with these systems (Harris and Balgopal, 1980).

Prevention Approaches

Epidemiological studies have revealed that as many as a third of all schoolchildren experience adjustment problems. Early school problems frequently persist, intensifying over time and becoming more severe mental health problems at later ages (Cowen and others, 1976). At the same time, traditional psychotherapy is not available to all who need it (Albee, 1970), is even less available to members of minority groups, and when available, may not be attuned to the context and needs of many members of ethnic minority groups (Sue, 1977).

Faced with this set of facts, many clinicians have joined other mental health professionals in developing interventions that will decrease the need for therapy by reducing the number of children who develop problems. Development of such programs would lessen the need for more expensive, time-consuming interventions that require the commitment of highly trained professionals, such as individual psychotherapy (Rickel and Allen, 1987).

Primary prevention programs have been designed to reduce the incidence (number of new cases) of nearly every category of diagnosable mental illness and have targeted children, parents, families, classrooms, and schools. Secondary prevention programs are designed to reduce the severity and duration of problems through early detection and intervention. Both primary and secondary prevention programs have occurred in a variety of settings, including hospitals (Minde, Shosenberg, and Marton, 1982), homes (Tableman, 1982), and schools (Rickel, 1977). Schools are particularly important sites for the delivery of prevention services because the vast majority of children in their elementary school years spend a good many of their waking hours there. Given the reluctance of many families to visit a place labeled "mental health center," the schools are a potential vehicle for reaching hard-to-serve groups and delivering services that reach more children than could be served even in group therapy within the same time frame.

The Yale–New Haven Primary Prevention Program is based in a school that serves a kindergarten through fourth-grade population that is 99 percent black; more than half the families receive Aid to Families with Dependent Children. The program's design is based on an ecological model and "focuses on creating a desirable climate or social environment in schools through application of mental health principles in a way that effects a coordinated management, curriculum, and staff development program" (Comer, 1985, p. 155). The mental health team—a psychiatrist, a psychologist, a social worker, and a psychologically oriented teacher—does not focus on children or families as "patients." Rather, the team addresses the organization and management of all aspects of the school environment, as well as intrapersonal and interpersonal issues involving pupils and/or staff.

Since the program began in 1969, it has had a measurable impact. The school moved from serious attendance problems in 1969 to a place in the top five schools in attendance in the city from 1976 on. On four occasions, the school was first in attendance for the entire city. Children who had gone through the intervention program more than three years earlier scored significantly better than matched controls on all nine subtests of the Iowa Test of Basic Skills. Furthermore, intervention-group children scored higher on a measure of school competence, had significantly higher grades in math, and had higher overall grade point averages (Comer, 1985).

Another type of primary prevention program that is sensitive to the importance of ecological and cultural factors is the family support program. The Yale Child Welfare Research Program (Seitz, Rosenbaum, and Apfel, 1985) is one example of such a program and is distinguished by its emphasis on outcome research. The interventions are delivered by an interdisciplinary team that works to enhance parents' ability to deal with their children as well as with their own lives. The target population, impoverished and predominantly African American families, received an array of services over a two-and-a-half-year period. A ten-year follow-up of program families and their equivalent controls showed that the program had positive and enduring effects. For example, intervention-group mothers were more likely than control-group mothers to be financially self-sufficient, had completed more years of school, and had had fewer children. Their children had better school attendance records, had better school and social adjustment, and required fewer costly social services.

An appreciable decrease in the prevalence of mental illness among black children would occur if primary prevention programs were fully implemented in appropriate community settings (Washington and Wilson, 1986). Yet even under the best of circumstances, there would still be children in need of services. Hence, the clinician who wants to promote the development of mental health among black children should be well versed in both individual and ecological approaches to treatment and intervention.

Complex problems often require complex solutions, such as the integration of theories on individual, family, classroom, and community determinants of adaptive and maladaptive behaviors in black children.

Conclusions and Recommendations

The intervention needs of African American children and their families can be better served under two conditions. First, more blacks should be encouraged and actively recruited for training as mental health professionals. For some clients, having a therapist of the same race is important for the success of treatment. In 1982, only 2 percent of American psychiatrists were black. Additionally, fewer than 10 percent were child psychiatrists, despite the fact that children constitute about 40 percent of the clientele in community mental health centers (Washington and Wilson, 1986). Blacks make up less than 1 percent of the psychologists in this country but are somewhat better represented in the professions of counseling and social work, for example. Blacks constitute about 9 percent of master's level social workers and make up about 4 percent of the total number of psychiatric nurses (Washington and Wilson, 1986).

A second factor that needs to be addressed in order to better serve the mental health needs of African American children is the training of mental health professionals, regardless of race or ethnicity. Most clinicians do not receive adequate training that increases their ability to understand how economic status, education, health care, housing, racism, and other ecological factors affect the functioning of the child and the child's social network (Comer and Hill, 1985). The need is great for course work that integrates cultural pluralist views into graduate theory and practicum work, rather than making discussion of such issues an "extra" that overburdened students have to try to squeeze into their schedules. Practicum courses must provide opportunities to work with black clients, with field- or university-based supervision from black clinicians and faculty members. Graduate programs must also include a critical mass of black graduate students in training programs, so that students can learn from one another and so that the pain of tokenism is not visited upon yet another generation of black achievers.

As we have suggested throughout this chapter, the state of knowledge of issues central to promoting mental health in African American and other children is in its infancy, at best. The entire mental health field would benefit from well-funded, careful research to produce reliable differential diagnostic procedures. To gauge the effectiveness of treatments and preventive interventions, we need better baseline data on the incidence and prevalence of psychological disorders in children, with particular emphasis on how rates vary for different sociodemographic groups. Finally, the effectiveness of therapies and preventive interventions must be more carefully and more often evaluated so that the scarce resources available to meet the tremendous need can be used most effectively.

References

Achenbach, T. *Developmental Psychopathology.* (2nd ed.) New York: Wiley, 1982.

Achenbach, T., and Edelbrock, C. "Behavioral Problems and Competencies Reported by Parents of Normal and Disturbed Children Aged Four Through Sixteen." *Monographs of the Society for Research in Child Development,* 1981, *46*(1), Serial No. 188.

Acosta, F. X., Evans, L. A., Yamamoto, J., and Wilcox, S. "Helping Minority and Low-Income Psychotherapy Patients 'Tell It Like It Is.'" *Journal of Biocommunication,* 1980, *7*, 13–19.

Albee, G. W. "The Uncertain Future of Clinical Psychology." *American Psychologist,* 1970, *25*, 1071–1080.

Bandura, A. *Social Learning Theory.* Englewood Cliffs, N.J.: Prentice Hall, 1977.

Bell, R. Q., and Harper, L. U. *Child Effects on Adults.* Hillsdale, N.J.: Erlbaum, 1977.

Billingsley, A. *Black Families in White America.* Englewood Cliffs, N.J.: Prentice Hall, 1968.

Bronfenbrenner, U. "Socialization and Social Class Through Time and Space." In H. Proshansky (ed.), *Basic Studies in Social Psychology.* Austin, Tex.: Holt, Rinehart and Winston, 1965.

Bronfenbrenner, U. *The Ecology of Human Development: Experiments by Nature and Design.* Cambridge, Mass.: Harvard University Press, 1979.

Comer, J. "The Yale–New Haven Primary Prevention Project: A Follow-Up." *Journal of the American Academy of Child Psychiatry,* 1985, *24*, 154–160.

Comer, J., and Hill, H. "Social Policy and the Mental Health of Black Children." *Journal of the American Academy of Child Psychiatry,* 1985, *24*(2), 175–181.

Cowen, E. L., and others. "Long-Term Follow-Up of Early Detected Vulnerable Children." *Journal of Consulting and Clinical Psychology,* 1976, *44,* 775–786.

Davis, A., and Havighurst, R. "Social Class and Color Differences in Child Rearing." *American Sociological Review,* 1946, *11,* 698–710.

Flaskerud, J. "A Comparison of Perceptions of Problematic Behavior by Six Minority Groups and Mental Health Professionals." *Nursing Research,* 1984, *33,* 190–228.

Flaugher, R. L. "The Many Definitions of Test Bias." *American Psychologist,* 1978, *33,* 671–679.

French, A. P. *Disturbed Children and Their Families: Innovations in Evaluation and Treatment.* New York: Human Sciences Press, 1977.

Gary, L., Beatty, L., and West, J. *The Delivery of Mental Health Services to Black Children.* Final report. Washington, D.C.: Mental Health Research and Development Center, Institute for Urban Affairs and Research, Howard University, 1982.

Gibbs, J. T. "Treatment Relationships with Black Clients: Interpersonal vs. Intrumental Strategies." In C. Germain (ed.), *Advances in Clinical Social Work Practice.* Silver Spring, Md: National Association of Social Workers, 1985.

Gillum, R., Gomez-Marin, O., and Prineas, R. "Racial Differences in Personality, Behavior, and Family Environment in Minneapolis School Children." *Journal of the National Medical Association,* 1984, *76,* 1097–1105.

Glidewell, J. C., and Swallow, C. S. *The Prevalence of Maladjustment in Elementary Schools.* Report prepared for the Joint Commission on the Mental Health of Children. Chicago: University of Chicago Press, 1968.

Gould, M., Wunsch-Hitzig, R., and Dohrenwend, B. S. "Estimating the Prevalence of Childhood Psychopathology." *Journal of the American Academy of Child Psychiatry,* 1981, *20,* 462–476.

Gray-Little, B., and Appelbaum, M. "Instrumentality Effects in the Assessment of Racial Differences in Self-Esteem." *Journal of Personality and Social Psychology,* 1979, *37,* 1221–1229.

Harris, D. C., and Balgopal, P. R. "Intervening with the Black Family." In C. Janzen and O. Harris (eds.), *Family Treatment in Social Work Practice.* Itasca, Ill.: Peacock, 1980.

Hill, R. *The Strengths of Black Families.* New York: Emerson Hall, 1972.

Hines, P. M., and Berg-Cross, L. "Racial Differences in Global Self-Esteem." *Journal of Social Psychology*, 1981, *113*, 271–281.

Hines, P. M., and Boyd-Franklin, N. "Black Families." In M. McGoldrick, J. K. Pearce, and J. Giordano (eds.), *Ethnicity and Family Therapy*. New York: Guilford Press, 1982.

Hollingshead, A. B., and Redlich, F. C. *Social Class and Mental Illness*. New York: Wiley, 1958.

Hraba, J., and Grant, G. "Black Is Beautiful: A Reexamination of Racial Preference and Identification." *Journal of Personality and Social Psychology*, 1970, *16*, 398–402.

Joint Commission on Mental Health of Children. *Crisis in Child Mental Health: Challenge for the 1970s*. New York: HarperCollins, 1968.

Jones, A., and Seagull, A. "Dimensions of the Relationship Between the Black Client and the White Therapist: A Theoretical Overview." *American Psychologist*, 1977, *32*, 850–856.

Langner, T., Gersten, J., and Eisenberg, J. "Approaches to Measurement and Definition in the Epidemiology of Behavior Disorders." *International Journal of Health Services*, 1974, *4*, 483–501.

Lewin, K. *Field Theory in Social Science: Selected Theoretical Papers*. New York: HarperCollins, 1951.

Lewis, D. "The Black Family: Socialization and Sex Roles." *Phylon*, 1975, *36*, 221–237.

Links, P. "Community Survey of the Prevalence of Childhood Psychiatric Disorders: A Review." *Child Development*, 1983, *54*, 531–548.

Luria, A. R. *The Role of Speech in the Regulation of Normal and Abnormal Behavior*. New York: Liveright, 1961.

McAdoo, H. P. "Family Therapy in the Black Community." *American Journal of Orthopsychiatry*, 1977, *47*, 75–79.

McCarthy, J., and Yancy, W. "Uncle Tom and Mr. Charlie: Metaphysical Pathos in the Study of Racism and Personal Disorganization." *American Journal of Sociology*, 1971, *76*, 648–672.

Meers, D. "Contributions of a Ghetto Culture to Symptom Formation: Psychoanalytic Studies of Ego Anomalies in Childhood." *Psychoanalytic Study of the Child*, 1970, *25*, 209–230.

Minde, K. K., Shosenberg, N. E., and Marton, P. "The Effects of Self-Help Groups in a Premature Nursery on Maternal Autonomy and Caretaking Style One Year Later." In L. A. Bond and J. M. Joffe (eds.), *Facilitating Infant and Early Childhood Development*. Hanover, N.H.: University Press of New England, 1982.

Moos, R. *Family Environment Scale Manual*. Palo Alto, Calif.: Consulting Psychologists Press, 1974.

Moynihan, D. P. *The Negro Family: A Case for National Action.* Washington, D.C.: U.S. Government Printing Office, 1965.

Nichols, P., and Anderson, E. "Intellectual Performance, Race, and Socioeconomic Status." *Social Biology,* 1973, *20,* 367–374.

Peters, M. F. "Parenting in Black Families with Young Children: A Historical Perspective." In H. McAdoo (ed.), *Black Families.* Thousand Oaks, Calif.: Sage, 1981.

Pierce, C. M. "Psychiatric Problems of the Black Minority." In G. Caplan (ed.), *American Handbook of Psychiatry.* Vol. 2: *Child and Adolescent Psychiatry, Sociocultural and Community Psychiatry.* (2nd ed.) New York: Basic Books, 1974.

Powell, G. J. "Self-Concepts Among Afro-American Students in Racially Isolated Minority Schools: Some Regional Differences." *Journal of the American Academy of Child Psychiatry,* 1985, *24,* 142–149.

Powell, G. J., and Fuller, M. "The Variables for Positive Self-Concept Among Young Southern Black Adolescents." *Journal of the National Medical Association,* 1972, *43,* 72–79.

President's Commission on Mental Health. Task Panel on Infants, Children, and Adolescents. *Report to the President.* Washington, D.C.: U.S. Government Printing Office, 1978.

Rickel, A. "Screening and Remediation of Preschool Children from Low-Income Families." *Perceptual and Motor Skills,* 1977, *45,* 757–758.

Rickel, A., and Allen, L. "Preventing Maladjustment from Infancy Through Adolescence." In A. E. Kazdin (ed.), *Developmental Clinical Psychology and Psychiatry,* no. 11. Thousand Oaks, Calif.: Sage, 1987.

Rosenberg, M., and Simmons, R. *Black and White Self-Esteem: The Urban School Child.* Rose Monograph Series. Washington, D.C.: American Sociological Association, 1971.

Rutter, M., Tizard, J., and Whitmore, K. *Education, Health and Behaviour.* London: Longmans, 1970.

Sattler, J. M. *Assessment of Children.* (3rd ed.) San Diego, Calif.: Jerome M. Sattler, 1988.

Schamess, G. "Group Treatment Modalities for Latency-Age Children." *International Journal of Group Psychotherapy,* 1976, *26,* 455–473.

Seitz, V., Rosenbaum, L., and Apfel, N. "Effects of Family Support Intervention: A Ten-Year Follow-Up." *Child Development,* 1985, *56,* 376–391.

Smith, E. "Cultural and Historical Perspectives in Counseling Blacks." In D. W. Sue, *Counseling the Culturally Different: Theory and Practice.* New York: Wiley, 1981.

Soares, A. T., and Soares, L. M. "Self-Perception of Culturally Disadvantaged Children." *American Educational Research Journal,* 1969, *6,* 31–45.

Spurlock, J. "Assessment and Therapeutic Interventions of Black Children." *Journal of the American Academy of Child Psychiatry,* 1985, *24,* 168–174.

Stack, C. *All Our Kin: Strategies for Survival in a Black Community.* New York: HarperCollins, 1974.

Sue, S. "Community Mental Health Services to Minority Groups: Some Optimism, Some Pessimism." *American Psychologist,* 1977, *32,* 616–624.

Tableman, B. "Infant Mental Health: A New Frontier." *Infant Mental Health Journal,* 1982, *3,* 72–76.

U.S. Bureau of the Census. *Statistical Abstract of the United States, 1996.* (116th ed.) Washington, D.C.: U.S. Government Printing Office, 1996.

U.S. Congress, Office of Technology Assessment. *Children's Mental Health: Problems and Services—A Background Paper.* Washington, D.C.: U.S. Government Printing Office, 1986.

Vincenzi, H. "Depression and Reading Ability in Sixth-Grade Children." *Journal of School Psychology,* 1987, *25,* 155–160.

Wall, S. M., and Paradise, L. V. "A Comparison of Parent and Teacher Reports of Selected Adaptive Behaviors of Children." *Journal of School Psychology,* 1981, *19,* 73–77.

Washington, A., and Wilson, S. "Providing Mental Health Services to Black Children and Youth." In L. Beatty (ed.), *Readings on Black Children and Youth.* Washington, D.C.: Mental Health Research and Development Center, Institute for Urban Affairs and Research, Howard University, 1986.

Wilkinson, C., and Spurlock, J. "The Mental Health of Black Americans: Psychiatric Diagnosis and Treatment." In C. Wilkinson (ed.), *Ethnic Psychiatry.* New York: Plenum, 1986.

Zigler, E., Abelson, W., and Seitz, V. "Motivational Factors in the Performance of Economically Disadvantaged Children on the Peabody Picture Vocabulary Test." *Child Development,* 1973, *44,* 294–303.

Zigler, E., and Butterfield, E. "Motivational Aspects of Changes in IQ Test Performance of Culturally Deprived Nursery School Children." *Child Development,* 1968, *39,* 1–14.

Chapter Six

African American Adolescents

Jewelle Taylor Gibbs

African American adolescents are one of the most vulnerable and victimized groups in contemporary American society. They have been mislabeled and miseducated by the schools, mishandled by the juvenile justice system, mistreated by mental health agencies, and neglected by the social welfare bureaucracy, until very recently. Their plight has been minimized by health care professionals and ignored by policymakers. Thus they have been labeled an "endangered species" (Gibbs, 1984, 1988b), members of a growing "underclass" (Glasgow, 1981; Wilson, 1987), and "at high risk for a variety of self-destructive and anti-social behaviors" (Dryfoos, 1990).

As a result of generations of discrimination and deprivation, African American adolescents have developed high rates of psychological and behavioral disorders, as well as certain problematic psychosocial behaviors. However, in spite of the high incidence of these problem behaviors, most African American youth have also managed to become competent, well-functioning young adults.

This chapter presents an overview of the psychological and psychosocial problems of African American adolescents, discusses issues of assessment and diagnosis, and describes intervention strategies that are appropriate and effective for this group. To avoid duplication of the previous chapter on African American children by Allen and Majidi-Ahi, this chapter focuses on African American adolescents and youth thirteen to twenty-one years of age, which basically consists of the school years from junior high school through college. Additionally, the discussion focuses primarily on non-Hispanic African American youth who are identified as African American rather than as Caribbean in their ethnic heritage, because the former group constitutes the great majority of black Americans.

The mental health problems and needs of these African American youth are discussed in the context of the historical, social, economic, and political factors that have shaped their experiences in American society. Further, the cultural values and adaptive behaviors that many African Americans have developed in response to these experiences are described.

The overarching conceptual framework of the chapter is a combination of two major perspectives: an ego-psychology perspective on adolescent development (Erikson, 1950, 1959) and an ecological perspective on the social environment in which this development occurs (Bronfenbrenner, 1979). Only through comprehension of the complex socioeconomic and political forces that impinge on African American youth and their families is it possible to understand their adaptive and maladaptive behaviors (Jones, 1989; Taylor, 1995). Thus this author proposes that the assessment and treatment of the psychological, behavioral, and psychosocial problems of African American youth should be carried out with particular attention to the interaction of intrapsychic, interpersonal, familial, cultural, and environmental factors, all of which have a significant impact on adolescent development, adaptation, and dysfunction.

Demographic Information

In 1995 there were approximately 5,699,000 African American youth aged ten to nineteen years old; 2,822,000 of them were in the fifteen-to-nineteen-years age bracket, and 2,638,000 were in the twenty-to-twenty-four-years age range (U.S. Bureau of the Census, 1996). The ratio of males to females was about equal. Because children and youth constitute nearly half of the total African American population, the median age for African Americans is 29.2 years, compared to a white median age of 35.3 (U.S. Bureau of the Census, 1996). Thus the African American population is a relatively youthful population, which has important implications for mental health policies, programs, and services that are targeted at the African American community.

In 1994, two of every five (43.3 percent) African American youth under eighteen lived in families whose incomes were below the poverty line, while more than half (52.9 percent) of African American youth in female-headed households were poor (U.S. Bureau of the Census, 1996). Nearly three of every five African American children lived in female-headed families, which were five times more likely than two-parent families to be welfare dependent. Although more than one-third of African American youth live in two-parent families, the remaining group also has higher rates than white youth of out-of-home placements in foster homes and institutions (Children's Defense Fund, 1987).

The median income of all African American families in 1994 was $24,698, which was 60 percent of the median white family income of $40,884 (U.S. Bureau of the Census, 1996). There were striking disparities, however, between the median income of intact families with two parents employed ($26,583) and that of female-headed families ($9,300). Thus, middle-class status for most African American youth is related to having two employed parents and a stable economy. The unemployment rate among African American adults is more than twice as high as the unemployment rate for white adults (U.S. Bureau of the Census, 1996). In 1995, the unemployment rate for African American teenagers, aged sixteen to nineteen, was over 35 percent, more than twice as high as the rate for white teenagers.

By 1994, 73.8 percent of all African Americans had completed high school and 13.2 percent had completed college or graduate school, compared to 83 percent and 24 percent of whites, respectively. High school dropout rates for blacks sixteen to twenty-four years old have dropped from 22.0 percent in 1970 to 15.5 percent in 1995 (U.S. Bureau of the Census, 1996).

Finally, African American youth are more likely than white youth to live in deteriorating central city neighborhoods, in substandard housing with poor sanitation located in urban areas with depressed economies, where they have much less access to adequate health and mental health facilities (Kasarda, 1985; Schorr, 1986; Children's Defense Fund, 1986a).

As several researchers have pointed out, these social and economic characteristics of inner-city neighborhoods generate chronic levels of stress for African American youth and their families (Comer and Hill, 1985; Myers, 1989; Wilson, 1987). Thus, an understanding of these ecological realities is essential for clinicians who deliver mental health services to African American youth (Spencer, 1995).

Historical, Social, and Political Influences

The current status of African Americans in the United States can be directly attributed to four major historical and social factors: slavery, segregation and discrimination, poverty, and urbanization (Franklin, 1967; Omi and Winant, 1986; Wilson, 1987). These factors have also contributed significantly to undermining the functioning of the African American family and major institutions of the African American community, which in turn has created a hospitable environment for the development of social, psychological, and behavioral problems among African American youth.

The effects of nearly 250 years of slavery on the African American family have been widely debated, but there is general agreement that slavery had a deleterious impact on the structure and functioning of the family as a unit, particularly on the role of the African American male as the head of the household (Frazier, 1966). The racial caste system introduced by slavery defined African Americans as inferior and subordinate to whites. This caste system has been reinforced by the educational and economic disparities between African Americans and whites, which have persisted since slavery was abolished in 1863 (Omi and Winant, 1986).

Even after legal segregation was eliminated by a series of Supreme Court decisions, culminating in the landmark school desegregation decision in 1954, discriminatory practices were still pervasive and pernicious, depriving African Americans of equal access to schools, jobs, housing, health care, political participation, recreation, and public facilities (Franklin, 1967; Omi and Winant, 1986). By enforcing the status of second-class citizenship for African Americans, the dominant society created a "separate and unequal" society that developed its own institutions, subcultural values, and behavioral norms, forcing African American parents to develop childrearing strategies that would enable them to promote healthy development in their children in spite of their minority status (Bowman and Howard, 1985; Cross, 1984; Peters, 1981; Spencer, 1982; Taylor, 1991).

A third factor that has significantly influenced the status of African American families is persistent poverty and low socioeconomic status. African American families are still three times more likely than white families to be poor. Poverty obviously has multiple adverse effects on African American youth, placing them at greater risk for a range of physical and mental health problems, conduct disorders, and psychosocial problems (Children's Defense Fund, 1987; Dryfoos, 1990; Gibbs, 1995; Kovar, 1982; Thompson, 1990).

Fourth, the mass migration of African Americans between World War I and World War II from the rural south to northern industrial centers transformed the African American population from a predominantly rural agrarian group to an urban working class. Although this rapid urbanization was accompanied by many positive benefits, including opportunities for educational and occupational mobility, it also resulted in the development of huge ghettos in most urban areas, the concentration of African American males in a few industries, and social and cultural isolation from the dominant society (Clark, 1965; Franklin, 1967). These negative outcomes of urbanization laid the foundation for the subsequent development of the so-called underclass two decades later (Glasgow, 1981; Wilson, 1987).

The more recent social forces that have shaped the experience of African American youth and their families have included three major socioeconomic and political developments: (1) the civil rights movement, (2) affirmative action legislation and backlash, and (3) radical structural and technological changes in the American economy. The civil rights movement, which began with the Montgomery bus boycott in 1955 and ended with the passage of two major civil rights bills in 1964 and 1965, signaled a new era of militancy among African Americans to obtain their full rights as citizens. Participation in the movement by thousands of college youth provided positive role models and raised the expectations and aspirations of millions of African American youth (Chambers, 1968).

After the successful passage of civil rights legislation, direct-action strategies were replaced in the early 1970s by legislative and administrative programs of affirmative action to promote equal opportunity in education and employment. These efforts were only moderately successful, however, before a widespread backlash developed among whites who perceived these efforts as "reverse racism" and as an organized effort to deprive them of their privileged status (Omi and Winant, 1986). Reinforcement of this backlash since 1980 by a conservative political administration has had a particularly negative impact on African American youth; their gains in employment rates and college enrollment rates achieved by the mid-1970s were virtually wiped out by the mid-1980s (Orfield and Ashkinaze, 1991).

Finally, post–World War II structural and technological changes in the economy, from a predominantly industrial and agricultural base to a high-technology and service base, have had devastating effects on the African American community. Northern industrial cities with large African American populations have suffered economic decline while the suburbs and the sunbelt cities have expanded their white-collar economies. The lack of fit between a largely unskilled African American labor market and the demands of a highly technical job market has resulted in high rates of unemployment, poverty, and family dysfunction, which have contributed to high levels of stress for African American youth and their families (Comer and Hill, 1985; Edelman, 1987; Wilson, 1987).

Cultural Attitudes, Values, and Norms

The literature has identified four major values of African American families, all of which can be understood as adaptive responses to their historical and social experiences in American society. These values are (1) the importance of religion and the church, (2) the importance of the extended family and kinship networks, (3) the importance of flexible family roles, and (4) the importance of education (Hines and Boyd-Franklin, 1996; Billingsley, 1968, 1992; Lewis and Looney, 1983; Cheatham and Stewart, 1990; Staples and Johnson, 1993).

Religion and the church. In the African American community, the church is often the central focus of social and civic activity

(Billingsley, 1992; Franklin, 1967; Lincoln and Mamiya, 1990). Most African Americans are Protestants and many participate in fundamentalist denominations (such as the Baptist Church, the Methodist Church, and the Church of God), which stress asceticism, tithing, and religious piety. In recent years the Black Muslims have made inroads in urban inner-city communities, while more liberal denominations have attracted upwardly mobile and professional African Americans. Even when African American families are not involved in a specific church, their religious heritage shapes their beliefs and values, and their views on marital relationships and divorce, abortion, adoption, childrearing practices, and so on. Awareness of a client's religious background will increase the clinician's understanding of attitudes and values that may affect treatment decisions. In addition, clinicians should identify the local African American ministers and view them as resources in helping clients to cope with problems.

Extended family and kinship networks. African Americans value their family ties and tend to maintain contact with a large network of relatives and fictive kin. This pattern is especially functional for low-income African American families, who exchange resources, services, and emotional support. Knowledge of this pattern is valuable for the clinician, who can often mobilize relatives to offer support to a troubled adolescent (Billingsley, 1992; Lewis and Looney, 1983; McAdoo, 1981; Stack, 1974; Staples and Mirande, 1980). It is not unusual for parents to send adolescents to live with other relatives in order to change their environment or to defuse a conflictual family situation.

Flexible family roles. Flexibility in family roles has always been an important aspect of African American family functioning, because most African American women have had to work in order to maintain an adequate standard of living for their families (McAdoo, 1981). Parents have divided their responsibilities less in terms of traditional gender-based roles and more in terms of household function. Traditional childrearing patterns also foster early independence in male and female children as well as less differentiation in roles and family tasks (Peters, 1981). While these patterns vary according to socioeconomic level and rural/urban residence, recent empirical studies generally support the descriptive accounts of role flexibility and non-gender-specific role functioning in

African American families (Allen, 1978; Staples and Mirande, 1980). These findings have obvious implications for the assessment of African American families, as well as for the interpretation of gender-related behaviors in male and female adolescents.

Education. African American families have historically valued hard work, education, and social mobility (Billingsley, 1992; Bowman and Howard, 1985; Franklin, 1967; Frazier, 1966; McAdoo and McAdoo, 1985). These values prompted the mass migrations from the rural agrarian south to the urban industrial north that offered greater educational and economic opportunities to African Americans. In spite of widespread discrimination and poverty, many African American families have sacrificed to send their children to college and prepare them for professional careers, often serving the African American community. Unfortunately, this impetus for higher education has slowed down in recent years due to several factors, including the social isolation of poor, inner-city African Americans who lack middle-class role models; the changing nature of the economy; and the government's declining commitment to affirmative action (Orfield and Ashkinaze, 1991; Wilson, 1996). These social changes have created a widening gap between middle-class African Americans, who are able to take advantage of educational opportunities, and poor African Americans, who are not even aware of these opportunities.

Mental Health Issues

There have been no large-scale epidemiological surveys of African American adolescent mental health problems, but there have been a few community surveys and clinical studies that have provided estimates of the incidence of psychological and behavioral disorders in this population group.

The incidence of depression among African American youth has been investigated by several researchers in a variety of school and community samples (Kaplan, Landa, Weinhold, and Shenker, 1984; Schoenbach and others, 1983; Gibbs, 1985b, 1986a). Rates of mild to moderate depression have ranged from 20 to 40 percent, while rates of severe depression have ranged from 5 to 15 percent in these nonclinical samples. Higher rates of depression have generally been found among males and low-income African American adolescents in these studies.

Eating disorders such as anorexia nervosa or bulimia are very rare among African American youth, with only sixteen cases reported in the clinical literature through 1985 (Pumariega, Edwards, and Mitchell, 1984; Robinson and Andersen, 1985). Primarily diagnosed as anorexia nervosa, these cases consisted of fourteen females and two males, but several were described as "atypical" in terms of their psychodynamics. Certain patterns characterized these cases, such as parental conflict and/or separation, conflicts around sexuality, underlying depression, and problems with autonomy.

While the prevalence of conduct disorders among African American adolescents is not known, it can be safely said that they have disproportionately high rates of conduct problems in school settings. African American teens are suspended or expelled from junior high and high schools more often than whites for fighting, extortion of money, verbal or physical abuse of teachers, vandalism, and truancy (Children's Defense Fund, 1985).

Psychiatric hospitalization rates of African American youth have traditionally been two to three times the rates for white youth (Myers, 1989). In a large-scale survey of public and private psychiatric facilities, Milazzo-Sayre and his colleagues (1986) found that while the rate of hospitalization had declined for all youth, it was still higher among nonwhites, and particularly for African American males. African Americans were more likely than whites to receive more severe diagnoses, such as affective disorders, schizophrenia, and personality disorders. Those African American males in public psychiatric institutions were six times more likely than whites to obtain a diagnosis of schizophrenia or other severe disorder.

Finally, suicide is increasing among African American adolescents and is now the third leading cause of death for African American youth ages fifteen to twenty-four. Between 1960 and 1992, the suicide rate for African American males in this age range more than quadrupled, from 4.1 to 17.3 per 100,000, while the rate for African American females nearly doubled, from 1.3 to 2.1 per 100,000 (U.S. Department of Health and Human Services, 1996). Although suicide rates are much lower than homicide rates for African American youth, they may be underestimated and many "undetermined deaths" may be misclassified as accidents due to the strong prohibition against suicide in the African American community (Warshauer and Monk, 1978; Shaffer and Fisher,

1981). Moreover, the symptoms of suicidal behavior in African American youth are often masked by extreme anger, acting out, and high-risk behaviors, making it more difficult for clinicians to assess suicidal intent. Thus it is essential for clinicians to recognize "depressive equivalents" and high-risk behaviors as potential clues to suicidal behavior in African American youth, and to conduct a suicide assessment whenever these symptoms are chronic or severe (Gibbs, 1988a; Weddle and McKenry, 1995).

Studies of the utilization of mental health facilities by African American college students indicate that these young people seek treatment for the same range of late adolescent problems as their white peers, including anxiety, depression, psychosomatic symptoms, interpersonal conflicts, sexual problems, and identity conflicts (Davis and Swartz, 1972; Gibbs, 1975). In addition, they are more likely than white students to express feelings of alienation, acculturation conflicts, academic anxieties, and feelings of victimization.

Psychosocial problems of African American youth are reflected in the statistics on social indicators, those conditions that cause social or legal difficulties for the youth and that usually have adverse consequences for the family and community, such as dropping out of school, juvenile delinquency, substance abuse, and unwed teenage pregnancy and parenthood. While the causal sequence is not clear, many of these youth experience anxiety, depression, and other emotional distress in connection with these problems (Gibbs, 1990, 1995).

School Dropout Rates

In 1994, dropout rates for African American youth ages eighteen to twenty-four had nearly reached parity with rates for white youth (15.5 percent versus 12.7 percent) (U.S. Bureau of the Census, 1996). Despite the overall improvement in school dropout rates among African American youth since 1960, the rates in many urban areas currently range from 40 to 60 percent, and some students leave school as early as seventh grade (Reed, 1988). Further, several surveys have found high rates of functional illiteracy, particularly among African American male adolescents (College Entrance Examination Board, 1985; Reed, 1988). Handicapped by educational deficiencies and lack of vocational training, inner-city African American youth have high unemployment rates and few opportunities for legitimate income.

Juvenile Delinquency

Official delinquency rates indicate that African American youth are more likely than white youth to be arrested for status offenses and index offenses. In 1960, African American youth accounted for 19.6 percent of all juvenile arrests, but that had increased to 28.1 percent in 1993 (U.S. Department of Justice, 1994). They were also more likely to be arrested for serious felony offenses than any other race-sex category. Although African American youth were more likely than white youth to be arrested, convicted, and incarcerated for the same category of offenses, a recent study concluded that there are no significant differences between African American and white youth in their rates of self-reported delinquency (Krisberg and others, 1986). Other researchers have concluded that the juvenile justice system discriminates against African American youth at several stages of the process (Hawkins and Jones, 1989; Walker, Spohn, and Delone, 1996).

African American juvenile delinquents also have higher rates than white youths of depression and of psychological and neurological symptoms that are often undetected and undiagnosed (Dembo, 1988; Gibbs, 1982; Lewis and Balla, 1976). As Dembo (1988) points out, the juvenile justice system is increasingly the channel for "handling" African American youth with behavioral disorders, while white youth with similar behaviors are more likely to be referred for treatment in the mental health system. The system of entry will obviously determine the nature and quality of the services offered, the assessment and diagnosis of the problem behaviors, and the effectiveness of the intervention used.

Substance Abuse

Community surveys of drug and alcohol use have consistently shown that relative to white youth, African American youth have lower rates of alcohol use and equal rates of marijuana use (National Institute of Drug Abuse, 1991; Benson and Donahue, 1989; Welte and Barnes, 1987). Rates of cocaine and heroin use, however, are generally reported to be higher among older African American youth than among whites (Brunswick, 1979). In large samples of junior high and high school students in New York and California, African American teenagers reported lower usage rates than whites of alcohol and drugs (Gibbs, 1985a; Kandel and others, 1977; Skager, 1986). An important limitation of these school-based surveys is that school dropouts are not included, probably resulting in an underestimation of drug use in this age cohort, because dropouts are more likely to be involved in deviant activities.

Drug use for many low-income African American youth is particularly problematic because it is often linked to a total lifestyle that includes delinquency and selling drugs (Brunswick and Messeri, 1986). Consequently, when these youth are referred for treatment, they are usually involuntary clients with multiple social, behavioral, and psychological problems, including low self-esteem, impulsivity, high levels of anger and hostility, psychosomatic symptoms, depression, and suicidal behaviors (Beschner and Friedman, 1986; Halikas, Darvish, and Rimmer, 1976; Lee, 1983).

Currently, young African American intravenous drug users who use unsterilized needles as well as those who engage in high-risk unprotected sex with homosexual or bisexual males face the threat of infection from the human immunodeficiency virus (HIV), which causes acquired immunodeficiency syndrome (AIDS). As of June 1996, non-Hispanic African American youth constituted 54.4 percent of the 5,366 children and adolescents under age twenty diagnosed with AIDS in the United States; 1,165 (11.8 percent) of these youth were adolescents between the ages of thirteen and nineteen (Centers for Disease Control and Prevention, 1996). Among the 4,474 youth under age twenty who have been diagnosed with an HIV-related infection, 2,809 (62.7 percent) are black. AIDS patients need counseling as well as long-term medical care to cope with their increasing disability and invariably fatal disease. Yet at this point there are inadequate services for counseling African American youth, their families, and their sexual partners about the chronic course of the disease, the behavioral and sexual changes necessary, and the prolonged grieving process (Honey, 1988; Mays and Cochran, 1987).

Teenage Pregnancy and Parenthood

Pregnancy is a major psychosocial problem for African American teenagers, particularly because it is often followed by a number of negative social and psychological sequelae (Rosenheim and Testa,

1992). In 1994, the birthrate for black adolescent females aged fifteen to nineteen was 104.5 per 1,000, compared to rates of 40.4 and 107.7 per 1,000 for white and Hispanic teenage females, respectively. About one out of ten African American young women aged fifteen to nineteen had a child, and they were 2.5 times more likely to give birth than their white same-age peers (Ventura, Clarke, and Mathews, 1996). In 1994, about 76 percent of all births to adolescent females occurred to unmarried mothers, with black females showing a rate of more than 90 percent of out-of-wedlock births among females aged fifteen to nineteen. African American teenage mothers had high rates of school dropout, welfare dependency, and unemployment (Children's Defense Fund, 1986b, 1986c). They were also more likely than girls who delayed their first pregnancy to experience health problems, psychological problems, and family problems (Rosenheim and Testa, 1992). Several studies have indicated that these teenage mothers need a range of comprehensive health, mental health, and educational-vocational services (Rosenheim and Testa, 1992; Murry, 1996). One of the major issues in counseling this group is that their own adolescent developmental needs are frequently in conflict with the needs of their infants and children.

It is interesting to note that statistics on African American youths' psychosocial problems are much more accessible than statistics on their psychological problems. This may reflect an actual difference between African American and white youth in their patterns of response to anxiety and stress, or it may reflect differential treatment and bias in their patterns of referral for evaluation; that is, African American youth are more likely to be referred through the social welfare and juvenile justice systems, and white youth are more likely to be referred through the mental health system (Dembo, 1988; Lewis and Balla, 1976; Myers and King, 1980).

Sociocultural Issues in Assessment

The assessment of African American youth will be discussed from three vantage points: (1) theoretical perspectives, (2) sociocultural issues, and (3) levels of assessment. First, the two theoretical perspectives that are useful in understanding the mental health issues of African American youth are the ego-oriented developmental theory of Erik Erikson (1950, 1959) and the ecological theory of Urie Bronfenbrenner (1979), as described in Chapter One. Both of these theories might predict differential outcomes for nonwhite and low-income youth, particularly because nonwhite youth are more likely than white and higher-income youth to experience greater socioeconomic deprivation, more prejudice and discrimination, and more restricted access to educational and vocational opportunities in American society. Thus Erikson (1959) suggests that teens growing up in these "disadvantaged" or minority families could develop "negative" identities and thus be at risk for dysfunctional or maladaptive behaviors.

Second, sociocultural factors must be considered in the assessment of all African American adolescents, particularly for those from socially segregated and economically disadvantaged families. A growing literature documents differences between African Americans and whites in definitions of mental health and mental disorders, help-seeking behaviors, symptomatology, distribution of psychiatric disorders, and response to treatment (Gardner, 1971; Griffith and Jones, 1978; Jones and Korchin, 1982; Neighbors, 1985; Ridley, 1984; Hall and Tucker, 1985).

Third, the four levels of assessment necessary to obtain a comprehensive picture of the African American adolescent are individual, family, school, and community. These levels are consistent with the dual individual and ecological theoretical perspective.

Individual Assessment

Erikson's (1959) view that African American adolescents may have greater difficulty in forming a positive identity because of negative societal feedback has been challenged by Chestang (1984), who distinguishes between "personal identity" and "racial identity" for African American youth, who have shown in a number of studies that they are able to separate their personal self-evaluations from the social evaluation of their racial identity (Cross, 1984; Foster and Perry, 1982; Rotheram-Borus and others, 1996; Spencer, 1982). Because the process of identity formation is intimately connected to the development of a self-concept and a sense of competence, the management of sexual and aggressive feelings, the establishment of autonomy from parental control, and the nature of educational aspirations, the clinician should evaluate these areas of adjustment in African American adolescents.

Attitudes toward self. African American children and adolescents develop their self-concept and self-esteem from the reflected appraisals of parents, relatives, and peers in their own ethnic communities (Spencer, 1982). Prior to the 1970s, many clinical and empirical studies found that African American youth had negative self-concepts and low self-esteem (Clark and Clark, 1940; Goodman, 1964). However, more recent studies of nonclinical samples of African American youth have consistently found that their self-concepts and self-esteem are as positive as or more positive than comparative samples of whites (Gibbs, 1985a; Powell, 1985; Rosenberg and Simmons, 1971; Smith, 1982; Spencer, 1982; Taylor, 1976). Contrary to predictions, African Americans in segregated school settings frequently express higher levels of self-esteem than African Americans in integrated settings (Nobles, 1973; Powell, 1985).

Clinicians are more likely to find evidence of negative self-concepts and low levels of self-esteem among African American youth referred for behavioral or psychological problems. These youth may develop negative feelings about themselves because of their physical appearance, their atypical family structures, their lack of competence in culturally valued skills, or their feelings of racial victimization (Franklin, 1982; Grier and Cobbs, 1968; Mayo, 1974). In assessing an African American adolescent's self-concept or self-esteem, the clinician should be cognizant of the significant sources of esteem for these youth, of parental and peer reinforcement, and of environmental factors. For example, studies indicate that athletic ability is a major source of esteem for African American male adolescents, while physical attractiveness and social skills are very important assets for African American females (Cauce, 1986; Mancini, 1980). Other abilities that are valued by both sexes are verbal skills (such as "rapping"), assertiveness, and fashionable dressing (such as "styling") (Jenkins, 1982; Ladner, 1971; Mancini, 1980; Schulz, 1969).

Intellectual achievement is valued in some settings while in other settings it is demeaned. High-achieving students in predominantly African American high schools are often ridiculed as "brainiacs" and accused of acting "like white folks" (Fordham and Ogbu, 1986). Boys who are physically small and girls who are precociously mature may become the targets of sarcasm and humor, sometimes causing them to develop overcompensatory behaviors. Social distinctions may be made on the basis of skin color or socioeconomic status, which can have damaging effects on the adolescent's self-concept and self-esteem, particularly for African American females (Foster and Perry, 1982; Heiss and Owens, 1976). Thus, an assessment of African American adolescent self-esteem must take into account the adolescent's subjective evaluation of assets and liabilities; the reflected appraisal of parents, peers, and significant others in the social environment; and whether the environment is a consonant or dissonant context, that is, whether the adolescent is in a majority or minority social context (Rosenberg, 1979).

Affect. African American adolescents are characteristically described as expressive, lively, and extraverted (Gibbs, 1985a; Ladner, 1971; Majors and Billson, 1992; Robinson and Ward, 1991). Yet in treatment situations they often appear angry and hostile or sullen and withdrawn (Franklin, 1982; Ridley, 1984). Angry, hostile teenagers may express a great deal of negative affect and appear to be physically intimidating, especially older youth who are referred for delinquent behaviors and substance abuse. Outwardly uncommunicative and uncooperative, the unresponsive demeanor of these youth often masks underlying depression over family problems, school failure, interpersonal rejection, or self-destructive behaviors (Franklin, 1982; Gibbs, 1981, 1982).

Speech and language. African American adolescents tend to have good verbal skills, but those reared in African American neighborhoods often speak a variety of "Black English" that may be unfamiliar to non–African American clinicians (Kochman, 1972; Labov, 1972; Smitherman, 1991). Because many youth are able to switch back and forth from Black English to Standard English, the clinician can usually communicate effectively by responding with flexibility and a willingness to clarify unfamiliar terms (Canino and Spurlock, 1994). Clinicians should also be aware that language serves many symbolic functions for African American youth, who utilize it as a means of artistic expression (as in "rapping") as well as a means of verbal assault (as in "playing the dozens") (Kochman, 1972; Labov, 1972; Mancini, 1980). Language can also be a source of conflict in schools and in the workplace, placing African American youth at a competitive disadvantage in both settings (Ogbu, 1985).

Interpersonal relations. The quality and intensity of relationships among African American adolescents must be evaluated in the context of their social and cultural environment. Same-sex peer groups have very close bonds with strong pressures to conform to group norms, particularly in situations where the peer group or gang also serves the functions of social identity and mutual protection (Mancini, 1980; Schulz, 1969). In areas with high rates of single-parent families and few community resources, peer group bonds among females function as social support networks (Belle, 1982; Ladner, 1971; Stack, 1974). However, these intense bonds can also cause intense rivalries and conflicts, reduce individual autonomy, and foster involvement in antisocial or self-destructive activities. For example, studies have found that high involvement of low-income African American teenagers in certain types of peer networks was inversely related to academic achievement and premarital sexual activity (Felner, Aber, Primavera, and Cauce, 1985). Moreover, the inner-city African American adolescent who is not a member of a cohesive peer group or gang is often excluded from activities, labeled negatively, and sometimes physically harassed (Schulz, 1969; Viadero, 1988; Way, 1996).

Sexuality. Both the expression of sexuality and sexual relationships are major issues for African American adolescents. They tend to initiate sexual activity about one year earlier, on the average, than white adolescents, and they are less well-informed about contraception, less positive about its use, and less effective in using it than whites (Chilman, 1983; Children's Defense Fund, 1986c; Gibbs, 1986b). Consequently, African American teenage females have higher rates of unintended pregnancy and higher birthrates than white females (Rosenheim and Testa, 1992). Attempts to cope with teenage parenthood often result in psychological problems for both males and females, including depression, anxiety, anger, psychosomatic symptoms, and feelings of helplessness (Chilman, 1983; Colletta, Hadler, and Gregg, 1981; Hendricks, 1980; Robinson, 1988). Because African American teenage females are often referred for issues of sexuality, pregnancy, and parenting, clinicians should be familiar with their cultural attitudes about premarital sexual activity, contraception, childbearing, and childrearing, and sensitive to the values they attach to these behaviors and the meaning of these behaviors in their lives (Anderson, 1995; Dash, 1989; Dougherty, 1978; Ladner, 1971).

Anxiety and patterns of defense. It is important to assess the levels of anxiety in African American youth, the ways in which it is expressed, and the situations in which it is most likely to occur. Anxiety may be triggered for African American youth by academic problems, family conflict, community violence, interpersonal and sexual relationships, or employment and career issues, so it is important for the clinician to assess the impact of all of these factors on the adolescent client. High levels of anxiety may not be evident in African American adolescents under direct observation, partly because culturally acceptable childrearing patterns, particularly in low-income African American families, often reinforce the externalization of anxiety (Franklin, 1982; Myers, 1989). Thus anxiety may be denied, projected, or displaced. Hyperactivity, acting out, and aggression in younger adolescents may be a clue to anxiety, while delinquent activity, substance abuse, and sexual promiscuity may be responses to underlying anxiety or depression in older adolescents (Franklin, 1982; Gibbs, 1982). Some clinical studies of African American college students suggest that they may have fairly high rates of somatic symptoms, so clinicians should be alert to signs of physical distress and psychosomatic complaints as possible evidence of anxiety (Davis and Swartz, 1972; Gibbs, 1974).

Coping and adaptive behaviors. African American adolescents have developed a number of coping skills and adaptive behaviors to compensate for their marginal minority status in this society. Young African American males have learned that athletic ability is one route to mobility, so many of them develop skills in a competitive sport (especially basketball, baseball, and track) that requires discipline, physical coordination, and motivation. Reinforced for social and interpersonal skills, young African American females may become sexually active as a route to premature parenthood, often foreclosing their educational and career opportunities (Apfel and Seitz, 1996; Gibbs, 1986b; Murry, 1996). In response to the uncertainties of their environment, many inner-city African American youth have developed a patterned set of behaviors known as "playing it cool" or "getting over." Researchers have identified a number of different coping styles that have enabled these youth to adapt to the realities of ghetto life but that may be maladaptive for success in mainstream society (Majors and Billson, 1992; Myers, 1989; Schulz, 1969). Nonetheless, they have consistently demonstrated much resilience, creativity, and persistence in the face of economic deprivation, social disorganization, and limited community resources, all of which reduce their opportunities and restrict their mobility.

The Family System

An assessment of the family environment of the African American adolescent should focus on the following factors: structure and roles of the family, socioeconomic status and living arrangements, degree of integration/acculturation, support system, communication patterns, and help-seeking patterns (Boyd-Franklin, 1989; Gwyn and Kilpatrick, 1981).

Family structure and roles. It will be helpful to the clinician to know whether the family is an intact nuclear family, a single-parent family with or without other adults in the household, or an extended family. Family structure not only helps to shape the psychosocial identity and social experiences of adolescents, but it also may place constraints on the development of their social roles (Cauce and others, 1996). For example, teenagers in single-parent families are often given more household and child-care responsibilities than those in two-parent families, creating potential detrimental effects on their health and school achievement. Teenagers living in extended families with several adult caretakers (such as mothers, grandmothers, and aunts) may experience conflicts over discipline and autonomy because of unclear lines of parental authority. In their study of African American adolescents' perceptions of family climate, Dancy and Handal (1984) found that those teenagers who perceived high levels of conflict in their families reported more psychological symptoms than those who perceived low levels of conflict.

Socioeconomic status and living arrangements. Occupational status and income of the parent or parents are important indicators of an adolescent's socioeconomic status, material resources, and lifestyle. Living arrangements should also be investigated to determine the size of the household, the sleeping arrangements, and the adolescent's household responsibilities. Many low-income African American youth live in crowded households with very little privacy and inadequate sleeping and study facilities, and many are exposed to negative role models, all of which have negative consequences for their physical and mental health.

Degree of integration and acculturation. The extent to which the family is integrated into society and has assimilated the values and the norms of the mainstream culture is also relevant to treatment of African American youth. Adolescents with varying levels of exposure to integrated schools and neighborhoods may present different patterns of symptomatology, problem behaviors, and adaptation to the community (Gibbs, 1974, 1986a; Powell, 1985).

Social support systems. The clinician should assess the wider kinship network and social support network of the adolescent's family. As noted earlier, church affiliation is an important source of social support for many African American families. Further, many African American families are involved in neighborhood associations, civic organizations, and fraternal lodges that can be valuable sources of support. Urban African American families also sometimes send troubled teenagers to live temporarily with relatives in more rural areas, so that northern-southern family ties are continually reinforced through mutual assistance (McAdoo, 1981; Stack, 1974).

Communication patterns. Interaction in African American families also varies by socioeconomic status and level of acculturation. There is some ethnographic evidence that in low-income families parent-child communication tends to be authoritarian, critical, unidirectional, and confrontational (Bartz and Levine, 1978; Cahill, 1966; Peters, 1981). African American parents and siblings sometimes engage in mutual teasing, sarcasm, and denigrating comments (Cauce and others, 1996; Ward, 1996). Overt expressions of affection, nurturance, support, and praise are not frequent in these families, and self-deprecating humor may be used as a protective mechanism to preserve one's self-esteem. Patterns of communication in middle-class families are more likely than in low-income families to be bidirectional, authoritative, and mutually supportive (Bartz and Levine, 1978; Durrett, O'Bryant, and Pennebaker, 1975; Peters, 1981).

Help-seeking patterns. African American families generally do not voluntarily seek psychiatric treatment for the emotional or behavioral problems of their children, who are more likely to be referred by schools, the juvenile court, and the social welfare system (Boyd-Franklin, 1989; Myers, 1989). Although this varies by socioeconomic status and level of acculturation, African American families are more likely to seek counseling initially from family doctors, ministers, and friends or relatives than from mental health professionals (Neighbors, 1985). Thus, by the time African American youth are referred for treatment, their symptoms may be more severe and the intervention required may be more intensive.

School Assessment

The school as an instrument of education and socialization has long been a source of conflict and controversy for African American youth (Fordham and Ogbu, 1986; McAdoo and McAdoo, 1985). That these youth are frequently referred for school-related academic or behavioral problems is not surprising, but the clinician's task is to disentangle the client's presenting problems from factors in the school environment that may have substantially contributed to or exacerbated those problems.

School environment. The milieu of the school can be a safe, orderly setting that facilitates learning and personal growth, or it can be a violent, chaotic setting that intimidates students and teachers and undermines both learning and social development. African American students may respond to these school environments with apathy and alienation, anger and hostility, or fear and anxiety, or by acting out and identifying with the antisocial elements in the school.

Educational program. African American students are overrepresented in special education programs and nonacademic tracks. Frequently mislabeled in elementary school, many African American adolescents either drop out or are "pushed out" of high school after experiencing years of academic failure or low achievement, low teacher expectations, high rates of suspension, and chaotic school environments (Committee for Economic Development, 1987; Reed, 1988; Rivers and others, 1975). Clinicians who suspect that students are performing below their abilities should use a culturally sensitive measure, such as the System of Multicultural Pluralistic Assessment battery, to assess their ability levels (Mercer, 1975; Samuda, 1975; Snowden and Todman, 1982). Should the clinician discover a discrepancy between the client's potential ability and the educational program, a recommendation for a more appropriate academic placement could be the most effective intervention.

Peer relationships. Attitudes and behaviors of peers are very influential in shaping the school experiences of African American adolescents (Cauce, Felner, and Primavera, 1982; Gibbs, 1985a; Ogbu, 1985; Way, 1996). Where the prevailing norms are anti-intellectual and college is not viewed as a realistic option, African American teenagers have an especially difficult time if they are viewed as high achievers (Fordham and Ogbu, 1986; Hare, 1988). Similarly, in many inner-city neighborhoods there are permissive attitudes toward early involvement in sexual activity and experimentation with drugs (Anderson, 1995; Brown, 1985; Hare, 1988; Murry, 1996). When students resist pressures to conform to these norms, they may be socially isolated and ridiculed. In these situations, clinicians should evaluate the students' psychological distress and ability to cope with the peer pressures, as well as the environmental supports or modifications necessary to reinforce their proactive behaviors.

Community Assessment

When African American children reach adolescence and venture beyond their immediate social environment, they may have their first experiences with racial discrimination. If they enter an integrated high school, seek a part-time job, or participate in community youth groups or athletic teams, African American teenagers may begin to sense racism and barriers to their opportunities and aspirations (Hare, 1988). Further, early exposure to unemployment, drugs, and illegal activities in inner-city communities often fosters cynicism, anger, and antisocial attitudes in these youth (Gibbs, 1984, 1988a; Wilson, 1987). In response to these environmental realities, African American youth often develop a sense of social isolation and hopelessness about their life chances, which increases their vulnerability to involvement in self-destructive activities such as drug abuse, unwed teenage pregnancy, suicide, and homicide (Gibbs, 1984, 1988a; Hare, 1988).

Clinicians who evaluate youth referred for antisocial or self-destructive behavior need to assess these adolescents' underlying feelings of alienation, depression, and rage in order to recommend appropriate treatment interventions (Franklin, 1982; Grier and Cobbs, 1968).

Intervention and Treatment

In this section, four modalities of treatment for African American adolescents are examined: individual, family, group, and crisis intervention.

Individual Treatment

Short-term ego-oriented psychotherapy is the model of individual treatment recommended for African American adolescents with nonpsychotic disorders who are usually seen in outpatient settings. As described by Norman (1980), this approach is appropriate for this group because it focuses on problem solving, strengthens coping skills, and is time-limited. This approach is also useful for a wide range of adolescent problems, ranging from anxiety and depression to identity conflicts and acting out behaviors.

Entry into Treatment

In the African American adolescent's initial contacts with the therapist, he will be judging the therapist's affect and behaviors while he is also being evaluated. Thus it is important for the therapist to project warmth, genuineness, and positive regard for the client, being especially attentive to cues that the client is testing the therapist for signs of prejudice, superiority, disapproval, and rejection (Gibbs, 1985c; Ridley, 1984). Therapists should be aware that African American youth are sensitive to how they are addressed (avoid overfamiliarity and excessive patronizing), how they are engaged in conversation (avoid using ethnic slang and an overly simplistic vocabulary), how the therapist's office is furnished (they appreciate attractive decor even if they live in projects), how the therapist is dressed (they believe that clothes reflect social status), and how respectful the therapist is toward them (do not keep them waiting interminably and do not answer a string of phone calls during their sessions) (Franklin, 1982). Clients will be more favorably disposed toward clinicians who demonstrate interpersonal competence rather than instrumental competence in the first sessions (Gibbs, 1985c).

African American adolescents may initially approach treatment with a great deal of misapprehension, suspicion, and anxiety due to lack of knowledge or prior treatment experience. The therapist can minimize the client's anxiety by spending a few minutes at the beginning of the first session in informal conversation, followed by a brief description of the treatment process through a "role induction" technique (Frank and others, 1978) or a patient-orientation program (Acosta, Yamamoto, and Evans, 1982). The goal is to demystify the therapeutic process for these clients and to be certain that they fully understand the "talking cure" before treatment proceeds.

Like all adolescents, African American youth are rarely psychologically sophisticated and generally have trouble distancing themselves from their own behaviors; that is, their observing egos are much less developed than their experiencing egos. They also tend to be less comfortable with self-disclosure than white adolescents, partly reflecting the African American cultural pattern of masking their true feelings and concerns from whites and authority figures (Jenkins, 1982; Pinderhughes, 1973; Ridley, 1984). Moreover, African American adolescents often have a history of conflict with authority figures, so they may appear unusually resistant, sullen, or hostile in the early sessions, especially because most of them have been referred by schools or social agencies.

To overcome this initial resistance and to establish rapport, the clinician needs to be fairly active, outgoing, directive, and open, encouraging adolescents to discuss their anger and ambivalent feelings about being referred for treatment, their fears about being labeled crazy by their peers, and their reluctance to reveal their true feelings and concerns to a stranger. By showing sensitivity to these issues and understanding of the youth's cultural context, the therapist can reassure the client that his or her concerns about treatment are fairly common among teenagers. At this point the therapist should reiterate the role of confidentiality in treatment and its specific limitations with minors and involuntary clients, so that these youth can clarify any concerns about freely discussing their problems. The following case provides an example of these issues in the initial phase of treatment.

Wanda, a fourteen-year-old African American female, was referred by her junior high school counselor because of her frequent somatic symptoms, her immature behaviors, and her problems in getting along with her peers. During her first session, Wanda seemed very anxious and fearful and responded very reluctantly when asked about her concerns. At the beginning of the second session, she blurted out that she didn't "want to be sent away to a special school." The therapist learned that Wanda's older brother had been abruptly institutionalized several years earlier for mental retardation when her mother remarried. Whenever her stepfather became angry with her, he would threaten to send her to join her brother. To please her very strict parents, Wanda had become excessively compliant at home, but she had frequent nightmares and physical symptoms. At school she was not able to contain her anxiety, so she frequently did inappropriate things to get attention from her teachers and peers. After the therapist clarified the referral and explained her role and her interest in helping Wanda, the teenager was able to feel more comfortable, to express her fears about being abandoned by her parents, and to set some short-term goals about improving her communication with her parents and reducing the frequency of her impulsive and inappropriate behaviors in the school setting.

Establishing the Working Alliance

To establish a working alliance with the African American adolescent, the clinician should proceed cautiously and anticipate a great deal of "testing" behavior, which may include wearing hats and sunglasses in sessions, refusing to remove heavy coats and jackets, using obscene or provocative language, coming late for appointments, terminating the session prematurely, being unresponsive, and acting hostile and rebellious. These behaviors will quickly diminish and usually disappear as the teenager becomes more comfortable in the relationship.

During this phase of treatment, the adolescent will expend a great deal of energy in challenging the therapist's authority and ability to maintain control of the sessions (see, for example, Franklin, 1982). The therapist must avoid being drawn into a power struggle with the client, while at the same time establishing structure and setting firm limits for the sessions. Male adolescent clients may try to intimidate the therapist with aggressive behaviors and sarcastic, street-style verbal responses, while adolescent females may act in a seductive or sullen manner. Franklin (1982) has described three types of urban African American adolescent clients as "reluctant talkers," who are difficult to engage in conversation, "babblers," who control sessions by compulsively talking about superficial issues, and "impressers," who brag about antisocial activities in an attempt to shock the therapist. Therapists should recognize some of these behaviors as "manipulative," but should avoid premature interpretations that will threaten the adolescent's fragile sense of self-esteem and weak defense mechanisms.

Therapists should also understand that many African American adolescents have adopted a demeanor of being "cool" and a repertoire of street-smart behaviors in order to survive in an environment that is stressful, frequently chaotic, and unpredictable (Majors and Billson, 1992). To facilitate rapport in the treatment relationship, clinicians should be familiar with the inner-city adolescent culture, with some of the slang, and with some of the characteristic behaviors. This does not imply that clinicians should use the language or engage in the behaviors, which would be condescending or patronizing to the client. Clinicians can also inquire about unfamiliar language or behaviors in order to determine whether these patterns are cultural or idiosyncratic in origin.

Humor is an important tool in forming a working alliance with the African American adolescent. African American culture has a highly developed oral tradition, in which humor has always played a prominent role, as exemplified in many contemporary soul and rock songs, "rapping," and routines of African American comedians (Kochman, 1972; Labov, 1972). Humor can be employed to foster insight in a client who might not be responsive to dynamic interpretations of his underlying conflict but who can see the irony of his self-defeating behaviors.

The following case provides an example of therapeutic strategies to facilitate a working alliance with an African American adolescent.

John, a sixteen-year-old high school sophomore, was referred by his probation officer for excessive truancy, failing grades, and constant conflict with his mother. Born out of wedlock to a teenage mother, John had a two-year history of minor delinquency and was suspected of drug use. He had begun to act out shortly after the death of his grandmother, who had actually reared him while his mother worked in a nearby city. John was initially hostile and rude to the therapist, clearly communicating that he was there against his will and did not intend to cooperate. In addition to coming late, he hummed popular songs, leafed through magazines, frequently said he was wasting his time, and answered questions in a sarcastic and condescending manner. After several un-productive sessions, the therapist learned that John had a collection of classic rock and roll records, which he had enjoyed listening to with his grandmother. He was encouraged to talk about this collection, which led to lively discussions about his interest in music and his aspirations to be a disc jockey. After his ini-tial resistance was overcome through limit setting on his disruptive behaviors and consistent reinforcement of his positive responses, the therapist was able to explore his unresolved feelings of grief over the loss of his grandmother, who had been very supportive of his school work and interests. The working al-liance was further strengthened when the therapist consulted with John's school counselor about developing a work-study plan that would enable him to work part-time at a radio station while taking courses more closely related to his vocational interests.

Issues in Individual Treatment

Clinical treatment of African American adolescents must recognize the impact of the social and political environment on these youth, as well as the culturally patterned coping strategies and defensive be-haviors that they have developed in response to their chronic levels of environmental stress (Franklin, 1982; Myers, 1989; Paster, 1985).

Once the working alliance has been established, the clinician must remain continuously sensitive and alert to the interaction of the intrapsychic, interpersonal, and environmental aspects of the problem. The clinician should encourage clients to describe their problems or issues as they view them, to explore the subjective ef-fects of the problems and the impact of their behaviors on others, and to identify specific ways to alleviate the symptoms and/or ame-liorate the problems. The problem-solving strategies should be rea-sonable and achievable within each adolescent's social context. The following cases provide examples of how these factors inter-act with each other and influence therapeutic interventions with black adolescents. These three cases also illustrate issues frequently presented by these clients: delinquent behavior, sexual problems, and aggressive behavior.

Bobby, a sixteen-year-old high school dropout, was referred by his probation officer while he was living in a group home. Bobby had been involved with the juvenile court system since the age of fourteen, when he was first arrested with two older boys for burglarizing houses in his neighborhood. In treatment Bobby was very street-wise, manipulative, and defensive, avoiding discussion of his chaotic family and his failures in a succession of schools. When the clinician learned that Bobby was a natural leader in the group home, she was able to support his efforts to obtain some athletic equipment and games for the residents. As he gained more confidence by organizing activities in the home, he became less defensive and was able to talk about his feelings of never having nice things and never being able to depend on his parents for anything. He had been recruited into a neighborhood gang at the age of thirteen and they had become his substitute family. The male clinician provided him with a model of warmth, acceptance, and consistency, as well as providing an expectable environment and setting limits on his manipulative behavior. A few weeks after the therapist confronted Bobby on the discrepancy between his obvious ability and his school failures, Bobby announced that he was going to go back to school "just to show these teachers and my parents that they were all wrong about me. I ain't dumb, I just didn't feel like working too hard." By challenging Bobby's negative self-image and supporting his competent behaviors, the clinician was able to help Bobby raise his self-esteem and his educational aspirations.

Juanita, a fifteen-year-old high school sophomore, was referred by her parents because she had recently become very depressed and withdrawn and had seemed to lose interest in everything. Juanita was overweight and very mature looking, but she seemed listless, slightly sullen, and unmotivated for treatment. In exploring the reasons for Juanita's recent mood change, the therapist noted that she was very uncomfortable discussing the topics of boys and social life, but she became more animated when she talked about one special girlfriend. Through careful probing, her confused feelings about this relationship emerged. After the therapist spent one session generally discussing the importance of having a "best friend" and normalizing her feelings, Juanita revealed that she was "turned off" from boys after a party where she had smoked some marijuana and two boys had fondled her, then later bragged about it to their friends. She had felt very ashamed but was grateful to her girlfriend, who was supportive. Following this session, Juanita formed a very positive relationship with the therapist, whose warmth and empathy contrasted with her mother's punitive and critical manner.

Andrew was a nineteen-year-old sophomore in a private "elite" college. He was referred to the counseling center for assaulting a white male student in his dormitory. After initially acting very suspicious and hostile toward the female therapist, he eventually formed a good working alliance with her, facilitated by a positive transference that was not interpreted. Andrew reported that he had attacked the student after a series of incidents in which several white students had made fun of his southern accent, his Afro haircut, and his clothes, all of which he interpreted as racist comments. The short-term treatment focused on helping Andrew to express his feelings about being a "token" African American who was always under a microscope, his doubts about his ability to achieve in the highly competitive environment, and his anger about being rejected by a white girlfriend. His self-esteem and feelings of competence were enhanced by encouraging him to identify the talents and skills that had gained him admission to college, and to review his actual college performance, which was above average. In addition, his ambivalence toward socializing with other African American students was explored and he was able to reevaluate and reframe his social options. Finally, the therapist helped Andrew to recognize those situations that particularly triggered his rather explosive temper, and to develop more socially acceptable ways of channeling his anger.

Family Treatment

Family treatment, increasingly viewed as an important modality for African American adolescents, has been described by several authors (Foley, 1975; Harris and Balgopal, 1980; Boyd-Franklin, 1989; Pinderhughes, 1982; Sager, Brayboy, and Waxenberg, 1970). Because many teenagers are struggling to separate from their families and to function autonomously, the clinician must make a careful assessment of the advantages and disadvantages of family therapy for a given client. It can be especially appropriate for pregnant teenagers or for those who are delinquent or predelinquent, depressed and suicidal, or substance abusers—cases in which the self-destructive behaviors may be symptomatic of a dysfunctional family system, a scapegoated teenager, or a breakdown in family communication. It is especially important to assess the family's involvement with all the systems impacting on its social, economic, political, and cultural well-being (Boyd-Franklin, 1989).

An eclectic blend of structural and strategic techniques is useful for African American families. In such techniques, attention is focused both on restructuring family roles and modifying family communication patterns (Hines and Boyd-Franklin, 1996; Minuchin and others, 1967). Frequently parents have singled out one child to bear the brunt of their own frustrations and feelings of victimization, scapegoating the adolescent by projecting all of their own anxieties and displacing their anger toward society on this particular child. The adolescent in turn has responded by acting out the negative impulses in a way that both reinforces his unworthiness in the family and confirms his negative identity in the community.

> Debbie, a pregnant sixteen-year-old school dropout, was referred by a counselor at her alternative high school because of depression. Debbie, who had a good academic record, had been pressured into a sexual relationship by her older boyfriend, who had dropped her soon after she discovered her pregnancy. Against her parents' wishes, she had decided to have the baby and now felt she didn't have any emotional support. Debbie's parents were an upwardly mobile working-class couple who wanted her to go to college, and they were quite angry about her "lower-class behavior." Family treatment, which was recommended after Debbie's evaluation, focused on helping Debbie and her parents to express their mutual feelings of anger, disappointment, and shame over her pregnancy, to explore alternative options for the baby, and to reevaluate Debbie's educational and vocational goals. After her parents recognized that Debbie's pregnancy was partly a response to their rigid rules and excessive expectations, their anger dissipated and they were able to show her more positive concern and support. When Debbie understood that her academic success was symbolic of upward mobility to her hard-working but poorly educated parents, she actively engaged with them to make plans to obtain child care while she returned to her regular high school and pursued her plans to attend a local community college.

Group Treatment

Group treatment is a popular modality for adolescents both in outpatient settings and residential treatment. There are some special factors to consider in forming groups for African American adolescents: whether the group should be mixed by gender, by race, and by social class; whether the therapists should also be mixed by gender and race; and whether the group members should be selected by diagnostic category or balanced to reflect a diverse range of problems.

Psychoeducational groups are especially appropriate for delinquents, school dropouts, and other troubled African American youth who need a comprehensive treatment program that includes counseling, remedial education, and vocational training (Franklin, 1982; MacLennan and Felsenfeld, 1968). Such groups are an integral part of many alternative high schools and residential treatment centers; they are also a core element in the "street academies" pioneered by the National Urban League in the 1970s (National Urban League, 1990).

Group leaders should foster a sense of cohesiveness and support in addressing the similar problems of the group members, encourage the development of appropriate problem-solving skills to replace acting-out and self-destructive behaviors, and promote an identification with constructive role models. Preferably, African American males with sexual identity problems, impulse disorders, or acting-out problems should be assigned to groups with African American male therapists who can be positive role models and will not be intimidated by aggressive or seductive behaviors. African American females can also benefit from relating to an African American female clinician who can offer an model for identification other than teenage motherhood as a route to adulthood.

Crisis Intervention

Crisis intervention is a modality that is particularly appropriate for adolescents who cannot control their violent impulses, who suffer toxic effects from alcohol or drug abuse, who are physically or sexually abused, who are extremely depressed or suicidal, and who have psychotic symptoms (Miller, 1980; Landau-Stanton and Stanton, 1985).

African American teenagers who have experienced a severe trauma or who have decompensated due to drugs or alcohol may present with extreme anxiety and paranoid symptomatology. As Ridley (1984) points out, many African American patients have a degree of "healthy cultural paranoia" due to their marginal status in society, yet this paranoid outlook has a tendency to become more pronounced under stress. Thus African American patients in crisis situations may appear very fearful and suspicious of the clinical staff, withhold pertinent information, engage in verbally abusive and threatening behaviors, and sometimes refuse medication or treatment. For those African American youth who are severely depressed and/or suicidal, the hospital emergency room may be a very frightening experience.

Sexual abuse and sexual exploitation of African American adolescents will probably increase as their ranks increase in the homeless population. As more African American youth become addicted to crack cocaine, there will be an increased number of drug overdoses and more victims of drug-related violence (Brunswick, 1988). It is important for emergency room doctors to refer these youth for follow-up counseling to help them to deal with their feelings of anger, shame, low self-esteem, worthlessness, helplessness, and despair.

In crisis intervention with African American youth, the clinician's task is not only to allay the immediate symptoms of distress and restore the client's ability to function, but also to assess the family environment and social support system available to the client when he or she returns home. Effective treatment will often require the clinician to intervene in a number of systems that impinge on the lives of African American adolescents, including the family, the school, the workplace, the juvenile justice system, and the social welfare system.

The following case illustrates a comprehensive approach to crisis intervention for an older female adolescent.

Mona, an eighteen-year-old high school dropout, was brought to the emergency room by her boyfriend after a suicide attempt. Mona had taken an overdose of sleeping pills, but she was conscious and she recovered after emergency treatment. She was admitted to the hospital on a forty-eight-hour hold for evaluation and follow-up. Mona had been very depressed for several weeks due to a number of traumatic events. First, she had a miscarriage after being beaten by her boyfriend, then she lost her job as a grocery clerk, and then her boyfriend threatened to leave her; so she felt that her life was hopeless and she could no longer cope with all her losses. The team of clinicians who evaluated her developed a plan that included four major aspects: (1) she was referred for outpatient counseling to deal with her grief over losing the baby; (2) she was referred for vocational counseling to discuss job training programs; (3) she was referred to a social service agency for temporary financial assistance; and (4) she and her boyfriend were encouraged to discuss the problems in their relationship and her boyfriend made a commitment to stay with her until the immediate crisis was resolved.

Crisis intervention obviously requires rapid assessment skills, sensitivity to the client's social and psychological problems, and knowledge of community resources that are accessible and affordable for African American clients.

Summary and Conclusions

The psychological and psychosocial problems of African American adolescents and youth have been described in this chapter. It is clear that African American youth are more likely to be identified for psychosocial than for psychological problems, although there is obviously a close relationship between these two types of presenting problems. Since African American youth are more likely than white youth to be identified through the juvenile justice system, they are also less likely to undergo a thorough psychological assessment, less likely to receive a psychiatric diagnosis, less likely to obtain therapeutic treatment, and more likely to experience long-term psychological impairments and behavioral and social deficits or dysfunctions.

The multiple risk factors for African American youth have been described, as well as the impact of social and cultural experiences on the values, norms, and behaviors of these young people. Knowledge of these factors will enable clinicians to understand the sociocultural influences on these youths' attitudes and beliefs about mental health and on their symptomatology, patterns of defense and coping strategies, help-seeking patterns, utilization of services, and responsiveness to therapeutic treatment.

Phases of the treatment process were discussed with a focus on the initial phase, the development of the working alliance, and examples of common issues in treatment of African American adolescents. Finally, four modalities of treatment of African American youth were described: individual, family, group, and crisis intervention.

In summary, the psychological and psychosocial problems of African American adolescents in America have increased rather than decreased in the past twenty-five years. These problems have been exacerbated by poverty, discrimination, economic dislocation, and social changes that have had disproportionate effects on the African American community. Many of these problems would be reduced or eliminated if there were a coordinated effort of federal, state, and local governments to develop comprehensive and humane social and economic policies to strengthen vulnerable families and provide adequate health and social services for all children and youth. In the absence of such policies and programs, African American youth will continue to need a wide range of social and mental health services to address their psychological and behavioral problems in a social environment that is far less than optimal for their psychosocial development.

References

Acosta, F. X., Yamamoto, J., and Evans, L. A. *Effective Psychotherapy for Low-Income and Minority Patients.* New York: Plenum, 1982.

Allen, W. R. "Black Family Research in the United States: A Review, Assessment and Extension." *Journal of Comparative Family Studies,* 1978, *9,* 167–189.

Anderson, E. "Sex Codes and Family Life Among Poor Inner-City Youths." In R. L. Taylor (ed.), *African-American Youth: Their Social and Economic Status in the United States.* New York: Praeger, 1995.

Apfel, N., and Seitz, V. "African American Adolescent Mothers, Their Families, and Their Daughters: A Longitudinal Perspective Over Twelve Years." In B. J. Leadbetter and N. Way (eds.), *Urban Girls: Resisting Stereotypes, Creating Identities.* New York: New York University Press, 1996.

Bartz, K. W., and Levine, E. S. "Childrearing by Black Parents: A Description and Comparison to Anglo and Chicano Parents." *Journal of Marriage and the Family,* 1978, *40,* 709–719.

Belle, D. (ed.). *Lives in Stress: Women and Depression.* Thousand Oaks, Calif.: Sage, 1982.

Benson, P. L., and Donahue, M. J. "Ten-Year Trends in At-Risk Behaviors: A National Study of Black Adolescents." *Journal of Adolescent Research,* 1989, *4,* 125–139.

Beschner, G., and Friedman, A. (eds.). *Teen Drug Use.* San Francisco: New Lexington Press, 1986.

Billingsley, A. *Black Families in White America.* Englewood Cliffs, N.J.: Prentice Hall, 1968.

Billingsley, A. *Climbing Jacob's Ladder: The Enduring Legacy of African-American Families.* New York: Simon & Schuster, 1992.

Bowman, P., and Howard, C. "Race-Related Socialization, Motivation, and Academic Achievement: A Study of Black Youths in Three-Generation Families." *Journal of the American Academy of Child Psychiatry,* 1985, *24,* 134–141.

Boyd-Franklin, N. *Black Families in Therapy: A Multisystems Approach.* New York: Guilford Press, 1989.

Bronfenbrenner, U. *The Ecology of Human Development: Experiments by Nature and Design.* Cambridge, Mass.: Harvard University Press, 1979.

Brown, S. V. "Premarital Sexual Permissiveness Among Black Adolescent Females." *Social Psychology Quarterly,* 1985, *48,* 381–387.

Brunswick, A. "Black Youths and Drug Use Behavior." In B. Beschner and A. Friedman (eds.), *Youth and Drug Abuse: Problems, Issues, and Treatment.* San Francisco: New Lexington Press, 1979.

Brunswick, A. "Young Black Males and Substance Use." In J. T. Gibbs (ed.), *Young, Black, and Male in America: An Endangered Species.* Westport, Conn.: Auburn House, 1988.

Brunswick, A., and Messeri, P. "Drugs, Life Style and Health." *American Journal of Public Health,* 1986, *76,* 52–57.

Cahill, I. D. "Child-Rearing Practices in Lower Socio-Economic Ethnic Groups." *Dissertation Abstracts,* 1966, *27,* 31–39.

Canino, I. A., and Spurlock, J. *Culturally Diverse Children and Adolescents: Assessment, Diagnosis and Treatment.* New York: Guilford Press, 1994.

Cauce, A. M. "Social Networks and Social Competence: Exploring the Effects of Early Adolescent Friendships." *American Journal of Community Psychology,* 1986, *14,* 607–629.

Cauce, A. M., Felner, R., and Primavera, J. "Social Support in High-Risk Adolescents: Structural Components and Adaptive Impact." *American Journal of Community Psychology,* 1982, *10,* 417–428.

Cauce, A. M., and others. "African American Mothers and Their Adolescent Daughters: Closeness, Conflict, and Control." In B. J. Leadbetter and N. Way (eds.), *Urban Girls: Resisting Stereotypes, Creating Identities.* New York: New York University Press, 1996.

Centers for Disease Control and Prevention. *HIV/AIDS Surveillance Report.* Atlanta, Ga.: U.S. Department of Health and Human Services, *8*(1), 1996.

Chambers, B. (ed.). *Chronicles of Black Protest.* New York: NAL/Dutton, 1968.

Cheatham, H. E., and Stewart, J. D. (eds.), *Black Families: Interdisciplinary Perspectives.* New Brunswick, N.J.: Transaction, 1990.

Chestang, L. "Racial and Personal Identity in the Black Experience." In B. White (ed.), *Color in a White Society.* Silver Spring, Md.: National Association of Social Workers, 1984.

Children's Defense Fund. *A Children's Defense Budget.* Washington, D.C.: Children's Defense Fund, 1985.

Children's Defense Fund. *A Children's Defense Budget.* Washington, D.C.: Children's Defense Fund, 1986a.

Children's Defense Fund. *Building Health Programs for Teenagers.* Washington, D.C.: Children's Defense Fund, 1986b.

Children's Defense Fund. *Welfare and Teen Pregnancy: What Do We Know? What Do We Do?* Washington, D.C.: Children's Defense Fund, 1986c.

Children's Defense Fund. *A Children's Defense Budget.* Washington, D.C.: Children's Defense Fund, 1987.

Chilman, C. *Adolescent Sexuality in a Changing American Society.* New York: Wiley, 1983.

Clark, K. B. *Dark Ghetto: Dilemmas of Social Power.* New York: HarperCollins, 1965.

Clark, K. B., and Clark, M. "Skin Color as a Factor in Racial Identification of Negro Pre-School Children." *Journal of Social Psychology,* 1940, 2, 154–167.

College Entrance Examination Board. *Equality and Excellence: The Educational Status of Black Americans.* New York: College Entrance Examination Board, 1985.

Colletta, N. D., Hadler, S., and Gregg, C. H. "How Adolescents Cope With the Problems of Early Motherhood." *Adolescence,* 1981, 16, 499–512.

Comer, J. P., and Hill, H. "Social Policy and the Mental Health of Black Children." *Journal of the American Academy of Child Psychiatry,* 1985, 24(2), 175–181.

Committee for Economic Development. *Children in Need: Investment Strategies for the Educationally Disadvantaged.* New York: Committee for Economic Development, 1987.

Cross, W. E. "A Two-Factor Theory of Black Identity: Implications for the Study of Identity Development in Minority Children." In J. Phinney and M. J. Rotheram (eds.), *Children's Ethnic Socialization: Pluralism and Development.* Thousand Oaks, Calif.: Sage, 1984.

Dancy, B., and Handal, P. "Perceived Family Climate, Psychological Adjustment and Peer Relationships of Black Adolescents: A Function of Parental Marital Status or Perceived Family Conflict?" *Journal of Community Psychology,* 1984, 12, 222–229.

Dash, L. *When Children Want Children: The Urban Crisis of Teenage Childbearing.* New York: Morrow, 1989.

Davis, K., and Swartz, J. "Increasing Black Students' Utilization of Mental Health Services." *American Journal of Orthopsychiatry,* 1972, 42, 771–776.

Dembo, R. "Delinquency Among Black Male Youth." In J. T. Gibbs (ed.), *Young, Black, and Male in America: An Endangered Species.* Westport, Conn.: Auburn House, 1988.

Dougherty, M. *Becoming a Woman in Rural Black Culture.* Austin, Tex.: Holt, Rinehart and Winston, 1978.

Dryfoos, J. *Adolescents at Risk: Prevalence and Prevention.* New York: Oxford University Press, 1990.

Durrett, M. D., O'Bryant, S., and Pennebaker, J. W. "Child-Rearing Reports of White, Black, and Mexican-American Families." *Developmental Psychology,* 1975, 11, 871–878.

Edelman, M. W. *Families in Peril: An Agenda for Social Change.* Cambridge, Mass.: Harvard University Press, 1987.

Erikson, E. H. *Childhood and Society.* New York: Norton, 1950.

Erikson, E. H. "Identity and the Life Cycle." *Psychological Issues,* 1959, *1* (entire issue 1).

Felner, R. D., Aber, M. S., Primavera, J., and Cauce, A. M. "Adaptation and Vulnerability in High-Risk Adolescents: An Examination of Environmental Mediators." *American Journal of Community Psychology,* 1985, *13,* 365–379.

Foley, V. "Family Therapy with Black Disadvantaged Families: Some Observations on Roles, Communication, and Techniques." *Journal of Marriage and Family Counseling,* 1975, *1,* 29–38.

Fordham, S., and Ogbu, J. "Black Students' School Success: Coping with the Burden of 'Acting White.'" *Urban Review,* 1986, *18*(3), 176–206.

Foster, M., and Perry, L. R. "Self-Valuation Among Blacks." *Social Work,* 1982, *27,* 60–66.

Frank, J. D., and others. *Effective Ingredients of Successful Psychotherapy.* New York: Brunner/Mazel, 1978.

Franklin, A. J. "Therapeutic Interventions with Urban Black Adolescents." In E. E. Jones and S. J. Korchin (eds.), *Minority Mental Health.* New York: Praeger, 1982.

Franklin, J. H. *From Slavery to Freedom: A History of American Negroes.* New York: Knopf, 1967.

Frazier, E. F. *The Negro Family in the United States.* Chicago: University of Chicago Press, 1966.

Gardner, L. "The Therapeutic Relationship Under Varying Conditions of Race." *Psychotherapy: Theory, Research and Practice,* 1971, *8,* 78–87.

Gibbs, J. T. "Patterns of Adaptation Among Black Students at a Predominantly White University." *American Journal of Orthopsychiatry,* 1974, *44,* 728–740.

Gibbs, J. T. "Use of Mental Health Services by Black Students at a Predominantly White University: A Three-Year Study." *American Journal of Orthopsychiatry,* 1975, *45,* 430–445.

Gibbs, J. T. "Depression and Suicidal Behavior Among Delinquent Females: Ethnic and Sociocultural Variations." *Journal of Youth and Adolescence,* 1981, *2,* 159–167.

Gibbs, J. T. "Personality Patterns of Delinquent Females: Ethnic and Sociocultural Variations." *Journal of Clinical Psychology,* 1982, *38,* 198–206.

Gibbs, J. T. "Black Adolescents and Youth: An Endangered Species." *American Journal of Orthopsychiatry,* 1984, *54,* 6–21.

Gibbs, J. T. "City Girls: Psychosocial Adjustment of Urban Black Adolescent Females." *SAGE: A Scholarly Journal on Black Women,* 1985a, *2,* 28–36.

Gibbs, J. T. "Psychosocial Factors Associated with Depression in Urban Adolescent Females: Implications for Assessment." *Journal of Youth and Adolescence*, 1985b, *14*, 47–60.

Gibbs, J. T. "Treatment Relationships with Black Clients: Interpersonal vs. Instrumental Strategies." In C. Germain (ed.), *Advances in Clinical Social Work Practice*. Silver Spring, Md.: National Association of Social Workers, 1985c.

Gibbs, J. T. "Assessment of Depression in Urban Adolescent Females: Implications for Early Intervention Strategies." *American Journal of Social Psychiatry*, 1986a, *6*, 50–56.

Gibbs, J. T. "Psychosocial Correlates of Sexual Attitudes and Behaviors in Urban Early Adolescent Females: Implications for Intervention." *Journal of Social Work and Human Sexuality*, 1986b, *5*, 81–97.

Gibbs, J. T. "Identity and Marginality: Issues in the Treatment of Biracial Adolescents." *American Journal of Orthopsychiatry*, 1987, *57*(2), 265–278.

Gibbs, J. T. "Conceptual, Methodological and Sociocultural Issues in Black Youth Suicide: Implications for Assessment and Early Intervention." *Suicide and Life-Threatening Behavior*, 1988a, *18*, 73–89.

Gibbs, J. T. (ed.). *Young, Black, and Male in America: An Endangered Species*. Westport, Conn.: Auburn House, 1988b.

Gibbs, J. T. "Mental Health Issues of Black Adolescents: Implications for Policy and Practice." In A. R. Stiffman and L. E. Davis (eds.), *Ethnic Issues in Adolescent Mental Health*. Thousand Oaks, Calif.: Sage, 1990.

Gibbs, J. T. "Health and Mental Health of Black Adolescents." In R. L. Taylor (ed.), *African-American Youth: Their Social and Economic Status in the United States*. New York: Praeger, 1995.

Glasgow, D. *The Black Underclass*. New York: Vintage Books, 1981.

Goodman, M. E. *Race Awareness in Young Children*. Reading, Mass.: Addison-Wesley, 1964.

Grier, W., and Cobbs, P. *Black Rage*. New York: Basic Books, 1968.

Griffith, M., and Jones, E. E. "Race and Psychotherapy: Changing Perspectives." *Current Psychiatric Therapies*, 1978, *18*, 225–235.

Gwyn, F. F., and Kilpatrick, A. C. "Family Therapy with Low-Income Blacks: A Tool or Turn-Off?" *Social Casework*, 1981, *5*, 259–266.

Halikas, J., Darvish, H., and Rimmer, J. "The Black Addict, Part 1: Methodology, Chronology of Addiction and Overview of the Population." *American Journal of Drug and Alcohol Abuse*, 1976, *3*, 529–543.

Hall, L. E., and Tucker, C. M. "Relationships Between Ethnicity, Conceptions of Mental Illness and Attitudes Associated with Seeking Psychological Help." *Psychological Reports*, 1985, *57*, 907–916.

Hare, B. R. "Black Youth at Risk." In J. D. Williams (ed.), *The State of Black America, 1988.* New York: National Urban League, 1988.

Harris, D.C., and Balgopal, P. R. "Intervening with the Black Family." In C. Janzen and O. Harris (eds.), *Family Treatment in Social Work Practice.* Itasca, Ill.: Peacock, 1980.

Hawkins, D. F., and Jones, N. "Black Adolescents in the Criminal Justice System." In R. L. Jones (ed.), *Black Adolescents.* Berkeley, Calif.: Cobb & Henry, 1989.

Heiss, J., and Owens, S. "Self-Evaluations of Blacks and Whites." *American Journal of Sociology,* 1976, *78,* 360–371.

Hendricks, L. E. "Unwed Adolescent Fathers: Problems They Face and Their Sources of Social Support." *Adolescence,* 1980, *15,* 862–869.

Hines, P. M., and Boyd-Franklin, N. "African American Families." In M. McGoldrick, J. K. Pearce, and J. Giordano (eds.), *Ethnicity and Family Therapy.* (2nd ed.) New York: Guilford Press, 1996.

Honey, E. "AIDS and the Inner City: Critical Issues." *Social Casework,* 1988, *69,* 365–370.

Jenkins, A. *The Psychology of the Afro-American.* New York: Pergamon Press, 1982.

Jones, E. E., and Korchin, S. J. (eds.). *Minority Mental Health.* New York: Praeger, 1982.

Jones, R. L. (ed.). *Black Adolescents.* Berkeley, Calif.: Cobb & Henry, 1989.

Kandel, D. B., and others. "Antecedents of Adolescent Initiation into Stages of Drug Use: A Developmental Analysis." *Journal of Youth and Adolescence,* 1977, *7,* 13–40.

Kaplan, S., Landa, B., Weinhold, C., and Shenker, I. "Adverse Health Behaviors and Depressive Symptomatology in Adolescents." *Journal of the American Academy of Child Psychiatry,* 1984, *23,* 595–601.

Kasarda, J. "Urban Change and Minority Opportunities." In P. E. Peterson (ed.), *The New Urban Reality.* Washington, D.C.: Brookings Institution, 1985.

Kochman, T. E. *Rappin' and Stylin' Out.* Urbana: University of Illinois Press, 1972.

Kovar, M. G. "Health Status of U.S. Children and Use of Medical Care." *Public Health Reports,* 1982, *97,* 3–15.

Krisberg, B., and others. *The Incarceration of Minority Youth.* Minneapolis: H. H. Humphrey Institute of Public Affairs, University of Minnesota, 1986.

Labov, W. *Language in the Inner City: Studies in the Black English Vernacular.* Philadelphia: University of Pennsylvania Press, 1972.

Ladner, J. *Tomorrow's Tomorrow.* New York: Doubleday, 1971.

Landau-Stanton, J., and Stanton, M. "Treating Suicidal Adolescents and Their Families." In M. Mirkin and S. Koman (eds.), *Handbook of Adolescents and Family Therapy*. Lake Worth, Fla.: Gardner Press, 1985.

Lee, L. J. "Reducing Black Adolescents' Drug Use: Family Revisited." *Child and Youth Services*, 1983, *6*, 57–69.

Lewis, D., and Balla, D. *Delinquency and Psychopathology*. Philadelphia: Grune & Stratton, 1976.

Lewis, J. M., and Looney, J. G. *The Long Struggle: Well-Functioning Working Class Black Families*. New York: Brunner/Mazel, 1983.

Lincoln, C. E., and Mamiya, L. *The Black Church in the African-American Experience*. Durham, N.C.: Duke University Press, 1990.

MacLennan, B. W., and Felsenfeld, N. *Group Counseling and Psychotherapy with Adolescents*. New York: Columbia University Press, 1968.

Majors, R., and Billson, J. M. *Cool Pose: The Dilemmas of Black Manhood in America*. San Francisco: New Lexington Press, 1992.

Mancini, J. K. *Strategic Styles: Coping in the Inner City*. Hanover, N.H.: University Press of New England, 1980.

Mayo, J. "The Significance of Sociocultural Variables in the Psychiatric Treatment of Black Outpatients." *Comprehensive Psychiatry*, 1974, *15*, 471–482.

Mays, V., and Cochran, S. "Acquired Immunodeficiency Syndrome and Black Americans: Special Psychosocial Issues." *Public Health Reports*, 1987, *102*, 221–231.

McAdoo, H. P. (ed.) *Black Families*. Thousand Oaks, Calif.: Sage, 1981.

McAdoo, H. P., and McAdoo, J. L. (eds.). *Black Children: Social, Educational, and Parental Environments*. Thousand Oaks, Calif.: Sage, 1985.

Mercer, J. R. *System of Multicultural Pluralistic Assessment Technical Manual*. New York: Psychological Corporation, 1979.

Milazzo-Sayre, L., Benson, P., Rosenstein, M., and Manderscheid, R. "Use of Inpatient Psychiatric Services by Children and Youth Under Age Eighteen, United States, 1980." *Mental Health Statistical Note*, No. 175. Washington, D.C.: U.S. Department of Health and Human Services, 1986.

Miller, D. "Treatment of the Seriously Disturbed Adolescent." *Adolescent Psychiatry*, 1980, *8*, 469–481.

Minuchin, S., and others. *Families of the Slums*. New York: Basic Books, 1967.

Murry, V. M. "Inner-City Girls of Color: Unmarried, Sexually Active Non-Mothers." In B. J. Leadbetter and N. Way (eds.), *Urban Girls: Resisting Stereotypes, Creating Identities*. New York: New York University Press, 1996.

Myers, H. F. "Urban Stress and the Mental Health of Afro-American Youth: An Epidemiologic and Conceptual Update." In R. L. Jones (ed.), *Black Adolescents*. Berkeley, Calif.: Cobb & Henry, 1989.

Myers, H. F., and King, L. M. "Youth of the Black Underclass: Urban Stress and Mental Health—Notes for an Alternative Formulation." *Fanon Center Journal,* 1980, *1,* 1–27.

National Institute of Drug Abuse. *National Household Survey on Drug Abuse, 1990.* Rockville, Md.: U.S. Department of Health and Human Services, 1991.

National Urban League. *Annual Report.* New York: National Urban League, 1990.

Neighbors, H. W. "Seeking Professional Help for Personal Problems: Black Americans' Use of Health and Mental Health Services." *Community Mental Health Journal,* 1985, *21,* 156–166.

Nobles, W. "Psychological Research and the Black Self-Concept: A Critical Review." *Journal of Social Issues,* 1973, *29,* 11–31.

Norman, J. S. "Short-Term Treatment with the Adolescent Client." *Social Casework,* 1980, *61,* 74–82.

Ogbu, J. "A Cultural Ecology of Competence Among Inner-City Blacks." In M. Spencer, G. Brookins, and W. Allen (eds.), *Beginnings: The Social and Affective Development of Black Children.* Hillsdale, N.J.: Erlbaum, 1985.

Omi, M., and Winant, H. *Racial Formation in the United States: From the 1960s to the 1980s.* New York: Routledge, 1986.

Orfield, G., and Ashkinaze, C. *The Closing Door: Conservative Policy and Black Opportunity.* Chicago: University of Chicago Press, 1991.

Paster, V. "Adapting Psychotherapy for the Depressed, Unacculturated, Acting Out, Black Male Adolescent." *American Journal of Orthopsychiatry,* 1985, *56,* 625–629.

Peters, M. F. "Parenting in Black Families with Young Children: A Historical Perspective." In H. P. McAdoo (ed.), *Black Families.* Thousand Oaks, Calif.: Sage, 1981.

Pinderhughes, C. "Racism and Psychotherapy." In C. Willie, B. Brown, and B. Kramer (eds.), *Racism and Mental Health.* Pittsburgh: University of Pittsburgh Press, 1973.

Pinderhughes, E. "Afro-American Families and the Victim System." In M. McGoldrick, J. K. Pearce, and J. Giordano (eds.), *Ethnicity and Family Therapy.* New York: Guilford Press, 1982.

Powell, G. J. "Self-Concepts Among Afro-American Students in Racially Isolated Minority Schools: Some Regional Differences." *Journal of the American Academy of Child Psychiatry,* 1985, *24,* 142–149.

Pumariega, A., Edwards, P., and Mitchell, C. "Anorexia Nervosa in Black Adolescents." *Journal of the American Academy of Child Psychiatry,* 1984, *23,* 111–114.

Reed, R. "Education and Achievement of Young Black Males." In J. T. Gibbs (ed.), *Young, Black, and Male in America: An Endangered Species.* Westport, Conn.: Auburn House, 1988.

Ridley, C. R. "Clinical Treatment of the Nondisclosing Black Client: A Therapeutic Paradox." *American Psychologist,* 1984, *39,* 1234–1244.

Rivers, L. W., and others. "Mosaic of Labels for Black Children." In N. Hobbs (ed.), *Issues in the Classification of Children: A Sourcebook on Categories, Labels, and Their Consequences.* Vol. 2. San Francisco: Jossey-Bass, 1975.

Robinson, B. *Teenage Fathers.* San Francisco: New Lexington Press, 1988.

Robinson, P., and Andersen, A. "Anorexia Nervosa in American Blacks." *Journal of Psychiatry Research,* 1985, *19,* 183–188.

Robinson, T., and Ward, J. V. "A Belief in Self Far Greater than Anyone's Disbelief: Cultivating Healthy Resistance Among African American Female Adolescents." In C. Gilligan, A. G. Rogers, and D. Tolman (eds.), *Women, Girls and Psychotherapy: Reframing Resistance.* New York: Harrington Park Press, 1991.

Rosenberg, M. *Conceiving the Self.* New York: Basic Books, 1979.

Rosenberg, M., and Simmons, R. *Black and White Self-Esteem: The Urban School Child.* Rose Monograph Series. Washington, D.C.: American Sociological Association, 1971.

Rosenheim, M. K., and Testa, M. F. (eds.), *Early Parenthood and Coming of Age in the 1990s.* New Brunswick, N.J.: Rutgers University Press, 1992.

Rotheram-Borus, M. J., and others. "Personal and Ethnic Identity, Values, and Self-Esteem Among Black and Latino Girls." In B. J. Leadbetter and N. Way (eds.), *Urban Girls: Resisting Stereotypes, Creating Identities.* New York: New York University Press, 1996.

Sager, C., Brayboy, T., and Waxenberg, B. *Black Ghetto Family in Therapy.* New York: Grove Atlantic, 1970.

Samuda, R. *Psychological Testing of American Minorities: Issues and Consequences.* New York: Dodd, Mead, 1975.

Schoenbach, V., and others. "Prevalence of Self-Reported Depressive Symptoms in Young Adolescents." *American Journal of Public Health,* 1983, *73,* 1281–1287.

Schorr, A. *Common Decency: Domestic Policies After Reagan.* New Haven, Conn.: Yale University Press, 1986.

Schulz, D. A. *Coming Up Black: Patterns of Ghetto Socialization.* Englewood Cliffs, N.J.: Prentice Hall, 1969.

Shaffer, D., and Fisher, P. "The Epidemiology of Suicide in Children and Young Adolescents." *Journal of the American Academy of Child Psychiatry,* 1981, *20,* 534–565.

Skager, R. *A Statewide Survey of Drug and Alcohol Use Among California Students in Grades 7, 9, and 11*. Sacramento, Calif.: Office of the Attorney General, 1986.

Smith, E. "The Black Female Adolescent: A Review of the Educational, Career and Psychological Literature." *Psychology of Women Quarterly,* 1982, *6,* 261–288.

Smitherman, G. "What Is Africa to Me: Language, Ideology, and African-American Speech." *American Speech,* 1991, *66*(2), 115–132.

Snowden, L. R., and Todman, P. A. "The Psychological Assessment of Blacks: New and Needed Developments." In E. E. Jones and S. J. Korchin (eds.), *Minority Mental Health.* New York: Praeger, 1982.

Spencer, M. B. "Personal and Group Identity of Black Children: An Alternative Synthesis." *Genetic Psychology Monographs,* 1982, *106,* 59–84.

Spencer, M. B. "Old Issues and New Theorizing About African-American Youth: A Phenomenological Variant of Ecological Systems Theory." In R. L. Taylor (ed.), *African-American Youth: Their Social and Economic Status in the United States.* New York: Praeger, 1995.

Stack, C. *All Our Kin: Strategies for Survival in a Black Community.* New York: HarperCollins, 1974.

Staples, R., and Johnson, L. B. *Black Families at the Crossroads: Challenges and Prospects.* San Francisco: Jossey-Bass, 1993.

Staples, R., and Mirande, A. "Racial and Cultural Variations Among American Families: A Decennial Review of the Literature on Minority Families." *Journal of Marriage and the Family,* 1980, *42,* 887–903.

Taylor, R. L. "Psychosocial Development Among Black Children and Youth: A Reexamination." *American Journal of Orthopsychiatry,* 1976, *46,* 4–19.

Taylor, R. L. "Childrearing in African American Families." In J. E. Everett, S. S. Chipungu, and B. R. Leashore (eds.), *Child Welfare: An Africentric Perspective.* New Brunswick, N.J.: Rutgers University Press, 1991.

Taylor, R. L. (ed.). *African-American Youth: Their Social and Economic Status in the United States.* New York: Praeger, 1995.

Thompson, C. L. "In Pursuit of Affirmation: The Antisocial Inner-City Adolescent." In A. R. Stiffman and L. E. Davis (eds.), *Ethnic Issues in Adolescent Mental Health.* Thousand Oaks, Calif.: Sage, 1990.

U.S. Bureau of the Census. *Statistical Abstract of the United States, 1996.* (116th ed.) Washington, D.C.: U.S. Department of Commerce, 1996.

U.S. Department of Health and Human Services. *Health, United States, 1996.* Washington, D.C.: National Center for Health Statistics, 1996.

U.S. Department of Justice. *Uniform Crime Reports for the United States, 1993.* Washington, D.C.: Federal Bureau of Investigation, 1994.

Ventura, S. J., Clarke, S. C., and Mathews, T. J. "Recent Decline in Teenage Birth Rates in the United States: Variations by State, 1990–94." *Monthly Vital Statistics Report: Supplement,* 1996, *45*(entire issue 5).

Viadero, D. "Big-City Gang Culture Spreading to New Turf." *Education Week,* 1988, *7*(1), 18–19.

Walker, S., Spohn, C., and Delone, M. *The Color of Justice: Race, Ethnicity, and Crime in America.* Belmont, Calif.: Wadsworth, 1996.

Ward, J. V. "Raising Resisters: The Role of Truth-Telling in the Psychological Development of African American Girls." In B. J. Leadbetter and N. Way (eds.), *Urban Girls: Resisting Stereotypes, Creating Identities.* New York: New York University Press, 1996.

Warshauer, M., and Monk, M. "Problems in Suicide Statistics for Whites and Blacks." *American Journal of Public Health,* 1978, *68*, 383–388.

Way, N. "Between Experiences of Betrayal and Desire: Close Friendships Among Urban Adolescents." In B. J. Leadbetter and N. Way (eds.), *Urban Girls: Resisting Stereotypes, Creating Identities.* New York: New York University Press, 1996.

Weddle, K. D., and McKenry, P. C. "Self Destructive Behaviors Among Black Youth: Suicide and Homicide." In R. L. Taylor (ed.), *African-American Youth: Their Social and Economic Status in the United States.* New York: Praeger, 1995.

Welte, J. W., and Barnes, C. M. "Alcohol Use Among Adolescent Minority Groups." *Journal of Studies on Alcohol,* 1987, *4*, 329–336.

Wilson, W. J. *The Truly Disadvantaged.* Chicago: University of Chicago Press, 1987.

Wilson, W. J. *When Work Disappears: The New World of the Urban Poor.* New York: Knopf, 1996.

Chapter Seven

Mexican American Children and Adolescents

Oscar Ramirez

Despite an accumulation of social science/mental health research spanning nearly thirty years, the knowledge base needed to guide and inform the process of providing effective mental health services to Mexican American youth and their families is small, fragmented, incomplete, and in some areas, nonexistent. This chapter addresses this substantial void in the psychotherapeutic literature on Mexican Americans by presenting some cultural characteristics of Mexican American family life that therapists should know about in order to provide effective, relevant, and culturally sensitive therapeutic services.

The chapter is organized around the following topics: first, a demographic profile of the Mexican American population; second, an overview of specific cultural and familial characteristics of Mexican Americans; third, the epidemiological research on the incidence and prevalence of psychological and behavioral disorders among Mexican American children and adolescents; fourth, the critical issues involved in providing effective and culturally relevant clinical intervention and treatment services to these young people

---

Note: The demographic profile of Mexican Americans is based on primary data from the following U.S. Bureau of the Census documents: *Statistical Abstract of the United States, 1996: March 1994 and 1995 Current Population Reports on Hispanics and Non-Hispanics, Size of Population, Age, Education, Income, and Poverty Level.*

and their families; and finally, future directions for the delivery of mental health services to the Mexican American population.

A Demographic Profile

In this chapter, a Mexican American is defined as any person residing in the United States who was born in Mexico or who is of Mexican descent. According to recent census figures, the Mexican American population in the United States comprises some 18 million people, which represents a growth of 30 percent from 1987 to 1995. People of Mexican origin account for 65 percent of the Hispanic population. The growth of the Mexican American population can be attributed to a high fertility rate, as well as to improved enumeration of illegal and undocumented individuals who continuously enter the United States from Mexico.

Mexican Americans tend to be younger than other ethnic groups and are in fact the youngest among Hispanic groups, with a median age grouping of twenty to twenty-four years, compared to twenty-five to twenty-nine years for Puerto Ricans, forty to forty-four years for Cuban Americans, and thirty to thirty-four years for non-Hispanics. The proportion of children and adolescents in this population is even more striking. Minors aged nineteen years and younger make up 43 percent of Mexican Americans. The comparable figures for other groups are 41 percent for Puerto Ricans, 19 percent for Cuban Americans, and 24 percent for non-Hispanics.

In 1995 the reported median income of Mexican American families ($23,609) was significantly lower than that of white non-Hispanic families ($40,884), lower than that of Cubans ($30,584), and higher than that of Puerto Ricans ($20,929). It is generally acknowledged that larger families suffer the burden of low income more severely. An earlier review reported that Mexican American families with four or more children had lower median incomes than Mexican American families with fewer or no children (Ramirez and Arce, 1981). The 1995 *Current Population Report* indicated that the proportion of Hispanic families whose income fell below the poverty level was more than double that of non-Hispanic families. However, there were consistent differences within the Hispanic population. Puerto Rican families had the highest poverty rate, with 33.2 percent of family incomes falling below the poverty level, while only 13.6 percent of Cuban American and 29.6 percent of Mexican American family incomes fell below the poverty level.

Measures of educational attainment, a closely related socio-economic variable, show that Hispanics, particularly Mexican Americans, have completed fewer years of formal education than non-Hispanics. The 1994 census reported that only 53 percent of Mexican Americans aged twenty-five and older had completed high school.

Geographically, the Mexican-descent population is largely concentrated in California, Texas, Illinois (primarily Chicago), New Mexico, Arizona, and Colorado. Two or three decades ago, Mexican Americans were characterized in the literature as being primarily a rural, agrarian subculture. However, in 1995 it was estimated that 60 percent of the Mexican American population now lives in the large metropolitan areas. Although this figure represents a major shift, it is highly significant that the remaining 40 percent of Mexican Americans continue to reside in smaller urban or rural settings.

In summary, recent demographic data indicate that Mexican Americans in the United States tend to be young, to be poor, to have high fertility rates, to live in large families, to have less than a high school education, and to confront problems of illiteracy and lack of facility in the English language. Even though a slight majority of Mexican Americans reside in large metropolitan areas, a substantial number continue to live in small urban and rural communities. This constellation of characteristics, as noted by Rogler, Malgady, Costantino, and Blumenthal (1987), makes this population highly vulnerable to the development of mental health problems. Thus the need for culturally sensitive mental health services is clearly evident.

Mexican American Cultural Family Patterns

Although Mexican American families are quite diverse, an attempt is made here to outline some characteristic patterns and values. It is important to note, however, that each family is unique and is at a different point on the continuum of acculturation, so these patterns are secondary to the individual differences and diversity within this population.

Recent research suggests that Mexican American families are currently undergoing substantial change. In a review of the contemporary Mexican American family, Ramirez and Arce (1981) examined multiple aspects of Mexican American family life and found a mixture of traditional and contemporary patterns. Such traditional values as the primacy of the family and extended kinship ties remained strongly entrenched. The structure and function of Mexican American families continued to be characterized by a strong, persistent familistic orientation; a highly integrated extended kinship system, even for families three or more generations removed from Mexico; and a strong reliance on this extended family system, including *compadres* (godparents), for emotional and social support, childrearing, financial support, and problem solving (see, for example, Sena-Rivera, 1979; Keefe, Padilla, and Carlos, 1978a, 1978b, 1979; Baca Zinn, 1977; Mindel, 1980). To facilitate the functioning of this kinship network, traditional Mexican American values of affiliation and cooperation are stressed, while confrontation and competition are discouraged. As LeVine and Padilla (1980) state, "According to the traditional Hispanic values of *personalismo*, it is not ability but, rather, goodness and the quality of personal relationships that are important in life" (p. 34).

In contrast to these more traditional values, Ramirez and Arce (1981) found some interesting variations in the area of male and female roles and conjugal decision making. Traditionally, men assumed the instrumental role of provider and protector of the family, and women assumed the expressive role of homemaker and caretaker of the children. To a certain degree this continues to be the dominant public norm (Falicov, 1982), and the concept of machismo continues to influence the role of the male and the patriarchal ideology in Mexican American families, though less so than in the past. Traditionally, this concept required men to be forceful and strong and to withhold tender or affectionate emotions; ideally, it encompassed a strong sense of personal honor, family, loyalty, and care for the children; however, it also connoted exaggerated masculinity and sexual virility and aggressiveness (Trankina, 1983). When this concept was carried to an extreme, family problems and dissatisfactions often ensued. In contrast to the male, the female's role was one of self-denial and abnegation, and her personal needs were considered subordinate to those of other family members. Ramirez and Arce (1981) found that the concepts of machismo and absolute patriarchy currently have diminishing influence on the dynamics and structure of the contemporary Mexican American family; instead, joint decision making and greater equality of male and female roles and opportunities are apparent. Of major significance is the increased frequency of women's employment outside the home, which seems to enhance a wife's status within the family and in decision-making processes (Cromwell and Ruiz, 1979; Ybarra-Soriano, 1977; Baca Zinn, 1980).

Parent/Child Relationships

It is the existence of children that validates and cements a marriage. Within this culture, *el amor de madre,* motherly love, is considered a much greater force than wifely love. Since the parent/child relationship is considered more important than the marital relationship, the Mexican American couple typically enjoys little freedom from parental functions during the childrearing stages.

During the family's early years, the home is usually child centered. Both parents tend to be permissive and indulgent with the younger children. In spite of an emphasis on good behavior, parents give a great deal of nurturance and protection to young children and adopt a relaxed attitude toward the achievement of developmental milestones or the attainment of skills related to self-reliance. Generally speaking, Mexican American parents seem less pressured than Anglo American parents to see that a child achieves developmental goals or to correct minor deviations from the norm. There is a basic acceptance of the child's individuality. Following this relatively permissive and indulgent phase, Mexican American parents begin to expect more responsible behavior from their children as they approach latency and the years beyond. During latency and adolescence, children are often assigned tasks or responsibilities in accordance with their age and ability. They are expected, for example, to help with housework, child care, cooking, and errands.

During the children's earlier years, the father is often playful and affectionate, but his primary role with older children is to discipline them and to expect obedience. This polarization of protective nurturance and authoritarian control between mother and father renders mother more accessible to the children and often places her in a position of mediator between father and children.

Sex-Role Socialization

Differences in sex-role socialization are clearly evident in this culture and become especially prominent at adolescence. The adolescent female is likely to remain much closer to the home than the male and to be protected and guarded in her contacts with others beyond the family, so as to preserve her femininity and innocence. The adolescent male, following the model of his father, is given much more freedom to come and go as he chooses and is encouraged to gain worldly knowledge outside the home in preparation for the time when he will assume the role of husband and father. As Murillo (1971) notes, "During this period of development, the young male is likely to join with others of his age in informal social groups known as *palomillas*. Through such associations, he gains knowledge and experience in holding his own with other males" (pp. 104–105).

Psychological and Behavioral Disorders

Epidemiological studies conducted before 1980 found a lower prevalence of psychiatric disorder among Mexican Americans than among other ethnic groups. In contrast, more recent epidemiological surveys (for example, Roberts, 1980) suggest that the prevalence of psychological distress among Mexican Americans is at least as high as in the overall population and in some instances is higher (Shrout and others, 1992). However, whether Mexican Americans are seeking mental health services at a rate commensurate with their actual prevalence of psychological disturbance remains an unanswered question.

Mexican American children and adolescents constitute the most rapidly growing group of young people in the Southwest and one about which relatively little is known as far as mental health issues are concerned. Unfortunately, comparative surveys of the prevalence of disorder in Mexican American and Anglo young people are disparate in focus and use different measures and different methods of data collection, making comparisons difficult and resulting in inconsistent findings. These studies do not offer any clear, consistent evidence that Mexican American youth have either higher or lower rates of behavior problems or psychopathology than their Anglo counterparts. In addition, because these few studies are not true epidemiological studies, they do not offer accurate estimates of the incidence or prevalence of psychological disorders in this population group.

In the absence of systematic epidemiological studies, incidence rates are estimated from clinic-based research. In their study of Mexican American and Anglo children matched for sex and family income in three Southwestern child guidance clinics, Stoker and Meadow (1974) found ethnic differences in the expression of behavior problems and psychopathology. While Mexican American boys were more frequently described as more aggressive and acting out, Anglo American boys were seen more frequently as neurotic. Mexican American girls, who were referred to the clinics at a later age than subjects in the other three groups, showed more depression overall. Further, these researchers reported that clinicians viewed Mexican American children as generally benefiting less from treatment than children from other groups.

An informal analysis of the diagnoses given children and adolescents at a county guidance center where I practice reveals a similar distribution of diagnoses for the Mexican American and non–Mexican American groups (see Table 7.1). In both groups, the diagnosis most frequently given was dysthymic disorder (neurotic depression), followed by oppositional disorder and, third, overanxious disorder. Among these three diagnoses, Mexican Americans received a diagnosis of depression more often than non–Mexican Americans; non–Mexican Americans received a diagnosis of oppositional disorder more frequently than Mexican Americans; and overanxious disorder was seen with equal frequency in the two groups. The diagnosis of conduct disorder (undersocialized or socialized, *aggressive*) was given slightly more frequently to Mexican Americans that to non–Mexican Americans, who were slightly more often given a diagnosis of conduct disorder, *nonaggressive*.

Table 7.1. Selected Primary Diagnoses Given to Children and Adolescents at the Community Guidance Center of Bexar County, Texas, from January 1984 through April 1987.

Diagnosis	Mexican Americans		Non–Mexican Americans		Total
Dysthymic disorder	140	(31.7 percent)	202	(24.8 percent)	342
Oppositional disorder	58	(13.2 percent)	150	(18.4 percent)	208
Overanxious disorder	55	(12.5 percent)	105	(12.9 percent)	160
Adjustment disorder with mixed disturbance of emotions and conduct	32	(7.3 percent)	61	(7.5 percent)	93
Schizophrenic disorder	8	(1.8 percent)	22	(2.7 percent)	30
Affective psychosis	11	(2.5 percent)	17	(2.1 percent)	28
Attention deficit disorder without hyperactivity	8	(1.8 percent)	16	(2.0 percent)	24
Attention deficit disorder with hyperactivity	29	(6.6 percent)	85	(10.4 percent)	114
Conduct disorder, undersocialized, aggressive	20	(4.5 percent)	30	(3.7 percent)	50
Conduct disorder, socialized, aggressive	36	(8.2 percent)	41	(5.0 percent)	77
Conduct disorder, undersocialized, nonaggressive	6	(1.4 percent)	15	(1.8 percent)	21
Conduct disorder, socialized, nonaggressive	38	(8.6 percent)	71	(8.7 percent)	109
Total	441	(100 percent)	815	(100 percent)	1,256

Substance Abuse

In his comprehensive report on drug use in the United States and along the United States–Mexico border, Adams (1986) notes that studies of drug use among Hispanics have been confined to small ethnic enclaves—that is, the barrios (neighborhoods). He cites a study that reported that Mexican American adolescents were at least fourteen times as likely to be abusing inhalants as their Anglo counterparts in a national sample. He also describes a pilot study conducted among eighth and twelfth graders in three small Southwestern communities and notes the "relatively high prevalence of inhalants in these towns" ranging in size from three thousand to eleven thousand people, where the reported use of inhalants among high school seniors was lower than among eighth graders, indicating the severity of drug use among younger Mexican American adolescents. When interpreting these studies, one must be careful not to generalize from school-based surveys to the entire Mexican American youth population, given the high dropout rate in the later school years. Adams also found that in Texas Hispanics account for almost 57 percent of heroin admissions and 88 percent of inhalant admissions to drug rehabilitation centers. Inhalant abuse is obviously a significant problem for the adolescent Mexican American population, especially those living in poor barrios, where the median age of first use among people admitted for treatment is about fourteen to fifteen years. Adams points to the isolation and relative poverty of some of these communities as important contributing factors, noting lower levels of education and higher levels of unemployment as two main indicators.

These observations are supported by Chavez, Beauvais, and Oetting (1986), who surveyed substance use among the youth of a small Southwestern town. In this survey, Mexican American and Anglo youth were compared on drug-use variables and gender differences and then compared with a national sample and a group of urban barrio youth. Use of alcohol, stimulants, tranquilizers, and heroin was significantly higher in the small-town sample than in the national sample. There were two other significant differences between the Hispanic small-town sample and the barrio sample: a higher percentage of small-town subjects had tried alcohol and a lower percentage had used inhalants. The researchers concluded that Hispanic young people with physical or psychological problems should be assessed for possible drug involvement, particularly because they have been found to be more vulnerable to drug use than their Anglo peers.

Adolescent Mothers

Recently, deAnda (1985) studied the life experiences of Mexican American adolescent mothers aged twelve to seventeen years who were pregnant or had delivered a child within the past twelve months. In general, deAnda found that, compared with the bilingual Mexican American group (N = 22), the Mexican American Spanish-speaking women (N = 19) received less support from their extended family; had fewer peer contacts; had more limited knowledge of child care, particularly about medical crises; and had lower incomes. Spanish-speaking subjects in this sample responded to upsetting situations with suppression of emotions and withdrawal, manifested by nervousness and somatic complaints, a pattern that has clinical implications.

Sociocultural Aspects of Assessment

In working with Mexican American patients, two sociocultural factors are of particular importance in the assessment of the child and family: family structure and level of acculturation.

Family Structure

As noted previously, Mexican American norms emphasize the parent/ child dyad over the marital dyad. Hence, during the initial stage of forming a therapeutic relationship, a focus on parent/child interactions will be accepted more readily than a focus on marital issues or on the parents' families of origin. Furthermore, a therapeutic focus on individual needs over familial needs may meet with resistance. For example, Falicov (1982) indicates that it is unwise to try to convince a Mexican American mother that she needs time for herself in an attempt to decrease her involvement with her children, as this is contrary to the cultural ideal of maternal self-sacrifice.

It is important that the therapist respect the traditional family age/sex hierarchies of power and convey a sense of *respeto* (respect) by addressing questions to the father first, then to the mother, then to other adults, and finally to the older and younger children. A neutral opening allowing the family to choose its own spokesperson is also appropriate; however, if an adolescent son or daughter begins or dominates a session, it may be symptomatic of a weakened parental subsystem and contrary to the public sociocultural norms. In this situation, the therapist might want to redirect the session toward the parents in order to strengthen culturally consonant generational boundaries, as well as to build the parents' trust in the therapist. Viewed from another perspective, initiation or domination of the session by an adolescent son or daughter may indicate a considerable gulf between the parents' and the children's levels of acculturation. These children may have been functioning in a translator/negotiator role with the outside world for quite some time, and this fact is relevant and is important to explore with the family.

Level of Acculturation

In addition to the usual family social and developmental history, it is important to obtain information on the patient's and family's immigration history and generational status in the United States. This information will influence interpretation of the data obtained throughout the assessment process. For example, a family that recently immigrated from Mexico may be unfamiliar with American customs and norms and may possess a distinctly traditional Mexican worldview. In contrast, ethnic differences may be insignificant in a later-generation family.

Family members often acculturate at different rates. Usually children adapt to American values and norms more readily than parents, often stimulating intergenerational acculturation conflicts. Within the parental dyad itself, there may also be acculturation differences, often related to degree of adherence to traditional family and sex roles or to different ages at migration. For these reasons, the various complexities of acculturation within the family need to be carefully assessed.

Issues in Treatment

Historically, Mexican Americans have shown low rates of mental health service utilization. In the past, this was partly explained by unfavorable attitudes toward these services. More recent studies have indicated that Mexican Americans in fact have a high positive regard for counseling and psychotherapy (Acosta and Sheehan, 1976; Karno and Edgerton, 1969). Explanations for low utilization have included language differences between Mexican Americans and staff members of mental health services, social-class and cultural differences, insufficient numbers of mental health services in the barrios, widespread use of physicians for primary help with psychological problems, lack of awareness of available services, and the tendency of this population to defer seeking help for mental health problems (Acosta, Yamamoto, and Evans, 1982).

Given these obstacles to using mental health services, it is imperative to attend to those factors that will facilitate establishing a good therapeutic relationship with Mexican American patients. The following discussion focuses on the concepts of personal distance and self-disclosure in this relationship, and on special concerns in the entry phase of treatment. Clinical cases are then presented to illustrate such issues as differing identity crises and different treatment modalities. Throughout this section, the emphasis is on the family, because intervention with Mexican American children and adolescents invariably involves the entire family.

Personal Distance

Therapists should be aware of certain characteristics of verbal and nonverbal communication in their initial face-to-face encounters with a Mexican American family that will facilitate forming a positive therapeutic alliance. *Personalismo,* a Mexican American concept denoting a preference for personal contact and individualized attention in social interactions, contrasts with the Anglo preference for impersonal regulations and the organizational "chain of command." Mexican Americans expect less physical distance in personal interactions and are accustomed to frequent physical contact (LeVine and Padilla, 1980). Handshakes between acquaintances and embraces between friends are the norm upon meeting and separating (Padilla, 1981). Even Mexican American children have been observed to engage in more physical contact than Anglo or African American children and to use less space between themselves and playmates (Aiello and Jones, 1971). Thus, when exchanging initial introductions, it is appropriate for the therapist to stand close to the person, exchange a warm handshake, and perhaps even place a hand on the client's shoulder, all of which tends to reduce the client's anxiety, to increase the client's comfort, and to facilitate openness in the early sessions. In greeting Mexican American clients, I find that I typically put my arm on the shoulder of the "identified child patient" and engage in casual conversation as the family and I walk toward my office. When this is not appropriate, such as when an older adolescent is the "identified patient," I usually engage one or both parents in casual conversation. These verbal exchanges offer vital information about language use and preferences of the various family members and give important information on how to direct the session.

When the family are settling down in the office to begin the interview, they usually move their chairs so that they can sit very close together. The therapist may also find it effective to move his chair closer to the family member or members he is addressing.

Self-Disclosure

Self-disclosure among Mexican Americans in therapy is another issue to which therapists should be sensitive. LeVine and Padilla (1980) and Falicov (1982), who emphasize that Mexican Americans will disclose personal information very slowly, propose several ways in which a therapist can facilitate self-disclosure. For example, a social phase that transmits the therapist's interest in the persons rather than focusing on procedures is essential. Falicov suggests that disclosure can be facilitated when the therapist becomes a philosopher of life through storytelling, anecdotes, humor, analogies, and proverbs.

Entering Treatment

Acosta, Yamamoto, and Evans (1982) stress the importance of the therapist's showing a sense of personal interest—that is, friendliness and warmth—when exploring the presenting problem and gathering information about the family's referral. During the initial stages, as Falicov (1982) suggests, the therapist should not challenge the family's statements that their lifestyle follows culturally prescribed norms, even if their actual behavior suggests otherwise. Falicov states: "For example, a wife may say that her husband is the 'boss' although the therapist and the rest of the family are all aware that she is dominating the therapy session and the family. These observations need to be placed in their cultural context and internally noted—but not verbalized" (p. 151).

In general, searching for strengths and praising the family's dignity will facilitate the development of a positive therapeutic alliance. Interpretations of dysfunction or direct confrontations tend to increase the Mexican American family's insecurity and may be perceived as disapproval rather than as a stimulus for change. Mexican American families usually provide enough information in the first interview to enable the therapist to formulate a working hypothesis that can be described summarily to the family. However, as Falicov (1982) warns, to close the first interview with an explicit "contract" may be too task oriented for Mexican Americans, who tend to be person oriented. There should be a general agreement about the proposed treatment approach and an estimate of the number of sessions needed; treatment objectives should be phrased clearly and focused either on the specific symptom or on improving parent/child relationships. In Burruel-Gonzalez's study (1975), Mexican American patients expected what they termed *platicas-consejos* (discussion/advice-giving) in therapy. *Platicas-consejos* signified a mutual, sharing relationship between the therapist and patient that resulted in learning and growth for the patient. Therapy was perceived in psychological terms, such as insight, development of the self, and increased reasoning capabilities of the patient. Burruel-Gonzalez pointed out that this finding is "not supportive of the common belief that lower-income and minority people expect primarily direction, concrete assistance, and tangible results from a psychiatric setting" (p. 175).

Acosta, Yamamoto, and Evans (1982) stressed the importance of educating Hispanic patients to the process of psychotherapy by explaining the treatment plan, what is expected of the patient, and approximately how long the treatment is expected to last.

Because of the cultural emphasis on cooperation and respect for authority, many Mexican Americans feel it is impolite to disagree, a value that may interfere with formation of a positive therapeutic alliance. A Mexican American family may seem to accept the treatment contract suggested by the therapist even though they are covertly resistant to the treatment plan, as in the following vignette.

Ana, a fourteen-year-old oldest daughter, was brought to the clinic by her parents for "rebelliousness"—namely, she was "boy crazy" and wanted to talk on the phone with boys, go to parties, and meet them at the mall. Ana's parents, who had moved to the United States ten years earlier from Mexico, had learned a little English but preferred to use Spanish in the sessions. Ana's father, who served as the family spokesperson, preferred to direct his answers to the Anglo male therapist, even though questions typically were asked of him by the Mexican American female therapist.

Ana and her siblings were extremely polite and reserved during the family interview, occasionally smiling as they were discussed. Ana's mother was also reserved and tended to agree with her husband's view of the problem. When seen alone, Ana described herself in a manner that reflected attitudes and interests typical for a girl her age reared in a predominantly Anglo culture. She talked a lot about socializing at school with both boys and girls, and wished that her parents would allow her to have contact with her friends outside school. She spoke enviously of her thirteen-year-old brother, who was being given considerably more freedom by their parents. She exhibited some guilt that her interest in boys went against her parents' wishes; on the basis of her interactions with peers, however, she perceived this interest as normal.

When the therapists met with the family after the assessment to provide feedback and recommendations, they discussed Ana's conflict between her parents' wishes and her peer culture. They recommended that Ana be seen individually by the female therapist to discuss her conflict, after which a family therapy session would be planned. The parents tentatively agreed with these recommendations but did not follow through. Neither Ana not the family returned for therapy.

This vignette brings up two important issues that are worth commenting on—one cultural, the other practical. The cultural issue, which apparently was not addressed adequately in formulating a treatment plan, was the substantial difference between Ana's level of acculturation and that of her parents. Certainly when viewed from an Anglo perspective, her behavior and attitudes appear typical for a girl her age; however, when viewed from a traditional Mexican American cultural perspective, her behavior would be considered very deviant, almost to the point of bringing shame on the family. If the difference in levels of acculturation between the parents and the daughter had been made explicit, so that the parents felt supported in their cultural values, a more mutual understanding might have been reached by the end of this initial assessment. Practically speaking, the patient should be encouraged to discuss with the therapist any disagreements with the therapeutic plan. The family's apparent resistance to the treatment plan was not addressed either by the family or by the therapist. The therapist should actively encourage any questions or uncertainties on the part of the patient or the family, encourage the patient to make specific requests, statements of need, and self-disclosure, and reward the patient for doing so.

Language is another important variable to consider when working with the Mexican American population. Language facility and preference are important indicators of level of acculturation. The various language preferences within a family may reflect significant family dynamics and points of acculturation, and intergenerational conflicts or harmony. Whether the family speaks Spanish or English, however, the Mexican American linguistic style tends to vary between public and private situations (Falicov, 1982; Paz, 1961). In public, it is prone to allusions, indirect statements, and guardedness, while in private conversations—reserved only for intimate relationships—it may be bolder, more straightforward, and more direct.

Treatment Modalities

The case vignettes that follow illustrate different treatment modalities to emphasize that a particular approach may be required for a particular problem. These vignettes highlight some common themes of conflict that frequently occur among Mexican American youth and their families.

LeVine and Padilla (1980) state that family therapy offers particular promise with Mexican Americans because of the importance of, and the support inherent in, kinship ties. In addition, Falicov (1982) has concluded that Mexican American families of lower socioeconomic levels tend to respond best to a brief and problem-oriented approach that redefines the problem in interactional terms centered on the relationship between parents and children. The cultural emphasis on hierarchies within the family lends itself to a structural family therapy approach that emphasizes generational boundaries (Minuchin, 1974).

The following case illustrates these issues and highlights a theme of conflict common among Mexican American youth that goes beyond the common identity issues of "Who am I?" In this particular case, the conflict manifests itself as an acculturational and generational problem between parents and children.

Sergio (fifteen), Laura (thirteen), and their family were seen because of the parents' concern about Sergio's "bad temper" and Laura's sexual behavior. The parents complained about Sergio's anger, poor impulse control, and self-destructive behavior, and Laura's overt interest in boys. Sergio, Mr. C. (forty-three, migrated from Mexico to the United States thirteen years before), Mrs. C. (thirty-four, born and raised in the United States), and Laura attended the first session. The Anglo intake therapist had reported that the mother was the family spokesperson, but later it was determined that the father spoke only Spanish, and the therapist was not Spanish-speaking. Accordingly, the family was transferred to the author for subsequent treatment.

The mother reported that the father was having difficulty as the children reached adolescence and began to assert themselves more, which he viewed as blatant disrespect. Both teenagers reported that they were doing well in school and related very well to the therapist. Mr. C. was emotional and articulate as he complained about his children's exposure to values and standards of morality that were considerably "lower" than what he wanted for them and what he had learned from his strict father. Sergio agreed that his father accurately described their defiant attitudes toward his values, and he explained that he and Laura constantly felt torn in two opposite directions. On the one hand was his father's strict, "old world" view of family life, in which children unquestionably accept the high moral and ethical standards set for them; on the other hand was the constant peer pressure to go along with the crowd. The adolescents pleaded with the therapist to help their father understand that they felt very conflicted emotionally and had resorted to hurting themselves as a way of releasing their tension and frustration. The therapist ended the session by translating for the father what his children had said in English and assuring him of their loyalty, love, and respect for him but also explaining the pressure they felt to be accepted by their peers at school. The therapist made three recommendations to the family: first, that all corporal punishment cease immediately; second, that the family members discuss in Spanish how they had been feeling so that the father could understand his children's emotional dilemma; and finally, that Sergio be allowed to stay temporarily with someone in the extended family in order to reduce the immediate tension in the home.

Over the next several sessions, the family improved dramatically, the level of tension decreased significantly, and there were no outbursts of aggression by anybody. Family therapy involved finding some middle ground for each teenager between the father's rules and the peer pressure to do "illicit" things for group acceptance. The mother, who was more modern in her views, acted as a mediator between her husband and the children. Finally, the father was encouraged to express nurturance and support toward his teenagers, whose earlier views of him as playful and affectionate had been replaced by experiences with him as angry and disapproving.

The complexity of the problems that Mexican American families present to a therapist often necessitates that the therapist play more than just a therapeutic role. For example, families who are referred for counseling are often involved with some other agency, such as the legal system or the child protective system. In order to work effectively with the family, the therapist must not only be the traditional clinician but must also work as a mediator, advocate, and resource finder. These roles are particularly critical when the "outside" agents are unfamiliar with and insensitive to Mexican American culture. The following vignette offers a good example of the delicate interplay between these issues.

Susana, age five, was referred for therapy with her mother, a forty-four-year-old single parent, after the child had been sexually abused by two teenage neighbors and, two years earlier, by a former boyfriend of the mother's. Susana was in foster placement, and the mother's service plan with the Department of Human Services (DHS) required that she recognize the seriousness of Susana's victimization, the child's needs, and the mother's responsibility to protect her. Although mother and daughter had a close relationship, the mother clearly lacked adequate parenting skills, evidently stemming from her own experience of inadequate parenting and protection (she, too, had been victimized as a child and young adult), and possible limited intellectual ability.

By conducting the sessions in Spanish, the therapist was able to elicit much more emotional material. Using Spanish also enabled the mother to maintain some sense of privacy from an Anglo DHS child advocate attorney who was vigorously seeking termination of parental rights. The therapist agreed with the mother that the grounds for seeking termination of her parental rights were culturally biased and insufficient to warrant such action. Examples of these grounds were that no playground was located close to the mother's home; that the mother worked and would not be home when Susana got out of school (she had arranged for a competent sitter); and that the mother would not be able to provide Susana with the kind of lifestyle she had in her Anglo foster home.

In this case, the therapist was a mediator between the mother and DHS, as well as an advocate, protecting the mother's interests and privacy and working with her toward fulfilling the DHS requirements that would allow Susana to return home.

In working with younger children or severely traumatized children, individual play therapy may be the modality of choice. Intensive and individually focused therapy is absolutely vital to helping the abused child work through the severe trauma and to reducing the probability of perpetuating the abuse syndrome in the next generation, as often happens. In the following case example, the therapist was an Anglo female with considerable experience with Mexican Americans.

Alma, a nine-year-old Mexican American girl, was referred for individual therapy by Child Protective Services after she had been severely physically abused by her stepfather, Javier, a Nicaraguan exile who had lived with the family for one year. The abuse occurred after Javier discovered Alma playing with his gun. He punished her brutally over a period of three days, breaking an arm and ribs and burning her palms by holding them over a stove burner.

Alma's hands were severely scarred, and she wore mittens throughout her therapy to keep scar tissue from constricting the extension of her fingers. Alma was seen for thirty individual play therapy sessions over a year.

When Alma started therapy, she was extremely frightened and shy, spoke little, initiated little, and had difficulty following through in her play. The therapist took a nondirective approach to the play therapy, participating as directed by Alma and asking questions or reflecting feelings as seemed appropriate. Early play involved issues of authority, submission, and self-assertion. For example, Alma played games in which she held the position of authority (such as teacher or therapist) and told the therapist to pretend she was Alma. In the process of therapy, she moved from an "abusive authority/submissive other" stance to a "moderate authority/assertive other" stance, appearing to model the behavior of the therapist. In her anger at Javier, she initially denied that she was Hispanic, viewing her mother and Javier as Hispanic and as "bad" and not wanting to identify with them. The therapist pointed out that her natural father, whom she liked, was also Hispanic (a fact she sometimes denied), and both her therapist and her Anglo foster mother encouraged Alma to be proud of her Hispanic heritage. She gradually became more comfortable with her ethnicity, no longer appearing to equate this with abusiveness.

In treatment, she frequently reenacted a drama in which she and the therapist alternated roles between a vicious, devouring wolf and a terror-stricken child. As Alma gradually developed the ability to tolerate and manage these powerful feelings, she also began using realistic problem-solving strategies in which she called the police or found other ways to escape or thwart her persecutors. Notable in these dramas, in contrast to Alma's early play, was her ability to organize and carry through a play theme involving two persons, and her comfort with assertiveness in both organizing and playing the parts. Around this same time, Alma began attempting to do chin-ups on the clothing bar in the closet, trying to get stronger despite the pain to her scarred hands.

Generally, by the time of termination of therapy, Alma's fear and anger appeared to be at manageable levels. She was more cognitively organized and more able to problem solve. She had internalized an image of a nurturant adult who was moderate in her use of power and authority, and she had developed a healthy self-esteem that included acceptance of her ethnicity and enabled her to be assertive about getting her needs met and protecting herself.

Conclusions and Future Directions

It behooves clinicians to operate from a philosophical framework that presumes that nothing about a culture is sacred or exempt from clinical and adaptational analysis. For example, this author considers traditional Mexican American norms that confine women to the status of lesser human beings to be dysfunctional and to be targets for change within psychotherapy. Differential (and discriminatory) socialization of Mexican American boys and girls is completely antithetical to successful living in a highly complex technological society that requires the full talents of all persons, regardless of gender. I make this personal value orientation explicit to my patients, when the time is right. Some patients actively oppose this position, and their view is respected; others respond favorably and enthusiastically.

Along these same lines, Rogler, Malgady, Costantino, and Blumenthal (1987) state, "It is our contention that when therapy modalities are modified to address the needs of Hispanic clients, the adapted therapy need not isomorphically reflect the client's cultural characteristics" (p. 569). Isomorphic reinforcement of cultural traits by therapists implies that those traits are adaptive, while departures from this position imply that some cultural traits serve as an obstacle to therapy and that acculturation to the values and norms of American society is an additional and valid standard of adjustment. The ultimate aim of psychotherapy should be relief from psychological distress and the adaptation of Mexican Americans to American society in such a way that ethnic identity and pride are not negated or diminished.

The clinical case examples offered in this chapter suggest that the therapeutic process can be facilitated greatly when the therapist is bilingual and bicultural. Unfortunately, there are not enough professionally trained bilingual and bicultural therapists to meet the mental health needs of the ever-growing Mexican American population. It is highly unlikely that this situation will change dramatically in the near future. However, there are other options: non–Mexican American, monolingual clinicians serving a Mexican American clientele can be trained, both didactically and experientially, through supervision and consultation with bilingual and bicultural Mexican American clinicians, to work more effectively with their clients. The sociocultural and socioeconomic gulf between the Mexican American client and non–Mexican American clinician may not be eradicated entirely, but it can be bridged by education and training and by providing clinicians with experience in culturally sensitive research and service delivery (Acosta, Yamamoto, and Evans, 1982; Malgady and Rogler, 1987).

Priorities should be refocused to include a renewed commitment to primary prevention programs. Low-income, predominantly Spanish-speaking, undocumented Mexican Americans are at high risk for the development of general health and mental health problems. The need for early intervention with this group is clearly established. Fortunately, there already exists a model for such a primary prevention program: the Houston Parent-Child Development Center (H-PCDC), reported on by Johnson and Walker (1987). The H-PCDC has been in operation since the early seventies, and its success in the area of prevention has been impressive. The center has had its greatest impact on conduct disorders, problems that clinicians have found the most difficult to treat. Without preventive approaches, these children tend to go on to more antisocial acts in adolescence and as adults. Prevention, as described in the H-PCDC program, is not coercive, but it frees the individual to participate harmoniously and autonomously in society.

Finally, in an excellent paper that offers an epidemiological perspective on the mental health of individuals of Mexican origin, Roberts (1986) proposes that future research efforts should include rigorous, large-scale epidemiological studies of the mental health of Mexican-origin children and adolescents. "First, and foremost, if we are interested in primary prevention of diseases that are the product of lifelong interactions of risk factors, the earlier such preventive efforts begin, the likelier they will have an impact. Both the design of intervention programs and the assessment of their impact require knowledge of incidence, prevalence, and putative risk factors in the target population" (p. 14).

In conclusion, I urge all clinicians working directly with Mexican American children and adolescents and their families to publish and share their clinical experiences. In this way, we can begin the important process of dialogue around the critical issues of providing these clients with the effective and culturally sensitive clinical services they need.

References

Acosta, F. X., and Sheehan, J. "Preferences Toward Mexican-American and Anglo-American Psychotherapists." *Journal of Consulting and Clinical Psychology,* 1976, *44,* 272–279.

Acosta, F. X., Yamamoto, J., and Evans, L. A. *Effective Psychotherapy for Low-Income and Minority Patients.* New York: Plenum, 1982.

Adams, E. H. "An Overview of Drug Use in the United States and Along the U.S.–Mexico Border." Paper presented at the U.S.–Mexico Border Public Health Association Conference, Monterrey, Mexico, Apr. 28, 1986.

Aiello, J., and Jones, W. "Field Study of the Proxemic Behavior of Young School Children in Three Subcultural Groups." *Journal of Personality and Social Psychology,* 1971, *19,* 351–356.

Baca Zinn, M. "Urban Kinship and Midwest Chicano Families: Review and Reformulation." Paper presented at annual meeting of the Western Social Science Association, Denver, Colo., Apr. 23, 1977.

Baca Zinn, M. "Employment and Education of Mexican-American Women: The Interplay of Modernity and Ethnicity in Eight Families." *Harvard Educational Review,* 1980, *50*(1), 47–62.

Burruel-Gonzalez, G. "The Definitional Process Among Mexican Americans and Its Effect on Utilization of Mental Health Services." Unpublished doctoral dissertation, Graduate School of Social Work, University of Denver, 1975.

Chavez, E., Beauvais, F., and Oetting, E. R. "Drug Use by Small-Town Mexican-American Youth: A Pilot Study." *Hispanic Journal of Behavioral Sciences,* 1986, *8,* 243–258.

Cromwell, R., and Ruiz, R. A. "The Myth of Macho Dominance in Decision-Making Within Mexican and Chicano Families." *Hispanic Journal of Behavioral Sciences,* 1979, *1*(4), 355–373.

DeAnda, D. "The Hispanic Adolescent Mother: Assessing Risk in Relation to Stress and Social Support." In W. A. Vega and M. R. Miranda (eds.), *Stress and Hispanic Mental Health: Relating Research to Service Delivery.* Rockville, Md.: National Institute of Mental Health, 1985.

Falicov, C. J. "Mexican Families." In M. McGoldrick, J. K. Pearce, and J. Giordano (eds.), *Ethnicity and Family Therapy.* New York: Guilford Press, 1982.

Johnson, D. L., and Walker, T. "The Primary Prevention of Behavior Problems in Mexican-American Children." *American Journal of Community Psychology,* 1987, *15,* 375–385.

Karno, M., and Edgerton, R. B. "Perception of Mental Illness in a Mexican American Community." *Archives of General Psychiatry,* 1969, *20,* 233–238.

Keefe, S. E., Padilla, A. M., and Carlos, M. L. *Emotional Support Systems in Two Cultures: A Comparison of Mexican-Americans and Anglo Americans.* Occasional Paper No. 7. Los Angeles: Spanish Speaking Mental Health Research Center, University of California at Los Angeles, 1978a.

Keefe, S. E., Padilla, A. M., Carlos, M. L. "The Mexican-American Extended Family as an Emotional Support System." In J. M. Casas and

S. E. Keefe (eds.), *Family and Mental Health in the Mexican-American Community*. Monograph No. 7. Los Angeles: Spanish Speaking Mental Health Research Center, University of California at Los Angeles, 1978b.

Keefe, S. E., Padilla, A. M., and Carlos, M. L. "The Mexican-American Extended Family as an Emotional Support System." *Human Organization*, 1979, *38*, 144–152.

LeVine, E. S., and Padilla, A. M. *Crossing Cultures in Therapy: Pluralistic Counseling for the Hispanic*. Pacific Grove, Calif.: Brooks/Cole, 1980.

Malgady, R. G., and Rogler, L. H. "Ethnocultural and Lingustic Bias in Mental Health Evaluations of Hispanics." *American Psychologist*, 1987, *42*(3), 228–234.

Mindel, C. H. "Extended Familism Among Urban Mexican Americans, Anglos, and Blacks." *Hispanic Journal of Behavioral Sciences*, 1980, *2*(1), 21–34.

Minuchin, S. *Families and Family Therapy*. Cambridge, Mass.: Harvard University Press, 1974.

Murillo, N. "The Mexican American Family." In N. W. Wagner and M. J. Haug (eds.), *Chicanos: Social and Psychological Perspectives*. St. Louis: Mosby, 1971.

Padilla, A. M. "Pluralistic Counseling and Psychotherapy for Hispanic Americans." In A. J. Marsella and P. B. Pedersen (eds.), *Cross-Cultural Counseling and Psychotherapy*. New York: Pergamon Press, 1981.

Paz, O. *The Labyrinth of Solitude: Life and Thought in Mexico*. New York: Evergreen Books, 1961.

Ramirez, O., and Arce, C. H. "The Contemporary Chicano Family: An Empirically Based Review." In A. Baron, Jr. (ed.), *Explorations in Chicano Psychology*. New York: Praeger, 1981.

Roberts, R. E. "Prevalence of Psychological Distress Among Mexican Americans." *Journal of Health and Social Behavior*, 1980, *21*, 134–145.

Roberts, R. E. "An Epidemiologic Perspective on the Mental Health of People of Mexican Origin." Paper presented (under the auspices of the Hogg Foundation for Mental Health) at fifth Robert Lee Sutherland Seminar, San Antonio, Tex., Sept. 24–26, 1986.

Rogler, L. H., Malgady, R. G., Costantino, G., and Blumenthal, R. " What Do Culturally Sensitive Mental Health Services Mean? The Case of Hispanics." *American Psychologist*, 1987, *42*(6), 565–570.

Sena-Rivera, J. "Extended Kinship in the United States: Competing Models and the Case of la Familia Chicana." *Journal of Marriage and the Family*, 1979, *41*, 121–129.

Shrout, P. E., and others. "Mental Health Status Among Puerto Ricans, Mexican Americans, and Non-Hispanic Whites." *American Journal of Community Psychology*, 1992, *20*(6), 729–752.

Stoker, D. H., and Meadow, A. "Cultural Differences in Guidance Clinic Patients." *American Journal of Social Psychiatry,* 1974, *20,* 186–202.

Trankina, F. "Clinical Issues and Techniques in Working with Hispanic Children and Their Families." In G. J. Powell, J. Yamamoto, A. Romero, and A. Morales (eds.), *The Psychosocial Development of Minority Group Children.* New York: Brunner/Mazel, 1983.

Ybarra-Soriano, L. "Conjugal Role Relationships in the Chicano Family." Unpublished doctoral dissertation, Department of Sociology, University of California at Berkeley, 1977.

Chapter Eight

Puerto Rican Adolescents

Jaime E. Inclán
D. Gloria Herron

In order to present issues in the assessment and treatment of Puerto Rican adolescents from an ecological point of view, this chapter begins by providing a picture of the unique sociocultural experience of Puerto Ricans living on the U.S. mainland. Against this background, the experience of mainland Puerto Rican adolescents is highlighted, followed by special considerations in the psychosocial assessment process. The chapter concludes with a presentation of clinical considerations in ecologically oriented individual, group, and family therapy with these adolescents.

Demographic Data

The U.S. Bureau of the Census (1996) estimated that in 1995 there were 27,521,000 Hispanics in the United States (excluding Puerto Rico), representing 10.3 percent of the U.S. population. The largest subgroup of Hispanics is Mexican American (17.9 million), followed by Puerto Ricans (2.7 million). Since the 1980 census, the Puerto Rican population has increased by more than 600,000, based on estimates of net movement of persons to and from Puerto Rico.

In 1995, Puerto Ricans represented about 10 percent of the total Hispanic population of the United States (U.S. Bureau of the Census, 1996). Puerto Ricans resided in every state; approximately 75 percent lived in urban areas. In 1985, the highest concentrations were found in New York and New Jersey (total of 61 percent)

(Perez, 1985). In New York State they represented 59.4 percent of the state's Hispanic population of 1.7 million. Of New York City's 1.4 million Hispanics, 61.2 percent were Puerto Rican (Governor's Advisory Committee for Hispanic Affairs, 1985).

More than 33 percent (2,420,000) of Puerto Rican families (or households of two or more people) lived below the poverty level in 1995, compared to 11.6 percent of the total population (U.S. Bureau of the Census, 1996). Of Puerto Rican families headed by females, 74.4 percent were below the poverty level. In 1995, the median family income of Puerto Ricans ($20,929) was the lowest of all Hispanic subgroups, because of such factors as family composition, educational level, and employment status of family members.

The Hispanic population is younger than the non-Hispanic population; median ages are 26.2 years for the former and 34.3 years for the latter, with the difference due to higher fertility levels among Hispanics. The median age of Puerto Ricans is 26 years, with 10.6 percent under age 5 and 26.5 percent between the ages of 5 and 17. In 1985, only an estimated 2.7 percent of Puerto Ricans were over 65 (U.S. Bureau of the Census, 1985).

In 1985, the mean family size among Puerto Ricans was 3.62 persons, compared to 3.23 in the general population and 3.18 for all non-Hispanics. Families of three persons or more accounted for 59.6 percent of all families, 58.5 percent of non-Hispanic families, and 75.6 percent of Puerto Rican families. Further, among Puerto Ricans a three-member family was very likely to be a mother with two children rather than two parents with one child, because 44 percent of Puerto Rican families were headed by a female. This is in sharp contrast to 16.2 percent in the general population and 15.7 percent among non-Hispanics.

In 1985, only 46 percent of Puerto Ricans older than twenty-five had completed high school (compared with 74 percent in the total U.S. population); 13 percent had completed less than five years of school. The median number of school years completed was 11.2. Of Puerto Rican males sixteen and older, 15 percent were unemployed, compared to 7.8 percent of the total population. The figures for females were 13.3 percent and 7.4 percent, respectively.

Population projections from the U.S. Bureau of the Census (1996) are based on varying estimates of fertility, life expectancy, and yearly net immigration. Projections for the Hispanic population in the year 2010 vary from 36,652,000 to 45,760,000, when Hispanics will replace African Americans as the largest ethnic minority group in the United States. Using the middle range of estimated growth, the Census Bureau projects that by 2010 Hispanics will account for approximately 13.8 percent of the population, or one of seven Americans.

Epidemiological Data

The majority of mainland Puerto Ricans reside in the greater metropolitan New York area. It is primarily this group that is the focus of this chapter. Unfortunately, despite the size of the mainland Puerto Rican population and its unique sociocultural problems, data on mental health issues are scarce.

One of the few studies of Puerto Rican children using mental health clinics in the New York area was conducted by the Hispanic Research Center at Fordham University (Canino, Earley, and Rogler, 1980). This study was based on cases reported to the New York State Department of Mental Hygiene during the fiscal year 1976–77. Puerto Rican children under thirteen years of age were represented in all fourteen of the most commonly indicated psychiatric problem categories. Among these 4,196 children, the percentages were as follows: antisocial attitudes, 5 percent; social withdrawal, 7 percent; dependency, 7 percent; speech articulation problems, 9 percent; sleep problems, 10 percent; depressed/inferiority, 11 percent; other physical problems, 15 percent; anger/belligerence, 16 percent; anxiety, fears, phobias, 17 percent; agitation/hyperactivity, 17 percent; social relations with other than family, 21 percent; social relations with family, 22 percent; inadequate intellectual development, 22 percent; social performance in school, 44 percent. In ten of these categories, percentages were higher for Puerto Rican children than for white children. The investigators advise caution in interpreting these data, because of the tendency to underreport cases and the difficulties of cross-cultural diagnoses; nevertheless, it seems valid to conclude that Puerto Rican children in New York are overrepresented in a significant number of psychiatric categories.

In a more recent study of Hispanic (N = 96) and African American (N = 53) children seen at a New York City hospital outpatient clinic, Canino, Gould, Prupis, and Shaffer (1986) found the children to be experiencing high levels of stress and family problems, as well as physical disorders. For the Hispanic group, Spanish was predominantly spoken in the home, and a high percentage of the children's mothers were homemakers born outside the United States. Twenty-two symptoms were examined for both groups. In the five categories in which the two groups differed significantly, a higher proportion of Hispanics than blacks had symptoms of morbid depression, fears and phobias, anxiety and panic, school refusal, and disturbances of relationships with other children. Thirty percent or more of the Hispanic children were represented in the following categories: withdrawal, disinhibition, disturbance of relationship with mother, disturbance of relationship with father, restlessness and fidgetiness, disobedience, and disturbance of sleep.

Comprehensive epidemiological studies specific to the mental health of Puerto Rican adolescents are lacking, but clinical reports have begun to identify typical problems in this population. Hardy-Fanta and Montana (1982) describe the impact of migration on female Hispanic adolescents as manifesting itself as "either sexual or aggressive acting-out or as depressed withdrawal or excessive withdrawal or excessive conformity. . . . rebelliousness, poor school functioning, and impulsively established male-female relationships" (p. 352).

Social indexes provide additional information indirectly related to the mental health of Puerto Rican youth. In 1986 the New York City Mayor's Commission on Hispanic Concerns reported that 47 percent of Puerto Rican households had incomes of less than $7,500. Almost one third of Hispanic families had dependent children under age eighteen, and 20.5 percent of the 100,000 registrants in the city's Child Health Program were Puerto Rican. In that program, the most common problems were iron deficiency anemia, growth problems, asthma, and English language difficulties. With the economic reality of Puerto Rican mothers needing to work outside the home, unable to afford child care, and leaving children unattended, accidents were found to be the single largest cause of death for Puerto Rican children under the age of sixteen.

Nationwide, 18 percent of the thirteen- to nineteen-year-old adolescent AIDS cases reported from June 1981 to June 1996 were Hispanic. During the same period, 23 percent of the reported cases in children under age thirteen were Hispanic. Of the AIDS cases of adolescents and adults under age 25 with the single risk factor of intravenous drug abuse, 35 percent were Hispanic, compared to 5 percent who were white and not Hispanic (Centers for Disease Control and Prevention, 1996).

Birth statistics for 1991 indicate that 21.7 percent of American-born Puerto Rican women who gave birth were under age twenty, and 57.5 percent were unmarried. These data compare with 13 percent teenage mothers and 29.6 percent unmarried mothers in the total population (Centers for Disease Control and Prevention, 1993).

Migration and Transculturation

Migration from Puerto Rico to the U.S. mainland began slowly early in the twentieth century. Mass migration did not begin until after World War II. In 1967 there was a net migration of 26,000 people, but a total of 3 million people had actually moved between Puerto Rico and the mainland. By 1970 the mainland Puerto Rican population was 1.5 million, about half of the island population, and New York City had a larger Puerto Rican population than San Juan, the island's largest city. There was negative migration again from 1972 to 1977. Growth of the mainland population continues and is now a function of early marriages and high fertility rates (Sowell, 1981).

Migration served the interests of capitalism in Puerto Rico as well as in the United States. In Puerto Rico, migration served to alleviate the structural problem of massive unemployment. In the United States, the immigration of Puerto Rican workers, like that of previous ethnic groups, helped to keep wages low. Puerto Ricans, migrating in search of job opportunities, assumed low-level jobs that nobody else wanted, with correspondingly meager salaries.

An understanding of the identity conflict experienced by Puerto Ricans in the United States is facilitated by a developmental evolutionary view of their migration and transculturation. The authors' observations in this regard coincide with those of others who have studied various ethnic groups and with those of family theorists (Bowen, 1976), who contend that change takes place over the generations—in particular, that it takes at least three generations for substantive change to be effected. In this evolutionary progression, the second and third generations, currently the numerical majority of Puerto Ricans, experience the most profound difficulties.

The first generation tends to uphold its culture of origin and values when in the new host culture. For Puerto Ricans, these traditional values include a family structure with very strong ties and great importance placed on the extended family. There is also a *compadrazgo* system of godparents and coparents. The nuclear family is patriarchal. The role of the husband is to protect and provide. *Machismo* is a virtue that encompasses courage and romanticism. The wife's primary role is to hold the family together. *Personalismo* upholds the dignity of the individual. It calls for the development of inner qualities to attain self-respect and gain the respect of others. Children are taught the importance of respect and the proper way to relate to others on the basis of age, sex, and social class. Aggression is to be controlled. Socially sanctioned channels for expression of anger include somatization, alcohol consumption, verbal threats, and loud discussions. Catholicism is the predominant religion, and the individual experiences a personal relationship with God. Many adhere to *spiritism,* which is a belief in good and evil spirits that can affect one's life. Time orientation is in the present, and "being" is valued above "doing" and "having" (Garcia Preto, 1982).

First-generation migrants exhibit predominantly traditional values. In the new host environment, the family experiences culture shock, to which the first generation reacts by attempting to make the family a tighter unit and by holding more strongly to those values. As a response to this culture clash, *barrios* come into being, where the native culture is recreated and preserved in the new environment.

The second and third generations, starting in adolescence and preadolescence, must cope with and adapt to the language, culture, and values of the new environment (Inclán, 1985). These constitute groundbreaking efforts, and stress, failure, and defeat are not uncommon. In clinical practice, many of the families and youths seen are victims of this culture clash.

At the macrosystemic level, there is a dearth of Puerto Rican institutions, business enterprises, labor unions, and political, cultural, and community groups that can reach out to the upcoming generation. In this vacuum, to whom can youth turn for role models, for material assistance? There are few apprenticeship possibilities that are easily reached through familial or community ties. Some can find opportunities outside their primary group, but then what are the consequences for family cohesion and personal identity?

Successful utilization of out-of-group resources implies a process of acculturation, the development of new and different sets of values and orientations, and an integration of new and old cultural values. Frequently this involves a stressful distancing from one's family, which lacks the framework to understand the desirability of the individual's movement and is thus likely to devalue and censure this development. For example, although many first-generation parents enjoy and take pride in their adolescent children's development of occupational and economic competence, they also find it difficult to accept the resocialization, the new values, and the behavior changes associated with success and acculturation. First-generation parents often interpret their children's acculturated lifestyle as indicating that they care less about their parent, that they are selfish, and that they prefer peers over family (Inclán, 1985).

At the family microsystemic level, similar dilemmas ensue. The parents present a model of success through nonassertive, loyal compliance that they trust will be rewarded by the benevolence and appreciation of superiors, usually "the boss" (Inclán, 1979). These values, adaptive in an agrarian, highly structured, and hierarchal society, are not conducive to success in the industrial, competitive, impersonal environment that exists in American urban centers. To compete in this society, young people must experiment with behaviors for which they lack role models and for which the parents, the primary guidance figures, cannot provide support. Again, the subjective experience for the adolescent is one not of progression and support but of discontinuity and isolation. A compromise for these youth often involves modulating the pace of acculturation over the generations in order to maintain the necessary familial connection.

This process of value transformation influences the frequency and pattern of use of mental health services. Although there is disagreement on the prevalence of psychiatric symptoms in the Puerto Rican community, there is general agreement that this population underutilizes services (Daykin, 1980). A recent nationwide report (Centers for Health Education and Social Systems Studies, 1985) provides epidemiological data obtained during the decade 1970 to 1980. Hispanics were found to underutilize mental health facilities, with the exception of inpatient use of public general hospitals. It appears that when symptoms are severe, the likelihood that mental health facilities will be used is greater. Less-than-severe symptoms are customarily dealt with in the family or within an informal support network. In addition, structural barriers may discourage use of service institutions unless the need is great. These barriers include geographical inaccessibility of services, ethnic and racial discrimination, language, and clinicians' unfamiliarity with the cultural diversity of Hispanic patients.

Rodriguez (1987) reviewed the literature on service utilization by Hispanic, black, and white residents in a low-income section of New York City. Results of the study supported two competing theories used to explain underutilization. The barrier theory suggests that people may want and need a service but their cultural values render bureaucratic agencies unattractive. Rodriguez found that acculturated Hispanics were more likely to use services than the unacculturated. The alternative-resource theory assumes that people want and need help but turn to providers in their own natural support system. Among Hispanics and blacks, it appeared that the support network encouraged utilization of formal services for serious psychiatric problems and viewed the informal system as an alternative for those with less serious symptoms.

Issues in Assessment

A valid psychological assessment of Puerto Rican adolescents requires an understanding of relevant sociocultural issues. The experience of these adolescents often differs significantly from that of mainstream white adolescents, and needless to say there is wide individual variation among Puerto Rican adolescents. However, one can begin to conceptualize the experience of these adolescents as a series of interrelated "clashes" that are cultural, generational, socioeconomic, and developmental.

Cultural Clash

The cultural clash has its roots in the political relationship between Puerto Rico and the United States. Until 1917, Puerto Rico was a colony of the United States. When citizenship was conferred on Puerto Ricans, the questions of cultural and political identity arose for the population. As American citizens, Puerto Ricans have voting privileges, benefit from entitlement programs, and have ease of travel between the mainland and the island. However, they have no congressional representatives, speak a different language, maintain a different culture, uphold different values, and are targets of constant racial and political discrimination. The question of political identity—Puerto Rican or American—is an ongoing dilemma. For adolescents, the juxtaposition of these two contrasting cultures renders self-definition an especially difficult process. The separation/ integration conflict on the political level indirectly influences the conflicting cultural pulls on adolescents.

Generational Clash

The generational clash is reflected in the schism between first-generation parents and their offspring, particularly adolescents. Moral standards and cultural practices of the parent generation differ greatly from those of adolescents, who rapidly become the reference group for Puerto Rican youth on the mainland. Sex-role differences, attitudes toward sexuality, and standards for drug and alcohol use are widely discrepant between the parental and the adolescent generations, rendering parental guidance and supervision ineffective. Peer pressures and the culture of the streets and the ghetto gain important influence over the adolescent's behavior and development. Whereas the generational clash is evident in many subgroups within the United States, it is intensified for Puerto Ricans by socioeconomic realities.

Socioeconomic Clash

The socioeconomic clash results from the contiguity of wealthy, affluent, mainstream communities and poor, disadvantaged ghetto communities. This clash incorporates Lewis's (1965) controversial concept of a "culture of poverty"[1] that coexists and competes with the mainstream culture, which often reflects the aspirations of first-generation parents, as a framework for identity and success.

At the level of the individual, the culture of poverty includes a primary orientation to the present; failure to postpone gratification; a tendency toward action and impulsivity; a sense of fate as predetermined and unchangeable; resentment of authority; a sense of being blamed; a feeling of aloneness and an inability to trust others; an underemphasis on rigor, discipline, and perseverance; and a tendency toward dependency. For Puerto Rican adolescents, the underlying fears and concerns are often characterized by this query: Why compete and struggle through school when I see no light at the end of the tunnel?

When working with Puerto Rican adolescents, therapists need to be aware of their own values and experiences and how these may influence their approach. Whereas for therapists the issue might present itself as *how* to succeed in the mainstream world, for their adolescent clients the issue may be a more basic one of *Should* I aim for the mainstream world as a framework for success?

The choice is not an easy one for the adolescent who is cognizant of the barriers to success for Puerto Ricans in mainstream society. The culture of poverty offers a here-and-now reward and access to status and commodities that might otherwise be out-of-reach. In our experience, recognizing and dealing with the dilemmas of this "choice" enable therapists to engage and more effectively treat Puerto Rican adolescents, who consequently experience their therapist as respectful and understanding of them.

It is also against the backdrop of the culture of poverty that therapists must operate when working with parents of Puerto Rican adolescents. In a middle-class culture, a therapist may view adolescence as a time for parents to relax their guidance and control in order to allow the children to find their way in society. However, in a community where the culture of poverty prevails, the therapist would need to be sympathetic with, and at times supportive of, the parents' demand for greater vigilance and control. At this juncture, concerned parents often call for military school, enlistment in the army, relocation to Puerto Rico, or other measures that may clash with a middle class–oriented therapist's values. The therapist must be able to understand this request as an attempt to thwart the attractions of the culture of poverty.

Developmental Clash

The fourth clash involves the process of individual development. Adolescence, as a discrete developmental stage, is a relatively recent concept (Erikson, 1963). It has been incorporated into the American ethos and is characteristic of a modern industrial society. However, for an agricultural economy, as Puerto Rico was in the 1960s, an apprenticeship model of passage into adulthood is functional and adaptive. Apprenticeship models of adolescence foster family cohesion and devalue individuality. When adolescence is conceived as a period of developing individualism and distancing from the family of origin, it is counterproductive to the labor demands of an agrarian economic system developed within a capitalist framework. The family's survival and economic growth require that the children stay within the family boundary and expand the productivity already achieved by the previous generation. Although Puerto Rican migrants live and work in the United States, and especially in its urban centers, they have not fully accepted the model of adolescence that is adaptive in this context.

Figure 8.1 presents the agrarian and industrial patterns of transition into adulthood. We have found this model helpful in understanding the difficulties often present in the therapy of Puerto Rican adolescents and their families. First-generation parents operate within a framework that considers offspring to be children, regardless of age or responsibilities, until they become adults. Adulthood is usually marked by marriage or leaving home, whichever comes first. Viewed as children, adolescents are expected to subordinate their views and interests to those of the parents, to show respect, and to follow the guidelines of behavior and etiquette that the parents provide. Therapists who are unaware of the social and historical roots of this point of view often find themselves quickly and simplistically blaming the parents for being overly controlling and restrictive with their adolescents. This blame-the-parent position can be exacerbated, as pointed out earlier, when the therapist fails to recognize the larger social dynamics of the ghetto. Puerto Rican adolescents reared in the United States and exposed to its socializing influences begin to expect and demand an adolescence, with its freedoms. This is an especially stressful demand to make for female Puerto Rican adolescents, whose requests are viewed within the cultural double standard that encourages sexual activity and increased freedom for the males, and abstinence and overprotectiveness of the females.

Puerto Rican adolescents of both sexes are often referred for treatment when the pattern of "irresponsibility," as defined by traditional norms, has escalated. At these times, a vicious, mutually reinforcing cycle between repressive parents and acting-out youth becomes entrenched.

**Figure 8.1. Agrarian and Industrial Patterns
of Transition to Adulthood.**

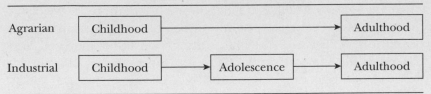

Treatment Modalities

In this section we present ecologically oriented individual, group, and family treatment considerations. The interventions we describe are based on existing theory and techniques but are modified in order to be more relevant to Puerto Rican adolescents and their families. Specifically, values, migration history, and sociocultural factors are introduced as significant intervening variables in treatment. This expanded point of view includes a historical and social-systems perspective of problems. Furthermore, it uses and manipulates these variables for therapeutic effect. This approach to the understanding and treatment of problems most closely approximates the ecological model of therapy proposed by Auerswald (1968, 1987).

The Context of Treatment

In work with Hispanic adolescents and families, the treatment setting is an important factor that can facilitate engagement in treatment. The Roberto Clemente Family Guidance Center was developed with this consideration in mind. This center is an outpatient public mental health facility that operates under the direction of a public health hospital in New York City. The center has its own storefront in the midst of the Hispanic community.

The center's characteristics include the following:

• *Culturally sensitive care.* Operationally, this means two things. First, the physical plant itself reflects the community it serves. Maps of Caribbean countries and Central and South America, as well as Latino posters and community-donated artwork reflecting the diversity and richness of the Hispanic cultures, adorn its walls. The center is named after a Puerto Rican hero, Roberto Clemente. Second, the staff at the center reflects the Hispanic community. All members are bilingual and bicultural. Currently, out of a total staff of twelve, seven nationalities are represented.

• *Systems-oriented therapy.* The general orientation of services at the center is an ecological-systems model, with emphasis placed on the family. The issues that patients present are analyzed and treated within the context of changing culture, history, family values, and multisystem involvements.

• *Community orientation.* Not only is the center in the midst of the Hispanic community, but it is also a participant in consortia and community networks. It has offered training opportunities for others in the community, it participates in street and health fairs, and it is continually active in community life.

• *Training and education.* Through its internship, externship, special seminar, field placement, and volunteer programs, the center provides training for Hispanic and other professionals who wish to further their skills in this area of work. The benefit is mutual, because new input and creativity are in turn made available to the center.

Although the concept of the "treatment setting" has often been ignored, especially in work with Hispanics and other minorities, the atmosphere, character, and staff of a center that serves poor and minority clients greatly influence its utilization rate.

Individual Treatment

Psychotherapy with poor Hispanic adolescents must reflect an awareness of the four intersecting clashes discussed earlier, because the presenting mental health problems are often embedded in complex sociocultural contexts. Immigrant status, cultural differences, and consuming poverty combine to isolate Puerto Ricans from mainstream society. Economically impoverished Puerto Rican adolescents recoil from integration into mainstream society, attempting to avoid the psychological disequilibrium associated with cultural conflict and with juxtaposing the familiar with the unfamiliar. However, this integration of the old with the new is the underpinning of psychological intervention and guides such issues as the nature of the setting, the choice of therapists, and the content of therapy.

At the Roberto Clemente Center, the physical setting embodies this concept. Maps, flags, and artwork depicting different historical eras and cultures convey the notion that the world is complex and varied and that one's reality can be set within a larger geographical, cultural, and historical perspective. Similarly, the center's therapists, though all are bilingual and bicultural, are of different nationalities and social classes. Inherent in this staff composition is the potential for dissension and conflict as well as for identification with the comfortable and familiar. This balance of the old and the new is often an objective of the therapeutic intervention. For example, Puerto Rican adolescents are more likely to reject the introduction of new ideas, values, or behaviors if they feel that their current ecological reality is not understood or validated by the therapist. Two examples from actual therapy situations serve to illustrate this point.

> Premature termination of treatment occurred after the second interview with Eric, an eighteen-year-old Puerto Rican adolescent. Examination of the therapeutic interaction revealed that the therapist, aware of Eric's involvement in lucrative yet illegal activity, had failed to understand the socioeconomic realities of the youth and his family and was ignorant of the attractions of the ghetto's underground economy. Instead, he had engaged Eric in a mild-mannered dialogue about the benefits of returning to school and using education as a tool to attain future economic sufficiency and autonomy. Clearly the therapist's agenda was strikingly remote from the realities of the adolescent. Without identification with the client's realities, interjection of new strategies may be futile.

> The therapist successfully engaged Ricardo, a sixteen-year-old Puerto Rican known to be involved in highly profitable, illicit street business, in a thorough exploration of the ghetto subculture, of the means to quick money, of the difficulty of resisting peer pressures, of the lack of rewards that Ricardo's father had experienced after twenty-two years of working two forty-hour jobs, of the racism and institutional discrimination that impede the success of minorities and the poor, of the bankruptcy of the community political leadership, and so on. This acknowledgment became the foundation for a therapeutic relationship that would eventually permit the introduction of new ideas and more constructive strategies for helping Ricardo to negotiate within society.

Therapists who work within this framework are encouraged to be active in relation to their clients, not only as role models but also as bridges between the familiar and the new. The clinical example of Sara and Noel, a young Puerto Rican couple, will highlight this process.

The presenting problem was that Noel had threatened Sara with physical abuse and Sara had threatened to divorce Noel. Penetrating beneath the presenting problem, the therapist observed the marked value differences and cultural polarizations in this couple's relationship. Noel maintained very traditional Puerto Rican values, while Sara was equally entrenched in American middle-class values.

The therapy proceeded first as couples therapy, then as individual therapy, and finally reconvened as marital therapy. The couple's therapist facilitated a process of problem redefinition that enabled the blame and frustration to be shifted from the individuals to the process of acculturation. This was a first step toward defusing the potential for violence. Individual therapy, with same-sex therapists, focused on the process of acculturation and the differences in level of acculturation and values transformation between the spouses. After eleven individual sessions with the husband and fourteen with the wife, the therapists reconvened the marital therapy. The couple reported symptom relief and increased understanding of themselves and each other.

This case underscores the role of the therapist as a bridge between the old and the new. The female therapist assisted the wife in crossing the bridge to the old set of values, while the male therapist helped the husband consider the new values.

Group Therapy

The Roberto Clemente Family Guidance Center's group therapy program adheres to an educational psychotherapy model, based on the assumption that migrant minority group populations need information and education as well as therapy. Oftentimes the clients' emotional problems are exacerbated by serious problems of living and real-life experiences. In this sense, the mental health professional is viewed not only as a therapist but also as an educator, adviser, and advocate who assists clients in dealing with individuals and agencies. Such multidimensional intervention requires that therapists be familiar with the real-life situation of their clients; that they use an active, directive therapeutic stance, which has been shown to be effective with this population; and that they divide therapy into time-limited segments (Acosta, Yamamoto, and Evans, 1982).

The educational psychotherapy group for adolescents is a time-limited experience. Each of the ten ninety-minute sessions focuses on a particular theme: (1) introduction and getting acquainted, (2) family and independence, (3) sexuality, (4) cultural identity, (5) school issues, (6) peers and peer pressure, (7) racism and discrimination, (8) jobs and job interviewing, (9) alcohol and drugs, and (10) self-revelation, trust, and therapy. During the first half of each session, the therapist presents selected stimulus materials, such as films, on the session theme. An unstructured discussion follows this guided presentation. Objectives of this group format include "breaking the ice" to facilitate group exchange and discussion, providing concrete information, generating a shared database for group members, normalizing contextualization of feelings, and facilitating engagement in ongoing therapy. The following highlights from an actual group session illustrate this process.

Before we developed the group program, issues of sexuality were particularly problematic in individual therapy with adolescents. Clinic therapists reported that the adolescents professed to know all about sex but wanted to share nothing. Ambivalence toward this topic was quite prominent. Sexuality was selected as the topic for session three of the group program. Presentation of a film proved very effective in opening the discussion, which was intense and proceeded with little guidance from the group leaders. Group members were able to focus on the film and talk about sexuality without experiencing the anxiety and resistance previously associated with personal disclosure. It was also clear that, contrary to their professed knowledge, there existed information lacunae, which the film addressed directly and indirectly, making subsequent discussion possible. Some members, typified by one young female, found great relief in normalization and contextualization of feelings about sexuality. The fifteen-year-old Puerto Rican teenager, Rosa, identified most with the feelings of guilt, isolation, and shame portrayed in the film. Until she viewed the film, Rosa had felt blemished and alone among her peers in having engaged in particular sexual acts. Group discussion revealed that she was not alone in having had these experiences or in feeling inadequate because of them.

Most important, however, were two general themes that surfaced during the discussion. One theme can be described as a group recalibration of the biological, peer, and social pressures for and against sexual behavior. What males and females desire, the differences between short-term and long-term effects of sexual activity on acceptance and esteem, questions of responsibility versus allocation of blame, feedback relative to peer perceptions of sexually active youngsters, and reactions to such perceptions were among the issues discussed.

The other important theme of the discussion was the adolescent/parental dynamics around questions of emerging sexuality. Surprisingly, when in a group context the adolescents were able to verbalize explicitly an understanding of changing values between their parents' generation and their own. More challenging was the question of what to do about the differences. The group was divided between those who opted for "respect" for the parents and accommodation to their values and experiences, and those who posited the need to act in accordance with individual beliefs and contemporary values. The belief of the latter group was that the parents needed to accommodate to them and the new morality. Rather than identifying a specific right or wrong position, the therapists highlighted and endorsed the group's framing of the problems within a context of familial and evolving values.

The ten-session educational psychotherapy group experience is designed to be a complete program in itself; however, it may also serve as an introduction to and preparation for continued therapy. Following the ten-session program, the adolescents are offered the opportunity to continue treatment in an ongoing group. Adolescents who choose to continue in group therapy often make use of and refer to the more structured experience of the educational psychotherapy group. Thus, an added advantage of the educational psychotherapy group is the minimizing of differences in therapeutic experience among participants in ongoing group therapy.

Ecologically Oriented Family Therapy

The family therapy literature includes some references to treatment issues in work with Puerto Rican families (Garcia-Preto, 1982; Inclán, 1985). In this section we discuss three issues of importance in treating poor Puerto Rican adolescents in the context of their families: value differences, the importance of siblings, and questions of role hierarchy.

Although all families experience value conflicts between the parent and child generations, this clash of values is exacerbated in poor migrant families and becomes most intense at adolescence (Inclán, 1985). This added stress for migrant families must be understood by the therapists who treat them.

When working with Puerto Rican adolescents and their families, therapists have found the technique of "cultural reframe" useful (Falicov and Karrer, 1984). In this technique the experience or demand that a parent or adolescent makes is analyzed in relation to the cultural values that constitute the background for the demand or expectation. For example, a mother's request that her daughter interact less frequently with peers is viewed as expressing a value that the family takes priority over the individual. The adolescent's demand for greater peer contact is viewed as expressing a value of individuality over family. Each value is understood to be functional, or adaptive, within its social context: the traditional value of the family over the individual is implicit in the mother's definition of the situation, while the middle-class American value of the individual above the group is implicit in the adolescent's request (Inclán, 1985).

Cultural reframing allows the focus of the blame to be shifted from the person to the acculturation process, which places different demands on the parent and adolescent generations. Contextualization of the problem is achieved when blame of the other person has been dissipated or transferred to blame of the acculturation process as it relates to adolescent expectations. Once this is attained, the therapist may proceed to the next stage of therapy, which involves presenting an objective and impartial model for family progression through the stages of adolescence. This model is based on the process of exchange and negotiation between parent and adolescent, for greater freedom, trust, and responsibility (Haley, 1980). For most families with adolescents, this is the normal developmental task, and it often needs clarification and therapeutic assistance. As discussed earlier, the Puerto Rican parent may view adolescence and its associated freedoms quite differently, making modifications of treatment necessary.

For example, in the family treatment of Carmen, a fifteen-year-old Puerto Rican girl who was angry and at odds with her parents, the therapist, through individual and family meetings, was able to sustain the girl's responsible behavior (no truancy or staying out beyond the agreed time) for a two-month period. Following this, the therapist supported Carmen in her "earned" request for greater freedom. Although the parents resisted at first, discussions resulted in permission for her to stay out later on weekend nights. At the same time, the rule governing exchange of privileges and responsibilities was further clarified and reinforced. Although Carmen observed the guidelines the first weekend, she failed to do so on the second one. As a result, the therapist insisted (to parents who were now, ironically, resistant) that a temporary curtailment of her new curfew privilege was indicated according to the previously agreed-upon rule guiding the exchange of responsibilities and privileges. This second stage of therapy, described by Haley (1980), is useful in work with families in which adolescent problems are present.

Because first-generation parents have limited ability to serve as a bridge between the old and new cultures, sibling relationships are very important in poor Puerto Rican migrant families. This is an underutilized resource in family therapy in general and in the therapy of minority adolescents in particular. Family dynamics and role distributions are usually such that some family member is able to differentiate from the family of origin earlier and/or more successfully than others. Often, young Puerto Rican women feel greater pressure than male adolescents to remain at home and help out. The sibling who has been able to differentiate successfully from the family of origin can be enlisted in family therapy to serve as a bridge between the parent's and children's generations, as in the following case example.

> In one Puerto Rican family of very traditional working-class parents who were distraught over and unable to cope with their son Eluid's use of drugs, the therapist used the older brother, Tomas, as a broker between the parental and young adolescent worlds and values. The parents, who operated within a closed-system definition of family and trust, were helped to surrender surveillance and guidance functions to Tomas. This move detriangulated the conflict and provided a successful approach to dealing with Eluid's drug problem.

Therapists need to be aware of the importance of siblings in family therapy and move beyond their initial reluctance to include well-differentiated siblings in treatment. Although these siblings often live elsewhere, are asymptomatic, hold jobs, and have families and other pressing commitments, they remain loyal to the family and tend to respond readily when an appeal is made for their assistance.

> Marta, aged seventeen, had become maladaptively entrenched in the role of executive of the family system, a role she had assumed as a result of the hospitalization of the male head of household and her mother's very limited social competence. Exploration revealed that an older brother, Ernesto, had moved out of the home but maintained good family ties. Efforts to engage him in the therapy were successful, and Ernesto was instrumental in helping his younger sister to reconnect with developmental tasks, issues, and priorities. Together they were able to redefine self and family needs, as well as to restructure family affairs so that family functioning could be maintained and Marta's autonomy and differentiation could proceed.

Work with poor migrant Puerto Rican families also suggests that traditional approaches to the question of hierarchy within the family be reviewed. In these families the adolescents often have a greater mastery of the language, behaviors, and social mores of the new culture than their parents. Thus they have sources of power within the society. A therapist who focuses on the family without considering its acculturative context may operate within a family model that assumes a generational hierarchy that is actually contradicted by the social and familiar reality.

Family therapy with poor Puerto Rican adolescents and their families may require a flexible and operational, as opposed to generational, basis of role relationships with the family. Although it is standard to support generational hierarchies, the process of rapid social transformation makes the substantive basis for this hierarchy tenuous in many migrant families, where children can quickly surpass parents in technical knowledge and expertise, status, marketability, and income.

Some adolescents, owing to level of acculturation, social achievement, or developmental maturity, are able to assume executive or other functional leadership roles within the family. The clinical criterion to be observed in such situations is whether this role is assumed with the implicit sanction of the parents or in a manner that undermines parental status and role, thus generating family dysfunction and psychopathology. Specifically, a socially contextualized family role for a functional and well-differentiated adolescent in a poor Puerto Rican migrant family is one of great responsibility for the family unit as a whole and for the parental and sibling subsystems in particular. In our experience, it is the lack of these types of family responsibilities and expectations that tends to correlate positively with antisocial behavior and social anomie. This view appears counter to the mainstream view of adolescence as a time when youngsters pay less attention to family affairs and seek out an identity of self in the social world. It is framed by an unquestioned value of individuality that constitutes a social-class and cultural bias that is nonadaptive socially and contraindicated therapeutically for Puerto Rican adolescents.

Summary and Conclusions

Puerto Rican adolescents are a significant and expanding at-risk population group. Sociohistorical, cultural, and migration characteristics differentiate Puerto Rican migrants from previous arrivals. Their role as second and third generations in the larger process of transculturation is to begin the integration of two cultures, value sets, and traditions. A significant number of adaptational problems can be expected at this stage. Mental health practitioners must be prepared for the challenge that providing services to Puerto Rican adolescents and their families constitutes.

Cultural factors, values, and clashes between parental and adolescent generations cannot be overemphasized as necessary considerations in the assessment and treatment of minority group adolescents and Puerto Rican adolescents in particular. Neglecting to pay attention to the processes of value orientation and value clashes can lead to an overemphasis on intrapsychic or family dynamics that may limit the effectiveness of treatment. An ecologically oriented approach expands and complements the training in individual, group, and family assessment and treatment of Puerto Rican and minority adolescents. It argues for the need to expand clinical areas of competence to include contextual issues of migration, history, social class, and the role of the community.

Like cultural- and value-orientation factors, social-class issues have been underemphasized in mental health treatment. The need to overcome this neglect in the field becomes most evident when one works with Puerto Rican adolescents. Therapists working with poor minority adolescents need to understand that more than one worldview competes for these clients' attention as a viable life course (Inclán and Ferran, forthcoming). Failure to understand this tends to result in ineffective therapies for minority groups.

Training of professional staff, Hispanics and others, to work with this large and growing at-risk population is a most important priority at this time. There is evidence of a decrease in training of Hispanic professionals in all the mental health disciplines. There is an equally alarming trend in the field toward the decontextualization of psychotherapy. Instead, "specialized" and biomedical approaches seem to be gaining acceptance. The combined effect of these two trends for the delivery of care to minority adolescents is of great concern. The system of organized therapy and training, in moving toward specialization and biotechnologies, may well be moving counter to the needs of Puerto Ricans and other minority populations, whose interests are best met by an ecologically oriented and contextualized treatment approach.

Community-based services and agencies for mental health care for minority groups are models for service delivery that are gaining prominence as cultural sensitivity is emphasized in the Hispanic mental health community (Rogler, Malgady, Costantino, and Blumenthal, 1987). These services could play an expanded role in training and research. The experiences obtained could in turn serve to develop further a mental health system that effectively addresses the needs of all segments of the population. Greater exploration and expansion of the roles and possibilities inherent in culturally sensitive community mental health centers would be opportune, given the accelerated increase in migration from countries and cultures with values very different from the American norms. Although many of these groups are currently first-generation immigrants, it can be expected that the second and third generations, as in the case of Puerto Ricans, will experience more difficulties and dysfunctions.

Note

1. Lewis's concept includes phenomenological description and etiological implications, the latter being controversial when introduced in 1965. Our experience partly supports Lewis's findings of a culture of poverty. We observe it in a subculture of the ghetto, not in the ghetto as a whole. With regard to etiological implications, we believe

with Lewis that societies that espouse a set of values for the dominant class that stresses the accumulation of wealth and property and simultaneously explains low socioeconomic status as the sole responsibility of the individual tend to foster a culture of poverty.

References

Acosta, F. X., Yamamoto, J., and Evans, L. A. *Effective Psychotherapy for Low-Income and Minority Patients*. New York: Plenum, 1982.

Auerswald, E. H. "Interdisciplinary Versus Ecological Approach." *Family Process*, 1968, *7*(2), 202–215.

Auerswald, E. H. "Epistemological Confusion in Family Therapy and Research." *Family Process*, 1987, *26*(3), 317–331.

Bowen, M. "Theory in the Practice of Psychotherapy." In P. Guerin, Jr. (ed.), *Family Therapy: Theory and Practice*. Lake Worth, Fla.: Gardner Press, 1976.

Canino, I. A., Earley, B. E., and Rogler, L. H. *The Puerto Rican Child in New York City: Stress and Mental Health*. Monograph No. 4. New York: Hispanic Research Center, Fordham University, 1980.

Canino, I. A., Gould, M. S., Prupis, S., and Shaffer, D. "A Comparison of Symptoms and Diagnoses in Hispanic and Black Children in an Outpatient Mental Health Clinic." *Journal of the American Academy of Child Psychiatry*, 1986, *25*(2), 254–259.

Centers for Disease Control and Prevention. *HIV/AIDS Surveillance Report*. Atlanta, Ga.: U.S. Department of Health and Human Services, *8*(1), 1996

Centers for Disease Control and Prevention. *Monthly Vital Statistics Report: Advance Report of Final Natality Statistics*. Washington, D.C.: U.S. Department of Health and Human Services, *42*(3), Supplement, September 9, 1993.

Centers for Health Education and Social Systems Studies. *Health Status of Minorities and Low-Income Groups*. Washington, D.C.: U.S. Government Printing Office, 1985.

Daykin, D. S. *Social and Community Support Systems in Hispanic Neighborhoods in New York City: A Public Policy Analysis*. Mental Health Policy Monograph Series, No. 3. Nashville, Tenn.: Center for the Study of Families and Children, Institute for Public Policy Studies, Vanderbilt University, 1980.

Erikson, E. H. *Childhood and Society*. (2nd ed.) New York: Norton, 1963.

Falicov, C. J., and Karrer, B. M. "Therapeutic Strategies for Mexican-American Families." *International Journal of Family Therapy*, 1984, *6*(1), 18–30.

Garcia-Preto, N. "Puerto Rican Families." In M. McGoldrick, J. K. Pearce, and J. Giordano (eds.), *Ethnicity and Family Therapy.* New York: Guilford Press, 1982.

Governor's Advisory Committee for Hispanic Affairs. *New York State Hispanics: A Challenging Minority.* Albany, N.Y.: Governor's Advisory Committee for Hispanic Affairs, 1985.

Haley, J. *Leaving Home: The Therapy of Disturbed Young People.* New York: McGraw-Hill, 1980.

Hardy-Fanta, C., and Montana, P. "The Hispanic Female Adolescent: A Group Therapy Model." *International Journal of Group Psychotherapy,* 1982, *32*(3), 351–366.

Inclán, J. "Family Organization, Acculturation, and Psychological Symptomatology in Second Generation Puerto Rican Women of Three Socioeconomic Class Groups." Unpublished doctoral dissertation, New York University, 1979.

Inclán, J. "Variations in Value Orientations in Mental Health Work with Puerto Ricans." *Psychotherapy,* 1985, *22*(2S), 324–334.

Inclán, J., and Ferran, E. "Poverty, Politics, and the Family." In M. Myrkin (ed.), *The Social and Political Context of Family Therapy.* Lake Worth, Fla.: Gardner Press, forthcoming.

Lewis, O. *La Vida: A Puerto Rican Family in the Culture of Poverty: San Juan and New York.* New York: Vintage Books, 1965.

Mayor's Commission on Hispanic Concerns. *Report of the Mayor's Commission on Hispanic Concerns.* New York: City of New York, 1986.

Perez, R. "The Status of Puerto Ricans in the United States." Paper presented at third National Puerto Rican Convention, Philadelphia, June 1985.

Rodriguez, O. *Hispanics and Human Services: Help-Seeking in the Inner City.* Monograph No. 14. New York: Hispanic Research Center, Fordham University, 1987.

Rogler, L. H., Malgady, R. G., Costantino, G., and Blumenthal, R. "What Do Culturally Sensitive Mental Health Services Mean? The Case of Hispanics." *American Psychologist,* 1987, *42*(6), 565–570.

Sowell, T. *Ethnic America: A History.* New York: Basic Books, 1981.

U.S. Bureau of the Census. *Persons of Spanish Origin in the United States: March 1985 (Advance Report).* Current Population Reports, Population Characteristics, Series P-20, No. 403. Washington, D.C.: U.S. Government Printing Office, 1985.

U.S. Bureau of the Census. *Statistical Abstract of the United States, 1996.* (116th ed.) Washington, D.C.: U.S. Department of Commerce, 1996.

Ventura, S. J., and Taffel, S. M. "Childbearing Characteristics of U.S.– and Foreign-Born Hispanic Mothers." *Public Health Reports,* 1985, *100*(6), 647–653.

Chapter Nine

Southeast Asian Refugee Children and Adolescents

Larke Nahme Huang

"Stranger in a strange land" is a theme played over and over again in the lives of refugees. Whether these refugees have fled their homes because of natural disasters such as drought or famine or because of political, religious, or racial repression, they enter host countries as aliens with mixed emotions of fear, anticipation, joy, and loss. By definition, refugees are subject to severe stress and problems of adjustment. In contrast to other people who migrate and resettle in foreign lands, refugees generally lack positive motives for abandoning their homes. As one Southeast Asian refugee succinctly stated, "We are not immigrants looking for a place where the grass is greener. For us refugees, the grass under our feet was burning" (Ferguson, 1984, p. 3).

Estimates of the number of refugees worldwide range from 10 to 15 million (Cohon, 1981; Loescher and Scanlan, 1986). It is generally estimated that children make up half the refugee population, although the proportions of children vary with the different waves of refugees (Huyck and Fields, 1981).

Since April 1975, more than 800,000 Southeast Asian refugees have entered the United States as part of the aftermath of the Vietnam War and the civil wars in Cambodia and Laos. Within this population are three groups of refugee children: slightly more than 2,000 orphans from Operation Babylift of April 1975, 7,637 unaccompanied minors (U.S. Department of Health and Human Services, 1987), and an untabulated number of children who entered with members of their families. Although the numbers are inexact, it has been estimated that children constitute 40 to 60 percent of the entering refugee population (Ahmed, Tims, and Kolker, 1980; Lee, 1987).

Consistent with the omission of youth in general from the psychological literature on refugees, systematic investigation of Southeast Asian refugee youth remains minimal. This is also evident in social policy documents, as reflected in the 1980 report by the Indochinese Refugee Consultation to the U.S. Department of Health and Human Services (Nguyen, Long, and Aylesworth, 1980). This report includes detailed and well-substantiated recommendations for training, service, and research programs but no recommendations specific to the issues, needs, and developmental concerns of refugee youth. Given that few crises are as traumatizing as rapid uprooting and forced migration due to war, it is important to understand the effects of this event on the development and mental health of children and adolescents.

This chapter focuses on these issues for refugee youth from Southeast Asia. Although the geopolitical term *Southeast Asian refugee* usually designates refugees from Vietnam, Cambodia, and Laos, in this chapter it will include only refugees from Vietnam and Cambodia, because these are the groups with which I have had the most clinical and research contact. Current demographic, epidemiological, and cultural information will be presented toward the goal of deeper understanding of these groups and development of appropriate psychosocial assessment and intervention strategies. When considering interventions, one must bear in mind that interventions for this group are not "proved" or well established, and to date one cannot definitely declare the "right" way to generate positive outcomes for these children, many of whom have experienced nightmares in real life beyond what helping professionals can even begin to imagine.

Demographics

The United Nations 1951 Refugee Convention defined refugees as persons outside the boundaries of their own countries who were not firmly resettled elsewhere and who maintained a well-substantiated fear of persecution based on race, religion, nationality, social class, or political opinion in their own country (United Nations, 1951). The Refugee Act of 1980, passed by the U.S. Congress, conformed to this international definition and clarified the legal parameters for refugee status (U.S. Department of Health and Human Services, 1987). However, this act did not readily translate legal definition into an organized resettlement policy at the national level. In contrast to well-defined, albeit fluctuating, policies for immigrants, who generally enter according to a system of preferences and do not feel the pressure of persecution in their homeland, U.S. government intervention with refugees has historically been piecemeal, lacking in continuity, and spearheaded by a few dedicated individuals influenced by humanitarian and political coalitions. These short-term rescue efforts have not evolved into a thoughtful, long-range policy.

By the end of 1986 there were 806,000 Southeast Asian refugees in the United States. Vietnamese continue to be the majority group among these refugees, although there is increasing ethnic diversity in the entering population. Vietnamese form 63 percent of the entering total, Laotians 19 percent, and Cambodians 17 percent (U.S. Department of Health and Human Services, 1987). In 1990, there were more than one million Southeast Asians in the United States, including nearly 615,000 Vietnamese, who accounted for 64 percent of the total group, followed by Laotians (20 percent) and Cambodians (16 percent). With a growth rate of 150 percent between 1980 and 1990, the Vietnamese constitute the sixth largest group of Asian Americans, after the Chinese, Filipinos, Japanese, Asian Indians, and Koreans (U.S. Bureau of the Census, 1995).

The age and sex composition reveals a relatively young population, 55 percent male. The median age of the refugees is twenty-five years. In 1986, 3.5 percent were preschoolers, 27 percent were school age, and 19 percent were young adults aged eighteen to twenty-four. Twenty-one percent of the Cambodians who arrived in 1986 were children under five years old, many of them born in refugee camps (U.S. Department of Health and Human Services, 1987).

Geographically, Southeast Asian refugees are concentrated in the West, with 316,200 (39.2 percent) in California, 61,100 (7.6 percent) in Texas, and 37,500 (4.7 percent) in Washington. Although refugees reside in every state, about 85 percent reside in eighteen states (U.S. Department of Health and Human Services, 1987). The initial government plan was to disperse refugees throughout the country in order to prevent an excessive burden on any particular community. However, secondary migration, in combination with the tendency of later refugees to seek already-existing refugee communities, worked against this plan. Secondary migration was spurred by employment opportunities, an established ethnic community, more desirable welfare benefits, better training opportunities, reunification with relatives, or a more attractive climate.

Turning to economic adjustment, refugee labor-force participation in 1986 was lower than in the general population, and the unemployment rate was higher. Forty-one percent of sampled refugees aged sixteen and older were in the labor force, compared to 65 percent of the U.S. population as a whole. Of those, 84 percent had jobs, compared to 93 percent of the total U.S. population. The jobs that refugees found in this country usually differed in type and status from the jobs they held in their country of origin. Whereas 37 percent had previously held white-collar jobs, only 19 percent were currently holding similar jobs in the United States, and significantly more refugees had blue-collar jobs or service jobs here than in their native countries. In 1982 the median family income for 1975 arrivals was $14,232, and for those who arrived between 1976 and 1979 it was $8,803. In 1984 these figures had increased to $16,377 for 1975 arrivals and to $11,105 for those who arrived between 1976 and 1979 (U.S. Department of Health and Human Services, 1987). In 1990, sociodemographic data indicated that Southeast Asians remain among the most economically stressed and impoverished population groups in the United States. In addition to economic strain, acculturation and disruption in the family system and roles are among the numerous psychological and social problems encountered by this population (Matsuoka, 1991).

Migration History

To comprehend the experience of the refugee, it is necessary to understand the conditions in the country of origin that necessitated flight, the sometimes circuitous and life-threatening journey, and the conditions and attitudes of the host country. For the three waves of Southeast Asian refugees, these circumstances were quite variable. The first wave of refugees were primarily Vietnamese who fled during the fall of Saigon in April 1975. These refugees and other Vietnamese who left before 1975, though a socioeconomically heterogeneous group, were generally well-educated white-collar workers and professionals who knew English and had had close contacts with Americans in Vietnam. Only 32 percent had been blue-collar workers in Vietnam (Aylesworth, Ossorio, and Osaki, 1980). Many were Roman Catholics from urban areas. With the pending collapse of the South Vietnamese government, the U.S. Congress agreed to evacuate 140,000 Vietnamese who were considered allies of the United States and whose lives would be endangered as a result of their contact with Americans during the war. Of this group, 50,000 were children under age fourteen (Le, 1983; Vietnamese Children's Resettlement Advisory Group, 1975). These refugees were received at military bases in the United States, where they were given medical examinations and an orientation to American customs and then assigned to one of nine voluntary agencies that assumed the task of locating sponsors to assist in resettlement (Loescher and Scanlan, 1986). Following a short-lived enthusiasm, public support for these refugees, who represented America's obligation and "legacy of guilt" (Loescher and Scanlan, 1986, p. 112), rapidly dissipated. A Gallup poll taken in May 1975 indicated that Americans were opposed to the resettlement of Vietnamese by 54 percent to 36 percent ("The New Americans," 1975). The United States was in an economic recession in mid-1975, and the reasons for opposition were ostensibly economic: refugees would take jobs from Americans, aggravate the already high unemployment rate, and compete for limited social services and federal assistance.

The second wave of refugees occurred between fall 1975 and fall 1978. Many of these refugees were considered high-risk persons—those who had fought in the South Vietnamese army or been associated with the United States or South Vietnamese government and had been unable to escape in April 1975. This group included many middle-class and politically elite persons, but the vast majority represented a broader cross-section of the population than the previous wave of refugees. Thousands of peasants uprooted by the war also managed to flee. In Cambodia, civil war resulted in the death of one-seventh to one-half of the nation's population. It is estimated that under the Pol Pot regime from mid-1975 to 1978, one to three million Cambodians died of executions, preventable malnutrition, disease, and exhaustion from forced marches and compulsory labor (Loescher and Scanlan, 1986). Pol Pot's Khmer Rouge army destroyed large segments of the middle and upper classes and forced the relocation and flight of the peasant classes. These conditions generated a steady stream of refugees to Thailand and subsequently to the West.

The third wave of refugees occurred between 1978 and 1980. The Communist restructuring of society in Vietnam and the elimination of a private entrepreneurial class stimulated the flight of many ethnic Chinese who had constituted the business class. Other Vietnamese fled in anticipation of being sent to "reeducation centers" or "new economic zones." Many parents, realizing their children would have no future in Vietnam, arranged for the children's escape although they themselves remained behind. These refugees came to be known as the "boat people," because they escaped by sea, usually to Malaysia, Indonesia, Singapore, or Hong Kong, where they were given temporary asylum in prison-like holding centers. In August 1978, the number of Vietnamese seeking asylum elsewhere in Asia averaged about 6,000 per month. By spring 1979, this number had reached 65,000 per month (Reimers, 1985).

Simultaneously, in Cambodia the bloodbath intensified with the Vietnamese invasion in 1978. All segments of the population fled on foot to Thailand, which begrudgingly established refugee camps on the Thai/Cambodian border. These land refugees arrived exhausted, malnourished, and brutalized by the army. At least 50 percent had already experienced the death of a family member. Before gaining entry to the United States, these land refugees remained in camps along the border, vulnerable to disease, robbery, rape, and extortion from inside and outside the camps (Oberdorfer, 1987).

The boat people and land refugees experienced more difficulties in adjustment to the United States than the first wave of refugees. Their conditions and methods of flight were harsher; they also came with less education and fewer employment skills, were predominantly rural, and had had little contact with Americans in their own countries. Overall they experienced greater culture shock than earlier refugees, which was exacerbated by direct entry into American communities without the orientation of the U.S. camp experience, which had been provided only for the first wave of refugees. On arrival in the United States, the refugees were entitled to government assistance for two years as a result of the 1975 Indochinese Migration and Refugee Assistance Act.

An Ecological Perspective

Understanding the experience of the refugee is an extremely complex process because it involves numerous systems, sometimes competing, sometimes complementary, all at different levels of proximity and awareness to the refugee. The social systems transcend national boundaries, often involve international law and politics, and blur humanitarian and political ideologies. On a more immediate level, the refugee has to maintain the family system in the context of a new cultural system, negotiate employment and educational systems, comprehend the intricacies of migration and naturalization laws, and maneuver through an impersonal social service system. Underlying all this is the need to master a new language, a new culture, and a new set of behaviors and expectations. Additionally, the refugee needs to integrate the experience of flight and the abandonment of homeland and loss of family and friends into his or her current state of existence. Where do professional helpers interacting with refugees begin? How do they start to understand the refugee's shattered world, the physical and psychological torment, and the attempt to construct a new, acceptable worldview? Can a professional helper whose life experiences are so extremely different from those of a refugee be truly helpful?

Bronfenbrenner's (1979) concept of the ecology of human development, as discussed in Chapter One, provides a conceptual framework that may help in organizing the vast complexities of the refugees' experience. This framework focuses on the reciprocal interaction of individual and environment, where the environment consists of immediate microsystems, such as family, work, and school settings; more remote systems, such as funding committees for English-language classes or legislative committees determining duration of federal assistance; and macrosystems, the "consistencies," "blueprints" (Bronfenbrenner, 1979, p. 26), or cultural attitudes underlying the various systems.

An ecological perspective also takes into consideration the less tangible psychological systems of the refugee. For example, in Asian cultures the extended family is a vitally important structure, and usually one thinks of the extended family as visible and accessible. For many refugees, however, the extended family has become an inaccessible system, because many members actually remain in the homeland but are psychologically, and sometimes disturbingly, present to the refugee in the new country. Thus many refugees are plagued by worry and regret about relatives left behind, while also confronting hostile communities that resent the competition for jobs and housing, well-meaning sponsors who are ignorant of the refugees' culture and behaviors, and established ethnic communities that resent an influx of bedraggled fellow countrymen.

Mental Health Issues

To date, there are few systematic studies of either the psychological and behavioral disorders or the positive adaptation and successful coping strategies of Southeast Asian youth. This lack may be attributed to several factors. First, until the early seventies, Asians in general had not been the focus of extensive psychological research, so there was little precedent and few methods for investigation of people from these cultures. Second, the refugees are recent arrivals, and adults, not children, seemed to be the more immediate targets for investigation. Finally, the language problem has posed a significant impediment for most researchers. The studies that have been conducted have been primarily clinical observations by mental health consultants working in refugee camps and clinics, or descriptive studies of adolescents in the foster care system.

The functioning of the significant adults in a refugee child's environment may have implications for the child's sense of well-being (Garmezy and Rutter, 1983). For this reason, studies of Southeast Asian adult refugees are briefly reviewed before a more detailed discussion of the literature on refugee youth is presented.

Studies of Adult Refugees

In a three-phase longitudinal study of 115 Vietnamese refugees, Lin, Masuda, and Tazuma (1982) documented high levels of physical and psychological dysfunction during the first two years of resettlement. Loss and culture shock seemed to be the primary components of the refugee experience and, when sustained for a prolonged period, seemed to result in clinically significant depression and anxiety. Paradoxically, refugees seemed to become more psychologically vulnerable when their lives became concretely more manageable and within their control. This finding is consistent with other studies of migration that report an early stage of heightened activity focusing on survival and satisfaction of daily needs, followed by a period of emotional distress, depression, and increasing anxiety (Sluzki, 1979). Lin, Masuda, and Tazuma (1982) also reported a disproportionate frequency of psychosomatic disorders and somatization, which may reflect the Asian concept of unity of mind and body and the tendency to avoid the stigma of mental illness. Frequent marital conflicts resulting in physical violence were also reported and were attributed to the breakdown of traditional age and sex roles due to differing rates and imperatives of acculturation within the family. Some reactive psychoses were reported; however, these individuals were usually symptom free within several months.

In a survey of fifty Vietnamese families that had recently resettled in the South, Vignes and Hall (1979) concluded that most of the refugees were adjusting well in spite of a number of specific sociological stresses: loss of role identity and self-esteem, social isolation due to language barriers, local prejudice directed toward the Vietnamese, and Vietnamese prejudices and suspicion of the local community, helping agencies, and the federal government. The individuals who seemed to have the poorest adjustment were those from the higher socioeconomic strata (income greater than $10,000) in both Vietnam and the United States, because they were least able to accept their downward mobility in occupation and status.

In an epidemiological study of refugees in Santa Clara County, California, Meinhardt, Tom, Tse, and Yu (1985–1986) surveyed 378 Cambodians, 563 Vietnamese, 120 Chinese, and 620 nonrefugee Chinese and arrived at the following conclusions:

• A poverty-level income was associated with refugee status. The median family income for Cambodians was $7,200; for refugee Chinese, $8,500; for Vietnamese, $10,000; and for nonrefugee Chinese, $31,005.

- Cambodians as a group seemed to have experienced the most life-threatening trauma; 91 percent of Cambodians reported that their lives had been in danger "three or more years."
- Depression and demoralization were repeated themes in the interviews. The post-1975 Vietnamese and Chinese refugees reported slightly higher mental health needs than those of the general county population, and 17 percent of the Cambodian population reported highly elevated needs for intensive help, including outpatient, day treatment, and inpatient services, for extreme psychological distress and dysfunction.
- Group differences in help-seeking patterns emerged. Cambodians used social workers, family counselors, and religious counselors to a significantly greater degree (28.3 percent) than the other Asian groups (4.1 percent). All of the Asian groups reported greater use of spiritualists and natural healers than the general population.

Studies of Child and Adolescent Refugees

The earliest studies of Southeast Asian refugee children emerged from camps set up for the first wave of Vietnamese refugees. After examining these children, Harding and Looney (1977) concluded that those who had departed with their families seemed to adapt well to their new environment. These children received the strong, steady emotional support characteristic of multigenerational families. The orderly sense of roles in the family kept the children occupied with duties and responsibilities and guarded against boredom, anomie, and antisocial behavior in the camps. There was no evidence of severe psychological disorder. In contrast, children who had fled without family members or significant adults—the unaccompanied minors—seemed to fare less well and were at much higher risk for psychological problems. These children ranged in age from eighteen months to eighteen years, were predominantly boys, and varied in background from the illiterate lower class to the most privileged upper class. Psychological and physical examinations found that many of these children were significantly depressed, manifesting somatic complaints, sleep disturbances, violent antisocial behavior, tantrums, and withdrawal. A general sense of sadness and hopelessness was observed in these youth (Harding and Looney, 1977).

Williams and Westermeyer (1983) studied the adjustment of twenty-eight Southeast Asian adolescent refugees who were seen at a psychiatric clinic. Six of these adolescents received a diagnosis of functional psychosis and six were diagnosed as mentally retarded; however, all twelve had exhibited these problems before migration. The migration process intensified these disorders and led to more flagrant psychoses, suicide attempts, disruptive behavior, and school crises. Other diagnoses of adolescents in this sample included depression, conduct disorder, somatic disorder, personality disorder, learning disorder, and no diagnosis. This last category included intergenerational conflicts typical of migrating families. Adolescents usually acculturate to a new society more rapidly than their parents, thus creating differences in behavioral and cultural expectations. While parents attempt to retain the language and ways of their home culture, adolescents are more actively exploring the roles and behaviors of the host culture and gradually reshaping their values and self-concepts. Intergenerational conflict was most severe in refugee families who had settled in rural areas isolated from their cultural peers, and in single-parent families, usually widowed mothers and their children (Williams and Westermeyer, 1983). In these situations, the parents were lacking a culturally similar and mutually supportive network.

Developmentally, adolescents are confronted with identity issues. From an ecological perspective, this task is intensified for the refugee adolescent, who must negotiate between family, peer, and societal expectations to resolve the question, Who am I? Given the unpopularity of the Vietnam War and the intense emotionality associated with it, Southeast Asian adolescents may have a particularly difficult time integrating a bicultural identity when confronted by the hostility and negative memories of the American mainstream society. Although they may begin to internalize "being American," fears of rejection by Americans may lead to emotional conflict. Similarly, though dependent on American aid they may simultaneously despise the Americans for their role in the war that generated the need to flee. This ambivalence may complicate formation of an identity and a positive self-concept. They may chronically feel they are unwelcome guests in someone else's home.

Carlin and Sokoloff (1985) have suggested that the concept of posttraumatic stress disorder applies to these refugee youth. Like the American veterans for whom this disorder has been recognized, these youth have undergone major stresses; witnessed atrocities, terrifying losses, and torture; and now need to adjust to a Western, technological society. Unexplained fears and night terrors may be expected, as well as an initial psychic numbing to block out these experiences.

Sokoloff, Carlin, and Pham (1984) conducted a five-year follow-up study of Vietnamese refugee children and concluded that developmental reversal of physical problems was quite rapid. Similarly, behavioral and emotional problems, nightmares, and generalized fears were initially severe in frequency and type; however, by the end of the first year, these had noticeably diminished. The older children in foster care showed more adjustment problems. Though functioning better than expected, they evidenced a high incidence of acting-out behaviors.

To date, the literature has not identified severe, long-term problems for refugee children. For the most part, these children show incredible resilience and healthy adaptation to a new environment. In contrast to many of the clinical studies, which tended to focus on maladjustment, Huang and Huang (1984) examined perceived competence in a comparison study of twenty-three Vietnamese refugee children and twenty-three white American children. They found no significant difference between the two nonclinical groups in reported levels of perceived competence in the cognitive, physical, and social domains, and no difference in general self-worth. Although this study started from a different set of assumptions, its findings were consistent with those in the clinical literature.

In my study of a nonclinical sample of fifty-one Vietnamese, Chinese, and Cambodian refugee school-age children, extensive interviews revealed serious concern about parents and their well-being. The children rated themselves as happier with the relocation than their parents and viewed their mothers as the least happy in the United States and the least adaptive to being American. Fathers were rated as slightly more willing to Americanize. The role of ethnicity in self-concept shifted with the children's situation. In the context of their home, they clearly viewed themselves as more ethnic; in school, as more American; and with "good friends," as equally ethnic and American. This finding echoes DeVos's (1980) hypothesis that peers play an important role in mediating acculturation. Furthermore, these context-dependent shifts in identification did not seem to affect feelings of general worth or competence.

When asked about the problems of most significance and difficulty for them, 32 percent of these refugee children cited physical altercations with peers in school; 20 percent indicated social interactions with peers; 20 percent described experiences of or concerns about physical injury, such as being hit by a car, being in an earthquake, or being stabbed in the neighborhood; 15 percent reported problems within the family; and 10 percent cited worries about family members, primarily grandparents, remaining in Vietnam. Again, the role of peers was especially significant. Surprisingly, cognitive and language difficulties were reported only when I specifically asked about problems related to school. The high reported incidence of physical altercations with peers was reiterated in testimony by California researchers before Congress ("Asian Immigrants. . . ," 1987). They reported that racial tension and brawls had become a regular aspect of school life for Asian children in California and that all the Asian immigrants interviewed reported being punched, mimicked, harassed, or robbed by non-Asian fellow students.

In contrast to the children and adolescents who migrated with parents or other adult relatives, the youth at most risk are clearly the unaccompanied minors. Some became separated from their families before or during their escape; others were sent away by their parents to avoid induction into the Communist army or assignment to the "new economic zones," which are noted for their extreme hardship and lack of any economic or social future. Still others escaped under the auspices of another family; however, when these families realized that sponsorship would be found earlier for smaller families, they relinquished these children to camp authorities. The vulnerability of unaccompanied minors is exacerbated by their longer stays in refugee camps. Observers have noted that these youth are depressed, restless, often hyperactive, and lacking in concentration. They are often grieving for their family and homeland while trying to adapt to a new, unfamiliar environment without the presence of familiar support systems. In their foster homes, their behavior often vacillates between periods of cooperativeness and periods of anger, aggressiveness, or withdrawal (Mortland and Egan, 1987; Redick and Wood, 1982).

Bachyun Nguyen, a Vietnamese social worker with the Catholic Charities of St. Paul and Minneapolis for thirty unaccompanied minors from Vietnam ranging in age from five to eighteen, cited the following as major problems for these youth (personal communication, 1987): (1) handling problems with foster parents, such as feeling unloved and "just a source of money," not being understood, and feeling ambivalent about forming an attachment to these parents while retaining a hope of being reunited with their biological parents; (2) having experienced the hardships of Communism and feeling that nobody really understands this experience; (3) harboring such questions as Who am I? and Where do I belong? which usually emerge after two years of rapid assimilation; and (4) integrating two disparate cultures and learning to flip-flop according to the situation.

During extensive clinical experience with refugee youth, Nidorf (1985) observed severe depression, hysterical conversion reactions, high levels of agitation, and antisocial and acting-out behaviors among unaccompanied adolescents. Lacking meaningful support from close adults and longing for parental nurturance, they remained vulnerable to feelings of shame, despair, and humiliation and a sense of being an outcast because of their lack of a family. In Asian cultures, the concepts of family and filial piety are essential for organizing one's experiences, social reality, and identity.

Nidorf hypothesized that certain events during the adolescent's escape may lead to specific types of maladjustment. The most traumatic aspect of the escape for many youth was physical and sexual assault by sea pirates, resulting in deep psychological wounds and traumatic memories. Adolescent females who experience this may later present as chronically suicidal, withdrawn, uninterested in social relationships, or rejecting of the cultural expectation of marriage. Still others, identifying with the aggressor in order to survive, may present as sexually promiscuous and inappropriately seductive. Adolescent males, overwhelmed by fear, shame, and rage, may present as physically or psychologically impotent, apathetic phobic, or anxiety ridden.

Nidorf (1985) also indicated that unaccompanied minors are at a higher suicide risk than other refugees. They are more vulnerable to maladaptive behaviors for which they may lose face, and suicide may become an alternative for resolving issues of shame.

Survivor guilt may also be a determinant of suicidal behavior. In some cases, survivor guilt is extremely reality based, as with one child whose mother died of starvation in a refugee camp, having given her food to her children so that they would survive. This child literally watched his mother die. Alienation in a strange culture and in the absence of one's family, and depression accompanied by the frustration and pressures of adaptation, may similarly play a role in the etiology of suicide.

In metropolitan areas with large populations of refugees, gangs of Vietnamese youth have recently become more prominent (Kelley, 1987). Detached from their native culture and unable to secure a niche in American society, these youth group together for reasons of identity, protection, and economics. These gangs include youth with and without families, but the latter are more vulnerable to the lure of gang membership, which becomes a substitute for the absent family. The hierarchy and loyalty expected within the gang resemble those of previous family roles. Additionally, the communal experiences and family separations under Communist rule, in labor camps, and in the refugee camps have provided precedents for this type of group bonding. Nidorf (1985) reports that the youth attracted to gangs have limited educational and vocational skills and are drawn by the prospect of experiencing a sense of belonging and excitement, gaining otherwise unattainable material possessions, and enjoying freedom and sexual experiences without adult constraints. Though gangs ostensibly provide protection for their members, they also provoke interracial tensions and endanger the members.

One other high-risk group is the Amerasians, the half-Vietnamese, half-American children fathered by U.S. servicemen during the Vietnam War. In 1988 it was estimated that there were eight to twelve thousand Amerasians, whose average age was 17.5 years, living in Vietnam (Hiebert, 1988). Some four thousand Amerasians were resettled in the United States under a program administered by the United Nations. With their dual ethnic identity, they were considered outcasts in Vietnam and unwanted reminders of the war. They were deprived of economic, educational, and social opportunities available to other Vietnamese. Some lived with families, but many were homeless street children. After much negotiating with members of the U.S. Congress, the Vietnamese government agreed in principle to an airlift of these children and their families to the United States (Hiebert, 1988). After enduring ostracism and discrimination for more than a decade, living in a Communist country in transition, and lacking a father in a culture where the family unit is paramount, these youth confronted a new set of stresses in the United States, including racism and discrimination, and at best, reluctant acceptance. The plight of these youth and its effect on their psychological well-being remain to be examined.

In general, available studies of Southeast Asian refugee youth are consistent with previous investigations of children living in violent, war-torn conditions (Garmezy and Rutter, 1983). Children separated from their families sustained the uprooting more poorly than those evacuated with their families. A prime factor in how children react to the stress of war is the behavior of their parents or significant adults, because the adults model the ability to exert control in the midst of crisis or upheaval. Thus the confidence of the adult community may have a significant impact on the well-being of the children.

These findings have mixed implications for Southeast Asian refugee children. In addition to relocations, their families undergo major sociocultural changes. Children and adolescents view the transformation of their parents from previously competent, autonomous caretakers to depressed, overwhelmed, and dependent individuals. Like children of other immigrants, refugee children more rapidly acculturate to the new country. The confidence of the parents is inevitably undermined when they become so dependent on their children, who more quickly acquire facility with the new language and customs. Extrapolation from earlier studies might predict poor adaptation of these children, who lose the critical resource of a strong parent to rely on. This may be the case for some youth. However, for others, the assumption of parental responsibilities may engender a sense of importance and competence and ward off feelings of despair and helplessness.

Sociocultural Issues in Assessment

The assessment approach to be presented here is based on an ecological framework, which focuses on interconnected systems dynamically interacting with an individual. Ecological transitions

occur when an individual's position in these systems is altered by
a change in role, setting, or both; the transitions are the joint function of individual and altered environmental circumstances (Bronfenbrenner, 1979). On the positive side, this process of mutual
accommodation between the individual and the environment represents the process of growth and change. However, ecological
transitions are inherently stress producing and may lead to maladaptive outcomes as well. For refugees, fleeing one's homeland,
migrating to unfamiliar places, and accommodating to a new society all represent major ecological transitions with the potential
for substantial growth or disorder.

The psychosocial assessment of Southeast Asian refugee youth,
as of other refugee groups, must take into consideration at least
three ecological contexts: premigration, migration, and post-
migration (Kinzie, 1981; Nidorf, 1985). Within each context, the
assessment includes larger, macrosystem issues, such as cultural and
societal expectations, as well as more focused microsystem structures, such as the family.

Premigration

The youth's perceptions of the world and ways of handling the
environment are to a large degree influenced by cultural values.
Although Vietnamese and Cambodians share some general characteristics of Asian cultures, the basic foundations of their respective cultures differ, leading to important cultural distinctions. The
culture of Vietnam is based on Confucian traditions imported from
China during its early history of Chinese domination. Roman
Catholicism, introduced by French missionaries and traders, became more widespread with the French conquest in 1958 (Chi,
1980). In contrast, Cambodia has been much more influenced by
Buddhism and isolated from Western influences.

In accord with Confucian traditions, the family is the basic social unit of Vietnamese society. As in Chinese culture (see Chapter
Two), the extended family and family interdependence are of critical importance. The family hierarchy and associated roles and responsibilities are clearly delineated; filial piety and respect for
elders, teachers, and authority are socially expected behaviors. Regardless of social status, children represent the future of the fam-

ily, and both children and adults feel a sense of inferiority if children do not achieve goals set by the family. Shame and loss of face are collectively shared by one's family, and avoidance of these is the motivator for much of one's behavior. Stoic attitudes, self-control, and avoidance of direct expression of emotions are highly valued. Harmony in interpersonal relationships is accomplished through tact, delicacy, and politeness, sometimes at the cost of honesty and forthrightness (Le, 1983).

The premigration culture of an Amerasian refugee may be quite dissimilar to that of other refugee youth. In a society in which family is of primary importance, the experience of these youth is one of rejection and degradation. They are scorned by most Vietnamese and lack the all-important sense of belonging. They and their families, usually mothers and siblings, are outcasts in an ethnically homogeneous country and devoid of the priceless commodity, family. Thus the premigration culture of an Amerasian refugee may instill values of self-preservation and basic survival, possible disdain for authority, and ambivalence toward one's country, culture, and family.

Cambodia is primarily a rural country whose society has been influenced by the teachings of Buddhism. The society is patriarchal, with the father the head of the family; but his is not an all-powerful role. His rights over the family are counterbalanced by duties prescribed by Buddhist morality and sanctioned by civil law. In many cases, husband and wife share authority (Garry, 1980). In contrast to other Asian cultures, Cambodia is a more open society in which the individual is not necessarily subordinate to the family or social group. Although the extended family is acknowledged, family structure is based more on the couple relationship. From Buddhist teachings the Cambodian people derive a respect for life in all its forms, a tolerance, gentleness, and honesty, and an indifference to material wealth (Garry, 1980). Buddhism suggests that all life involves suffering; however, one can influence this condition by morally upright behavior and thoughts and good deeds. In contrast to Vietnam, Cambodia has had less exposure to Western technological societies and remains a less modernized, underdeveloped country. For example, the stringent examination system for education and the strong values of competition in Vietnam are not as apparent in Cambodia.

These cultural attributes of Vietnam and Cambodia are, by necessity, generalizations. One can expect wide individual and social-class variation. Additionally, these historical patterns are being increasingly challenged and diluted as new values are introduced or imposed by Western countries.

Another relevant aspect of the Vietnamese and Cambodian cultures is attitude toward mental health. In general, the conceptualization of mental disorders is bimodal. The less severe emotional and behavioral disorders are believed to reflect a combination of youthfulness, life circumstances, and unusual and excessive problems in living. Whenever possible, these disorders are handled within the family to avoid embarrassment and shame. When the family can no longer contain the confusion, agitation, or acting-out behavior, outside assistance is usually sought from priests and village elders or shamans and fortunetellers (Aylesworth, Ossorio, and Osaki, 1980). The more severe psychopathological disorders are believed to be of mysterious origin and are also handled within the family whenever possible. These abnormal behaviors are sometimes believed to be a result of some physical ailment, and occasionally help from a physician is sought. More likely, the family contacts the traditional cultural healers. Only as a last resort is the individual taken to a psychiatric helper or admitted to a psychiatric facility.

Understanding the resources that were available to a youth's family in their homeland is important, because this may significantly affect the psychological and practical coping capabilities of the refugee (Nidorf, 1985). Occupational status in the homeland has been considered a predictor of socioeconomic status in the country of resettlement, as well as a weak predictor of psychological adjustment (Vignes and Hall, 1979).

Further, the child's age at the time of departure has implications for how the child comprehends and copes with the emigration experience. Preschoolers and adolescents are in particular need of a stable, predictable environment as they undergo significant physiological changes and major psychological upheavals. Preverbal memories of terror and disrupted language patterns may plague the preschooler, and the identity crisis of the adolescent may be intensified (Le, 1983).

Determining the age at departure may also provide important information on the youth's experiences in the homeland. Youth who remained in Vietnam or Cambodia after the Communist regimes became entrenched, around 1977, endured numerous hardships, such as disintegration of the family unit, witnessing of torture, forced internment in labor camps, and conscription into children's armies, events not experienced by those who left earlier (Nguyen, 1982; Sheehy, 1986).

Migration

Of critical importance in the assessment is the microsystem of flight: With whom did the youth migrate and who was left behind? As seen in the studies reviewed earlier, whether or not one is accompanied by an intact family during the migration process will affect later psychosocial development.

Examination of this microsystem also includes the process of flight—preparation for and means of escape and any dangerous situations or losses encountered during the escape. The trauma incurred during flight may significantly transform a youth's perception of self, others, and the world in general. Many children, often for reasons of safety and security, were not informed of the plans to leave. For example, one child in my study was told that they were going to his grandmother's, only to find that they were escaping by boat at night and he would never see his grandmother again. Subsequently, this child harbors obsessive concerns about his grandmother, and several years after resettlement the intensity of his desire to see her has not subsided. Children and adolescents who witnessed or experienced brutality at the hands of pirates or soldiers often feel a betrayal of their expectation that adults, particularly family members, will protect them. Their trust in the goodness and predictability of the world has been deeply wounded, and their sense of powerlessness in the world has been deeply accentuated. For parents, these incidents of brutality, including repeated rapes and beatings, underscored their inability to perform the sacred duty of protecting their children. Their sense of rage and helplessness is apparent to the children. For many of the youth and the adults, the fleetingness of life becomes a reality, and subsequently many of these children, like other traumatized children (Terr, 1979), do not view life as long.

In an ecological framework, the refugee camp can be considered another microsystem affecting the development of refugee youth. The camp experience was characterized by overcrowded, unsanitary conditions; makeshift shacks overrun by rats; frequent outbreaks of bubonic plague, tuberculosis, and malaria; food and clothing shortages; absence of privacy; and prolonged periods of boredom (Borton, 1984). Nevertheless, it provided a psychosocial respite during which refugees were able to put their escape in perspective and begin to worry about the future. My brief observation at Camp Jubilee in Hong Kong in 1980 found the young children to be hungry and poorly clothed but playful and curious. Even in the squalor and poverty of the camp, the children played in small groups and converted the meager resources of the camp into instruments of play. In contrast, the adolescents seemed more remote and distant. They eyed the visiting observers warily and seemed to spend much of their time in bed listening to music. There were few activities for them, and their idleness and boredom were particularly striking.

In assessing the camp experience, one must be sensitive to the quality of the experience as it is subjectively viewed by the youth (Nidorf, 1985). Although media reports describe horrendous conditions, for the youth the camp may have been a safe haven from the previous horror of their flight. Conversely, it may represent the first context for recognizing their loss of family, home, and homeland and thus may be associated with the deepest sense of pain and tragic memories. While remaining attuned to the youths' subjective experiences, clinicians must also be cognizant of the tendency to idealize or vilify the camp experience.

The macrosystem phenomena within the migration period can be considered a "trauma culture." Straddling the uncertain line between life and death and between freedom and captivity, many refugees develop behaviors that would be uncharacteristic of them in normal situations. Basic survival skills, such as scrounging for food and shelter, become preeminent. Vigilance and mistrust become ubiquitous. When confronted with life-threatening situations, people are often forced to do things they would normally consider unacceptable; eventually these behaviors must be integrated into an acceptable self-concept. Anticipating the role of victim and readily capitulating to more dominant personalities are behaviors associated with a trauma culture. The degree to which an individual remains immersed in a trauma culture is related to the duration and intensity of the traumatic events and the disruption of normality. This is especially pertinent for unaccompanied minors and Amerasian children, whose lives have usually been the most shattered and disrupted. Though occasionally adaptive, the learned behaviors from this stage may interfere with normal development and adjustment to a new society.

Postmigration

The categories of assessment for refugee youth may be similar to those used with nonrefugee youth: age, general appearance and size, speech and language, affect, interpersonal relatedness, level of anxiety, patterns of defense, and management of aggression and sexuality. However, the interpretation of these data needs to incorporate cultural and experiential differences. For example, determining the true age of the individual, usually considered a simple and routine question, may be quite difficult. For many refugee children, the age stated on official documents is several years lower than the child's actual chronological age. The rationale for this deception has to do with survival and resources. In refugee camps, younger children were usually given priority for food and shelter, and in the countries of resettlement they would receive educational and welfare benefits for a longer period. In school, however, this age deception may be a source of problematic behavior because, particularly for adolescent males, the sixteen-year-old in a class with twelve- and thirteen-year-olds may feel isolated and awkward (Nidorf, 1985).

In the other assessment categories, judgments about the range of normality may be subject to cultural bias. For example, the form and intensity of affect may be more constricted and halting, as dictated by cultural norms. Interpersonal relatedness may be guarded and unusually cautious owing to emigration experiences of betrayals, multiple losses, and loss of faith in adult providers. The interviewer must be cautious in interpreting the assessment data and must carefully distinguish between culturally determined behavior and maladaptive psychopathological behavior.

When considering the family microsystem, the clinician must remember that refugee families are families in transition, presenting a wide range of issues: culture, communication, depression, grief, disorganization, and separation (Lappin and Scott, 1982). The hierarchy of roles within the family is often in disarray as children more readily acculturate to the host country and become emissaries for the parents with the outside world. Additionally, wives are often forced to work for economic survival. These age-role and sex-role reversals upset the prescribed distribution of power within the family, leading to tension and conflict. In addition, there is the stress of having left family members behind. The efforts toward family reunification are relentless and time- and resource-consuming.

Refugee youth assigned to foster families encounter yet another set of stresses that needs to be included in any assessment. The expectations of the youth and the foster family need to be carefully examined. The child's hopes and dreams of America had often been a sustaining influence during the emigration. Inevitably, these idealizations will be met by disappointment with the reality. Similarly, foster parents' excitement and good intentions may become tarnished as they encounter a bewildered youth who is psychologically numbed, emotionally distant, and distrustful. Frequently the youth's anger toward the biological parents for abandonment is displaced onto the foster parents. In Asian cultures, the concept of foster parenting has no counterpart, as this task is usually assumed by the extended family. Consequently, refugee youth may have difficulty comprehending this Western form of family and determining their role in this structure. Cultural clashes are to be expected and need to be assessed. For example, the primacy of the youth's biological family may be hurtful to the foster family, who, for example, may resent the youth's sending money and medicine to the family in Asia. Meanwhile, the refugee youth may be struggling with divided family loyalties. Underlying these potential areas of conflict is the ever-present language difficulty, a source of repeated frustration and continual misunderstanding.

For these foster families, there are predictable times of stress that may trigger increased anxiety in the refugee youth (Rudnick and Harmatys, 1987). Receiving letters from home may raise feelings of guilt and depression; ethnic holidays, such as Tet, the Vietnamese New Year, may similarly trigger intense affect. School events, such as beginning a new academic year, meeting new teachers, or taking exams, may be particularly difficult for the refugee. American holidays, when all the children come home to "one big, happy family," intensify the refugee youth's loneliness and isolation, and school vacations present the refugee with much unstructured time to ruminate about personal losses and worry about the future and the family back home.

Another important microsystem is the school. For children and adolescents, the school is the most frequent source of referral to mental health agencies. It behooves the mental health worker to obtain a thorough assessment of the youth's functioning in the school, including cognitive and social skills.

The ethnic/racial composition of the school has implications for the refugee child's adjustment and acculturation. The presence of other ethnically similar children may ease the refugee's transition. However, it must be kept in mind that ethnic sameness does not guarantee a support system for the refugee. Earlier refugees or American-born ethnic Chinese, Vietnamese, or Cambodians, wishing to acculturate to mainstream America and disregard memories of a painful past, may be reluctant to associate with newer refugees. School-age children driven by the need to belong and to be accepted tend to avoid the unusual or unfamiliar. Amerasian children may be especially vulnerable targets of hostility, given their often unknown parentage and their physical features and color, which set them apart from other groups. These difficulties in ethnic/racial identity, in combination with significantly different school histories and pervasive language problems, give rise not only to academic problems but to emotional and behavioral problems as well.

A final area of assessment is societal issues. Despite federal provision of funds for refugee resettlement, the public has been less than receptive to the refugees. Although this country was built on the concept of an "open door," refugees of color seem to be only reluctantly welcomed. Southeast Asian refugees also bear the stigma of association with the United States' "lost war" and deep dissension and divisiveness in the country.

In recent years, the United States has experienced a resurgence of racial tension and violence that had been subdued following the civil rights gains of the late 1960s. The refugees encounter racism from multiple directions, often stemming from economic and political tensions and cultural ignorance. At many inner-city schools, daily verbal and physical clashes between Southeast Asians and other racial minority groups have become habitual (Fong, 1987). Many of the refugees, who came from rural, racially homogeneous countries, had no previous contact with blacks or Hispanics or with urban lifestyles. As the refugees moved into predominantly minority communities, cultural clashes were inevitable. In Davis, California, racial tensions between Southeast Asian students and white students escalated without intervention, resulting in the stabbing death of a Vietnamese refugee high school student in the spring of 1984. Although the incidents of violence remain isolated, they are becoming disturbingly more frequent and routine. Children and adolescents do not remain impervious to this atmosphere of increasing interracial tension, and their developmental experiences may be directly or indirectly affected.

Intervention and Treatment

In developing an intervention approach with Southeast Asian refugee youth, several critical issues should be considered: (1) the concept of mental health is alien to these youth, and associated treatments are viewed warily; (2) disclosure of problems beyond family boundaries is considered inappropriate and damaging to the reputation and integrity of the family; (3) trust in professionals, whether ethnic or nonethnic, is usually only superficial, given the history of misunderstandings, bureaucratic entanglements, and repeated disappointments; and (4) a request for help places one in the culturally eschewed position of "debtor." These issues form major impediments to effective intervention and therefore need to be acknowledged if the clinician is to engage the refugee client in treatment.

An ecological perspective is the basis for the intervention strategies to be presented here. Identifying the pertinent systems that intersect with the individual provides the beginning points for intervention. For the child or adolescent, these systems invariably include the family, the school system, social service agencies, or self-help, social support groups, such as mutual aid associations, within the community. The therapist needs to have a conceptual map of the individual's ecological niche and may need to work simultaneously with different systems. Essential to the therapist's successful engagement with the refugee are two elements: the therapist's credibility and the development of a working relationship based on an "active exchange."

As noted by Sue and Zane (1987), the therapist enters the situation with an *ascribed* credibility based on such characteristics as age, sex, ethnicity, and status in the agency. To sustain the refugee client in the treatment relationship, the therapist must attain a higher *achieved* credibility, which is based on effective therapeutic skills and a feeling of progress on the part of the client. Although one can delineate the traits that contribute to ascribed credibility, it is not always possible to predict the direction of influence. For example, many agencies automatically assume that a Southeast Asian refugee client would prefer an Asian therapist. In some instances, this assumption is correct. However, one Vietnamese client, for example, was deeply offended when assigned a Chinese therapist. This client harbored much hatred toward Chinese, reflecting the history of antagonism between these two ethnic groups in Vietnam. He resented the economic domination of the ethnic Chinese in Vietnam and more recently despised the role of Chinese Communists in the political situation in his homeland. For the client, the assignment of a Chinese therapist dramatically reflected the agency's insensitivity to him and confirmed his preconceptions that they would neither understand nor help him.

Matching client and therapist ethnicity does not guarantee augmenting the therapist's credibility. Some refugees are hesitant to interact with a therapist of their own ethnicity because of differing stages of loyalty to their ethnic group, fears of breaches in confidentiality if the therapist lives or works in their community, or reluctance to confront reminders of a painful past. Other refugees, however, find comfort in a shared culture and history with the therapist, and language obstacles may be minimized.

The combination of a white therapist with a refugee client similarly has its advantages and disadvantages. The refugee may ascribe higher status to the white therapist and thus may be more cooperative with a treatment plan, believing that this therapist possesses the power or expertise to obtain the desired resources or resolve the presenting problem. Conversely, the refugee may have much ambivalence toward Caucasian Americans stemming from their role in escalating the war in Vietnam, abandoning the country, and then begrudgingly providing assistance to refugees. The refugee may seriously question the trustworthiness and motives of the therapist.

An alternative to the usual combinations is a cross-cultural team approach that employs a nonrefugee American therapist and a bilingual refugee trained as a mental health paraprofessional. DeMonchy and Pin-Riebe (1987), a cross-cultural counseling team in the Department of Mental Health in Boston, report that bicultural teams are a visible symbol to their clients of the interaction between two worlds. The ethnic therapist provides familiarity with the culture and the language, a shared history, and an example of "making it" in the new country. In addition, this therapist may possess important knowledge and contacts within the ethnic community and may be instrumental in linking the client with a system of social support. The nonethnic therapist provides a link to the social service system, knowledge of laws and policies, and support and energy from a less traumatized perspective. Often this therapist is able to instill new hopes and dreams. Advocates of this method suggest that the integration and process between the team members are essential for effective intervention and are a critical model for the refugee clients.

A second critical component of the helping relationship with refugee clients is the concept of *active exchange*. For many refugees, who are unfamiliar with Western mental health practices, the efficacy of "talking" is not readily apparent. Rather, the refugee client expects some form of advice, advocacy, immediate symptom relief, or change in the problematic situation. When this does not occur, the clients, as documented with minority groups in general (Acosta, Yamamoto, and Evans, 1982; Sue and McKinney, 1975), often terminate the relationship prematurely. Most clients are familiar with the physician/patient relationship, which entails a brief encounter, a series of questions from the doctor, concrete answers from the patient, and subsequently some sort of symptom relief. Refugee and minority clients often generalize from this relationship to that with the mental health worker. When these expectations are not met, the client becomes disillusioned with the process. To establish a working alliance with the client, the therapist or mental health worker needs to engage the client in an active exchange, in which the client perceives giving and receiving on the part of both client and helper. This reciprocal exchange enables the client to experience tangible gains as a result of participation in the interaction. As discussed in Chapter Two, components in this exchange on the client's side include willingness to meet with the helper, self-disclosure and receptivity, and some form of payment for the services, be it a nominal fee or a third-party payment. The therapist demonstrates a willingness to meet with and listen to the client, shares personal credentials or qualifications, empathizes with the client's emotional pain or frustration, and acknowledges the client's explanations for the problem. On a concrete, practical level, the therapist may also provide specific information about social services, refugee resources, and social support groups in the community.

Construing the working relationship as an active exchange also serves to counter the notion of the client as debtor. Inherent in most Asian cultures is the unwillingness to incur obligation. The fear of being indebted to someone often drives Asian clients from a helping relationship. The active exchange promotes a sense of partnership in the helping process and transforms the client from a passive recipient to an active participant, attempting to regain control over his or her life situation.

The following two cases represent composites from my clinical and research experience. The objective of these presentations is to provide a sense of the refugee youth's experiences and presenting problems and to illustrate the concepts of therapist credibility and active exchange in the helping process. The first case focuses on a refugee child experiencing a psychological disorder akin to posttraumatic stress disorder, and the second highlights issues for unaccompanied minors in foster care.

Thuy, a twelve-year-old Vietnamese girl, was referred to the child and adolescent unit of a community mental health center by her teacher and counselor. Her teacher had noticed a marked deterioration in her academic performance and that she frequently complained of headaches and asked to leave the class, seemed to lack energy, showed a loss of appetite, and nonverbally conveyed a general feeling of hopelessness. During the previous six months she had changed from a good student, actively involved with peers, to a withdrawn, depressed preadolescent. More recently, for days at a time she would not talk unless pressured to, and frequently stared off into space.

Thuy was from a middle-class family in Saigon, where until the downfall of South Vietnam her father had been a lower-level clerk with the army. He fled Saigon with his family, a wife and three children, in 1978; however, during the escape, the family became separated and the wife and two younger children remained in Vietnam. Thuy and her father escaped by boat. Their boat was intercepted by Thai pirates, and Thuy's father was beaten and several women were raped. Although Thuy observed this, she herself was not physically assaulted. Eventually Thuy and her father reached Malaysia, where they remained in a refugee camp for nearly a year until they located relatives in the United States. They have been in the United States for two years and reside in a small apartment with a cousin's family of five in the inner city of a West Coast metropolitan area.

Thuy's father has had a particularly difficult time adjusting to the United States. He struggles with English classes and has been unable to maintain several jobs as a waiter. He attributes these difficulties to the assault during his escape, saying blows to the head impaired his memory and crippled him physically.

Just before the onset of Thuy's problems, she received a letter from her mother informing them of the death of her five-year-old brother. Complications from a childhood disease combined with malnutrition had contributed to his death. Thuy remained impassive on receiving this news, while her father wept uncontrollably, mourning the loss of his only son. Soon after that, her father was fired from yet another job, seemed to lose interest in English classes, and just languished around the small apartment.

At the insistence of the school and accompanied by her father, Thuy came to the clinic most reluctantly. She was reticent and scowling. Her father immediately began to plead with the therapist to help Thuy because she was all he had and he depended on her to make it in this country. He vacillated between sadness and anger toward Thuy. The therapist decided that father and daughter needed to be seen separately and arranged for the father to see another therapist, ostensibly to deal with Thuy's problems, but also to address his own issues.

This case is not atypical of the refugee children who present at mental health clinics. Their histories are replete with losses, trauma, and unrelenting family pressures. They are also usually very young.

In this case, establishing credibility took a long time. Thuy was initially quite distrustful of the therapist, assuming her to be yet another adult putting pressure and demands on her. Lacking knowledge about therapists, Thuy assumed she was another teacher or tutor for remedial students. Additionally, Thuy questioned the motivation of the female therapist, who was Asian but not Vietnamese and who simultaneously reminded her of her distant mother. The therapist gave Thuy permission not to trust her, recognizing that mistrust was a healthy reaction in this situation and that she would have to earn Thuy's trust.

Noticing Thuy's reticence and her tendency to doodle during the early sessions, the therapist made pencils, markers, and paper available. Thuy was too old for the playroom, but simple art supplies could promote nonverbal symbolic expression. The doodling seemed to be an outlet for some anxiety, and Thuy began to banter with the therapist, first about seemingly inconsequential matters such as objects in the office, bus routes, and procedures in her classroom. The therapist addressed these issues at face value, realizing they were questions about American ways. The beginning of an active exchange, a reciprocal relationship, was occurring; though remaining silent in the early sessions, Thuy continued to come. In turn, the therapist gave her time, patience, no pressure, and concrete materials—paper, markers, pencils—with no explicit expectation. Each party was contributing to the interaction.

On the next level, Thuy shared her perplexity about American ways; the therapist reciprocated with education about customs, behaviors, and attitudes of Americans. They then moved on to more disturbing matters, such as racial incidents on the bus and harassment by other children in her classroom. Over the next two months, Thuy experienced the therapist as dependable, regular, genuinely listening, and when asked, willing to give advice and suggestions for handling different experiences in the new country.

Of critical importance to intervention with refugees is allowing them to "tell their story" (Carlin and Sokoloff, 1985; Kinzie, 1981, Rudnick and Harmatys, 1987). Refugee youth rarely have the opportunity to do this, because family rules implicitly advocate "Don't talk about it." Community pressures to keep the "secrets" hidden and not incur shame for unavoidable events similarly inhibit disclosure about the emigration. However, the ventilation of their often remarkable and horrifying stories of flight may be cathartic and essential to the building of trust.

Thuy eventually recounted her story of flight, which included severe deprivations of food and water when on the boat as well as in the camp, and as already mentioned, severe brutality by sea pirates. Although Thuy herself was not attacked, she cringed in fear, hearing the screaming, and cried out for her own mother. The details of the stories are not as important as the accompanying emotions and associations. Thuy was only nine years old at the time of the pirate attack; however, she still has nightmares about it and currently associates the women's screaming with the plight of her mother in Vietnam. Until the notice of her brother's death, Thuy had maintained a positive image of her mother, believing that she was safe, comfortable, and happy in Vietnam, much as Thuy remembered her to be prior to their flight. Thuy firmly wanted to believe this; however, her brother's death penetrated this denial, and her fears and longing for her mother reemerged. She held much disdain for her father's perceived weaknesses: failure to bring the entire family out of Vietnam, inability to thwart the pirates, inability to maintain a job and save money to achieve family reunification, and excessive reliance on Thuy.

Adhering to a model of active exchange, what did the therapist give? With the child's continued disclosure, the therapist provided consistency, predictability, and support, things currently absent from this child's life. The therapist was an attentive listener and acknowledged the child's pain and suffering. Of particular importance at this point is the careful monitoring of the therapist's reactions to the child's story of horror and inhumanity. The therapist was careful not to show natural feelings of revulsion or to act on tendencies to be outraged at the persecutors or to overidealize the refugee's endurance. Strong emotions from the therapist may inhibit the child's own expression of emotion.

For many refugee children, the opportunity to grieve over significant losses is inhibited. This was the case with Thuy, who on arrival in the United States was immediately thrust into the role of caretaker for her father and "hope of the future" for her family. The therapist facilitated the delayed grief process for Thuy, for the loss of her brother, her homeland, and her mother and sister. This process was begun with gentle yet firm questioning about her life in Vietnam. Thuy's grief was manifest as anger and rage toward her father for breaking up the family and failing to adequately protect her. Expression of these feelings was particularly difficult for Thuy, because it is culturally unacceptable to speak disrespectfully of one's father or other family members. However, when these feelings were legitimized by the therapist's acceptance and reassurance that many children in this situation would have similar feelings, Thuy seemed noticeably relieved. Thus, in the process of active exchange, the therapist gave Thuy permission to grieve; in turn, Thuy entrusted the therapist with culturally prohibited feelings. Working through the grief also involved instilling hope for the future. For refugees, the grief process often remains incomplete because the prospects for family reunification are uncertain. In these circumstances, the therapist gives the youth ways to cope—for example, to anticipate and prepare for the feelings associated with receiving a letter from home or to anticipate the anxiety around birthdays or ethnic holidays.

The outcome of the intervention with Thuy was not complete symptom relief. Her presenting symptoms did subside and her schoolwork improved. However, she continued to have nightmares occasionally and felt anxiety in new situations. Some days her intense longing for her mother became so painful that she sank into periods of despair and weeping. However, she had discovered ways to live with her memories and the sense of disconnectedness in her life, so that her daily functioning was considerably improved.

In addition to the individual work, the therapist had regular contact with Thuy's teacher, who said Thuy had been indirectly involved in several interracial skirmishes at school. With the assistance of the mental health clinic, the school was initiating interracial student panels to address cultural differences and to discuss reasons for racial hostility. Thuy was selected to participate in these panels.

Thuy's family situation also improved. Her father, though still unemployed, periodically saw a therapist and became more involved in the community mutual assistance association. His physical symptoms and complaints, the culturally acceptable manifestation of psychological distress and anxiety, diminished. The emerging difficulties in the family revolved around cultural and generational conflicts. Thuy acknowledged the cultural imperative to respect and obey one's father; however, given her superior competence in American society relative to her father's diminished coping, this became a point of conflict. As Thuy became more bold, assertive, and self-initiating, adopting more Western behaviors, her father viewed this as a repudiation of her cultural heritage and family identity. Thuy received the confusing message that she was expected to succeed in America but to avoid becoming American.

This case discussion has focused primarily on the process of active exchange in individual therapy. In addition, the intervention was ecologically focused, targeting several systems pertinent to Thuy's life.

Sann, a fifteen-year-old Cambodian male, came to the attention of the community mental health clinic through the Department of Social Services. Sann had a history of poor school performance and truancy and had been in three foster homes in two years. Most recently, he was apprehended by juvenile authorities for petty theft.

Sann had been in the United States for two years. He had come in 1982 as an unaccompanied minor. His family had been middle-class residents of Phnom Penh until driven to the countryside by Khmer Rouge guerrillas under the Pol Pot regime. During this forced march, his mother, who had recently given birth, the newborn baby, and a younger sister died of starvation, dehydration, and exhaustion. Sann, his older sister, and his father were sent to a labor camp for nine months, where they witnessed regular beatings and deaths, until their escape, which involved walking across Cambodia and into Thailand. During this escape, Sann's father was killed by a land mine, and Sann and his sister became separated. To this day, he is unsure of the whereabouts of his sister or even whether she is alive. Sann spent two years in refugee camps in Thailand, where he learned rudimentary English.

Entering foster care at age thirteen, Sann found it difficult to accept his new parental figures. He resented their authority and concern, and he reacted with sullenness and suspicion. His caseworker described both sets of foster parents as highly motivated, caring couples who were unable to develop a relationship with Sann and requested his reassignment after he was caught stealing money from them. Similar problems were occurring in his third placement.

The caseworker described Sann as a highly intelligent yet very vigilant and mistrustful child suffering from severe depression related to his traumatic and tumultuous life experiences. He vacillated between a sense of hopelessness and a strong will to survive. His coping skills were derived from his escape and camp experiences and had not been modified to fit his current living situation. He was a loner and seemed uninterested in peer relationships.

Mollica (1987), of the Indochinese Psychiatry Clinic in Boston, suggests that therapeutic objectives with refugees are (1) to increase the client's ability to cope in family, community, school, and work settings, acknowledging that the symptoms and memories from the trauma may last indefinitely; and (2) to assist the client in re-creating a future that was destroyed by the trauma. For Sann, it would also have been ideal to regain some of the childhood that had been destroyed; however, connecting him with new elements in his present society took precedence. Adhering to an ecological model, the intervention with Sann was multifocused. In contrast to the work with Thuy, the individual therapy was a much smaller component of the intervention. The therapist occasionally met with Sann, but her role was more that of a resource broker. She linked him with a therapy group for Cambodian refugee adolescents, consulted with the caseworker who was doing family work with the foster family, advocated for a special tutorial program as he was struggling in school, and connected him with refugee community agencies that could assist him in a strategy to determine his sister's whereabouts.

Initially, credibility was not an issue for the therapist: in Sann's eyes, she had none. However, Sann knew that she had authority and that in order to avoid juvenile hall, he had to comply with the treatment program. The turning point for Sann was brought about by the group program. The refugee adolescents had the opportunity to share their stories with others who could understand on a personal level. After initial hesitation, they began readily to discuss events in their homeland, life before the political disruptions, and incidents during the escape. Their growing camaraderie, built on shared experiences and shared memories, tended to dissipate the powerful grip and intrusiveness of these traumatic memories. The Cambodian adolescents, all males and in foster placements, were on the verge of regaining a sense of positive control in their lives.

The issues in the foster family system included differing expectations, cultural misunderstandings, and conflicts around independence and control. Sann's foster family was a middle-class Caucasian American family associated with a church organization that sponsored refugees. Finances were a first source of conflict. As a survivor, Sann existed by looking out for himself and taking whatever he could get. His efforts to gain money and material possessions were thwarted by the foster family. Each month there was conflict over the disposition of the foster care stipend. This is an issue that seems common to many refugees' foster care arrangements (Mortland and Egan, 1987).

Second, there was continual conflict over Sann's role in the family. Still bewildered by American customs and confused about his own identity, Sann resisted integration into the family. He remained distant and aloof, uncommunicative, and erratic in complying with family chores and responsibilities. Sann assumed the role of an uninvolved boarder, which made the family feel unappreciated, used, and annoyed. In their frustration, the foster parents became less sensitive to Sann's emotional needs and inadvertently belittled his heritage with such comments as "You should consider yourself lucky you're in America; a lot of kids your age are still living in primitive conditions in Cambodia."

Third, after being on his own since age eleven, Sann had difficulty accepting the authority of the foster parents and their infringement on his independence. Like other refugees in foster care (Mortland and Egan, 1987), Sann resented family rules, the inability to handle his own federal stipend, and being forced to adapt to a family that was not really his. He felt angry and ashamed that he did not have his own family, and he resented the family in which he had been involuntarily placed. With consultation from the therapist, the caseworker addressed these issues with the family and tried to develop contractual agreements between Sann and the family. The caseworker tried to prepare the family for emotional assaults stemming from Sann's displacement of anger about his own family and situation onto the foster family. Clarification of the roles, the cultural meanings of family, and the preconceptions of each other's cultures were addressed by the caseworker.

The intervention with the school was unsuccessful, as neither the school nor Sann was motivated. The counselor felt that Sann's needs were beyond the school's limited and already strained resources and that his age would soon make him "eligible to drop out." Although his school was racially and ethnically mixed, Sann felt like an outcast. He was embarrassed to be in classes with students several years younger than he and avoided contact with other refugees because of his status as a "foster kid," a refugee without a family. In his life experiences, he could find little to share with his nonrefugee peers. In spite of the joint efforts of the therapist and counselor to devise a special program, Sann eventually dropped out.

Sann's withdrawal from school coincided with his increased involvement in the group of Cambodian adolescents and entry into the refugee community. At the therapist's insistence, Sann enrolled in English-language courses and became active at a community center serving Cambodian refugees. Here he made contacts and learned of refugee agencies that could assist him in locating his sister. Sann was beginning to assemble pieces for a future. While acknowledging that she might have died, Sann could at least begin to talk about her, his longing for her, and his fears for her demise. And most important, he had reconnected with his culture and his community.

To reengage Sann, the concept of active exchange was applied repeatedly and in various settings. He was retrieved from his isolation by the mutuality in the group program for Cambodian adolescents, the caseworker negotiated the give-and-take with the foster family, and the ethnic community gave him a sense of belonging and hope for the future in exchange for his renewed motivation and contributions to the center. In essence, the overall intervention represented a balance and reciprocity between helpers and client.

Conclusions

With few exceptions, Southeast Asian refugee youth have spent a significant portion of their lives in violent conditions, experiencing serious loss, fear of the unknown, prolonged periods of waiting, and discontinuities in their schooling and health care. The escape from their homeland was usually precipitous, with little warning or time for preparation and farewells. The journey itself was often traumatic and at times life threatening. These experiences were intensified by the dynamic interaction of these frightened children with their traumatized parents or other accompanying adults (Huyck and Fields, 1981). In general, the dramas of refugee youth are extreme and tragic, and their stories are a testimony to both the brutality of human beings and the resilience of the human spirit. Professionals in a range of fields can learn much about survival and coping from these children.

This chapter has presented the developmental and psychosocial conflicts of Southeast Asian refugee youth in the context of their unique migration and sociocultural histories. Although many of these children and adolescents have adapted well to their new life circumstances in the United States, some are still struggling with memories of the past, psychological wounds from the trauma, and new intercultural and intergenerational dilemmas. The effects of war and uprooting are subject to individual variation, ranging from major disruptions in development to incidental annoyances. The degree of risk for psychological disturbance also varies and seems correlated with economic and familial resources. The common finding in many studies identifies unaccompanied minors and Amerasian children as high-risk groups.

An ecological model for intervention is based on the assumption that an individual's development is both the cause and the effect of multiple system interactions. The task for the therapist working with refugee youth is to identify the unique systems and cultural frameworks to be incorporated into the intervention. In this sense, the clinician's role may range from individual therapist to school consultant to advocate; the arenas for investigation may be not only the individual and the family but also schools, work settings, social service agencies, and community organizations. In my experience, therapist credibility and active exchange are essential ingredients in a working relationship. Because there are no definitive routes to successful outcomes, therapists must be innovative in developing appropriate interventions for this unique population.

References

Acosta, F. X., Yamamoto, J., and Evans, L. A. *Effective Psychotherapy for Low-Income and Minority Patients.* New York: Plenum, 1982.

Ahmed, P., Tims, F., and Kolker, A. "After the Fall: Indochinese Refugees in the United States." In G. Coelho and P. Ahmed (eds.), *Uprooting and Development: Dilemmas of Coping with Modernization.* New York: Plenum, 1980.

"Asian Immigrants Say Schoolmates Harass Them." *San Francisco Chronicle,* Mar. 28, 1987.

Aylesworth, L., Ossorio, P., and Osaki, L. "Stress and Mental Health Among Vietnamese in the United States." In R. Endo, S. Sue, and N. Wagner (eds.), *Asian-Americans: Social and Psychological Perspectives.* Vol. 2. Palo Alto, Calif.: Science and Behavior Books, 1980.

Borton, L. *Sensing the Enemy: An American Woman Among the Boat People of Vietnam.* New York: Doubleday, 1984.

Bronfenbrenner, U. *The Ecology of Human Development: Experiments by Nature and Design.* Cambridge, Mass.: Harvard University Press, 1979.

Carlin, J., and Sokoloff, B. "Mental Health Treatment Issues for Southeast Asian Refugee Children." In T. Owan (ed.), *Southeast Asian Mental Health: Treatment, Prevention, Services, Training, and Research.* Washington, D.C.: U.S. Department of Health and Human Services, 1985.

Chi, N. H. "Vietnam: The Culture of War." In E. Tepper (ed.), *Southeast Asian Exodus: From Tradition to Resettlement—Understanding Refugees from Laos, Kampuchea and Vietnam in Canada.* Ottawa: Canadian Asian Studies Association, Carleton University, 1980.

Cohon, D. "Psychological Adaptation and Dysfunction Among Refugees." *International Migration Review,* 1981, *15*(1), 255–275.

DeMonchy, M., and Pin-Riebe, S. "Cross-Cultural Team Therapy with Cambodian Trauma Survivors." Paper presented at third annual meeting of the Society for Traumatic Stress Studies, Baltimore, Oct. 1987.

DeVos, G. "Ethnic Adaptation and Minority Status. *Journal of Cross-Cultural Psychology,* 1980, *11*(1), 101–124.

Ferguson, B. "Successful Refugee Resettlement: Vietnamese Values, Beliefs, and Strategies." Unpublished doctoral dissertation, School of Social Welfare, University of California at Berkeley, 1984.

Fong, T. "Cultural Dialogue Program Eases Tensions Between Blacks and SE Asians at Oakland's Fremont High." *East/West News,* June 18, 1987, p. 6.

Garmezy, N., and Rutter, M. (eds.). *Stress, Coping and Development in Children.* New York: McGraw-Hill, 1983.

Garry, R. "Cambodia." In E. Tepper (ed.), *Southeast Asian Exodus: From Tradition to Resettlement—Understanding Refugees from Laos, Kampuchea and Vietnam in Canada.* Ottawa: Canadian Asian Studies Association, Carleton University, 1980.

Harding, R., and Looney, J. "Problems of Southeast Asian Children in a Refugee Camp." *American Journal of Psychiatry,* 1977, *134*(4), 407–411.

Hiebert, M. "Hanoi Said Ready to Speed Amerasians' Exit." *The Washington Post,* Jan. 21, 1988, p. 1.

Huang, K.H.C., and Huang, L. N. "Perceived Competence and Self-Worth in Vietnamese Refugee and Caucasian-American Children: A Comparison Study." Unpublished paper, 1984.

Huyck, E., and Fields, R. "Impact of Resettlement on Refugee Children." *International Migration Review,* 1981, *15*(1), 246–254.

Kelley, B. "Vietnam's 'Lost Generation' of Youth New Focal Point for Racial Conflicts." *East/West News,* Apr. 30, 1987, p. 4.

Kinzie, J. "Evaluation and Psychotherapy of Indochinese Refugee Patients." *American Journal of Psychotherapy,* 1981, *35*(2), 251–261.

Lappin, J., and Scott, S. "Intervention in a Vietnamese Refugee Family." In M. McGoldrick, J. K. Pearce, and J. Giordano (eds.), *Ethnicity and Family Therapy.* New York: Guilford Press, 1982.

Le, D. "Mental Health and Vietnamese Children." In G. J. Powell, J. Yamamoto, A. Romero, and A. Morales (eds.), *The Psychosocial Development of Minority Group Children.* New York: Brunner/Mazel, 1983.

Lee, E. "Assessment and Treatment of Southeast Asian-American Survivors of Mass Violence." Paper presented at third annual meeting of the Society for Traumatic Stress Studies, Baltimore, Oct. 1987.

Lin, K. M., Masuda, M., and Tazuma, L. "Adaptational Problems of Vietnamese Refugees. Part III: Case Studies in Clinic and Field: Adaptive and Maladaptive." *Psychiatric Journal of the University of Ottawa,* 1982, *7*(3), 173–183.

Loescher, G., and Scanlan, J. *Calculated Kindness: Refugees and America's Half-Open Door, 1945 to the Present.* New York: Free Press, 1986.

Matsuoka, J. "Vietnamese Americans." In N. Mokuau (ed.), *Handbook of Social Services for Asian and Pacific Islanders.* Westport, Conn.: Greenwood Press, 1991.

Meinhardt, K., Tom, S., Tse, P., and Yu, C. Y. "Southeast Asian Refugees in the 'Silicon Valley': The Asian Health Assessment Project." *Amerasia Journal,* 1985–1986, *12*(2), 43–66.

Mollica, R. "A Worldwide Survey of the Psychological Impact and Treatment of Refugee Trauma and Torture." Paper presented at third annual meeting of the Society for Traumatic Stress Studies, Baltimore, Oct. 1987.

Mortland, C., and Egan, M. "Vietnamese Youth in American Foster Care." *Social Work,* 1987, *32*(3), 240–245.

"The New Americans: Are They Welcome? A Refugee Referendum." *Gallup Poll Index,* May 1975, pp. 2–5.

Nguyen, N. N. *The Will of Heaven: A Story of One Vietnamese and the End of His World.* New York: NAL/Dutton, 1982.

Nguyen, T., Long, P. B., and Aylesworth, L. *The ADAMHA Role in ADM Service, Training and Research for Indochinese Refugees.* A report by the Indochinese Refugee Consultation to the Alcohol, Drug Abuse, and Mental Health Administration. Washington, D.C.: Indochinese Refugee Consultation, 1980.

Nidorf, J. "Mental Health and Refugee Youths: A Model for Diagnostic Training." In T. Owan (ed.), *Southeast Asian Mental Health: Treatment, Prevention, Services, Training, and Research.* Washington, D.C.: U.S. Department of Health and Human Services, 1985.

Oberdorfer, D. "Indochinese Americans Seek Help for Refugees." *The Washington Post,* Mar. 3, 1987, p. A18.

Redick, L. T., and Wood, B. "Cross-Cultural Problems for Southeast Asian Refugee Minors." *Child Welfare,* 1982, *61*(6), 365–373.

Reimers, D. *Still the Golden Door: The Third World Comes to America.* New York: Columbia University Press, 1985.

Rudnick, J., and Harmatys, J. "The Young Immigrants: Treating PTSD in Refugee Adolescents." Paper presented at third annual meeting of the Society for Traumatic Stress Studies, Baltimore, Oct. 1987.

Sheehy, G. *Spirit of Survival.* New York: Morrow, 1986.

Sluzki, C. "Migration and Family Conflict." *Family Process,* 1979, *18*(4), 379–390.

Sokoloff, B., Carlin, J., and Pham, H. "Five-Year Follow-Up of Vietnamese Refugee Children in the United States." Part I. *Clinical Pediatrics,* 1984, *23,* 565–570.

Sue, S., and McKinney, H. "Asian-Americans in the Community Health Care System." *American Journal of Orthopsychiatry,* 1975, *45*(1), 111–118.

Sue, S., and Zane, N. "The Role of Culture and Cultural Techniques in Psychotherapy: A Critique and Reformulation." *American Psychologist,* 1987, *42*(1), 37–45.

Terr, L. "Children of Chowchilla: A Study of Psychic Trauma." *Psychoanalytic Study of the Child,* 1979, *34,* 547–623.

United Nations. *U.N. Convention Relating to the Status of Refugees, 1951.* No. 2545, 189 UNTS (U.N. Treaty Series) 137, Article 1A (1), July 28, 1951.

U.S. Bureau of the Census. *The Nation's Asian and Pacific Islander Population, 1994.* Washington, D.C.: U.S. Dept. of Commerce, Nov. 1995.

U.S. Congress. *Refugee Act of 1980.* Public Law 96–212. Hearings, 96th Congress, Mar. 17, 1980.

U.S. Department of Health and Human Services. *Refugee Resettlement Program: Report to the Congress.* Washington, D.C.: U.S. Department of Health and Human Services, 1987.

Vietnamese Children's Resettlement Advisory Group. *Recommendations of the Vietnamese Children's Resettlement Advisory Group.* Unpublished report submitted to the Interagency Task Force for Indochinese Refugees (Senator Edward Kennedy, Chairperson), Washington, D.C., 1975.

Vignes, J., and Hall, R. "Adjustment of a Group of Vietnamese People to the United States." *American Journal of Psychiatry,* 1979, *136*(4A), 442–444.

Williams, D., and Westermeyer, J. "Psychiatric Problems Among Adolescent Southeast Asian Refugees: A Descriptive Study." *Journal of Nervous and Mental Disease,* 1983, *171,* 79–85.

Chapter Ten

Biracial Adolescents

Jewelle Taylor Gibbs

Since the early 1960s, American society has undergone some profound social, cultural, and demographic changes. As a natural consequence of the civil rights movement, the counterculture movement, and the Vietnam War protests, conventional social barriers were weakened and contacts between diverse racial and ethnic groups were greatly increased. As social interactions among members of different ethnic groups expanded, interracial marriages and partnerships inevitably increased (Cretser and Leon, 1982; Root, 1992; Stuart and Abt, 1973; Washington, 1970). These mixed marriages have produced a growing number of biracial children, many of whom are now adolescents and young adults.

This chapter describes biracial adolescents as an emerging population of young people who have some unique characteristics, some potential problems, and some special needs, all of which are related to their ambiguous ethnicity and their need to define their identities in a society where race has always been a significant social dimension (Benson, 1981; Bradshaw, 1992). As this group has increased in the population, there has been a concomitant blurring of racial distinctions and an increasing societal tolerance toward interracial marriage (Cretser and Leon, 1982; Daniel, 1992; Ladner, 1977). Despite these changes, we lack information about these biracial youth, who are faced with the developmental task of integrating two ethnic identities and, frequently, two distinct cultural heritages (Gibbs and Moskowitz-Sweet, 1991; Kich, 1992). Because adolescence is the stage during which these issues emerge as major psychosocial tasks, it is important for mental health clinicians, educators, and other human service professionals who serve youth to understand the impact of biracial identity on the attitudes, behaviors, and problems of these youth.

Demographic data on the population of biracial children are subject to a number of statistical biases because the validity of self-professed racial labels on marriage applications and birth certificates is questionable, particularly for children born out of wedlock. Because the federal government has collected statistics on black/white interracial marriages for a longer period than on other interracial marriages, this chapter focuses on adolescents who are offspring of black/white unions.

In 1995 there were more than 1,392,000 interracial married couples in the United States, including 328,000 black/white couples (U.S. Bureau of the Census, 1996). Although black/white married couples constituted only 23.6 percent of all interracial married couples in 1995, the actual number had increased five-fold from 65,000 in 1970. The majority of these families reside in urban areas of the North, Midwest, and West Coast, where they have found less overt racial prejudice and greater tolerance for diversity in family structures and lifestyles. Metropolitan areas with a significant number of interracial families are New York, Boston, Chicago, Minneapolis–St. Paul, Denver, Seattle, San Francisco, and Los Angeles (Collins, 1984).

Estimates of the number of biracial children and adolescents in the United States have ranged from 600,000 to 5 million, but these estimates included offspring of other interracial unions. Most recently, the population of biracial children has been estimated at two million (Holmes, 1997), but this probably understates the actual number due to methodological difficulties in identifying mixed-race children from birth certificates or from visual appearance (Root, 1992; Spickard, 1992).

Nearly a decade ago, a series about interracial families in *The Los Angeles Times* (Njeri, 1988) described the experiences of these families, the varied ways in which they cope with their uniqueness, and the complex challenges faced by biracial teenagers in their efforts to separate from their families and establish their own identities. Quoting from several of these articulate young people, Njeri noted the emerging sense of community among biracial persons and the perceived need for a new racial category to describe themselves (Gay, 1987). Advocates of a new label for biracial people have become increasingly vocal in the 1990s and have lobbied the U.S. Census Bureau to broaden its categories to account for mixed-race people (Daniel, 1992; Mathews, 1996).

Historical Background

Interracial families are a relatively recent phenomenon in American society, primarily because of three historical factors. First, many states passed laws before and after the Civil War prohibiting marriage between whites and nonwhites. As Gay (1987) points out, these laws were based on theories of white supremacy and myths about racial mixing that were frequently supported by conservative political and religious writings. Second, even after the Supreme Court declared these antimiscegenation laws unconstitutional in 1967, social sanctions continued to operate against interracial marriages, and the costs of defying these sanctions were very high, including family disapproval and alienation, social exclusion, and discrimination in housing, employment, and public accommodations (Gay, 1987). Third, social and economic discrimination against African Americans and other nonwhites resulted in the development of two essentially separate, castelike communities, so that blacks and whites had few opportunities for social relationships and shared activities. Thus, although informal contacts and nonmarital sexual liaisons between blacks and whites occurred despite these barriers, marriages between these groups were relatively rare before World War II (Root, 1992).

After World War II and the Korean War, African American soldiers brought home European and Korean war brides. Coinciding with a number of other significant changes in American society, these interracial couples settled in communities that seemed more hospitable to them and that were generally more open than other communities to the other postwar innovations in the economy, science and technology, and the social structure. These communities included the newly expanded suburbs with housing developments tailored to the needs of returning veterans with low-interest mortgages, such as the Levittown planned communities in the Northeast, which were among the first to promote integrated middle-income housing (Jaynes and Williams, 1989).

During the postwar period of the late 1940s and early 1950s, landmark Supreme Court decisions overturned many of the legal underpinnings of discrimination in housing, public accommodations, and education, further generating a social climate of tolerance and equal opportunity that was beneficial for interracial couples as well as for all nonwhites (Farley and Allen, 1989; Omi and Winant, 1986).

After the Supreme Court outlawed school segregation in 1954 and the Montgomery, Alabama, bus boycott began in 1955, the nation witnessed a remarkable alliance between young blacks and whites who mounted a successful decade of civil rights protests, which culminated in two major federal civil rights bills in 1964 and 1965 (Chambers, 1968). Although these protests and the ensuing legislation met with much resistance, the important legacy of this era was the breaking down of institutional barriers to African Americans, as well as the opening up of greater opportunities for interracial social interaction in educational, employment, recreational, and cultural settings. These opportunities inevitably led to more interracial dating and more interracial marriages, as can be inferred from the dramatic increase in the black/white marriage rate in the past three decades (Daniel, 1992; Porterfield, 1982).

As noted earlier, the social upheaval brought about by the counterculture movement of the late 1960s and 1970s, the black student protests on predominantly white college campuses, and the Vietnam War protests was accompanied by significant shifts in black/white relationships and radically different norms of social behavior regarding sexuality, drug use, and marital patterns. Antiestablishment attitudes and massive rejection of middle-class norms among young whites and blacks fostered an environment of social and political experimentation, including interracial relationships, communes, and political organizations. In some liberal communities and on many college campuses, it became a sign of "radical chic" to date interracially, so the incidence of black/white affairs and marriages rose, with a corresponding increase in biracial children (Cretser and Leon, 1982; Pope, 1985).

In more recent years the trend toward interracial marriages appears to have increased, perhaps for a number of reasons, including the greater number of unions between black females and white males, the weakened sanction against unions between black males and white females, and the general decrease in societal disapproval of interracial marriages (Gibbs and Hines, 1992). In fact, a recent Gallup poll analysis of changes in American attitudes toward interracial marriage found that between 1972 and 1997 the proportion of whites who expressed approval increased from 25 percent to 61 percent, while the proportion of blacks who expressed approval increased from 60 to 77 percent (Holmes, 1997). Although half of the American public may still disapprove of interracial marriage, the trend is clearly toward a more tolerant viewpoint.

Social and Cultural Issues

One of the major issues for interracial families is the transmission of a coherent sense of a cultural heritage and an ethnic identity to their children. In contrast to other minority families, these parents do not share the same racial or cultural heritage even if they are from the same socioeconomic background and educational level. Whites and blacks in America have different historical roots, have different social experiences, and are reared in different subcultural contexts (Hacker, 1992; Omi and Winant, 1986). As the descriptions in Chapters Five and Six clearly show, the predominant influences shaping the experiences of African Americans have been slavery, discrimination, and poverty. Blacks were forced to develop a separate and unequal set of social institutions (for example, churches, schools, social and health services, small businesses, and fraternal, social, and political organizations) and have maintained many of these institutions even after segregation was legally abolished. This quasi caste system required most African Americans to become familiar with the institutions of the dominant society to the extent that this knowledge facilitated their educational or economic activities, but few whites found it necessary or useful to acquire any knowledge about black cultural or social institutions. Even for most middle-class African Americans, this legacy has left its imprint in many social, psychological, and behavioral characteristics that reflect an adaptation to prejudice and social exclusion (Cose, 1993; Grier and Cobbs, 1968; Jenkins, 1982; Pierce, 1970; Pinderhughes, 1982; Willie, Brown, and Kramer, 1973).

By contrast, whites came to America voluntarily as immigrants or refugees and so were able to maintain much of their cultural heritage while adjusting to a new country. Regardless of their country of origin, white immigrants were eventually able to become fully acculturated and assimilated into the mainstream society through educational and economic mobility. Thus, while few blacks have enjoyed the full benefits of citizenship, most whites have been able to enjoy at least a part of the American dream. This disparity in social and cultural backgrounds sometimes makes it quite difficult for whites and blacks to communicate and to understand each other's viewpoints. More relevant to interracial families, it poses a special challenge to parents, who must transmit to their children knowledge about their family history and continuity, a positive sense about their dual cultural heritage, and an integrated sense of an ethnic identity. As McGoldrick (1982, p. 5) asserts, "Ethnicity is a powerful influence in determining identity. A sense of belonging and of historical continuity is a basic psychological need. We may ignore it or cut it off by changing our names [and] rejecting our families and social backgrounds, but we do so to the detriment of our well-being."

Despite evidence of more liberal societal attitudes toward interracial marriage, some studies of these couples and their children suggest that they frequently encounter problems of family approval, community acceptance, job discrimination, and social isolation (Brown, 1987; Gay, 1987; Porterfield, 1978, 1982; Stuart and Abt, 1973; Washington, 1970). These studies have suggested or implied that biracial children and adolescents are particularly vulnerable to differential treatment by their parents and relatives, social rejection by their peers, and ambivalent attention in their schools and communities. However, more recent empirical studies have found that these youth are not significantly different in their psychosocial adjustment and family relationships from their black or white peers of the same age (Cauce and others, 1992; Gibbs and Hines, 1992). It is important to note that most of these studies are based on clinical samples or small community-based nonrandom samples, limiting their generalizability to all mixed-race youth and their families. Nonetheless, the contrasting findings provide alternative perspectives for viewing the mental health issues of biracial youth.

Mental Health Issues

Biracial children and adolescents have legitimate claims to majority and minority ethnicity, yet society forces them to define and label themselves as members of a minority group. The existence of a dual racial identity and a dual cultural heritage poses dilemmas for these youth as they enter adolescence. Erikson (1959) proposes that the central task of adolescence is to form a stable identity, which he describes as "a sense of personal sameness and historical continuity." He delineates a series of developmental tasks to be successfully negotiated: development of a personal identity (a sense of uniqueness and self-esteem), establishment of a sense of autonomy and independence from parents, development of the ability to relate to same-sex and other-sex peers, and commitment to a vocational choice.

Several African American authors have pointed out that identity formation for black adolescents may be a more difficult and problematic task, particularly in view of the message they receive from the dominant society that they are members of a disadvantaged and devalued minority group (Erikson, 1968; Jenkins, 1982; Logan, 1981; Taylor, 1976). Chestang (1984) notes that blacks must integrate their "personal" and "racial" identities in order to form a cohesive total identity. Recent history offers numerous examples of African Americans who have overcome the barriers of discrimination and social devaluation by whites to achieve remarkable accomplishments that reflect an internal sense of purpose and personal worth—for example, Bill Cosby, Jesse Jackson, Colin Powell, Marian Wright Edelman, and Alice Walker.

Empirical studies of biracial children indicate that their racial attitudes and self-concepts develop differently than those of either black or white children (Jacobs, 1992; Logan, 1981; Payne, 1977). However, most studies have found that biracial children have equivalent or higher self-esteem compared to their monoracial peers (Chang, 1974; Duffy, 1978; Jacobs, 1992). In his study of ten biracial children, Jacobs (1992) identified three stages of racial identity development with increasing levels of cognitive maturity, from the first stage of precolor constancy to the second stage of postcolor constancy and racial ambivalence to the third stage of a unified biracial identity.

If identity formation is more problematic for black than for white adolescents, then one can hypothesize that it would be even more difficult for adolescents with a biracial background (Sommers, 1964; Piskacek and Golub, 1973). By their teen years, these youth are fully cognizant of the differential prestige accorded to blacks and whites in America, the differential opportunities available to each group, and the advantages and disadvantages of belonging to each. Moreover, their normal identity conflicts will inevitably be exacerbated by their feelings of love and loyalty to each parent, especially when they can easily attribute ambivalent feelings toward either parent as a sign of racial rejection rather than as an expression of the normative separation process (Adams, 1973; Lyles and others, 1985; Sebring, 1985).

Community surveys of biracial children and adolescents have also produced conflicting findings. Whereas earlier researchers focused on the incidence of low self-esteem, confused racial or ethnic identity, and psychological or behavioral problems among these youth (Benson, 1981; Gordon, 1964; Henriques, 1974; Ladner, 1977; Piskacek and Golub, 1973), more recent authors have emphasized their adaptability, resiliency, and creativity (Gay, 1987; Johnson and Nagoshi, 1986; Poussaint, 1984) and their overall positive psychosocial adjustment (Cauce and others, 1992; Gibbs and Hines, 1992). Positive outcomes are predicted for those youth who are reared in supportive families, have a sense of competence and high self-esteem, and are involved in supportive social networks (Adams, 1973; Gibbs and Hines, 1992; Ladner, 1984; Lyles and others, 1985; Sebring, 1985).

Biracial children in school settings have also been characterized as having a high incidence of academic and behavioral problems as well as identity conflicts (McRoy and Freeman, 1986). Further, these problems have been noted among black or racially mixed children who have been adopted by white parents (McRoy, Zurcher, Lauderdale, and Anderson, 1984; Simon and Alstein, 1977; Silverman and Feigelman, 1981). Although the majority of these adopted children appear well adjusted, those who do have problems are more likely to reveal them as they enter adolescence.

Clinical studies of biracial children are sparse, but a pioneer study by Teicher (1968) noted that these children had problems of identification with the minority parent, sexual-identity conflicts, and problems of adjustment to a predominantly white environment. These observations have been supported by reports of clinicians who have treated a variety of biracial children, adolescents, college students, and interracial families (Adams, 1973; Faulkner and Kich, 1983; Gibbs, 1973; Lyles and others, 1985; Sebring, 1985). In addition, these latter studies have described a range of psychological and behavioral problems in these youth, including conduct disorders, substance abuse, academic problems, psychosomatic disorders, depression, and suicidal behaviors.

Finally, in a 1986 survey of fifty social service, mental health, special education, and probation agencies located in the San Francisco area, 60 percent of the thirty-one responding agencies reported that referrals of biracial adolescents had increased during the past ten years and that this group was overrepresented among their adolescent client population (Gibbs, 1987). These clients had been referred for a broad spectrum of problems similar to those described earlier in the clinical literature. Not only had the incidence of referrals in this group increased, but their presenting symptoms had also become more severe.

Despite the obvious limitations of clinical studies and the difficulty of drawing any generalizations from so few studies of biracial children and adolescents, some issues have been identified across a wide range of studies, as have some themes of potential problems and protective coping mechanisms. First, these biracial youth must integrate dual racial and/or cultural identifications while also learning how to develop a positive self-concept and sense of competence. Second, as they enter adolescence, they must synthesize their earlier identifications into a coherent and stable sense of a personal identity as well as a positive racial identity. In accomplishing this task, they must deal effectively with the related tasks of developing peer relationships, defining their sexual orientation and sexual preference, making a career choice, and separating from their parents, all of which may be more problematic for this group.

In conceptualizing the process of identity development for biracial adolescents, I have proposed that they may experience conflicts in their efforts to resolve five major psychosocial tasks: (1) conflicts about their dual racial/ethnic identity, (2) conflicts about their social marginality, (3) conflicts about their sexuality and choice of sexual partners, (4) conflicts about separation from their parents, and (5) conflicts about their educational or career aspirations (Gibbs, 1987; Gibbs and Moskowitz-Sweet, 1991). Both clinical studies and community surveys indicate that these conflicts may be expressed in a variety of psychological and behavioral symptoms, ranging from mild symptoms of anxiety and depression to moderate symptoms of academic underachievement and peer conflicts to severe symptoms of delinquency, substance abuse, and suicidal behaviors. At the milder end of the spectrum, these symptoms reflect a pattern of identity confusion; the moderate level of symptomatology reflects a form of identity diffusion or foreclosure; and the severe symptoms reflect the formation of a negative identity (Hauser, 1972).

The consensus of clinicians is that the teenagers who experience difficulties in negotiating their identity process are those most likely to be referred for assessment and treatment (Adams, 1973; Lyles and others, 1985; Sebring, 1985). Further, some clinicians would predict that biracial adolescents are at greater risk for problematic outcomes because of their potential vulnerability to conflicts in each of the central developmental tasks. Although there are no epidemiological data to support this hypothesis, clinical evidence suggests that an understanding of this important developmental process in biracial adolescents will increase clinicians' sensitivity to the unique concerns of this emerging group and will enable clinicians to serve them more effectively.

In the following section these identity conflicts are illustrated with case vignettes and guidelines for assessment. The case examples are drawn from my experiences over a twenty-five-year period as a clinician, consultant, and supervisor in college mental health clinics, outpatient psychiatric clinics, and private practice. The clinical material is supplemented by interpretations of the developmental, empirical, and clinical studies summarized earlier.

Conflicts and Coping Strategies

In this section I propose that the central issue for the clinician to assess in evaluating biracial adolescents is their underlying attitudes toward their dual racial/ethnic heritage, which must be successfully integrated before they can resolve the developmental tasks in the four related areas of identity achievement. The defense mechanisms and coping strategies employed by these teenagers to handle these conflicts are also described. An ecological framework is used to examine four other important domains of assessment, encompassing individual, family, school, and peer areas.

Conflicts About Racial/Ethnic Identity

Racial identity is the most widespread conflict encountered by clinicians when treating biracial adolescents, who describe themselves variously as "half and half," "Heinz 57 varieties," or "Oreos." The basic question in this area is *Who am I?* In these cases, there has been a partial or complete failure to integrate both parental racial backgrounds into a cohesive racial/ethnic identity. These teenagers may identify with the white parent as the symbol of the dominant majority, rejecting the black parent even if there is a closer physical resemblance. Typically, the racially mixed teens seen by clinicians express ambivalent feelings toward the racial/ethnic backgrounds of both parents, alternately denigrating and praising the perceived attributes of both groups (Benson, 1981; Lyles and others, 1985; Sebring, 1985). As with other racially mixed adolescents, they may experiment with "passing" as white or adopting an alternative identity as "jock" or "punk rocker" or "druggie" (Daniel, 1992; Kich, 1992; Gibbs and Moskowitz-Sweet, 1991; Wilson, 1992).

Adolescent females are more likely than males to feel ashamed of their black physical traits, such as dark skin, curly hair, or broad facial features (Boyd-Franklin, 1989; Pinderhughes, 1982). As a consequence of incorporating negative attitudes and stereotypes about African Americans, they often try to distance themselves from black peers in school and social situations, and they may reject any identification with African American culture as it is expressed in the music, dance, and dress styles of those peers.

When biracial teens have overidentified with their black parents, the similar phenomenon of rejecting white culture and white friends is played out. This overidentification may take the form of adopting the attitudes, behaviors, styles of dress, and styles of speech stereotypically associated with low-income African Americans rather than with their own middle-class lifestyle. Because many of the racially mixed adolescents referred for treatment are from middle-class families, these behaviors not only are quite dissonant with the family lifestyle but also tend to result in a negative identity formation. That is, the negative identity is associated with the dissonant and devalued social status of the black parent's culture, which is not congruent with the reality of these clients' life experiences.

> Thirteen-year-old Marcia, born out of wedlock to a white mother and black father, was referred by her white adoptive parents because of rebellious behavior, truancy, and stealing from family members. The parents also suspected she was sexually active and using drugs. In individual sessions, Marcia, who had very light skin but black facial features and hair, spoke of always feeling inferior to her younger sister, who was part Asian and had always been favored by the adoptive parents. Her behavioral problems had surfaced when she entered junior high school and felt she did not belong with any of the cliques, was rejected by her former white neighborhood friends, and drifted into a group of "dopers" who were alienated from school and society. In family sessions it was clear that Marcia had assumed the role of the "bad child," identifying with the negative stories she had been told about her African American father, who had been imprisoned for drugs and burglary, and playing out an unspoken script to fulfill the negative expectations communicated to her by her parents. Marcia tried to resolve her racial identity conflict through assuming a negative identity and seeking out deviant peers whose antisocial behaviors reinforced that identity. By "acting just like my dad," Marcia was identifying with her natural black parent while punishing her adoptive white parents for their ambivalence toward her blackness.

Conflicts About Social Marginality

A conflict about social marginality is inextricably related to the core identity conflict, but it can be assessed as a separate problem. The basic question in this area for these biracial teens is *Where do I fit?* This question is especially salient as they enter adolescence and begin to participate in heterosexual social and extracurricular activities. During this phase of development, teens are particularly vulnerable to the twin terrors of anxiety about social acceptance and fear of social rejection.

In elementary school these children may have had a close-knit peer group and satisfying social relationships. However, social problems will often emerge when they enter junior high school and later when they go to high school. Typically, girls seem to experience more anxiety than boys about social acceptance, because they are more often excluded from social activities and extracurricular school activities.

In a stage where conformity is expected and valued, these biracial teens are often rejected by both majority and minority peer groups because they are neither fish nor fowl, their physical appearance is "exotic" or unusual, their family background is unorthodox, and they often feel torn between two competing sets of cultural norms and values (Benson, 1981; Ladner, 1977; Porterfield, 1978; Stuart and Abt, 1973).

> Jill, the nineteen-year-old daughter of a black mother and white father, was from a well-do-to Eastern family. After growing up in a white neighborhood and attending an exclusive prep school, she enrolled in a West Coast university for a "change of scenery." Her first year was difficult because she preferred to socialize with the white students from similar backgrounds and felt that the African American students were very hostile to her. After an unsuccessful affair with an older white male who physically abused her, she became very depressed and stopped going to classes. She was brought into the student mental health clinic by her roommate after she took an overdose of sleeping pills, and she was hospitalized for several days. Jill confided in the therapist that she felt as if she had a foot in two worlds but couldn't stand on both feet in the white world or the black. She was very angry at her parents "for treating me like I was white and not preparing me for the real world as a black person."

Conflicts About Sexuality

Conflicts about sexuality emerge in tandem with the conflicts of racial identity and social marginality. The basic question in this area is *What is my sexual role?* This conflict finds expression in several ways—in issues of sexual orientation, gender identity, choice of sexual partners, and patterns of sexual activity. Uncertainties about gender identity and/or sexual orientation sometimes seem to be an extension of a more general identity confusion of biracial adolescents. Females may exhibit very masculine mannerisms in speech, dress, and behavior long beyond the normal "tomboy" stage; males may appear effeminate and engage in traditionally feminine activities. Sexual orientation is a conflictual issue with some of these teens, particularly those who failed to make appropriate sex-role identifications during the oedipal phase of development, perhaps as a result of negative feeling toward the black parent of the same sex.

Choice of sexual partners and patterns of sexual activity are also highly charged issues for these teens. Biracial females often perceive that their dating options are limited to black males, a group toward which they are often ambivalent and from which they frequently feel alienated. Although black males feel they have a broader range of options, they are also acutely aware of the risk of rejection from white females.

Patterns of sexual activity also tend to be an "all or none" situation. For some biracial adolescents, sexual promiscuity represents a negative identification with their African American heritage, while others choose the path of celibacy and avoid the risks of sexual relations.

> Brenda, a sixteen-year-old eleventh grader, was the daughter of a white mother and a black father who had divorced when she was ten. She physically resembled her father, with light brown skin and dark, curly hair, but streaked her hair blond like her mother's. After she entered high school, she became friendly with a group of older teens who liked to party, were using drugs, and were sexually active. When she became pregnant after a casual date, she told her mother that boys expected her to have sex with them because she was black. She was referred for counseling from a family planning clinic.

Conflicts over Autonomy

Biracial adolescents may experience an exaggerated version of the normative adolescent separation/individuation conflict over the balance between autonomy and dependency in parent/teen relationships. The basic question in this area is *Who is in charge of my life?*

Particularly vulnerable to external assaults on their self-esteem, these adolescents are often overprotected by their parents, who try to shelter them from the social realities of prejudice and discrimination. They may respond either by becoming overly dependent on their parents and using home as a haven against the mixed signals of society, or by rebelling and establishing their independence prematurely.

Adolescents who prolong their dependency on their parents are usually also more immature physically and socially, as expressed in their tendencies to be more obedient, more conforming, and more passive in their relationships with adults and peers. Clinically, members of this group appear to be more depressed or emotionally constricted and do not seem to be handling the task of separation very effectively, accepting the parental message that they need protection from a potentially hostile society.

The more rebellious adolescents assume an overt posture of pseudosophistication and maturity, engaging in more assertive, more confrontational, and more risk-oriented behaviors. More frequently involved in delinquent behaviors, school problems, and interpersonal conflicts with parents, siblings, and peers, these teenagers challenge society to acknowledge them and to validate them, refusing to accept parental discipline or protection.

Conflicts over Educational and Occupational Aspirations

The source of conflicts over aspirations for many of these adolescents is their ambivalence toward achievement and upward mobility. The basic question for them is *Where am I going?* Some biracial teens, fearing rejection by their black peers if they are perceived as "bookworms" or "nerds," lose interest in school achievement or activities (Fordham and Ogbu, 1986; Irvine and Irvine, 1995). Others become involved in truancy and deliberately fail their courses. For those teens who identify with white middle-class culture, academic achievement may be one area in which they excel in order to prove that they are as smart as their white peers. In the clinical setting, the more typical pattern is nonachievement, negative attitudes toward school, and unclear or unrealistic career aspirations.

The aspirations of many of these teens seem to be shaped by their unstated awareness of prejudice and discrimination toward their racial or ethnic minority group. In some cases, they apparently impose self-limiting constraints on their educational achievement and mobility aspirations in response to these perceptions.

> David, a seventeen-year-old high school senior, was the son of a German American woman and a black soldier. He had grown up on army bases in Europe until he moved to the States to complete high school. David had attended base schools, where there were children of many nationalities, and he thought of himself as a "military brat." A good student, he particularly enjoyed athletics and tried out for several teams. His teammates were friendly at school but rarely included him when they were out on weekends after games. White girls rejected his overtures to date, and he gradually withdrew and lost interest in school. His parents encouraged him to apply to college, but he said he couldn't make up his mind about what he wanted to study. When his counselor referred him for treatment, he was quite apathetic and refused to talk. After a few sessions, he confided that he had always felt "more white than black" because he spoke German and had very light skin. He said he didn't like living in the States because "you have to choose to be something you would rather not be." He didn't want to go to college at this point because "most black people don't go to college, and anyway nobody expects me to set the world on fire."

In summary, these cases illustrate the types of identity conflicts experienced by biracial adolescents who are referred for psychological treatment. These conflicts may be mild, resulting in some level of identity confusion and maladaptive behaviors; they may be moderate, resulting in more serious symptoms of identity diffusion or identity foreclosure; or they may be severe, resulting in a negative identity with more serious behavioral problems.

It is important to emphasize, however, that clinicians should not assume that psychological or behavioral problems presented by biracial adolescents are necessarily responses to conflicts over their ethnic identity. In fact, clinicians must be particularly cautious in inferring a causal relationship between biracial ethnicity and psychosocial maladaptation. Adolescents of all races may experience emotional distress because of normative developmental and social experiences, interpersonal relationships, academic problems, family conflicts, and a host of other causes. In assessing biracial adolescents, clinicians must rule out all of these usual stressors before concluding that the adolescents' psychological symptoms are the result of ambivalence or rejection of their dual racial heritage.

Defense Mechanisms and Coping Strategies

Given the adolescent's task of developing a stable identity, a biracial background can create anxiety and confusion. If the ethnic identities of both parents are not integrated, the adolescent may feel pressure to assume one identity at the expense of the other, precipitating anxiety or guilt over rejecting one parent and identifying with the other.

The defense mechanisms and coping strategies employed by these adolescents to deal with anxiety may be maladaptive or adaptive, depending on their context and the function they serve in the adolescent's overall psychological adjustment. Many of the behavioral strategies are aimed at protecting the adolescents' fragile self-esteem and warding off the anxiety associated with their feelings of identity diffusion. To cope with their conflicts over racial/ethnic identity and social marginality, they employ denial (for example, "I'm not black, I'm mixed"), reaction formation ("I don't like to hang around with the black kids at school because they always segregate themselves"), and overidentification with the idealized racial group ("I prefer to go to white parties").

Their fears of social rejection may result in social withdrawal as "loners" or in overconformity to group norms. They may be especially vulnerable to peer pressure to become involved in high-risk behaviors in order to achieve group membership and social acceptance.

To cope with their sexual identity conflicts, they may employ two contrasting sets of defense mechanisms and behaviors. On the one hand, some exhibit a pattern of repression (for example, asceticism and lack of any interest in sexual activity) or sublimation (for example, excessive involvement in sports of extracurricular activities); on the other hand, others exhibit a pattern of promiscuity and, in a few instances, experimentation with homosexuality, bisexuality, or prostitution.

To cope with their autonomy/dependency conflicts, they also adopt contrasting defenses and behaviors. Those youth who use reversal to deal with their anxieties about separation from their parents behave in a pseudomature manner, insisting on independence from parental supervision and rejecting parental rules and values. This pattern may occur more frequently in single-parent homes and adoptive homes where the teenager is defending against fears of abandonment in a problematic or unstable family situation.

For those youth who employ regression as a defense, excessive dependency emerges, and they appear childish, clinging, and fearful. In families where parents have been extremely overprotective, adolescents may unconsciously choose to delay their second separation/individuation process.

Biracial youth also may use rationalization and projection or intellectualization and identification with the aggressor to cope with their conflicts over educational and career goals. Rationalization ("I'm not going to waste my time studying because I probably won't be able to get a good job anyway") or projection ("None of the teachers like me because I'm different") are used more frequently by underachievers. This group are also more likely to be negatively invested in their black identity, to have problematic relationships with their teachers, to blame external causes for their erratic academic record, to have a record of truancy and/or acting-out behaviors in school, to express low aspirations for college, and to have no clearly articulated career goals.

Intellectualization ("I spend all my time studying and don't have energy to worry about what people think of my race or color") and identification with the aggressor ("White people run the country because they are smarter than blacks") are sometimes employed as defenses by those youth who are consistent overachievers. This group are more likely to be positively invested in their white identity, to feel committed to academic achievement, to be "superstudents," to be heavily involved in extracurricular activities, and to express high aspirations for college and future career plans.

In evaluating this spectrum of defense mechanisms, and coping strategies, three trends emerge. First, those adolescents who assume a negative identity tend to exhibit more primitive defense mechanisms (for example, denial, acting out), and their coping strategies are more maladaptive and socially dysfunctional (for example, sexual promiscuity, low school achievement). Second, those youth who develop a negative identity usually identify with the most devalued and deviant stereotypes of their African American heritage and then pattern their behaviors to achieve a self-fulfilling prophecy. Third, those teens who identify with their white racial heritage tend to maintain an overt facade of adaptation to the majority culture but experience some degree of identity confusion, which exacts a high psychic cost. Thus they are more likely to be sexually and emotionally inhibited, overenmeshed in their families, and perfectionistic in school and community contexts.

Sociocultural Issues in Assessment

In the assessment of biracial adolescents, it is important to evaluate four specific areas: (1) age-appropriate developmental behaviors and concerns, in contrast to identity conflicts and problems; (2) parental and family attitudes toward their biracial identity; (3) school and community resources and social networks; and (4) peer relationships. As McRoy and Freeman (1986) suggest, assessment of mixed-race children should have two goals: to isolate the factors that influence the child's racial identity, and to identify environmental supports to reinforce a positive racial identity.

Age-Appropriate Behaviors and Concerns

Normal adolescents have a host of concerns that may induce periods of transitory anxiety or depression, minor rebelliousness in the family, and some fluctuations in school performance, peer relationships, and community activities. Such symptoms and mood shifts are not indicative of severe pathology or maladjustment (Oldham, Looney, and Blotcky, 1980).

However, more severe psychological or behavioral problems should not be confused with age-appropriate developmental problems and concerns. These behaviors should be evaluated for evidence of successful identity achievement, in contrast to identity foreclosure, identity diffusion, or negative identity. As described earlier, the latter three outcomes tend to be expressed in exaggerated, deviant, or self-destructive behaviors in the areas of personality functioning, family and peer relationships, school achievement, and antisocial activities.

These adolescents call attention to themselves because they are *oversocialized* (overachieving, constricted, and overconforming) or *undersocialized* (impulsive, antisocial, and alienated). Even if they are superficially adapted, they may be paying a high psychological price for their external conformity. Alternatively, their behaviors may be dysfunctional and maladaptive to the environment in which they are living.

Parental and Family Attitudes

Biracial adolescents often receive conflicting messages about their identity from parents and family members on both sides (Adams, 1973; Benson, 1981; Lyles and others, 1985; Porterfield, 1978). This may be particularly true of white parents who cannot accept society's definition of their children as black and who give their children mixed messages about their skin color and nonwhite physical appearance. Some parents handle their child's biracial identity through denial, while other parents assume a Pollyannaish attitude, behaving as if the society were truly color blind and minimizing evidence of differential treatment.

Assessment of parental racial attitudes is especially important in family treatment so that these attitudes can be confronted and clarified in order to provide clear, consistent, and positive feedback to their children about both sides of their racial heritage. It is also essential to determine what steps parents have taken to expose their teens to both racial/ethnic backgrounds.

Attitudes of relatives and close family friends must also be assessed. Relatives sometimes treat the biracial child in an ambivalent, demeaning, or rejecting manner, or they may express their ambivalence by teasing the child or making racist statements about either parent's racial background.

School and Community Resources

Several researchers have proposed that biracial children and adolescents are happier and better adjusted in schools and neighborhoods where there are other mixed families and minority families with similar socioeconomic backgrounds, primarily because they can identify with other children who look like them and have similar family compositions (Gibbs and Hines, 1992; Ladner, 1984; Porterfield, 1978; Stuart and Abt, 1973).

In addition to assessing the racial and socioeconomic composition of the school's student body, it is important to evaluate the racial/ethnic balance of the faculty and staff and their experience in teaching from a multicultural perspective as well as in dealing with children of varied racial and cultural backgrounds. Further, the community should be evaluated for its educational, cultural, and social resources that would be helpful to interracial families in supporting their efforts to develop positive identities in their adolescents.

Peer Relationships and Social Networks

Because relations with peers are a particularly critical area for biracial youth, it is important to evaluate not only the size and cohesiveness of the current social networks but also the group dynamics to determine whether the adolescent is playing an unhealthy role or being scapegoated in order to be accepted by the group.

The adolescent's self-perception in relation to peer groups in the neighborhood and the school should be assessed. If the current relationships are not satisfactory, alternative group experiences such as youth organizations that promote multicultural goals and focus on building self-esteem and competence should be sought.

Implications for Intervention and Treatment

The clinician must first develop a working relationship with the adolescent, following the general principles of short-term, ego-oriented adolescent treatment (Norman, 1980). In addition, the clinician must be particularly sensitive to the possibility of mistrust and hostility based on racial factors in the therapeutic relationship (Gardner, 1971; Gibbs, 1985; Jones and Seagull, 1977; Ridley, 1984). In the case of Marcia, for example, the African American female therapist had to explore Marcia's negative transference feelings toward her and confront her testing behaviors, simultaneously establishing a therapeutic climate of warmth and nonjudgmental acceptance to elicit Marcia's trust.

Second, the clinician must permit these adolescents to ventilate feelings about their biracial identity and its meaning in our society, and they must be able to provide confirmation and assurance that those feelings are not irrational or paranoid (Lyles and others, 1985; Sebring, 1985). In these sessions the clinician must demonstrate cognizance of the social realities and be aware of his or her own attitudes and feelings about majority/minority race relations. In the case of Jill, for example, the therapist's knowledge of the particular problems of middle-class African American students on integrated college campuses was useful in establishing rapport and encouraging Jill to express her ambivalence and anger toward both her white and black classmates.

Third, the clinician should help these youth to build up their self-esteem as unique individuals by identifying and supporting their positive coping mechanisms, their abilities, and their interests that are independent of their racial heritage (Adams, 1973; Lyles and others, 1985; Sebring, 1985). In this process, the clinician will have to help these adolescents to distinguish between their own personal interests and abilities and those they have adopted out of a stereotyped notion of their racial identity. In David's case, for example, the therapist encouraged him to describe his interests in sports and languages. By reinforcing his basic feelings of competence and exploring his individual aspirations, she was able to help him sort out his own interests as distinct from the negative ethnic stereotypes he had internalized.

Fourth, the clinician must help these youth to see the link between their confusion over their racial identity and their confusion in other areas of behavior or developmental tasks (Gibbs, 1987; Sebring, 1985). It is important to challenge those adolescents who have foreclosed or negative identities in order to unlock their potential for growth in a positive direction. They should be encouraged to discuss alternative scenarios for their current behaviors and to project reasonable options for their future; they should be confronted with the realistic fact that continued dysfunctional or antisocial activities will result in a self-fulfilling prophecy for their negative or foreclosed identities. Brenda's self-destructive behaviors, for example, though motivated by a need for social acceptance, represented a negative identification based on a stereotype of black female sexuality. The therapist focused on helping Brenda to understand this connection and to channel her considerable energies into more constructive activities.

Fifth, the clinician should encourage these youth to explore both sides of their racial heritage in order to form a positive sense of identification with their diverse ethnic and cultural roots (Lyles and others, 1985; Sebring, 1985). They can be assigned "homework," to read and report on heroes and achievements of both groups for school essays; they can be assisted in drawing a family tree to illustrate the various facets of their heritage; they can be encouraged to put together scrapbooks about their family, friends, and neighbors to illustrate the cultural diversity in their lives; and they can be urged to participate in holiday celebrations and other community activities that recognize the contributions of both of their racial groups.

Finally, parents and siblings should be involved in treatment if at all possible, particularly so that one child can avoid being stigmatized as the family problem (Adams, 1973; Lyles and others, 1985). If the adolescent is seriously confused about his racial identity, he has probably received mixed signals from his immediate family. By exploring the parents' attitudes toward race in general and toward the teenager specifically, the therapist can attempt to clarify and modify attitudes so that a more supportive family environment can be developed.

In addition, the clinician can involve the entire family in activities that will promote individual self-esteem and family pride, such as recreational and cultural activities involving ethnic themes, church-based interracial activities, and political activities to enhance the status of the African American minority group.

Other strategies that are effective in working with these youth to help them consolidate their identities and to improve their self-esteem include role-playing, keeping diaries to record feelings and concerns, expressing conflictual feelings in creative writing or other forms of creative endeavor, storytelling about the past, and fantasizing about the future. More traditional psychodynamic techniques can also be supplemented by behavioral techniques such as contracting for short-term behavioral goals, giving homework assignments for specific behavioral change, and self-monitoring of negative attitudes and feelings.

Implications for Clinical Training and Practice

The increase in the number of biracial children and adolescents in the community poses a new set of challenges for mental health professionals. Given the inadequacy of classroom and clinical training in minority mental health in most professional schools, it will be necessary for clinicians to expand their knowledge in this area through continued education, workshops, in-service training, and consultation. It is also important for clinicians to examine their own racial stereotypes and biases as well as their attitudes toward interracial relationships so that they can confront their own prejudices in working with these youth and their families.

Graduate training programs for mental health professionals need to strengthen their course offerings in the area of minority mental health, to integrate this information into their regular curriculum, to sponsor colloquia on these topics, and to provide clinical opportunities for students to gain experience and skills in working with these clients.

Demographic trends suggest that rates of marriages between blacks and whites will increase as the two groups come into closer contact and as social attitudes continue to become more cosmopolitan (Root, 1992). Intermarriage between whites and other nonwhite groups will also increase as the proportion of nonwhites increases because of immigration, high birthrates, and low mortality rates. Thus the proportion of biracial and bicultural children in our society will continue to rise, and as they enter adolescence they may prove to be particularly vulnerable to the vicissitudes of this developmental stage. This chapter offers a conceptual framework for the understanding of the special issues these adolescents face, as well as a set of therapeutic goals and techniques for the effective treatment of these clients. As these biracial youth increase in the population, many will manage to achieve truly integrated identities, while others will experience chronic identity conflicts. This latter group will pose a growing challenge to mental health professionals in the twenty-first century.

References

Adams, P. "Counseling with Interracial Couples and Their Children in the South." In I. R. Stuart and L. E. Abt (eds.), *Interracial Marriage: Expectations and Reality.* Old Tappan, N.J.: Grossman, 1973.

Benson, S. *Ambiguous Ethnicity.* London: Cambridge University Press, 1981.

Boyd-Franklin, N. *Black Families in Therapy: A Multisystems Approach.* New York: Guilford Press, 1989.

Bradshaw, C. K. "Beauty and the Beast: On Racial Ambiguity." In M. P. Root (ed.), *Racially Mixed People in America.* Thousand Oaks, Calif.: Sage, 1992.

Brown, J. A. "Casework Contacts with Black-White Couples." *Social Casework,* 1987, *68,* 24–29.

Cauce, A. M., and others. "Between a Rock and a Hard Place: Social Adjustment of Biracial Youth." In M. P. Root (ed.), *Racially Mixed People in America.* Thousand Oaks, Calif.: Sage, 1992.

Chambers, B. (ed.). *Chronicles of Black Protest.* New York: NAL/Dutton, 1968.

Chang, T. "The Self-Concept of Children of Ethnically Different Marriages." *California Journal of Educational Research,* 1974, *25,* 245–253.

Chestang, L. "Racial and Personal Identity in the Black Experience." In B. White (ed.), *Color in a White Society.* Silver Spring, Md.: National Association of Social Workers, 1984.

Collins, G. "Children of Interracial Marriage." *The New York Times,* Mar. 20, 1984, p. 17.

Cose, E. *The Rage of a Privileged Class.* New York: HarperCollins, 1993.

Cretser, G. A., and Leon, J. J. (eds.). *Intermarriage in the United States.* Binghamton, N.Y.: Haworth Press, 1982.

Daniel, G. R. "Beyond Black and White: The New Multiracial Consciousness." In M. P. Root (ed.), *Racially Mixed People in America.* Thousand Oaks, Calif.: Sage, 1992.

Duffy, L. K. "The Interracial Individual: Self-Concept, Parental Interaction, and Ethnic Identity." Unpublished master's thesis, University of Hawaii, 1978.

Erikson, E. H. "Identity and the Life Cycle." *Psychological Issues,* 1959, *1*(entire issue 1).

Erikson, E. H. "Race and the Wider Identity." In E. H. Erikson, *Identity, Youth and Crisis.* New York: Norton, 1968.

Farley, R., and Allen, W. R. *The Color Line and the Quality of Life in America.* New York: Oxford University Press, 1989.

Faulkner, J., and Kich, G. "Assessment and Engagement Stages in Therapy with the Interracial Family." *Family Therapy Collections,* 1983, *6,* 78–90.

Fordham, S., and Ogbu, J. "Black Students' School Success: Coping with the Burden of 'Acting White.'" *Urban Review,* 1986, *18*(3), 176–206.

Gardner, L. "The Therapeutic Relationship Under Varying Conditions of Race." *Psychotherapy: Theory, Research and Practice,* 1971, *8,* 78–87.

Gay, K. *The Rainbow Effect: Interracial Families.* New York: Franklin Watts, 1987.

Gibbs, J. T. "Black Students/White Universities: Different Expectations." *Personnel and Guidance Journal,* 1973, *51,* 463–469.

Gibbs, J. T. "Treatment Relationships with Black Clients: Interpersonal Versus Instrumental Strategies." In C. Germain (ed.), *Advances in Clinical Social Work Practice.* Silver Spring, Md.: National Association of Social Workers, 1985.

Gibbs, J. T. "Identity and Marginality: Issues in the Treatment of Biracial Adolescents." *American Journal of Orthopsychiatry,* 1987, *57*(2), 265–278.

Gibbs, J. T., and Hines, A. M. "Negotiating Ethnic Identity: Issues for Black-White Biracial Adolescents." In M. P. Root (ed.), *Racially Mixed People in America.* Thousand Oaks, Calif.: Sage, 1992.

Gibbs, J. T., and Moskowitz-Sweet, G. "Clinical and Cultural Issues in the Treatment of Biracial and Bicultural Adolescents." *Families in Society,* 1991, *72*(10), 579–592.

Gordon, A. *Intermarriage.* Boston: Beacon Press, 1964.

Grier, W., and Cobbs, P. *Black Rage.* New York: Basic Books, 1968.

Hacker, A. *Two Nations: Black and White, Separate, Hostile, Unequal.* New York: Scribner, 1992.

Hauser, S. "Black and White Identity Development: Aspects and Perspectives." *Journal of Youth and Adolescence,* 1972, *1,* 113–130.

Henriques, F. *Children of Conflict: A Study of Interracial Sex and Marriage.* New York: NAL/Dutton, 1974.

Holmes, S. A. "A Rose-Colored View of Race." *The New York Times* (National Edition), June 15, 1997, p. 4E.

Irvine, J. J., and Irvine, R. W. "Black Youth in School: Individual Achievement and Institutional/Cultural Perspectives." In R. L. Taylor (ed.), *African-American Youth: Their Social and Economic Status in the United States.* New York: Praeger, 1995.

Jacobs, J. H. "Identity Development in Biracial Children." In M. P. Root (ed.), *Racially Mixed People in America.* Thousand Oaks, Calif.: Sage, 1992.

Jaynes, G. D., and Williams, R. M., Jr. (eds.). *A Common Destiny: Blacks and American Society.* Washington, D.C.: National Academy Press, 1989.

Jenkins, A. *The Psychology of the Afro-American.* New York: Pergamon Press, 1982.

Johnson, R. C., and Nagoshi, C. J. "The Adjustment of Offspring Within Group and Interracial/Intercultural Marriages: A Comparison of Personality Factor Scores." *Journal of Marriage and the Family,* 1986, *48,* 279–284.

Jones, A., and Seagull, A. "Dimensions of the Relationship Between the Black Client and the White Therapist: A Theoretical Overview." *American Psychologist,* 1977, *32,* 850–855.

Kich, G. K. "The Developmental Process of Asserting a Biracial, Bicultural Identity." In M. P. Root (ed.), *Racially Mixed People in America.* Thousand Oaks, Calif.: Sage, 1992.

Ladner, J. A. *Mixed Families.* New York: Anchor Books, 1977.

Ladner, J. A. "Providing a Healthy Environment for Interracial Children." *Interracial Books for Children Bulletin,* 1984, *15,* 7–8.

Logan, S. L. "Race, Identity and Black Children: A Developmental Perspective." *Social Casework,* 1981, *62,* 47–56.

Lyles, M., and others. "Racial Identity and Self-Esteem: Problems Peculiar to Bi-Racial Children." *Journal of the American Academy of Child Psychiatry,* 1985, *24,* 150–153.

Mathews, L. "More Than Identity Rides on a New Racial Category." *The New York Times* (National Ed.), July 6, 1996, p. A1.

McGoldrick, M. "Ethnicity and Family Therapy: An Overview." In M. McGoldrick, J. K. Pearce, and J. Giordano (eds.), *Ethnicity and Family Therapy.* New York: Guilford Press, 1982.

McRoy, R. G., and Freeman, E. "Racial Identity Issues Among Mixed-Race Children." *Social Work in Education,* 1986, *8,* 164–174.

McRoy, R. G., Zurcher, L. A., Lauderdale, M. L., and Anderson, R. E. "The Identity of Transracial Adoptees." *Social Casework,* 1984, *65,* 34–39.

Njeri, I. "A Sense of Identity." *The Los Angeles Times,* June 5, 1988, p. C-1.

Norman, J. S. "Short-Term Treatment with the Adolescent Client." *Social Casework,* 1980, *61,* 74–82.

Oldham, D. G., Looney, J. G., and Blotcky, M. "Clinical Assessment of Symptoms in Adolescents." *American Journal of Orthopsychiatry,* 1980, *50,* 697–703.

Omi, M., and Winant, H. *Racial Formation in the United States: From the 1960s to the 1980s.* New York: Routledge, 1986.

Payne, R. "Racial Attitude Formation in Children of Mixed Black and White Heritage: Skin Color and Racial Identity." *Dissertation Abstracts International,* 1977, *38*(6-B), 2876.

Pierce, C. M. "Offensive Mechanisms." In F. Barbour (ed.), *The Black Seventies.* Boston: Porter Sargent, 1970.

Pinderhughes, E. "Afro-American Families and the Victim System." In M. McGoldrick, J. K. Pearce, and J. Giordano (eds.), *Ethnicity and Family Therapy.* New York: Guilford Press, 1982.

Piskacek, V., and Golub, M. "Children of Interracial Marriage." In I. R. Stuart and L. E. Abt (eds.), *Interracial Marriage: Expectations and Reality.* Old Tappan, N.J.: Grossman, 1973.

Pope, B. R. "Black Men in Interracial Relationships: Psychological and Therapeutic Issues." *Journal of Multicultural Counseling and Development,* 1985, *5,* 10–16.

Porterfield, E. *Black and White Mixed Marriages.* Chicago: Nelson-Hall, 1978.

Porterfield, E. "Black Intermarriage in the United States." In G. A. Cretser and J. J. Leon (eds.), *Intermarriage in the United States.* Binghamton, N.Y.: Haworth Press, 1982.

Poussaint, A. "Study of Interracial Children Presents Positive Picture." *Interracial Books for Children Bulletin,* 1984, *15*(6), 9–10.

Ridley, C. R. "Clinical Treatment of the Nondisclosing Black Client: A Therapeutic Paradox." *American Psychologist,* 1984, *39,* 1234–1244.

Root, M. P. (ed.). *Racially Mixed People in America.* Thousand Oaks, Calif.: Sage, 1992.

Sebring, D. "Considerations in Counseling Interracial Children." *Journal of Non-White Concerns in Personnel and Guidance,* 1985, *13,* 3–9.

Silverman, A. R., and Feigelman, W. "The Adjustment of Black Children Adopted by White Families." *Social Casework,* 1981, *62,* 529–536.

Simon, R. J., and Alstein, H. *Transracial Adoption.* New York: Wiley, 1977.

Sommers, V. "The Impact of Dual Cultural Membership on Identity." *Psychiatry,* 1964, *27,* 332–344.

Spickard, P. R. "The Illogic of American Racial Categories." In M. P. Root (ed.), *Racially Mixed People in America.* Thousand Oaks, Calif.: Sage, 1992.

Stuart, I. R., and Abt, L. E. (eds.). *Interracial Marriage: Expectations and Reality.* Old Tappan, N.J.: Grossman, 1973.

Taylor, R. L. "Psychosocial Development Among Black Children and Youth: A Reexamination." *American Journal of Orthopsychiatry,* 1976, *46,* 4–19.

Teicher, J. "Some Observations on Identity Problems in Children of Negro-White Marriages." *Journal of Nervous and Mental Disease,* 1968, *146,* 249–256.

U.S. Bureau of the Census. *Statistical Abstract of the United States, 1996.* (116th ed.) Washington, D.C.: U.S. Department of Commerce, 1996.

Washington, J. R. *Marriage in Black and White.* Boston: Beacon Press, 1970.

Willie, C., Brown, B., and Kramer, B. (eds.). *Racism and Mental Health.* Pittsburgh: University of Pittsburgh Press, 1973.

Wilson, T. P. "Blood Quantum: Native American Mixed Bloods." In M. P. Root (ed.), *Racially Mixed People in America.* Thousand Oaks, Calif.: Sage, 1992.

Chapter Eleven

Multicultural Perspectives on Two Clinical Cases

Larke Nahme Huang
Jewelle Taylor Gibbs

Perceptions of reality are shaped in part by ethnicity, culture, and social class. Rather than embodying a singular valid truth, a given event or circumstance may generate multiple perceptions and multiple truths. This concept has often been called the *Rashomon* model, after a famous Japanese movie in which various characters present their own interpretations of a particular incident. This phenomenon, or perhaps reality, is what we illustrate in this chapter.

We presented a child or adolescent clinical case to the contributing authors of this book and requested that they comment on the case from a particular ethnic and sociocultural perspective. In the two cases, the details of the presenting problems remained constant for all discussants; only the youths' ethnicity and migration history differed. The discussants were asked to address three topics: issues of referral, issues of assessment, and issues of treatment.

Referral issues were addressed by the following questions: What questions would you ask concerning the pattern of referral to the clinic? What data would you gather about previous attempts to resolve the problem? What attitudes and beliefs would you evaluate concerning the client's symptoms and how they should be treated?

Assessment issues were addressed by the following questions: What is a valid theoretical framework for evaluation of the symptoms and behaviors? In what ways are these behaviors adaptive or maladaptive? What cultural norms need to be considered? What developmental norms need to be considered? How do these norms interplay with the ethnic minority status of the child or adolescent? What are the hypotheses regarding the areas of impaired functioning? What are the issues of differential diagnosis?

Treatment issues were addressed by the following questions: What intervention would you recommend for this client? What approach would be most culturally relevant? Who or what systems should be involved in the treatment? What modifications or innovations in treatment would be indicated and what strategies would be inappropriate or contraindicated?

Our objective in this chapter is to demonstrate multicultural perspectives on a given stimulus—the clinical case material. When we set out to do this chapter, we did not know how the various discussants would respond to the material. We remained receptive about the areas of similarity or difference and were hopeful that the final product would elucidate the themes presented in the earlier chapters, generating a useful comparative analysis of clinical material across cultures and ethnic groups.

The child case and the adolescent case in this chapter are each discussed from three different ethnic vantage points. The primary discussant in each case is of a similar ethnic background to the child or adolescent. Presenting issues in each case are typical of the age group. The child case is presented first, followed by three discussions that treat the child as Native American, African American, or Japanese American. The adolescent case is then presented, followed by three discussions that view the adolescent as African American, Puerto Rican, or Chinese American. The discussions are grouped by referral, assessment, and treatment issues, and each section is followed by our brief commentary.

The Child Case

John is a nine-year-old [Native American/black/Japanese American] boy who was referred by his school to the psychology clinic in January for evaluation. His fourth grade teacher complained of unmanageable behavior, including fighting with other children, disruptive noises and talking during class, angry outbursts, and uncooperative behavior. He seemed to have trouble concentrating on assigned tasks, and his schoolwork had rapidly deteriorated during the past three months. He showed no motivation or interest in improving his performance.

John's parents also reported a change in his behavior in the past several months. He seemed more easily frustrated at home, displayed more temper tantrums, and fought continually with his siblings. When he wasn't being angry and hostile, he tended to seclude himself in his room and remain uncommunicative, or wander off with a friend for long periods of time, often coming home late in the evening. According to his parents, John stole money and small items from his siblings and evidenced persistent lying.

[*For the black and Native American cases:* John lives with his parents, his grandmother, his aunt, two older sisters, and one younger brother. His parents relocated to an urban area from a primarily rural district two years ago, and his grandmother and aunt migrated last year and immediately moved in with the family. John's parents and his aunt work in skilled labor positions while the grandmother stays home with the children.]

[*For the Japanese American case:* John, his parents, his aunt, and his two older sisters were born in this country. John and his sisters are Sansei, or third-generation Japanese American, while his parents and aunt are Nisei, from the second generation. The grandmother immigrated to the United States in the early 1900s. Although his grandmother and aunt recently came to live with the family, they are not recent immigrants from Japan. John's parents and aunt speak English but can understand Japanese. The grandmother speaks only Japanese and understands some English, while John speaks English but does not understand Japanese. John's family has recently moved from one community to another. His parents and his aunt work in skilled labor positions, while the grandmother stays home with the children.]

In contrast to John, his siblings are described as "model children." They are good students, well liked among their peers, easily managed, and well behaved and respectful at home. They have been a source of pride to their parents, but John has been disappointing and frustrating.

According to John's mother, his developmental history is normal, with developmental milestones attained within the expected periods and no unusual illnesses or problems during his early years. Prior to this year, John had been an average student and well behaved and obedient at home.

Referral Issues

LaFromboise and Low (Native American)

Several questions arise regarding John's referral. First, although it is clear that the referral came from John's school, it is not clear who referred him. Did a school counselor evaluate John's behavior? If so, valuable information might be available from this liaison. Second, the level of family involvement should be assessed. How supportive is John's family of the referral? Are they willing to participate in therapy or a behavioral program with John? Third, was the referral an attempt to avoid serious dysfunction or adjustment problems, or was John referred because he can no longer function in the classroom context? Fourth, the therapist should ascertain the ethnic composition of the school and the class and solicit information about classroom structure and management that might be relevant.

Information about previous attempts to resolve the problem, particularly any previous therapeutic experiences, is crucial. In addition, the degree of involvement of his extended family in these interventions should be documented. Because John has recently relocated to an urban area, information regarding the amount of contact with the reservation and potential tribal resources would be helpful. If other interventions have been tried, some measure of their effectiveness is crucial.

The therapeutic problem may be defined at a number of different levels. For example, it is important that John's conceptualization of the problem be elicited, with particular attention to the attitudes of his family and his culture toward acting out, misbehavior, rebellion, and disrespect. The therapist must also evaluate the family's attitude toward psychotherapy, and specifically the level of cooperation and compliance they are realistically able to offer.

Majidi-Ahi and Allen (African American)

The teacher's chief complaints—disruptive behavior, deterioration in academic work, concentration problems, and attention-seeking behavior—are symptoms one sees in many children diagnosed as having attention deficit disorder (ADD) with hyperactivity. Has this child been tested before? If yes, were there any signs of attention deficit or any indications of learning disabilities? We would recommend a complete neuropsychological evaluation aimed at assessing the child's learning impairments, if any. One question to investigate thoroughly is, Was there a sudden change in John's classroom behavior and academic performance, or are his preexisting difficulties more elaborate and evident now? Usually around fourth grade there is a shift in what is expected from a student, from learning skills to performing and producing. Often learning impairments become more pronounced around this time. Previous test and school reports should shed light on this question.

If there has been a sudden change within the past three months, a medical evaluation and a neurological exam for the presence of tumors or other neurological deficits is strongly recommended. The nature of the "disruptive noises" and "angry outbursts" should be investigated in relation to the presence of a neurological condition.

Finally, a history of the family's attempts to seek help for John's problem behaviors should also be obtained. We would want to assess the family's experiences with formal mainstream services and helpers within the black community. Given the frequent dissatisfaction and distrust among blacks stemming from their experiences with formal services and predominantly white institutions and schools, it would be important to assess this family's particular experiences and attitudes. This assessment might provide useful information regarding their attitudes about the present referral.

Nagata (Japanese American)

Referral information for this case indicates that although John's parents had noticed a change in his behavior, they did not seek services themselves prior to the school referral. This is not surprising given their cultural background and should not be interpreted as a sign of defensiveness or resistance to therapy. However, because John has now been referred to the psychology clinic by the school, it is possible that his parents will experience a sense of shame and embarrassment. Japanese American culture emphasizes the belief that an individual's behavior reflects on his entire family, so John's parents might feel that the referral indicates their own failure to raise their son properly. To investigate these possibilities, it is important to explore the significance of the referral to the parents and to John himself. For example, does John see the referral as an indication of personal failure, or does he show relief in receiving services?

It is also important to know how John and his parents conceptualize the referral problem itself. Many Japanese Americans feel that difficulties can be overcome through hard work and dedication, and John's parents may view his problem behavior as something that he could change on his own if he tried hard enough. If that is how they see it, their previous attempts to deal with the problem may have been focused on his motivation rather than on more emotional or systemic issues. Assessment of previous intervention strategies should also explore the potential role of the extended family. The presence of multiple generations may have influenced the degree to which previous interventions have been attempted, encouraged, or discouraged. Because John's grandmother lives with him, it is quite possible that she, being the eldest family member, has a great deal of power in influencing his upbringing. For example, even if John's mother wanted to talk to him about his emotional difficulties, his grandmother might suggest that the best way to handle John is to impose restrictions or exclude him from family activities. If his grandmother is from the paternal side of the family, John's mother may defer to her, because a deferential role is culturally expected of a daughter-in-law.

Commentary

In their discussions of referral issues, LaFromboise and Low and Nagata focus on understanding the presenting behavior within a cultural framework. They place much emphasis on the family's reaction to the referral and on the meaning of such a referral given the family's cultural belief systems and their understanding of John's behavior.

LaFromboise and Low highlight the importance of the ethnic composition of John's school and, more particularly, his classroom, and they encourage the clinician to determine the familial and cultural attitudes toward acting-out behavior. Nagata follows a similar line of thought, focusing on how both John and his parents conceptualize the problem. She also underscores the role of multiple generations in the referral process and the potential for conflict given John's extended family situation. In contrast, Majidi-Ahi and Allen devote less attention to family and referral issues, focusing instead on developmental processes and the importance of ruling out neurological or organic factors in John's behavior. Secondarily they suggest assessing the family's history and experience with help-seeking in both the mainstream white and the black communities in order to understand the family's attitude about the present referral.

Assessment Issues

LaFromboise and Low (Native American)

The selection of specific assessment strategies is difficult to make on the basis of the available information. We assume that John's move from a rural/reservation environment two years before and the recent arrival of members of the extended family have created some cultural dissonance for John. Initially the therapist should assess the level of acculturation among various members of John's family and the level of cultural congruity between John's family and the new community in which they live. John may be trying to maintain a cultural identity in direct conflict with his family or his community environment.

Clearly John is aggressive, acting out, and having difficulty controlling his impulses. Without knowing more about the surrounding circumstances, it is difficult to formulate a diagnosis based on the information provided. There may be circumstances (for example, a very hostile school environment or a prejudiced teacher) in which such acting out may be adaptive. Misbehavior is not adaptive in an Indian home, however, where children are expected to be socially responsible, kind, and honest and to represent an extension of the reputation and pride of the entire family. John's position in the birth order should be examined, along with his level of responsibility in the family and his relationship with various family members, particularly with the grandmother responsible for his care. Almost any Indian child having difficulty in school should be tested for hearing loss and language difficulties. Having recently come to an urban area, John may have difficulty with English or with Anglo classroom learning styles. If he is repeatedly asked to read aloud or overtly demonstrate expertise in class, he may feel awkward and anxious. Developmentally, a nine-year-old is acquiring concrete operations and learning important verbal and mathematical skills. So it is important that John have some success at this stage to facilitate literacy and the acquisition of related skills.

To formulate a working diagnosis, the therapist should rule out physical problems, learning disabilities, and attentional problems (hyperkinetic behavior). If these organic and developmental issues could be eliminated during assessment, we could conclude that John is acting out as a result of cultural conflicts. For example, there may be cross-generational conflicts (for example, the grandmother and parents may disagree on his upbringing); there may be differences between John's early childhood cultural experiences and his current environment; and finally, John himself may have trouble "deciding" which behaviors are appropriate in the school setting.

Majidi-Ahi and Allen (African American)

It is reported that John's parents have noted a change in John's behavior at home, too. How much is change and how much is an elaboration of preexisting problems needs to be investigated. The statement "John has been disappointing and frustrating" leads us to think that John has had problems all along, because a sudden appearance of behavior problems does not usually result in such a global statement. What was the nature of those problems? What changes have taken place in the demands on John at home that may have contributed to his acting out? When parents say, "He had been well behaved and obedient," what do they really mean? In other words, we need to reevaluate the parents' assessment of how normal he has been until now.

With regard to the stealing and lying behaviors, we need to assess the parents' observations; specifically, how long has this been going on? In addition, it is useful to consider and evaluate the possibility of drug involvement, which may account for John's stealing, lying, seclusive behavior, and staying out late with friends, patterns that are not uncommon in urban inner-city neighborhoods.

It is important to evaluate the family system: Have there been any recent changes in the patterns within the family system to which John may be reacting? How did he react to the family relocation that occurred two years ago and to the move of his aunt and grandmother into his home one year ago? If John's behavior changes are sudden and recent, what changes have occurred at home or in the family system? Have there been any changes in authority or new demands? Does John exhibit any behavior indicative of physical or sexual abuse? Is he secluding himself in his room or coming home late to avoid something unpleasant in the household? Is his acting out at home and school his cry for help?

Nagata (Japanese American)

John's presenting problem requires asking many additional questions, including the following: What are the roles expected of John and others in this extended family household? Of males and females? Sons and daughters? The young and the old? Are the aunt and grandmother relatives of the father or of the mother, and how is their presence accommodated by the nuclear family? To what degree is Japanese spoken in the home, and is this a potential source of embarrassment for John? Were one or more of John's parents, aunt, or grandmother in internment camps during World War II?

Information concerning the changes precipitated by the family's recent move is also clearly significant. John may have moved from a predominantly Japanese or Asian American community to one in which there are no or few Asian Americans and he may feel pressure (for example, from peers) to minimize his Japanese heritage. In this situation, although John's behaviors appear to be maladaptive, they may also be viewed as adaptive. His disruptiveness and poor school performance are a far cry from the "model" Japanese American child, but they may indicate an attempt to establish his own identity and/or meet his need for acceptance in the new community. As the eldest son, John is likely to have experienced particular pressure to carry on the family name, reputation, and responsibilities. His recent seclusion from the family, disruptive behavior, and wandering off with friends could, again, reflect a separation from his cultural and family identity. Since verbal challenging of parents and elders is rare or minimal in Japanese American families, John may not have felt comfortable confronting his family with verbal expressions of distress, but instead may demonstrate his emotional struggle through overt actions.

A preliminary *DSM-IV* diagnosis based on the sketchy case information is clearly difficult. Although John does not meet the full criteria for conduct disorder, an alternative diagnosis might be adjustment disorder with disturbance of conduct. However, the case does not include a clearly identifiable stressor three months prior to John's change in behavior. One problem with the *DSM-IV* classification is that it does not take into account cultural variables when specifying the time frame in which a stressor needs to have occurred to create a significant impact. In John's case, it is possible that aspects of his Japanese American background (for example, keeping emotions within and not troubling others with one's own concerns) may have delayed the overt display of stress-induced behavior precipitated by his family's move and the arrival of his grandmother and aunt.

Commentary

Perhaps the most striking similarity among the various discussions on assessment is the tendency of each discussant to examine the presenting behavior in a cultural context and to consider the "adaptiveness" of this troublesome behavior in the pertinent sociocultural environment. LaFromboise and Low address the need to assess the cultural congruity between John's family and the new community, as well as the level of acculturation among family members, with the explicit assumption being that cultural dissonance may be involved in the etiology of his disturbing behavior. Similarly, Majidi-Ahi and Allen raise the hypothesis that the presenting behaviors reflect socioenvironmental problems common to urban inner-city neighborhoods. Nagata further raises the possibility that the behavior reflects identity issues and a need for acceptance in the new community. She emphasizes the possibility that John's disturbing behavior may reflect personal and familial acculturation conflicts, a hypothesis that needs to be examined in the assessment process.

Interestingly, the discussants arrive at different tentative diagnoses. LaFromboise and Low, as well as Majidi-Ahi and Allen, raise the possibility of ADD, although the former two discussants mention this primarily as a diagnosis to rule out and instead strongly emphasize cultural and cross-generational conflicts. Similarly, Nagata proposes an adjustment disorder with disturbance of conduct, while acknowledging the limitations of the diagnostic criteria for different ethnic groups. Two of the three sets of discussants mention the need to evaluate and rule out the possibility of organic or neurological causes for John's problematic behaviors.

Treatment Issues

LaFromboise and Low (Native American)

A family systems approach—including the extended family members who interact with John—is recommended. The goals of therapy would be to identify cognitions, communication patterns, and family roles that are maladaptive; to enhance communication between John and his family; and to reduce John's acting-out behaviors. Extended family members who could provide John with support and direction even from afar (for example, through letters, phone calls, and visits) might be mobilized. If acculturation is a problem for this family, the "talking circles" intervention, which clarifies family roles in the context of the larger community, would be helpful. In addition, we would offer to do some consultation with John's teachers, including classroom observation. If these interventions do not facilitate change, nonconfrontational individual therapy techniques like mutual storytelling could be employed to facilitate the exploration of John's cognitions and behaviors. Social cognitive interventions designed to increase John's confidence and ability in school (see our chapter) might also be employed in therapy. One-on-one psychodynamic approaches or client-centered therapies would be contraindicated in this case.

Majidi-Ahi and Allen (African American)

Once a diagnostic evaluation is completed, treatment alternatives can be considered for John. If ADD is diagnosed, the primary intervention is an appropriate school placement and an individualized educational plan plus the possibility of stimulant medication on a trial basis. Parent guidance work in such a case is often useful. Individual play therapy may also help the child to work through some of the emotional problems that often accompany or result in learning difficulties, such as low self-esteem. If the child, as the identified patient, represents the psychopathology of the family system, family treatment is strongly indicated. If the child's behavior problems are in reaction to a change or dysfunction in the family system, then the intervention must address the system and not the individual.

Nagata (Japanese American)

Early on, the therapist for this case should work to elicit the concerns and questions John and his parents have about therapy and address those concerns as clearly as possible. The therapist should also identify a time frame for the therapy and adopt an active rather than a passive role. Given the central role of the family in Japanese American culture, family sessions would be especially useful. However, sensitivity to the multigenerational issues present in John's family is also crucial. For example, if assessment information reveals the existence of tension between the grandmother and other family members, simply counseling the parents to have the grandmother move out could be countertherapeutic, because Japanese American culture stresses an indebtedness and responsibility to one's elders. Likewise, instructing John's parents to disregard the grandmother and implement their own intervention strategies could be threatening. A more sensitive approach might include the enlistment of the grandmother's support in carrying out interventions within the family and providing a role for her in the change process.

Finally, the therapist should be especially attentive to both verbal and nonverbal messages from John and his family. Because many communications within Japanese American families are unspoken, the therapist must recognize that the dynamics of family interaction during therapy may not be overt.

Commentary

The section on treatment issues elicited the most variation among the discussants. A full range of treatments was suggested, including individual and family treatment, school consultation, and medication. The common element in all the treatment recommendations was the need for family intervention. Specifically, LaFromboise and Low recommended a family systems intervention as the primary treatment of choice; Nagata proposed this as well, though less emphatically; and Majidi-Ahi and Allen recommended this in conjunction with a primary emphasis on school consultation, involving determination of an appropriate school placement and an individualized educational plan.

The Adolescent Case

Maria is a fifteen-year-old female, the oldest daughter in a middle-class [black/Puerto Rican/Chinese American] family. Her father is a salesman, and her mother works part-time as a sales clerk. Maria's parents have moved frequently in search of better opportunities for their children. [*For the Puerto Rican and Chinese American cases, the previous sentence reads:* Maria's parents have recently immigrated to the United States in search of better opportunities for their children.] Until recently, Maria has been a "model child," helping her mother with the household chores and care of her three younger siblings, doing average work in school, and spending time with her friends at a neighborhood youth center.

In the last six months, Maria's behavior and moods have radically changed. She is moody and irritable much of the time, quarrels constantly with her mother, and has lost interest in her schoolwork. She also complains about sleeping and doesn't have much appetite, so she has lost some weight. She has begun to stay out late with a new group of older friends, whom her parents don't like. Maria's teacher called Maria's mother and requested that the parents come to the school for a conference. Maria's parents were surprised to learn that she had been truant several times, was failing in several classes, and was hanging around with a group of teenagers who were known to be involved with drugs and delinquent activities. The teacher suggested that Maria needed counseling because she was "headed for trouble." The teacher addressed her comments primarily to Maria's mother, virtually ignoring the father.

Maria's parents reacted very differently to the teacher's disclosures. Her father was very angry and threatened to discipline Maria very harshly "to bring her into line," but Maria's mother felt that Maria was just getting adjusted to a new school and that she would "get back to herself soon." The teacher referred the family to a local mental health center, but they seemed very reluctant to comply.

Referral Issues

Gibbs (African American)

The case of fifteen-year-old Maria includes a number of issues that would be viewed with particular concern by an African American clinician.

First, the clinician would want to explore the feelings of Maria and her parents toward the teacher's referral for counseling. It would be important to ascertain whether or not Maria's parents had consulted with any other members of their family, their minister, or their family doctor before finally following through on the referral. If they had, the clinician should encourage the parents to discuss their feelings of ambivalence over the referral, their attitudes toward being stigmatized by their friends, and their need to seek information about and support for counseling from significant members of their family and from professionals in the black community. This information will enable the clinician to evaluate parental attitudes and beliefs about mental health problems and their solutions, to identify prior sources of help with the problem, and to verbalize their fears and anxieties about the treatment process. Questions to be asked about the referral include the following: (1) How did they initially feel when the teacher recommended counseling for Maria? How did Maria herself feel? (2) How did they view Maria's behavior before the discussion with her teacher? After the discussion? (3) What did they do to deal with Maria's behavior before the teacher called them in? What have they done since the meeting? (4) What alternative sources of advice or help did they seek for Maria before the referral? After the referral?

Inclán (Puerto Rican)

In view of Maria's acting-out behaviors and personality changes, the teacher's decision to refer this family for treatment was a correct one. The fact that she called for a meeting with the parents to discuss the referral is equally commendable. It is more common in a middle-class Puerto Rican family like Maria's than in a poor family for both parents to attend the meeting. However, the teacher made an error of process by addressing the mother exclusively. Cultural awareness and sensitivity dictate addressing either the father first or both parents equally in Puerto Rican families. This subtle behavior is an important one that may influence the father's, and subsequently the family's, engagement in treatment, so it is important for teachers and therapists to acknowledge these cultural patterns.

Ying (Chinese American)

Because Maria's parents are recent immigrants to this country, they are unlikely to have much knowledge of counseling. Thus they are likely to view the teacher's recommendation as an accusation that they have been bad parents and that their daughter is "crazy." The referral, as well as Maria's behavior, certainly represents a major loss of face for the family, so it is understandable that the parents would feel most reluctant to follow up on the teacher's referral.

It is important to assess how Maria and her parents understand her change in behavior. Do they view the change as reflective of physical problems or difficulty adjusting to the new environment? It is likely that Maria's bad temper and loss of interest in schoolwork have been most disturbing to her parents, because obedience and respect toward one's parents and academic excellence are expected from children in Chinese culture. It is unclear whether Maria is experiencing difficulty in school because of difficulties with English, so it would be important to talk with Maria and her parents separately about what they view as the cause of her behavior change and how they have tried to deal with it. Have they sought help from other family members or from Western and/or traditional Chinese doctors? It is unlikely that they would be willing to go to a mental health clinic unless other avenues for help have been exhausted.

Commentary

In their discussions of referral issues, Gibbs, Inclán, and Ying are in general agreement regarding the appropriateness of the referral and the importance of including the family in the intervention. Gibbs and Ying focus on understanding the meaning of the referral for the family in a sociocultural context, and they suggest that a history of the family's help-seeking behavior be obtained in order to determine what has been attempted before this referral, particularly because members of these ethnic groups often initially seek out informal and indigenous sources of help for psychological problems. Ying and Inclán additionally present specific cultural issues such as the role of language and generational and gender hierarchy within the family, all of which must be addressed in the assessment process.

Assessment Issues

Gibbs (African American)

Assessment issues are also influenced by the social and cultural context of the family's socioeconomic status. The clinician would note that Maria is entering middle adolescence and is becoming more concerned about peer relationships, group norms, and heterosexual activities. Because her family has been very mobile, Maria may not have a strong sense of roots and/or an extended family to support her parents' childrearing. If she is living in a racially integrated neighborhood and attending an integrated school, she may feel pressure to identify with other black teenagers, even if they come from lower-class backgrounds. Alternatively, if she attends a primarily black school and lives in a segregated neighborhood, she may be adjusting to a completely new racial environment in her school and neighborhood, and her behaviors may reflect some confusion over adapting to the norms of new peer groups.

The clinician should evaluate the norms of Maria's new neighborhood and peer group to determine whether parents exercise little supervision over their teenage children and whether many of the teenagers engage in minor delinquency as an adaptation to their social milieu. Further, the clinician should explore parental expectations for Maria to assume a mother's-helper role with her siblings. Are these expectations reasonable or is Maria assuming the role of a surrogate parent? As the eldest daughter in a black middle-class family, Maria may be rebelling against becoming a surrogate parent.

The level of Maria's self-esteem and her identity development as a minority adolescent should also be evaluated. Is her acting-out behavior a symptom of low self-esteem? Is she assuming a "negative identity" as a black teenager in a white society? How have her parents handled her transition to puberty—that is, what discussions have they had with her about sexual feelings and learning how to respond to peer pressures about drugs and delinquent activities?

Maria's functioning is impaired in several major areas: mood changes, relationship with her parents, schoolwork, and impulse control. These symptoms and behavioral signs suggest that Maria is suffering from depression, perhaps as an adjustment reaction to her family's most recent move. Because her parents have moved frequently in search of better opportunities for their children, they may not be aware of the difficulties for black adolescents of finding a supportive peer group and making an adjustment to a new school where teachers may have ambivalent feelings and low expectations for black students. Further, Maria may have been ridiculed by other black students in her school because of her previous academic achievements, so she now experiences conflict about being a good student.

A tentative formulation in this case is that Maria is depressed as a result of several factors, including her recent move, her excessive household responsibilities, and her parents' lack of empathy with her situation. Her acting-out behavior serves several functions. First, it is a way of externalizing her inner conflicts and warding off the depressive feelings that threaten to overwhelm her. Second, the delinquent behaviors may be a route to acceptance by a peer group whose approval she seeks. Third, her labile moods and her eating and sleeping irregularities are symptoms to alert her parents that she is very unhappy. Because both of her parents work, it may be necessary for Maria to find multiple ways to express her depression in order to gain their attention and sympathy.

Inclán (Puerto Rican)

Assessment of this family situation is facilitated by an ecosystemic point of view that conceptualizes the young adolescent and her family, community, and society as coevolving and mutually interacting. Maria is in midadolescent development, and as the first-born daughter of working parents, she occupies an instrumental, mother-substitute role at home. Following the usual pattern of acculturation of migrants to the United States, the mother's adaptation to the new host culture and its values precedes the father's. The family's migration, acculturation, and idiosyncratic coevolutionary development take place in a society still evolving with regard to male/female roles and their implications for work life, family life, and power relations in general.

The initial working hypothesis in this case is that of a Hispanic family in transition from a preadolescent to an adolescent stage, in which transitional problems and symptoms are manifest in the young adolescent. The family would be followed up in therapy and observation to determine whether the problem subsides and the family coevolves or the adolescent behavior rigidifies into a conduct disorder.

Further assessment considerations would focus on the acculturation—that is, values incorporation—of the spouses. It should be noted that social-class mobility usually involves the incorporation of values, norms, and attitudes that go with that social-class status. Moreover, the process of acculturation proceeds at different paces for male and female parents. This often results in conflict and argument between parents in regard to what each believes is appropriate and most functional for the family.

Ying (Chinese American)

From an ecological perspective, Maria has recently undergone major changes. Along with the physiological and cognitive changes of adolescence, Maria finds herself in a new environment with conflicting values that seriously burden the normal task of identity formation. The family has been involved in a number of moves recently, possibly hampering Maria's ability to form close peer relationships crucial for the development of a sense of self during adolescence. In addition, Maria's recognition of being an ethnic minority member in a predominantly white society and the need to master a new language and adapt to a new peer culture may compound the already difficult task of finding a comfortable niche for herself in her new world. Moreover, her parents have probably had to devote much of their attention to the financial and physical survival of the family and are less available to assist her in this difficult transition.

In Western societies, adolescence is generally recognized as a time of turmoil for the child and of heightened parent/child struggles around independence. In Chinese culture, this developmental stage is much less well accepted or acknowledged than in U.S. culture. Although Chinese and Chinese American adolescents may experience the urge to test their independence, it is often a covert process. Generally they do not leave home, and they do not openly form romantic relationships. If they challenge authority, they are severely reprimanded. Overtly they do what they have been expected to do all along—that is, go to school, do well, and conform to the rules at home. They may be extremely idealistic and philosophical, but that is well tolerated as long as their behavior conforms to the norms just stated.

In Maria's case, she may be struggling to make sense of these divergent views of adolescence and of the greater tolerance for nonnormative behavior outside the home (which is not to say that peer culture does not have its own set of norms). Finding herself now in a Western culture, Maria may be wishing for the independence she observes among her peers, yet she is unable to reconcile her parents' disapproval of it. Her conflict is compounded by the fact that, as the firstborn in her family, she is expected to implement the family norm and to serve as surrogate parent to her siblings during her parents' absence, particularly if they are working long hours struggling for the family's economic survival.

Maria's behavior and mood changes strongly suggest the presence of depression. Appetite and sleep disturbances and irritability are common first signs of depression among Chinese. The severity and duration of the symptoms need to be assessed to determine whether they are manifesting major depression. It is, of course, important to rule out the presence of organic causes.

Commentary

In discussing assessment, Inclán focuses on the family as a coevolving system, a family in transition in its acculturation and its establishment of new cultural/social roles. He arrives at a diagnostic formulation that focuses on the family system, identifying it as a family adjusting from the preadolescent to the adolescent stage of development. Maria's acting-out behaviors are thus viewed as an expression of family disequilibrium, exacerbated by cultural conflicts.

Gibbs highlights other contextual and developmental factors within an ego-psychological framework that examines the ongoing and new tasks of the adolescent. She also focuses on the influence of social and ecological factors such as the family's socioeconomic status and the racial environment in which Maria is functioning. She highlights the need to understand Maria's symptoms in context, especially in the context of her peer relations, and to evaluate her self-esteem and identity formation as a minority adolescent. Proceeding from a dynamic interpretation of Maria's behavior and symptoms, Gibbs arrives at a tentative diagnosis of depression.

Ying examines the contextual stressors, such as Maria's recent move, her ethnic minority status, the possibility of language difficulties, a change in the peer culture, and developmental changes consistent with adolescence. She also points to the need to assess acculturation stresses and divergent cultural views of the various generations within the family. Through a similar analysis of Maria's symptomatology, Ying also arrives at a tentative diagnosis of depression.

The three discussants employ a developmental perspective, emphasizing the tasks and pressures associated with adolescence. Ying, however, also focuses on the different meanings of adolescence across cultures. Although all three discussants attend to Maria's mother-surrogate role and how this may conflict with drives for her own autonomy, Ying points out that the different cultural meaning of adolescence for some Chinese families may compound the more conventional generational conflicts stimulated by emergence into adolescence.

Treatment Issues

Gibbs (African American)

The treatment modality that would be most appropriate developmentally and culturally for Maria is a combination of individual and family treatment. The initial phase of treatment should involve the entire family so that the parents can clearly communicate their expectations and aspirations to Maria and, simultaneously, become more sensitive to her developmental needs for greater autonomy and social relationships. The family needs to explore the multiple pressures that black teenagers experience in integrated rather than segregated school environments to determine whether Maria's rebellious behavior is a way of identifying with a specific black peer group. Individual sessions should be time-limited and should focus on three issues: (1) helping Maria to express her ambivalent feelings toward her parents, (2) helping her to express feelings of insecurity and anxiety about being accepted in a new environment, and (3) helping her to develop a positive self-concept and coping skills that will enable her to resist peer pressures, to identify with her parents' aspirations, and to sublimate her energies into more constructive activities.

Inclán (Puerto Rican)

The whole family should be seen in treatment, particularly the father, mother, and Maria. Additionally, Maria should be referred to an adolescent-transition group in which she may be able to work on developmental issues regarding family and self from the vantage point of her peers.

Treatment of the family would begin with engagement of the father. Then the therapist should focus on reaching a common understanding of the demands and issues involved in migration/acculturation and social-class transition. As suggested in our chapter, specific techniques, such as a visual mapping-out process, should be considered. Following this stage of therapy, a more focused discussion of the developmental issues facing Maria and her family, and the systemic triangulation that appears to be present, would be encouraged. Expected adolescent behaviors such as attending school would be examined from the privileges/responsibility continuum that was, again, discussed in our chapter.

Individual therapy for Maria would not be recommended at this time.

Ying (Chinese American)

It would be important to involve at least Maria and her parents in treatment. Given that Maria is an adolescent and likely to feel uncomfortable speaking openly in front of her parents, I would recommend a primarily individual orientation. However, if only she is seen and her parents are not, the treatment is very likely to fail. Maria's parents may be expected to sabotage the treatment if they are uninformed about what is being done with their daughter. Thus it is important to involve the parents, especially initially, by engaging them as partners in the treatment process. I might exchange with them perspectives on what is going on with Maria, to help them recognize normal developmental changes and the stresses and losses she and the family have suffered, and to praise their efforts in providing for her. A major challenge for the therapist will be to maintain confidentiality within Maria's treatment while also conveying an openness to the parents when they feel a need to contact the therapist. Further, it would be important to assess Maria's immediate needs (for example, for language skills) and her potential sense of estrangement from her current world.

Commentary

The most striking difference among the discussants is in their recommendations for treatment. Whereas there was some similarity in their comments on assessment and in their tentative diagnoses, they clearly differ on treatment formulation. This may be more a function of the discussant's philosophical and theoretical orientation and clinical training than of the ethnicity of either the presenting adolescent or the discussant. Inclán recommended an educationally and developmentally oriented family intervention. Gibbs would combine the family and individual modalities with different agendas for each form of intervention. Interestingly, she focused more explicitly than either of the other discussants on Maria's probable ambivalence toward the parents. Ying recommended an individually focused intervention, with Maria as the target of treatment and her parents as collaborators but not the identified clients. All these discussants emphasize the need to develop a treatment plan that involves Maria's parents, reflecting their shared understanding of the importance of an ecological perspective and of the crucial need for family involvement in the treatment of minority adolescents.

Conclusions

Our objective in this chapter was to begin to examine how different clinicians respond to the same clinical material, with one varying attribute: the ethnicity of the presenting child or adolescent. The chapter is also an initial attempt to present a comparative analysis across clinicians whose ethnicity also differs. Of course this was not a controlled study, and many factors differed besides ethnic/racial identity. For example, the clinician-discussants varied in their training and professional backgrounds, their theoretical perspectives, their treatment expertise, their personal backgrounds, and their involvement with ethnic minority populations. Though not intended to be an experimental design, the comparative analysis can be viewed as a beginning exchange among clinicians who serve minority youth and their families.

Moreover, the discussants functioned under the following limitations: first, there was no dialogue about the case between us and the discussants or among the discussants; second, they were merely sent the case with a brief set of questions to which they were to respond; and third, they were given stringent limitations of space and time and asked to reach conclusions from limited data.

We feel that in spite of these limitations some valuable information has emerged in this initial look at clinical responses to ethnic minority clients who are children and adolescents. Some similarities and differences emerged, although of course these may not be due solely to the ethnic variable but may reflect other factors, as noted earlier.

Each discussant assumed a primarily ecological perspective, examining the child or adolescent in the relevant sociocultural context. Less attention was given to individual psychodynamics independent of the familial and cultural environment, leading to a tentative conclusion that ethnic and sociocultural factors, as considered by this set of clinicians, are significant factors in the etiology of psychological problems, the symptomatology expressed, the familial attitudes toward these problems and symptoms, and the help-seeking patterns of these youth and their families.

In summary, among the factors to consider are understanding the presenting behavior in a cultural framework; determining the cultural and familial attitudes toward the problem and toward help-seeking behaviors and services; considering the adaptiveness of the presenting behavior in the ecological and developmental environments; assessing the cultural congruity among the child/adolescent, the family, and the community; considering the possibility of identity conflicts in culturally dissonant contexts; examining the appropriateness of the treatment in a cultural context; and applying, with caution, the conventional differential diagnostic criteria. Consequently, ethnic factors should be seriously and carefully considered in every phase of the assessment and treatment process.

Although it is clear that the Rashomon model is pertinent to clinicians and clinical data, the present chapter has also illustrated striking areas of similarity and commonality in the process of assessment and treatment of minority youth. The integration of these two perspectives has provided a useful glimpse into the clinical reasoning process within an ethnic/sociocultural context.

Chapter Twelve

Future Directions: Implications for Research, Training, and Practice

Larke Nahme Huang
Jewelle Taylor Gibbs

The overall objective of this book has been twofold: first, to provide in-depth information about the mental health of youth from selected ethnic and racial minorities in the United States; and second, to present culturally appropriate and sensitive forms of mental health assessment and intervention. While the primary focus has been on the individual child or adolescent, we have consistently examined this individual in his or her pertinent contexts. It is our contention that, as in figure-ground perceptual tasks, one cannot understand the child divorced from the environment, nor can one comprehend the environmental context devoid of the individual. Accordingly, throughout the book we have attempted to place the ethnic or racial group in a historical and societal context; this in turn has provided the backdrop for understanding the individual within the more immediate and personal ecological system.

Emerging Themes

From the theoretical, empirical, and clinical material discussed in the various chapters, several themes emerge that have direct implications for ethnic minority youth: (1) the relationship of changing demographics to social, economic, and mental health imperatives;

(2) the balance between universalism and pluralism; (3) the resilience and adaptation of ethnic minority groups; and (4) minority status as a stressor on the growth and development of individual youth.

Changing Demographics

Although the ethnic minority population in the United States is increasing as a proportion of the total population, the patterns and directions of growth among the separate groups are quite variable. In 1995, African Americans remained the largest minority group in the country, with more than one-third (35.7 percent) of their total population, 33.1 million, being youth under 20 years of age, and with a median age of 29.2 years (U.S. Bureau of the Census, 1996). This group experiences steady but limited growth due more to high fertility rates and increased longevity than to immigration. Key social indicators highlight a relatively dismal socioeconomic picture for African American youth in terms of education, employment, teen pregnancy, substance abuse, and delinquency (Gibbs, 1989; Taylor, 1995). Additionally, in 1994, 43.3 percent of African American children, as opposed to 41.1 percent of Hispanic and 16.3 percent of white children, lived below the poverty level (U.S. Bureau of the Census, 1996).

Hispanics are the most rapidly growing minority group, due primarily to immigration and high fertility rates. It is anticipated that by the year 2010 this will be the largest minority group (U.S. Bureau of the Census, 1996). Since 1970, the Hispanic population has evidenced a 6.1 percent average annual growth rate, and in 1995 it numbered 26.9 million, with a median age of 26.2 years (U.S. Bureau of the Census, 1996). Nearly 40 percent of this Hispanic population are children under 20 years of age. This rapid population increase has significant implications for the allocation of physical health, mental health, and educational resources. For example, in 1995, minority students constituted 35 percent of the U.S. public school population, grades K to 12, and ranged from 40 to 60 percent in states like California, New York, New Mexico, Florida, Maryland, and Texas ("Quality Counts," 1997). In some school districts, particularly in California, Hispanics are nearly 50 percent of the enrollment. Mexican Americans are the most numerous of the Hispanic population, followed by Puerto Ricans. These two Hispanic groups are unique in their ease and frequency of movement between their homelands and the mainland United States. Thus, while statistics show an annual net growth of Hispanics, the actual composition of this group is quite fluid and the degree of acculturation is quite variable across subgroups.

Asian Americans have actually registered the highest rate of growth of all ethnic minority groups in the past decade, currently numbering nearly 9.3 million and constituting more than forty-three distinct ethnic and cultural groups, including Pacific Islanders (Lee, 1996; U. S. Bureau of the Census, 1996). Nearly half (49.3 percent) of Asian Americans are under 20 years of age, with a median age of 30.4 years. Growth for these various groups has been bidirectional. For example, Japanese Americans have a low fertility rate, minimal immigration, and high rates of out-of-group marriage. Thus their overall rate of growth is nominal. In contrast, the Southeast Asian population is expanding rapidly over a short, concentrated period. Except for Japanese Americans, in 1990 the largest Asian American groups were composed mainly of immigrants: 56 percent of Chinese, 64 percent of Filipinos, 71 percent of Koreans, 92 percent of Vietnamese, and 80 percent of Cambodians are immigrants (Lee, 1996). Although all of these highly diverse groups fall under the designation Asian American, their needs and rates of acculturation are quite different.

In 1995, there were an estimated 2.2 million American Indians, a minority group that has nearly doubled in size since the census of 1980 (U.S. Bureau of the Census, 1996). This increase is more likely due to shifts in racial identification and rising consciousness about Native American identity rather than to incorrect enumeration or birthrates (Wilson, 1992). Nearly 40 percent of this population is under 20 years of age, with a median age of 26.8 years. Similar to other minority groups, American Indians are becoming increasingly urban.

Changing demographics influence the degree of sociopolitical attention accorded to individual minority groups, which in turn is a determinant of the allocation of resources. As the needs of a particular group are highlighted, funds are channeled in that direction. However, the crisis-oriented approach, characteristic of much of the distribution of federal funds, renders one group a national priority, then without warning replaces this group with another. Such has been the situation with mental health funding, thus resulting in the expansion and contraction of services to minorities, independent of careful assessment and consideration of need.

About one in every four Americans (26.4 percent) is from one of the four major ethnic groups of color (U.S. Bureau of the Census, 1996). This minority population in the United States tends to be younger as a group, with a higher proportion of youth than the nonminority population. In 1995, 34 percent of children under age eighteen were from one of the four minority groups. It is projected that in 2020, 48 percent, or just under half, of the children in the United States will be children of color (Child Trends, Inc., 1996). As of the 1990 census, African American youth constituted the largest minority population group at 15 percent of the total U.S. child population, with Hispanics following at 12 percent, Asian Americans at 3 percent, and Native Americans at 1 percent (U.S. Bureau of the Census, 1996). Hispanics are projected to surpass African Americans as the largest minority among children by the year 2010. By 2020, more than one in five American children are expected to be Hispanic, with the Asian American youth population also expected to continue its rapid growth, increasing to 8 percent (Child Trends, Inc., 1996). Currently, 35 percent of public school students are ethnic minorities. Given that the school system is the major source of referral to mental health agencies for youth, it is likely that a significant number of the referrals will be minority students, thus dramatically changing the clientele of these agencies. Furthermore, a significant proportion of these children will live below the poverty line and come from non-English-speaking families.

These changes in clientele will necessitate changes in mental health priorities and policies. This was in fact evident in the recommendations of the President's Commission on Mental Health (1978). Nearly twenty years ago, the commission urged that attention be focused on the needs and problems of racial and ethnic minorities and that innovative strategies be developed, acknowledging the unique cultural and racial experiences of Asians, African Americans, Hispanics, and Native Americans, in order to promote their mental health and social well-being. As minority status emerged as a priority in mental health care, funds were allocated for minority research centers, minority training centers, and minority scholarships in mental health. The shift in demographics had in fact signaled changes in mental health care and delivery systems. Of course, the funds were limited and the various minority groups struggled among themselves for pieces of the proverbial pie. With the changing political winds and the arrival of a new administration, however, mental health priorities once again shifted. Biological factors were "in," social factors were "out." Thus, while the changing demographics and the emergent political clout and visibility of these minority groups brought about a rearrangement of priorities, this was only short-lived. Since the early 1980s, the federal and state legislatures have become increasingly conservative, emphasizing welfare reform, balanced budgets, and creative incentives for reduced health care costs. Combined with the movement toward managed health care in the private sector, these forces have further threatened funds for community mental health centers and reduced support for mental health training programs and innovative research projects in the area of minority mental health.

Another result of growing ethnic and racial minority populations is the increasing number of biracial and multicultural children. These children encounter a different set of problems and issues in development, and accordingly may present different mental health needs and concerns (Gibbs and Moskowitz-Sweet, 1991; Root, 1992). While these children may be symbolic of the harmonious and positive blending of cultures, they may also experience painful crises of identity and alienation. Mental health services will need to be attuned to the special problems and competencies of this unique group.

Balancing Universalism and Pluralism

The focus on evolving demographics serves to underscore the increasing diversity in American society. The Western European origins of this society are being challenged by new belief systems and cultures emanating from different parts of the world. The twenty-first century has already been declared the "century of the Pacific" as third-world countries in Asia gain economic stature and prominence, thus redirecting American economic and sociopolitical interests from Europe to Asia (Kotkin and Kishimoto, 1988; Powell and others, 1988). As people, products, and joint business endeavors are imported from third-world countries, the blending of new and old cultures is inevitable. Whether the relationship will be egalitarian remains to be seen.

These economic and population trends reawaken the continuing debate of universalism versus pluralism in the field of mental health (Berry, 1969; Draguns, 1989; Jones and Korchin, 1982; Sue and Morishima, 1982; Triandis and Brislin, 1984). The uniqueness of the various ethnic minority groups in the United States is reflected in their manifestation of psychological problems, in their conceptualizations and explanations of these problems, in their problem-solving strategies, and in their help-seeking patterns. Proponents of pluralism contend that the mere application of mainstream services for these culturally and historically different populations is inadequate and unacceptable. Rather, specific programs and services, tailored to the unique needs of these various groups, are necessary. In part, pluralism has arisen in reaction to the universalist assumptions that human functioning is largely governed by uniform processes and modes of expression and that group-related differences are insignificant (Mindel and Habenstein, 1981; Snowden, 1982).

In this book our intent has been to highlight cultural diversity and to suggest that it is an important value in our society in general and in the mental health field in particular. We are not proposing that every racially or ethnically different group requires their own specific programs or mental health strategies. If this were so, the number and categories of intervention would become unwieldy and this approach would obfuscate the important variations within minority groups, thus reducing them to unidimensional stereotypes. Rather, we are proposing that diversity be acknowledged and that a balance between universalism and pluralism be attained. In the past, diversity has been a difficult concept to accept, and in most fields, including education and psychology, attempts have been made to fit people of different races and cultures into previously existing schemas. The homogenization of races and cultures has been a predominant American ethic (DeAnda, 1984;

Green, 1982; Root, 1992; Smedley, 1993; Takaki, 1994). This was most clearly exemplified by the psychological testing movement, which utilized instruments standardized on white populations for all racial and ethnic minorities, totally ignoring the question of cultural relevance, appropriateness, and validity (Helms, 1992; Jones, 1988; Jones and Thorne, 1987; Mercer and Lewis, 1978; Oakland, 1977; Samuda, 1975; Snowden and Todman, 1982). More recently, this has been an issue in college education. There has been increasing dissatisfaction on university campuses with the classical liberal education, which is viewed as too white, too male, and too Western (Nakao, 1987; Glazer, 1997). Critics assert that changing demographics in the United States and growing internationalization warrant a more globally oriented curriculum that better reflects human and cultural diversity, taking into consideration the contributions to Western culture of women, minorities, and other "nonelite" groups. Our intent in this book has been to highlight the unique cultural characteristics of ethnic and racial groups of color and to suggest methods of assessment and intervention that reflect a blending of traditional, mainstream knowledge and techniques with innovative, culture-specific conceptualizations and strategies. The ability to differentiate the general from the specific, the universal from the unique, is critical to effective work with children of all cultures and backgrounds.

Each of the preceding chapters has included a discussion about the unique cultural and historical factors of a minority group and about the role of those factors in the assessment and treatment process. It is important to note that while special considerations have been highlighted, these have been presented in conjunction with established mainstream techniques. For example, LaFromboise and Low, in their chapter on American Indians, combine traditional Indian techniques such as sweat lodge and talking-circle ceremonies with more conventional group and social cognitive therapies. In the chapters on Chinese Americans and Southeast Asian refugees, the concept of active exchange was presented in collaboration with conventional individual and family therapy to counter the stigma of obligation in these cultures. In the chapter on Puerto Rican youth, Inclán and Herron combine the established family therapy techniques of Jay Haley (1980) with the cultural reframe technique espoused by Falicov and Karrer (1984). And in the chapter on African American adolescents, Gibbs highlights the need to blend interpersonal competence with an instrumental, task orientation in order to overcome the African American youth's initial mistrust, an often justified product of previously negative experiences with bureaucracies and mainstream institutions.

Thus the emerging theme reiterates Kluckhohn and Murray's (1956) observation that every individual is in certain respects like all other persons, like some other persons, and like no other person. One may alternately emphasize shared qualities or individual differences; however, a complete picture requires a balancing of universals and specifics.

Resilience and Adaptation of Groups of Color

A common thread in the history of these populations of color is the experience of racism, oppression, and exclusion. Each group individually has encountered subtle to violent acts of racism by segments of the dominant white community, and occasionally several groups have been lumped together. In the 1854 California Supreme Court decision in the case of *People* v. *Hall,* the court declared that African Americans, mulattoes, Indians, Chinese, and any other persons of color were prohibited from being witnesses against whites (Heizen and Almquist, 1971). A few years prior to that decision, President Rutherford Hayes had analyzed the "Chinese problem" within the context of race in America, declaring the present Chinese labor invasion pernicious and destructive and likening the problem to that of the other "weaker races," the Negroes and Indians (Takaki, 1979, p. 220).

Three of these groups—the American Indians, the African Americans, and the Japanese—were subjected to forced removals and relocations with the intent to "protect" the dominant white society and disempower these groups by weakening their cultures and communities. The systematic removal and extermination of American Indians decimated entire Indian tribes and vanquished them to reservations. The slavery of African Americans disrupted family and kinship ties and denied them their African language, their culture, and even remembrance of their country. Alexis de

Tocqueville, describing the white or European character, writes in *Democracy in America* ([1835] 1945) "The European is to the other races of mankind what man himself is to the lower animals; he makes them subservient to his use, and when he cannot subdue, he destroys them" (p. 370). Tocqueville predicted that Indians would perish in their refusal to conform to white civilization, but African Americans would continue to be dependent and "fastened" to whites but would not intermingle (Takaki, 1979). During World War II, Japanese Americans were dispossessed of their land and their belongings and forcibly interned in relocation camps (Bosworth, 1967; Daniels, 1971; Girdner and Loftus, 1969).

In spite of the attempts of the dominant white group to enslave or dispossess entire populations, these minority groups have survived and even flourished. In the face of severe oppression and unrelenting efforts to disperse and divide communities, these groups have maintained their culture and heritage. As minority groups coexisting in a predominantly white society, they have demonstrated impressive resilience and adaptation. Confronted with implicit or explicit attempts at segregation, they have developed their own communities and social structures, such as African American churches, Vietnamese mutual assistance associations, Chinese family associations, Japanese language schools, Indian "bands" and tribal associations, and Mexican *compadrazgo* (fictive kin) systems, while simultaneously learning to negotiate with mainstream societal structures. In essence, they have mastered two cultures, two competing realities, and have developed competencies and strategies for dealing with an unaccepting oppressor. In the United States, race has been the persistent determinant of advantage and privilege throughout every generation in history (Duster, 1987; Farley and Allen, 1989; Hacker, 1992; Omi and Winant, 1986); thus the resilience and adaptation of these groups can teach us much about coping and survival in the face of overwhelming adversity. The dynamics of race and ethnicity must be viewed as potential sources of strength and resources. The negative experiences of racism, discrimination, and restricted access to goods and services has often resulted in the development of personal and group resources, such as a strong collective identity, a sense of personal and collective resilience, and creative and flexible coping strategies

(Billingsley, 1992; Garcia-Preto, 1996; Lee, 1996; Attneave, 1996; Stack, 1974; Takaki, 1994).

The Stress of Minority Status

Moritsugu and Sue (1983) have conceptualized minority status as a stressor, suggesting that individuals who are members of groups of color potentially encounter hostility, prejudice, lack of effective support during times of crisis, and the development of ineffective cognitive coping styles based on these experiences. Minority status has been associated with alienation, social isolation, heightened stress, and decreased social structure resources. These character-istics have in turn been associated with increased psychological dysfunction in communities (Dohrenwend, 1978; Tafoya and Del Vecchio, 1996; Wilson, 1987) and in youth (Farrington, 1986; Garmezy and Rutter, 1983; Wolkind and Rutter, 1985).

A number of studies reviewed by Moritsugu and Sue (1983) have confirmed the relationship between minority status and heightened risk of mental disorder. Bloom (1975) found that in Pueblo, Colorado, the 1970 psychiatric hospitalization rates for Spanish-surnamed individuals were highest where these individu-als were in a minority, and the same was found for non-Spanish-surnamed people in a minority position. Analyzing the relationship between ethnic group size within a community and psychiatric hos-pitalization rates in New York City, Rabkin (1979) consistently found that for whites, African Americans, and Puerto Ricans, the smaller their group was in an area, the higher was their rate of hos-pitalization. Mintz and Schwartz (1964) found that whites living in African American areas demonstrated a rate of psychosis 313 per-cent higher than whites living in white areas; and African Ameri-cans residing in white areas had a 32 percent higher rate than African Americans who lived in African American areas. Numer-ous studies over several decades have supported this relationship; however, most have been of a correlational nature and thus have not established cause and effect. Specifically, one may hypothesize that disturbed persons, or those so predisposed, may tend to re-side in communities where they are in the minority; or alterna-tively, one may assume that minority group status creates stress and related disorders. While the direction of the relationship is yet to be determined empirically, Moritsugu and Sue (1983), drawing upon the concept of stress, have provided a sound conceptual argument based on the latter hypothesis.

In addition, the evolving demographics of minority populations stimulate the potential for clashes on several levels. As upwardly mobile families of color begin to leave the cities and penetrate historically all-white neighborhoods, interracial tensions increase. Similarly, racial tensions and hostility flourish among the various ethnic and racial minorities as they each struggle for limited housing and employment opportunities and a fair share of the limited market (Hacker, 1992; Rieff, 1991; Takaki, 1994). Clashes become inevitable as Korean family markets spring up in African American urban neighborhoods; as Vietnamese extended families displace Hispanic and African American apartment dwellers; and as the increasing enrollment of Asian students on college campuses is perceived as a threat to affirmative action policies by other nonwhite minority students. Although race relations in the United States have historically been conceptualized as African American versus white, this is no longer the sole combination of racial animosity. As Hispanics and Asians have increased in number and as Native Americans have crossed the boundaries of reservations, the visibility and mobility of these groups have brought them into contact not only with mainstream white society but with each other as well. Depending on the circumstances, this contact has been variably harmonious or antagonistic. Children and adolescents are not immune to these experiences of racial and ethnic antagonism, which affect one's self-esteem and, in turn, mental health (Canino and Spurlock, 1994; Comer, 1972; Phinney and Rotheram, 1987; Stiffman and Davis, 1990).

The experiences of many minority youth include exposure to early traumas that can be attributed to the dynamics of race and poverty (Dohrenwend and Dohrenwend, 1970; Myers, 1989). Myers (1989) contends that patterns of early deprivation due to low-income and minority status continue throughout the person's life, which is characterized by instability and unpredictability as the fate of the individual and family are often controlled by factors beyond their influence and control (such as unemployment due to cutbacks, changes in policies governing welfare, job training, language courses, immigration, health care, changes in college admission quotas, and so on). Recent research on community samples of ethnic minority youth in urban areas suggests that there are high rates of undiagnosed cases of posttraumatic stress disorder among youth who are frequently exposed to environments that contain drugs, guns, gangs, and school and family violence (Breslau, Davis, Andreski, and Peterson, 1991; Singer, Anglin, Song, and Lunghofer, 1995; Myers, 1989). Minority youth are also often the targets of individual acts of ethnic and racial prejudice, as discussed in the previous chapters. Allport (1954) outlines three levels of rejection aimed at out-group members: verbal rejection, discrimination, and physical attack. These forms of behavior, as well as the perception of prejudice, have obvious negative effects on minority youth.

Thus, in addition to the normative tasks of development, ethnic minority youth need to master the stress of being "different" and to overcome the labels "inferior" and "second-class." They need to selectively internalize the range of "reflected appraisals" (Rosenberg, 1979) from their surroundings in order to establish a strong self-concept and positive self-esteem. They need to constantly negotiate between at least two distinct cultures and value systems, and to modulate the attendant ambivalence from the social environment (Gibbs and Moskowitz-Sweet, 1991; Kich, 1992). A study by Cross (1983) that analyzed the commonplace parent-child activities conducted in the homes of African American and white families with young children found that a white-oriented monocultural frame was found in most white homes and a dual cultural perspective—that is, African American and white—was found in African American homes. African American families, responding to social realities, seemed to be promoting the development of bicultural competence in their children.

The concept of biculturality focuses on the extent to which an individual is able to understand and step into and out of two cultural environments, adjusting his or her behavior according to the norms of each culture in order to attain his or her objectives (DeAnda, 1984). While many minority youth do attain a healthy bicultural identity, for others this is a particularly difficult and problematic task, especially in view of the disparaging messages received from the mainstream society (Gibbs and Hines, 1992). Many of these youth must develop and differentiate between a "personal" identity and an "ethnic" or "racial" identity in order to form a cohesive sense of self. In the past, biculturality was considered synonymous with a diffuse or marginal identity and was associated with insecurity, anxiety, distrust, hostility, and defensiveness (Paz, 1961; Stevenson and Stewart, 1958; Stonequist, 1935). More recent theories emphasize the benefits of dual socialization (McFee, 1968; Phinney and Rotheram, 1987; Ramirez and Castaneda, 1974). However, while theorists suggest that children with bicultural competence may have higher self-esteem, greater understanding, and higher achievement than others (Ramirez, 1983), they also acknowledge, as discussed in Chapter Ten by Gibbs, the additional stress of straddling two disparate cultures (Welsh, 1988).

A Model for Mental Health Intervention

The themes just discussed underscore the need for changes in mental health intervention for minority youth and their families. Although the majority of these youth will probably not require such services, the number that do come to the attention of mental health providers will be increasing (Canino and Spurlock, 1994). With the ethnic minority population in the United States growing from 17 percent in 1970 to 23.3 percent in 1980 to an estimated 40 percent in 2030 (U.S. Bureau of the Census, 1973, 1996), mental health providers can expect to see more children and adolescents from these various groups. As pointed out in the previous chapters, each ethnic or racial group possesses different conceptualizations of psychological disorder, manifests different help-seeking patterns, and encounters different barriers and facilitators to services. While there are many similarities among the various groups, such as the value of interdependence over independence, the primacy of the group over the individual, the emphasis on extended family networks as opposed to nuclear family units, and the clashes of roles and values in relation to those of the mainstream society, there are also significant differences, not all of which can be detailed here.

In view of these complexities, we propose a model of intervention that delineates a process of inquiry and investigation. Consistent with the ecological perspective represented throughout this book, this model draws heavily on Bronfenbrenner's (1979) model of the person in environment. At the center of this model is the developing individual. This individual is embedded in a complex array of systems dynamically interacting with the individual and with one another. The individual and the environmental systems are mutually shaping one another, each changing over time and each adapting in response to changes in the others (Garbarino, 1982). The interaction is reciprocal and ongoing throughout development. Figures 12.1 and 12.2 depict the two orders of interaction.

Figure 12.1 displays an ecological network for a developing child or adolescent, with the significant microsystems being the family, the school, the community (neighborhood or peers), and the religion. For our purposes, we have added the indigenous helping system and the mental health provider system. Another system not pictured but also significant for these youth is the social service system. For children and adolescents who require the latter services, these systems also become microsystems affecting and affected by these youth. As demonstrated by the bidirectional arrows in the figure, the direction of influence is two-way. The geometric shapes around each microsystem and the individual symbolize the different history, origin, and culture of each system. The culture of each system represents a blend of the subcultures of race, ethnicity, social class, and institutionalism. Except for youth in foster families, the shape around the central individual and the family microsystem should be the same, reflecting a shared history and culture.

The shapes encompassing the individual and the microsystems are particularly significant because they represent the basis for the functioning and values of the specific microsystems. These shapes are distinct in order to highlight the differences and potential for conflict among the various systems. For example, returning to Figure 12.1, the individual comes from the "Culture of the Triangle," attends a school in the "Culture of the Rectangle," and participates in a community characterized by the "Culture of the Pentagon." In this sense, the child or adolescent negotiates among three distinct cultural systems. Unlike this child's family, the values and beliefs of the school system are founded on the Rectangle culture and the concept of institutionalism, which emphasizes the organization at the expense of other factors, including individual characteristics. To be successful in school, the child must accommodate

**Figure 12.1.   An Ecological Framework for Intervention:
First-Order Interactions.**

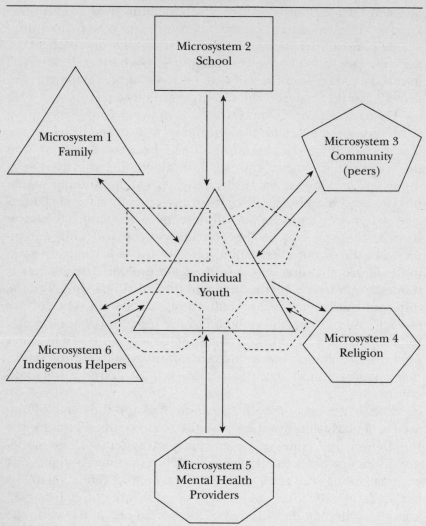

to the norms of the Rectangle culture; to maintain harmony in the family, the child must adhere to the values and norms of the Triangle culture; and to gain acceptance in the community, the child must abide by the norms of the Pentagon culture.

The individual's culture, the Triangle, is superimposed on the other shapes, thus representing the different cultures exerting an influence on the developing individual. Aspects of these various cultures may be incorporated into the child's self-concept. Eventually, in order to develop a coherent sense of self, the child must meaningfully integrate these diverse cultural systems. The added complexity for the individual youth in a multicultural environment is represented by the imposition of various geometric shapes on the triangle, the individual's home culture. The experience of this child would differ significantly from that of a child whose family, school, community, and peer systems all emanated from the same cultural basis. Obviously this geometric description of a child's ecology oversimplifies the reality. However, it is parsimonious, provides a starting point for assessment and intervention, and reflects our assumption that race, ethnicity, and the associated culture form the foundation for one's values and perceptions, and therefore of one's attitudes and behaviors in the world. In working with ethnic minority youth, the determination of the ecological map and relevant cultural systems is of paramount importance.

This map also targets the points for intervention. It is particularly critical in working with children and adolescents that one identify the relevant systems impinging on the individual. Although the child or adolescent is most frequently the focus of the intervention, in some instances this may be inappropriate. Rather, the school, family, or peer system, or some combination of these systems and the individual, or even intersystemic interaction not actually involving the individual, may more appropriately be the target of an intervention. Again, this model presents the range of possibilities appropriate for a single or multipronged intervention. Figure 12.1 displays the first-order of interaction between the individual and the various systems. Figure 12.2 shows the second-order interaction, or what Bronfenbrenner (1979) refers to as the mesosystem. The figure represents interactions between the various microsystems that have an impact on the individual and vice versa. For example, the interaction between the school and family

Figure 12.2. An Ecological Framework for Intervention: Second-Order Interactions (Solid Lines).

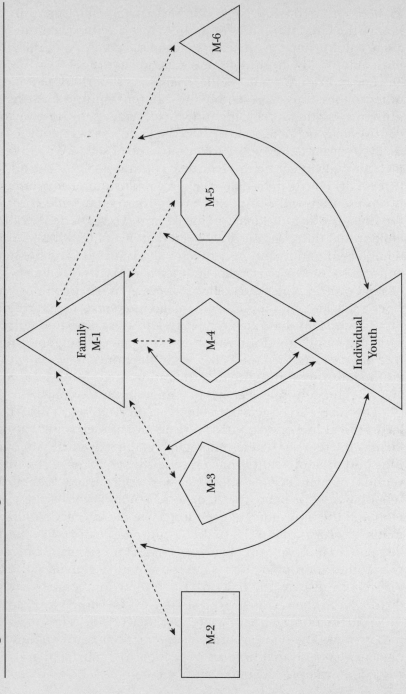

system, whether mutually supportive and positive, absent, or hostile, will have an impact on the child. Reciprocally, the child will also have an effect on this relationship. Similarly, the relationship between the family and the peer group, and between the family and the mental health provider, will affect the individual child or adolescent. As in the first-order interactions, the consonance or dissonance of cultures may potentially affect the nature of these interactions. This relationship is represented again by the various geometric shapes. The mental health provider must adequately assess these complex relationships, which may have a bearing on the problems presented by the individual youth.

Although this model of intervention, which focuses on the individual in an ecological context, is not a new idea, it is particularly pertinent to ethnic minority youth for a number of reasons. First, it emphasizes the youths' subjective field of experience, possibly generating essential data not normally tapped by conventional, mainstream methods of inquiry. Second, it focuses attention on both the immediate and the more distant, albeit embedded, cultural environment (Canino and Spurlock, 1994; Garbarino, 1982; Vargas and Koss-Chioino, 1992). Third, by focusing on intersystem relationships and their effects on the individual and vice versa, the model reveals connections that might otherwise be overlooked and enables one to look beyond the immediate first-order interactions. In this sense, it also mandates an interdisciplinary perspective that potentially minimizes the "holes" in one's data. Fourth, this model cuts across theoretical orientations and modalities of treatment. It does not prohibit the psychodynamic theorist, enjoin the behaviorist, or ignore the social cognitive advocate. Rather, it provides a comprehensive, systematic way of viewing intervention. The provider may, in fact, utilize a psychodynamic approach with the individual while developing a psychoeducational consultation with the school. Similarly, the model does not limit the target of intervention. On the contrary, it renders the individual, the family, the couple, the group, or the institution equally appropriate targets of change, depending on the circumstances.

This model has important implications for the roles of mental health providers. The task for providers working with children of color is to identify the unique systems and cultural frameworks to be incorporated into the intervention. The clinician's role may range from individual therapist to family therapist to school consultant to advocate; the arenas for intervention may be the individual, the family, the school, the work setting, the social service agency, or the community organization. Although a single provider may not be able to fulfill these various roles, it is critical to acknowledge the necessity of these functions and the need to work in multiple contexts, and if necessary, in multidisciplinary teams and with indigenous helpers. Most important, however, is the need to acknowledge one's own limitations given the demands of this model of intervention.

Preparing a "Wish List" and Understanding the Obstacles

A new model of intervention necessitates changes in the preparation of mental health service providers. This final section addresses a number of recommended changes, some of which have been discussed in the previous chapters. Many of these recommendations have been proposed previously and several have already been implemented in some mental health settings. However, they do represent ideals and in some instances would require major reconceptualizing and restructuring in mental health settings and training arenas. Nevertheless, we feel that these are important directions that need to be delineated. In conjunction with this discussion, we address some of the impediments to these recommended changes.

Multicultural Competence in Service Delivery

Throughout this chapter we have emphasized the need to obtain a balance between pluralism and universalism, and the value of diversity. These values have been promoted at both the societal and the individual levels. Accordingly, they should be prominent in the foundations of a mental health care system and manifest throughout all levels of its operation. Making this happen would involve the integration of culture-specific beliefs and healing practices with conventional, mainstream treatments, and increased collaboration between cultural healers and mainstream service providers. The precise blend of these two components would be tailored to the needs of the client. In this sense, knowledge of different cultures is necessary but not sufficient; rather, this approach must be supplemented with an understanding of the client's unique and personal history of acculturation. For example, as implied by Nagata in Chapter Three, for the third-generation Japanese American client who is highly assimilated to American society and fluent only in English, conventional, mainstream approaches may be appropriate, while a different blend of services may be appropriate for that individual's second-generation parents. In contrast, the recent Hispanic immigrant may require a bicultural, bilingual provider or intercultural team who, as Inclán and Herron state, can serve as a bridge between the old and the new. The important point here is the *availability* of the different combinations of services, which in turn reflects the agency's or service provider's attitude toward diversity.

Multicultural competence in a helping service can be attained in a variety of ways, two of which are the recruitment of bicultural providers and the establishment of intercultural teams (Fong and Gibbs, 1995). The increase of ethnic providers of color in the mental health field was a priority of the 1960s and 1970s; however, as the result of changing priorities and decreases in funds for minority training, much of this gain may soon be reversed (Korchin, 1976; Snowden, 1982). As concluded by Allen and Majidi-Ahi in Chapter Five, a "critical mass" of minority providers and trainees in the field is necessary to diminish the societal patterns and socioemotional pain of tokenism. Among other obstacles, bicultural providers may experience difficulty locating a meaningful position in the field. Although they are representatives of a minority race or ethnicity, in most instances their training has been predominantly mainstream. Therefore, upon completion of training many of these young professionals struggle with conflicts of professional identity (Am I a minority professional? Am I a minority person trained only in white conventional methods?) and finding institutions that will recognize and value their bicultural interests and competencies. This dilemma is akin to that of the scientist-practitioner in the field of clinical psychology. After the landmark Boulder Conference (Raimy, 1950) in which the scientist-practitioner model was established, training programs embraced this image of the psychologist. However, the eventual work settings for the graduates of this model were limited in number. Universities wanted the scientist-researcher and provided few incentives for the practitioner; clinical and community settings wanted the practitioner and provided minimal resources for the scientist. Thus, in some ways this model remained an ideal paradigm rather than becoming an actuality. It is hoped that this will not be the outcome for the bicultural provider.

Intercultural teams have been used in a variety of settings to address the needs of bicultural or biracial clients. As Huang described in Chapter Nine, this was a highly effective approach with the Southeast Asian refugees. Utilizing combinations of providers enables each helper to concentrate on their area of expertise so that the breadth and depth of the intervention are maximized. Intercultural teams, as well as bicultural helpers, are important role models for ethnic minority youth who see and experience these minority individuals in positions of competence, authority, and expertise. The drawback to this approach is the tendency of intercultural teams to inadvertently reenact the political dynamics of the larger society. Rather than assuming positions of equality, the "leader" of the team is often from the dominant, white culture and is the "professional-in-charge"; the "helpers" are often the minority or bicultural providers, translators, or paraprofessionals. Many of the latter individuals have accumulated extensive experience in mental health that they cannot transform into policy or programs due to their lack of necessary titles or influential positions (Munoz, 1982). It is therefore imperative that these individuals be identified and given the opportunity for continued training and education, because this would move the mental health system toward the goal of multicultural competence.

These are small suggestions for improving the cultural competence of a service delivery system. A much broader perspective is needed, however, to generate a culturally competent system of mental health care. A culturally competent system of care values diversity, is capable of cultural self-assessment, understands the dynamics of difference, institutionalizes cultural knowledge, and makes adaptations to diversity (Cross, Bazron, Dennis, and Isaacs, 1989). These elements must function at every level of the system, including the institutional, administrative, managerial, and provider levels, and they must be inherent in attitudes, policies, and practices. Culturally competent, effective, quality services require that service providers and policymakers recognize the cultural complexity and rich diversity that exists among ethnically and racially diverse populations, and that services be provided within a cultural context (Isaacs and Benjamin, 1991).

The "Whole Child" Versus Professional Preciousness

As mentioned throughout this book, mental health providers working with children and adolescents need to be familiar with the total ecology of the child. Without knowledge of the settings that foster or impede psychological development, our understanding of youth, particularly ethnic minority youth, will remain limited and incomplete (Bronfenbrenner, 1979) and our system of service delivery will continue to be fragmented and poorly coordinated (Namir and Weinstein, 1982). For example, there are specialists who work with children in medical settings, in school settings, in recreational settings, in family settings, in community settings, in juvenile justice settings, and in advocacy. Rarely is a specialist trained or given the opportunity to work with the whole child or to gain access to the child's total ecology. Services are created and delivered based on pieces of the children's lives, and providers become setting specialists as opposed to child specialists (Namir and Weinstein, 1982). This approach serves to promote "professional preciousness" (Sarason, 1974), the conceptualizing of problems in ways that professionals have been trained to treat them; impedes the coordination of multiple and disparate services; and leads to further specialization and polarization.

The model of intervention we have proposed requires that providers be familiar with the ecological map of an individual child or adolescent. This requires either familiarity with more than one setting, or interdisciplinary collaboration, both in training and service delivery, across settings. Providers must be sensitive to the cultural diversity of these various systems, and to the influence of economic, educational, and racial factors on the operation of these settings and the functioning of the children within these settings. Unfortunately, these suggestions are readily apparent but discouragingly difficult to implement. Professionals are entrenched in their specific bodies of knowledge and zealously guard their areas of expertise, assuming that sharing resources and territories is antithetical to a well-delineated and protected professional domain. Thus, if these ideas are to be implemented, they need to be introduced early in a provider's training and professional development.

Systematic Changes in Curriculum and Training

The concepts of multicultural perspective and interdisciplinary collaboration need to be part of the socialization of the mental health provider. Cultural diversity and interdisciplinary orientations should be integrated into the content and process of training and education.

A core curriculum in mental health should include knowledge not only from psychology, social work, and psychiatry, but also from the fields of education, public policy, sociology, anthropology, and history (Levine and Levine, 1970; Pinderhughes, 1989). This knowledge should be conveyed by experts in these disciplines who can help interface their respective areas with the psychology of the developing child or adolescent. Similarly, training experiences should span a range of settings so that the provider will gain familiarity with the different approaches and priorities of the collaborating disciplines. As stated by Namir and Weinstein (1982), "interdisciplinary collaboration in learning, as well as in the delivery of services, is a critical factor in the training of specialists of the whole child" (p. 65).

For the most part, culture and diversity have been accepted as legitimate topics of scientific inquiry and training. Ethnicity is recognized as an important independent and dependent variable associated with different value systems, learning histories, philosophical outlooks, social structures, life experiences, and behaviors (Suinn, 1987). The content areas include such topics as the values and practices of minority cultures, the historical experiences of minority groups, the impact of institutional racism on childrearing practices and the psychosocial development of minority children, the effects of discrimination and racism on the individual and the group, minority family structures and values, and identity development of minority individuals and groups (Bronstein and Quina, 1991). In the field, however, the continuing debate is how best to incorporate ethnic minority content into the education and training of mental health providers.

There are usually two options for curriculum development: a single course or series of specialized courses focusing only on minority content, or an integration of minority content into the existing courses (Gibbs, 1985; Suinn, 1987). Obviously the former option is easier to implement; however, the latter may be more effective in terms of reaching a larger number of students and socializing both ethnic minority and mainstream white students to the value of diversity and cultural pluralism. Proponents of the specialized course approach argue that faculty cannot be expected to offer other than superficial coverage of ethnic topics, and that under the auspices of "academic freedom" they will proceed to teach their courses as they always have. Thus, until a new generation of faculty emerges, one that has been socialized in our increasingly multicultural society with the value of and appreciation for cultural diversity, little change will be possible.

It is our contention, however, that faculty, like curricula, will have to evolve to meet the changing needs and demands of our society. Ethnicity should be a relevant topic to all faculty and students, not just to minority faculty and students. Suinn (1987) argues that education, as demonstrated by the curriculum and the faculty, imparts attitudes as well as knowledge. Students in research sequences learn the basic tools of statistics while also acquiring the attitude of investigative curiosity to guide future research endeavors. Similarly, ethnic content should convey the attitude that ethnicity is an important, integral part of a core curriculum, not a specialized subtopic of limited value. If ethnic content is distributed across all or most courses, students will accept it as valued, relevant academic material rather than viewing it as a token session on minority mental health or a perfunctory lesson on social awareness.

Research Directions

In the best of all possible research-funding worlds, the topics for investigation could fill several chapters! Acknowledging the limits of time, space, and resources, we suggest three areas that are especially pertinent to the themes of this book.

First, what consistently emerges from each of the previous chapters is the need for epidemiological data to indicate the incidence and prevalence of psychological and behavioral disorders among ethnic minority children and adolescents. Without this information it is difficult to determine who we are serving, who we are underserving, and what interventions we need to develop. This problem is embedded in a general lack of epidemiological data for all children and adolescents, which stems in part from the problems of definition, diagnosis, and differentiation between psychological disorder in childhood and cognitive or social lags in development (Achenbach, 1974; Namir and Weinstein, 1982).

Second, consistent with the themes of changing demographics, increasing multicultural contact and diversity, and recognition of minority status as a stressor, it is important to further our investigations of bicultural identity development and competence (DeAnda, 1984; Phinney and Rotheram, 1987; Root, 1992). It is critical to examine the developmental processes that facilitate or detract from bicultural competence in order to develop primary prevention programs for children in situations of risk, and more effective intervention strategies for children and adolescents already succumbing to the stresses and pressures of being ethnic or racial minorities in a white dominant society.

Finally, research must focus on the helping relationship in the context of the child's or adolescent's ecological environment (Farrington, 1986; Huang and Gibbs, 1992; Wolkind and Rutter, 1985). The effectiveness of the proposed multicultural, multisetting model of intervention must be assessed so that the limited resources in the field will be utilized most efficiently and effectively. This assessment involves systematic investigation of intercultural and intracultural helping relationships with youth.

Conclusion

The idea for this book initially arose from our frustrations as university professors who were repeatedly asked to teach graduate students how to provide mental health services to children and youth of color yet found it difficult to locate adequate research or clinically based studies of ethnic minority families and their children. Since the first edition of this book, other authors have focused on this high-risk population and there is a growing literature in this field. In this revised edition of our book, we have attempted to consolidate theoretical, clinical, and empirical information about six established ethnic minority youth populations and two emerging populations in the United States, drawing upon recent studies and our own varied clinical and research experience. What we have presented represents "sketches" of these youth, a further attempt to increase our understanding of youth of color, the problems they encounter, and the competencies they display. We have offered ways to intervene and a systematic method of assessment and inquiry. We have raised some significant issues and advanced a number of proposals in the hope that others will continue these efforts. As Edelman (1987) proclaims, children are the easiest people in American to ignore. While the knowledge base has certainly expanded in the past decade, there remains much more to be done. Sketches are only a beginning; we remain a significant distance from the finished portraits. It is hoped that the momentum will be sustained and that the conclusions drawn in our endeavor will provide additional impetus for new frameworks of inquiry and investigation in this field.

References

Achenbach, T. *Developmental Psychopathology*. New York: Wiley, 1974.

Allport, G. *The Nature of Prejudice*. Reading, Mass.: Addison-Wesley, 1954.

Attneave, C. L. "American Indians and Alaska Native Families: Emigrants in Their Own Homeland." In M. McGoldrick, J. K. Pearce, and J. Giordano, (eds.), *Ethnicity and Family Therapy*. (2nd ed.) New York: Guilford Press, 1996.

Berry, J. W. "On Cross-Cultural Comparability," *International Journal of Psychology*, 1969, *4*, 119–128.

Billingsley, A. *Climbing Jacob's Ladder*. New York: Simon & Schuster, 1992.

Bloom, B. *Changing Patterns of Psychiatric Care*. New York: Human Science Press, 1975.

Bosworth, A. P. *America's Concentration Camps*. New York: Norton, 1967.

Breslau, N., Davis, G., Andreski, P., and Peterson, E. "Traumatic Events and Posttraumatic Stress Disorder in an Urban Population of Young Adults." *Archives of General Psychiatry*, 1991, *48*, 216–222.

Bronfenbrenner, U. *The Ecology of Human Development: Experiments by Nature and Design*. Cambridge, Mass.: Harvard University Press, 1979.

Bronstein, P., and Quina, K. *Teaching a Psychology of People: Resources for Gender and Sociocultural Awareness*. Washington, D.C.: American Psychological Association, 1991.

Canino, I. A., and Spurlock, J. *Culturally Diverse Children and Adolescents: Assessment, Diagnosis and Treatment.* New York: Guilford Press, 1994.

Child Trends, Inc. *Trends in the Well-Being of America's Children and Youth: 1996.* Washington, D.C.: U.S. Department of Health and Human Services, 1996.

Comer, J. P. *Beyond Black and White.* New York: Quadrangle Books, 1972.

Cross, T., Bazron, B., Dennis, K., and Isaacs, M. *Towards a Culturally Competent System of Care: A Monograph on Effective Services for Minority Children Who Are Severely Emotionally Disturbed.* Washington, D.C.: CASSP Technical Assistance Center, Georgetown University Child Development Center, 1989.

Cross, W. "The Ecology of Human Development for Black and White Children: Implications for Predicting Racial Preference Patterns." *Critical Perspectives of Third World America,* 1983, *1,* 177–189.

Daniels, R. *Concentration Camps U.S.A.: Japanese Americans and World War II.* Austin, Tex.: Holt, Rinehart and Winston, 1971.

DeAnda, D. "Bicultural Socialization: Factors Affecting the Minority Experience." *Social Work,* Mar.–Apr. 1984, 101–107.

Dohrenwend, B. P. "Social Stress and Community Psychology." *American Journal of Community Psychology,* 1978, *6,* 1–14.

Dohrenwend, B. S., and Dohrenwend, B. P. "Class and Race as Status-Related Sources of Stress." In S. Levine and N. Scotch (eds.), *Social Stress.* Hawthorne, N.Y.: Aldine de Gruyter, 1970.

Draguns, J. G. "Dilemmas and Choices in Cross-Cultural Counseling: The Universal Versus the Culturally Distinctive." In P. B. Pedersen, J. G. Draguns, W. J. Lonner, and J. E. Trimble (eds.), *Counseling Across Cultures.* (3rd ed.) Honolulu, Hawaii: University of Hawaii Press, 1989.

Duster, T. "Purpose and Bias." *Society,* 1987, *24*(2), 8–12.

Edelman, M. W. *Families in Peril: An Agenda for Social Change.* Cambridge, Mass.: Harvard University Press, 1987.

Falicov, C. J., and Karrer, B. M. "Therapeutic Strategies for Mexican-American Families." *International Journal of Family Therapy,* 1984, *6*(1), 18–30.

Farley, R., and Allen, W. R. *The Color Line and the Quality of Life in America.* New York: Oxford University Press, 1989.

Farrington, D. P. "The Sociocultural Context of Childhood Disorders." In H. C. Quay and J. S. Werry (eds.), *Psychopathological Disorders of Childhood.* (3rd ed.) New York: Wiley, 1986.

Fong, L., and Gibbs, J. T. "Facilitating Mental Health Services to Multicultural Communities in a Dominant Cultural Setting: An Organizational Perspective." *Administration in Social Work,* 1995, *19*(2), 1–24.

Garbarino, J. *Children and Families in the Social Environment.* Hawthorne, N.Y.: Aldine de Gruyter, 1982.

Garcia-Preto, N. "Latino Families: An Overview." In M. McGoldrick, J. K. Pearce, and J. Giordano, *Ethnicity and Family Therapy.* (2nd ed.) New York: Guilford Press, 1996.

Garmezy, N., and Rutter, M. *Stress, Coping and Development in Children.* New York: McGraw-Hill, 1983.

Gibbs, J. T. "Can We Continue to Be Color-Blind and Class-Bound?" *Counseling Psychologist,* 1985, *13*(3), 426–435.

Gibbs, J. T. "Black Adolescents and Youth: An Update on an Endangered Species." In R. Jones (ed.), *Black Adolescents.* Berkeley, Calif.: Cobb & Henry, 1989.

Gibbs, J. T., and Hines, A. M. "Negotiating Ethnic Identity: Issues for Black-White Biracial Adolescents." In M. P. Root (ed.), *Racially Mixed People in America.* Thousand Oaks, Calif.: Sage, 1992.

Gibbs, J. T., and Moskowitz-Sweet, G. "Clinical and Cultural Issues in the Treatment of Biracial and Bicultural Adolescents." *Families in Society,* 1991, *72*(10), 579–592.

Girdner, A., and Loftis, A. *The Great Betrayal.* Old Tappan, N.J.: Macmillan, 1969.

Glazer, N. *We Are All Multiculturalists Now.* Cambridge, Mass.: Harvard University Press, 1997.

Green, J. W. *Cultural Awareness in the Human Services.* Englewood Cliffs, N.J.: Prentice Hall, 1982.

Hacker, A. *Two Nations: Black and White, Separate, Hostile, Unequal.* New York: Scribner, 1992.

Haley, J. *Leaving Home: The Therapy of Disturbed Young People.* New York: McGraw Hill, 1980.

Heizen, R. F., and Almquist, A. F. *The Other Californians.* Berkeley: University of California Press, 1971.

Helms, J. E. "Why Is There No Study of Cultural Equivalence in Standardized Cognitive Ability Testing?" *American Psychologist,* 1992, *47,* 1083–1101.

Huang, L. N., and Gibbs, J. T. "Partners or Adversaries: Home-School Collaboration Across Culture, Race, and Ethnicity." In S. Christenson and J. Conoley (eds.), *Home-School Collaboration: Enhancing Children's Academic and Social Competence.* Silver Spring, Md.: National Association of School Psychologists, 1992.

Isaacs, M., and Benjamin, M. *Towards a Culturally Competent System of Care.* Vol. II: *Programs Which Utilize Culturally Competent Principles.* Washington, D.C.: CASSP Technical Assistance Center, Georgetown University Child Development Center, 1991.

Jones, E. E., and Korchin, S. J. "Minority Mental Health: Perspectives." In E. E. Jones and S. J. Korchin (eds.), *Minority Mental Health*. New York: Praeger, 1982.

Jones, E. E., and Thorne, A. "Rediscovery of the Subject: Intercultural Approaches to Clinical Assessment." *Journal of Consulting and Clinical Psychology*, 1987, *55*(4), 488–495.

Jones, R. L. (ed.). *Psychoeducational Assessment of Minority Group Children: A Casebook*. Berkeley, Calif.: Cobb & Henry, 1988.

Kich, G. K. "The Developmental Process of Asserting a Biracial, Bicultural Identity." In M. P. Root (ed.), *Racially Mixed People in America*. Thousand Oaks, Calif.: Sage, 1992.

Kluckhohn, C., and Murray, J. "Personality Formation: The Determinants." In C. Kluckhohn (eds.), *Personality in Nature, Society and Culture*. New York: Knopf, 1956.

Korchin, S. *Modern Clinical Psychology: Principles of Intervention in the Clinic and Community*. New York: Basic Books, 1976.

Kotkin, J., and Kishimoto, Y. "America's Asian Destiny." *The Washington Post*, July 3, 1988, pp. C-1, C-4.

Lee, E. "Asian American Families: An Overview." In M. McGoldrick, J. K. Pearce, and J. Giordano (eds.), *Ethnicity and Family Therapy*. (2nd ed.) New York: Guilford Press, 1996.

Levine, M., and Levine, A. *A Social History of Helping Services: Clinic, Court, School, and Community*. Englewood Cliffs, N.J.: Appleton-Century-Crofts, 1970.

McFee, M. "The 150 Percent Man: A Product of Blackfeet Acculturation." *American Anthropologist*, 1968, *70*, 1096–1103.

Mercer, J., and Lewis, J. *System of Multicultural Pluralistic Assessment*. New York: The Psychological Corporation, 1978.

Mindel, C. H., and Habenstein, R. W. (eds.). *Ethnic Families in America: Patterns and Variations*. (2nd ed.) New York: Elsevier, 1981.

Mintz, N., and Schwartz, D. "Urban Ecology and Psychosis: Community Factors in the Incidence of Schizophrenia and Manic-Depression Among Italians in Greater Boston." *International Journal of Social Psychiatry*, 1964, *10*, 101–118.

Moritsugu, J., and Sue, S. "Minority Status as a Stressor." In R. Felner, L. Jason, J. Moritsugu, and S. Farber (eds.), *Preventive Psychology: Theory, Research and Practice*. New York: Pergamon Press, 1983.

Munoz, R. F. "The Spanish-Speaking Consumer and the Community Mental Health Center." In E. E. Jones and S. J. Korchin (eds.), *Minority Mental Health*. New York: Praeger, 1982.

Myers, H. F. "Urban Stress and the Mental Health of Afro-American Youth: An Epidemiologic and Conceptual Update." In R. L. Jones (ed.), *Black Adolescents*. Berkeley, Calif.: Cobb & Henry, 1989.

Nakao, A. "Western Culture Faces Decline—At Least on Campus." *San Francisco Examiner,* April 5, 1987.

Namir, S., and Weinstein, R. "Children: Facilitating New Directions." In L. Snowden (ed.), *Reaching the Underserved: Mental Health Needs of Neglected Populations.* Thousand Oaks, Calif.: Sage, 1982.

Oakland, T. (ed.). *Psychological and Educational Assessment of Minority Children.* New York: Brunner/Mazel, 1977.

Omi, M., and Winant, H. *Racial Formation in the United States: From the 1960s to the 1980s.* New York: Routledge, 1986.

Paz, O. *The Labyrinth of Solitude: Life and Thought in Mexico.* New York: Evergreen Books, 1961.

Phinney, J. S., and Rotheram, M. J. *Children's Ethnic Socialization: Pluralism and Development.* Thousand Oaks, Calif.: Sage, 1987.

Pinderhughes, E. *Understanding Race, Ethnicity and Power: The Key to Efficacy in Clinical Practice.* New York: Free Press, 1989.

Powell, B., and others. "The Pacific Century." *Newsweek,* Feb. 22, 1988, pp. 43–51.

President's Commission on Mental Health. *Report to the President.* Washington, D.C.: U.S. Government Printing Office, 1978.

"Quality Counts: A Report Card on the Condition of Public Education in the Fifty States." *Education Week,* 1997, *16,* 61.

Rabkin, J. "Ethnic Density and Psychiatry Hospitalization Hazards of Minority Status." *American Journal of Psychiatry,* 1979, *136,* 1562–1566.

Raimy, V. C. (ed.). *Training in Clinical Psychology.* Englewood Cliffs, N.J.: Prentice Hall, 1950.

Ramirez, M. *Psychology of the Americas: Mestizo Perspectives on Personality and Mental Health.* Orlando, Fla.: Academic Press, 1983.

Ramirez, M., and Castaneda, A. *Cultural Democracy: Biocognitive Development and Education.* Orlando, Fla.: Academic Press, 1974.

Rieff, D. *Los Angeles: Capitol of the Third World.* New York: Simon & Schuster, 1991.

Root, M. P. (ed.). *Racially Mixed People in America.* Thousand Oaks, Calif.: Sage, 1992.

Rosenberg, M. *Conceiving the Self.* New York: Basic Books, 1979.

Samuda, R. *Psychological Testing of American Minorities: Issues and Consequences.* New York: Dodd, Mead, 1975.

Sarason, S. *The Psychological Sense of Community: Prospects for a Community Psychology.* San Francisco: Jossey-Bass, 1974.

Singer, M., Anglin, T., Song, L., and Lunghofer, L. "Adolescents' Exposure to Violence and Associated Symptoms of Psychological Trauma." *Journal of the American Medical Association,* 1995, *273*(6), 477–482.

Smedley, A. *Race in North America: Origin and Evaluation of a World View.* Boulder, Colo.: Westview Press, 1993.

Snowden, L. "Services to the Underserved: An Overview of Contemporary Issues." In L. Snowden (ed.), *Reaching the Underserved: Mental Health Needs of Neglected Populations.* Thousand Oaks, Calif.: Sage, 1982.

Snowden, L., and Todman, P. A. "The Psychological Assessment of Blacks: New and Needed Developments." In E. E. Jones and S. J. Korchin (eds.), *Minority Mental Health.* New York: Praeger, 1982.

Stack, C. *All Our Kin: Strategies for Survival in a Black Community.* New York: HarperCollins, 1974.

Stevenson, H. W., and Stewart, E. C. "A Developmental Study of Racial Awareness in Young Children." *Child Development,* 1958, *29,* 399–409.

Stiffman, A. R., and Davis, L. E. (eds.). *Ethnic Issues in Adolescent Mental Health.* Thousand Oaks, Calif.: Sage, 1990.

Stonequist, E. V. "The Problem of the Marginal Man." *American Journal of Sociology,* 1935, *41,* 1–12.

Sue, S., and Morishima, J. K. *The Mental Health of Asian Americans: Contemporary Issues in Identifying and Treating Mental Problems.* San Francisco: Jossey-Bass, 1982.

Suinn, R. M. "Minority Issues Cut Across Courses." *APA Monitor,* 1987, *18,* 3.

Tafoya, N., and Del Vecchio, A. "Back to the Future: An Examination of the Native American Holocaust." In M. McGoldrick, J. K. Pearce, and J. Giordano, (eds.), *Ethnicity and Family Therapy.* (2nd ed.) New York: Guilford Press, 1996.

Takaki, R. *Iron Cages: Race and Culture in Nineteenth-Century America.* Seattle: University of Washington Press, 1979.

Takaki, R. *From Different Shores.* (2nd ed.) New York: Oxford University Press, 1994.

Taylor, R. L. (ed.). *African-American Youth: Their Social and Economic Status in the United States.* New York: Praeger, 1995.

Tocqueville, A. de. *Democracy in America.* Vol. 1. New York: Knopf, 1945. (Originally published 1835.)

Triandis, H., and Brislin, R. "Cross-Cultural Psychology." *American Psychologist,* 1984, *39,* 1006–1016.

U.S. Bureau of the Census. *1970 Census of Population: Characteristics of the Population.* Washington, D.C.: U.S. Department of Commerce, 1973.

U.S. Bureau of the Census. *Statistical Abstract of the United States, 1996.* (116th ed.) Washington, D.C.: U.S. Government Printing Office, 1996.

Vargas, L. A., and Koss-Chioino, J. D. (eds.). *Working with Culture: Psychotherapeutic Interventions with Ethnic Minority Children and Adolescents.* San Francisco: Jossey-Bass, 1992.

Welsh, P. "The Black Talent Trap." *The Washington Post,* May 1, 1988, p. C1.

Wilson, W. J. *The Truly Disadvantaged.* Chicago: University of Chicago Press, 1987.

Wilson, T. P. "Blood Quantum: Native American Mixed Bloods." In M. P. Root (ed.), *Racially Mixed People in America.* Thousand Oaks, Calif.: Sage, 1992.

Wolkind, S., and Rutter, M. *Sociocultural Factors in Child and Adolescent Psychiatry.* Boston: Blackwell Scientific, 1985.

About the Authors

Jewelle Taylor Gibbs is the Zellerbach Family Fund Professor of Social Policy, Community Change, and Practice at the School of Social Welfare, University of California at Berkeley. She received her A.B. degree *cum laude* from Radcliffe College and subsequently was awarded an M.S.W. degree in social welfare as well as M.A. and Ph.D. degrees in psychology from the University of California at Berkeley. She is a licensed clinical psychologist whose areas of specialization are the psychosocial problems of adolescents and the social and mental health issues of low-income and minority populations. Gibbs is editor of *Young, Black and Male in America: An Endangered Species* (1988) and author of *Race and Justice: Rodney King and O. J. Simpson in a House Divided* (1996) as well as numerous book chapters, articles, and essays. In 1987, Gibbs was the recipient of the McCormick Award from the American Association of Suicidology for her research on minority youth suicide. She has served on the board of directors of the American Orthopsychiatric Association and on the editorial board of the *American Journal of Orthopsychiatry*. Gibbs is a fellow of the American Psychological Association and a founding member of the Advisory Board of the National Center for Children in Poverty. A former fellow of the Mary I. Bunting Institute at Radcliffe College, Gibbs has also been a visiting professor at the University of Toronto and a visiting scholar at the University of London, at McGill University, and in the Claremont College system.

Larke Nahme Huang is currently a consulting psychologist with the National Technical Assistance Center for Children's Mental Health Services at Georgetown University Child Development Center. She conducts research, training, and consultation in the areas of child development, systems of care for culturally diverse youth, cultural competence in behavioral health and education systems, outcome

389

measurement, and acculturation for multicultural youth. She has published in these areas and has been a practicing clinician in both private and public settings. Huang received her A.B. degree with highest honors from the University of Maryland and her M.S. and Ph.D. degrees in psychology from Yale University. She completed a two-year clinical fellowship at the Langley Porter Psychiatric Institute of the University of California Medical School, San Francisco. Huang has served as grants reviewer for the National Institute of Mental Health, as cochair of the Advisory Board for the National Asian American Psychology Training Center, as consultant for the Head Start Validation Program, as chair of the Advisory Board of the American Psychological Association Minority Fellowship Program, and as a member of the Governor's Advisory Committee on the Policy Implications of California's Increasing Minority Populations.

LaRue Allen, a clinical psychologist, received her A.B. degree *cum laude* from Radcliffe College and her Ph.D. degree in clinical-community psychology from Yale University. She is currently professor and chair of the Department of Applied Psychology in the School of Education at New York University. She is also director of education and training of the National Consortium on Violence Research.

D. Gloria Herron, a native of Cuba, received her B.S. degree from Indiana University and her M.S. degree in psychology from Purdue University. She received her Ph.D. degree in clinical psychology from Fairleigh Dickinson University.

Jaime E. Inclán, a clinical psychologist, received his B.A. degree from Georgetown University and his Ph.D. degree in clinical psychology from New York University. A native of Puerto Rico, Inclán has served since 1983 as director of the Roberto Clemente Family Guidance Center in New York City. He is also clinical associate professor of psychiatry at the New York University School of Medicine, and he maintains a private practice specializing in family and individual psychotherapy.

Teresa D. LaFromboise, a counseling psychologist, received her M.A. degree from the University of North Dakota and her Ph.D. in counseling psychology from the University of Oklahoma. She is currently associate professor of counseling psychology in the School of Education at Stanford University, and she currently serves as chair of the American Indian and Alaska Native Program at Stanford.

Kathryn Graff Low, a counseling psychologist, received her M.A. degree from Harvard University and her Ph.D. in counseling psychology from the School of Education at Stanford University. She is currently associate professor of psychology at Bates College in Lewiston, Maine.

Shayda Majidi-Ahi received her Ph.D. degree in clinical psychology from the University of Maryland, College Park. She completed a postdoctoral fellowship at the Massachusetts Mental Health Center in Boston. From 1989 to 1993 she worked at a community mental health center in Northshore, Massachusetts, and conducted private practice with adults and families. She continues her private practice in Wenham, Massachusetts, and consults to public and private schools.

Donna K. Nagata, a clinical psychologist, received her Ph.D. degree in clinical psychology from the University of Illinois, Champaign-Urbana. She is currently associate professor of clinical psychology at the University of Michigan, Ann Arbor. She is the author of *Legacy of Injustice: Exploring the Cross-Generational Impact of the Japanese American Internment* (1993).

Oscar Ramirez, a clinical psychologist, received his B.A. degree from the University of Texas, Austin, and his M.A. and Ph.D. degrees in clinical psychology from the University of Michigan, Ann Arbor. Ramirez is currently clinical associate professor of psychiatry at the University of Texas Health Sciences Center at San Antonio. He also maintains a private practice specializing in the treatment of children, adolescents, and families.

Yu-Wen Ying, a clinical psychologist, received her B.A. degree *magna cum laude* from Barnard College, Columbia University, and her Ph.D. in clinical psychology from the University of California at Berkeley. She is currently professor at the School of Social Welfare, University of California at Berkeley. Ying is a fellow of the American Psychological Association, coauthor of *The Prevention of Depression: Research and Practice* (with R. F. Munoz, 1993), and currently serves on the editorial board of the *American Journal of Community Psychology.*

Name Index

Subject Index